ALCOHOL USE AND WORLD CULTURES:

A COMPREHENSIVE BIBLIOGRAPHY OF ANTHROPOLOGICAL SOURCES

ADDICTION RESEARCH FOUNDATION BIBLIOGRAPHIC SERIES

This series is a service to individuals concerned with problems of alcohol and drug abuse. The following bibliographies are available from the Marketing Department, Addiction Research Foundation, 33 Russell Street, Toronto M5S 2S1

No.	2	An Interim Guide to the Cannabis (Marihuana) Literature	(1968)	$ 3.00
No.	3	Interaction of Alcohol and Other Drugs. Second Edition Revised	(1972)	$17.50
No.	3a	Interaction of Alcohol and Other Drugs. Supplement 1	(1973)	$ 4.50
No.	4	Non-Alcoholic Drugs and Personality: A Selected Annotated Bibliography	(1972)	$ 4.00
No.	5	Solvent Abuse: An Annotated Bibliography with Additional Related Citations	(1973)	$ 5.50
No.	6	Teratogenic and Chromosomal Damaging Effects of Illicit Drugs	(1973)	$ 5.50
No.	7	Drug Use and Driving	(1974)	$ 4.50
No.	8	Amphetamines and Related Drugs: Clinical Toxicity and Dependence. A Comprehensive Bibliography of the International Literature	(1974)	$ 5.50
No.	9	The Benzodiazepines - Patterns of Use	(1975)	$ 7.00
No.	10	Behaviour Modification for the Treatment of Alcoholism	(1975)	$ 8.00
No.	11	Women and Psychoactive Drug Use: An Interim Annotated Bibliography	(1976)	$ 7.00
No.	12	Therapeutic Communities for the Management of Addictions: A Critically Annotated Bibliography	(1976)	$ 7.00
No.	13	The Ethical Pharmaceutical Industry and Some of its Economic Aspects	(1977)	$10.00
No.	14	Disulfiram in the Treatment of Alcoholism	(1978)	$ 8.00
No.	15	Alcohol Use and World Cultures	(1981)	$10.00

ALCOHOL USE AND WORLD CULTURES:

A COMPREHENSIVE BIBLIOGRAPHY OF ANTHROPOLOGICAL SOURCES

Dwight B. Heath
Professor of Anthropology, and
Program Director,
"Social Science Research Training on Alcohol",
Brown University

and

A.M. Cooper
Brown University

Bibliographic Series No. 15

R.J. Hall, Series Editor
Addiction Research Foundation
Toronto, Ontario, Canada

© 1981 by the Addiction Research Foundation of Ontario. No part of
this book may be reproduced in any form, except for brief quotation in
a review or professional work, without permission in writing from the
publisher.

I.S.B.N.   0-88868-045-7
I.S.S.N.   0065-1885

PRINTED & BOUND IN CANADA

CONTENTS

Foreword vii

Introduction ix

Acknowledgements xiii

Citations xv

Appendix 177

Index of Authors 185

Index of Subjects 213

FOREWORD

For at least two reasons, it is a pleasure to write a foreword to this bibliography. First, it is gratifying that the rather formidable and onerous task which the indefatigable team of Heath and Cooper so willingly assumed has now been accomplished, and accomplished with the care and thoroughness characteristic of all their work. Second, from a personal standpoint, the publication of the Heath and Cooper bibliography serves to remove a long-standing sense of discomfort that nothing had been done to up-date its predecessor, <u>Culture and alcohol use</u>, published 13 years ago and out of print for some time.

It is true that, in 1967, Carole Yawney and I considered that the need for future editions of our bibliography would be obviated by the International Bibliography of Studies on Alcohol, the first volume of which (covering the period 1901-1950) had just appeared. However, further volumes did not materialize and, in the meantime, the amount of literature increased very greatly. In 1967 we listed 448 references; Heath and Cooper have listed nearly four times as many. While the difference no doubt reflects an exponential growth of interest in anthropological aspects over the period, it probably also reflects - one might as well admit - the relatively greater bibliographic skills of Heath and Cooper.

In any event, we were delighted when these distinguished anthropologists - renowned for their own numerous contributions to the topic - agreed to prepare a new edition. Professional researchers and many others interested in the problems of alcohol are in their debt for undertaking what may be aptly termed 'a labor of love', and thereby providing a ready reference to the large and widely scattered literature on <u>Alcohol use and world cultures</u>.

Robert E. Popham

Addiction Research Foundation
Toronto, May 21, 1980.

INTRODUCTION

Among the many psychoactive drugs that have been tried by human beings, none is more widely used than alcohol, and none has been used for so many centuries. There is probably no other substance that has also been used so widely as a food, as a sacrament, as a symbol of friendship and hospitality, or as a tranquilizer, an anesthetic, or an adjunct to recreation. The wide variety of roles that alcoholic beverages play in the lives of peoples throughout the world is reflected in the writings of anthropologists, travelers, historians, classicists, and others. Their attention to the subject reflects the importance of drinking in the lives of the people they study, probably more than it does their own preconceptions. For these reasons, the study of alcohol in world cultures has a significance that transcends even the enormous concern with health and social welfare that dominates much of the writing that deals with drinking in any modern nation.

PURPOSE

This bibliography has been compiled with the aim of providing easier and more comprehensive access to the large, diverse, and widely scattered literature that deals with alcoholic beverages in relation to human behavior among various populations throughout the world. In recent years, it has become a truism that the effects of alcohol can only be understood through a combination of biological, psychological, and sociocultural perspectives. Although there have been many attempts to make biological and psychological viewpoints about alcohol clear and accessible to non-specialists, there has been less emphasis placed on the sociocultural approach. This is especially ironic because it is, in some senses, the most interesting and exciting -- although people are dealing with the same substance (ethanol), it has very different meanings and uses among different populations. These are associated with very different values and attitudes, and they also lead to very different effects.

This is not the context in which to summarize the rich variation of alcohol-related beliefs and behaviors that occur around the world, or to analyze the reasons for certain limited similarities among the enormous differences. A recent anthology that offers a sampling of data is Mac Marshall's book (see citation no. 813), available in paperback. An account of how this literature evolved through time is provided in an article by Heath (521), and a detailed review of the theoretical implications of it is available in another article by Heath (520).

In a very real sense, this volume is an extension of the pioneering work of Robert E. Popham and Carole D. Yawney, whose Culture and alcohol use (968) made invaluable contributions in many respects. For those in many disciplines who are interested in the literature on alcohol and other drugs, their compilation made accessible a rich corpus of cross-cultural evidence that had been largely ignored because it was scattered so widely in such varied and sometimes recondite sources. For anthropologists, it

made clear the wealth of data that were already available on this important
subject, and made it easier to find salient studies on which to base comparisons, regional surveys, tests of hypotheses, and so forth. For the Addiction
Research Foundation, it set a high standard at the very beginning of their
venture into publishing bibliographies, an enterprise that is often viewed
as a labor-of-love but that contributes significantly both in terms of
general education and in terms of furthering research.

SCOPE

No bibliography can be truly comprehensive, but we have attempted to
provide an up-to-date list of most of the sources that deal with alcohol in
sociocultural perspective, throughout time and space. Coverage is intentionally
broad and inclusive in every respect. In temporal terms, it ranges from
prehistory to mid-1978; we expect that revised editions or addenda will be
issued from time to time to update the coverage. In spatial terms, no area
of the world has been ignored. To be sure, the amount available dealing
with various continents and countries is highly variable, but that reflects
the work that has been done at least as much as the interests of the compilers.

In topical terms, selectivity has been more problematic. Our general
aim has been to include all that we could find that describes the range of
beliefs and behaviors with respect to alcoholic beverages, written with an
essentially anthropological orientation. Following the effective precedent
that Popham and Yawney concisely spelled out in their second edition, we are
"... concerned with drinking behavior (whether customary or pathological)
in particular cultural contexts (whether literate or non-literate, past or
present), or with the theoretical implications of cross-cultural similarities
and differences in such behavior" (968, p. iii). Not only are tribal and
peasant peoples represented, but so are non-Western civilizations. Not only
are classical and other ancient peoples included, but so are our contemporaries.
It may be worthwhile in this context also to note a few categories that are
not included. Surveys of political jurisdictions (such as provinces, states,
counties, etc.) are omitted, as are sociological or epidemiological studies
among culturally heterogeneous categories that are sometimes referred to as
special groups or populations (such as "women", "the aged", "students",
"chronic drunkenness offenders", etc.), histories (other than those that
emphasize alcohol use), and general ethnographic studies (except those that
pay special attention to the analysis of patterns of beliefs and behavior
concerning alcohol).

In qualitative terms, the materials listed are frankly uneven. A few
items that were patently redundant, or almost certainly inaccurate, have been
omitted, but there are many references here that provide little beyond
simplistic description, often distorted by religious or ethnic biases, and
some of the interpretations or analyses are also questionable. Such inclusion
was made on the basis of our feeling that a few data may be better than none,
especially with respect to weakly documented times or places, and that some
topics are of sufficient sociological importance (e.g., ceremonial exclusion
from one's natal caste in India) that even a fragmentary account may be

significant for theoretical or conceptual purposes.

This bibliography should serve students and laypersons as well as the international and multidisciplinary scholarly community. Although several languages are represented, English predominates. This is appropriate because so much is written by people for whom English is the first language, and because English-translations are often more readily accessible than an other-language original, unless one is working in a major research library.

Books, monographs, chapters in books, and articles in scientific journals comprise the bulk of the items that are cited. There is no intention that this be an exhaustive check-list, so reprintings and pre-publication versions are not cited. In those instances where a revised version is available, it is usually cited rather than the original, because the revision is usually more accurate and/or more detailed. In order to keep the list within manageable bounds, we have elected to be highly selective in our inclusion of unpublished materials. In a few instances, we have included reports to organizations, papers read at professional meetings, theses, dissertations, and so forth. Such inclusion was made on the basis of our estimation that the source was relatively important despite difficulty of access -- either exceptionally rich in data, or useful in addressing a topic that had otherwise been virtually neglected.

In short, our aim in this volume has been to make it easier for people to learn more about what is known -- and what remains to be known -- about patterns of beliefs and behavior with respect to alcoholic beverages among the many and diverse cultures of the world.

FORMAT AND USE

The bulk of this volume is a listing of citations, each identified with a unique citation number to the left of each entry. An index of authors and an index of subjects should be helpful to users who want to find the works of a particular individual, to explore a particular topic, to learn about drinking among a given population, and so forth.

The citations are listed in alphabetical order, by the surname of the senior author. For an author who has written more than one item, the sequence of entries under his/her name is chronological. Among various jointly authored items by the same senior author, the same order applies, i.e., chronological sequence, not names of junior authors, determines the order. Among items by the same senior author which appear in the same year, the order is alphabetical by title. Prefixed names e.g., Mac and Mc, are not ordered separately, but are interspersed alphabetically throughout the citations. Some authors use only initials for names other than surnames; in instances where the compilers feel confident, we have completed the names [in brackets]. Unsigned articles and editorials are listed under "Anonymous", regardless of the source in which they appeared. In those instances where a report from a government agency, corporation, or other such entity lacks any indication of authorship, on front and back of the title page, the corporate name is used as author.

In a few citations, we have provided additional data that is not available in the original source. For example, non-English titles are translated [in brackets]. Date of publication seems so important a fact that we have inserted it [in brackets] in those instances where we are confident, on the basis of independent evidence, even though the title page lacked a date. We have not, however, changed the date of those citations for which the date of imprint is incorrect in the original.

Indexing is intended to help an interested person, even one with little prior knowledge of the subject, to find relevant sources. Abundant use of cross-references avoids the limitations sometimes posed by professional jargon. For example, someone interested in drinking among "American Indians" would quickly find that they are here called "Native Americans", and could then look at the full range of sources listed under that broad rubric, or could select a particular region or culture-area from among these named, or even an individual tribe. A student with specific interest would presumably begin with the tribal name and could quickly find the relevant numbers listed under that entry.

Different authors sometimes use the same word with different meanings, however, so one should be aware that, for example, some of the sources indexed under "anomie" emphasize confusion about norms, whereas others emphasize frustration about non-achievement of goals. It also deserves mention that an index-entry signals only that a source includes important discussion of a topic, and does not necessarily mean that that variable in any way causes drinking or alcohol problems. For example, although many entries under "acculturation" and "urbanization" treat them as significant factors in connection with alcohol-related social or psychological pathologies, some other sources take pains to emphasize the absence of such a linkage.

Readers who are interested in pursuing a particular topic in greater depth should be able, with a little extra effort, to seek out other relevant publications, using the Classified Abstracts Archive of the Alcohol Literature (see citation no. 646), or the excellent index of Journal of Studies on Alcohol.

In a sense, a bibliography should be thought of as a tool. The measure of its worth is the success of those who use it. And it must be kept honed if it is to serve over any length of time. We hope that anyone who has occasion to use this bibliography will find it helpful, and we also hope that anyone who knows of other relevant sources will notify us in order that subsequent editions may be more complete.

Dwight B. Heath
A.M. Cooper

Brown University
Department of Anthropology
Providence, Rhode Island
02912   U.S.A.

ACKNOWLEDGEMENTS

A volume such as this is always the outgrowth of many years' interest and work on a subject. The Addiction Research Foundation has provided an appropriate opportunity through publication in its Bibliographic Series, for us to share this compilation with others who may find it useful. Brown University has provided an institutional context that has allowed us to pursue alcohol studies and our other interests, in the company of good students and colleagues.

It was Mark Keller, then editor of the Quarterly Journal of Studies on Alcohol, who originally sparked our interest in the field; he continues to set a good example in his diligence, breadth, wit, stamina, and respect for documentation. Clyde Kluckhohn at Harvard University, and George Murdock and Floyd Lounsbury at Yale, effectively taught anthropology by effectively doing anthropology. At Brown, Roswell Johnson, David Lewis, and Sidney Cobb have helped sustain our involvement with alcohol studies in recent years, and Paul Freund contributed to expanding the list of references.

Robert Popham, at the Addiction Research Foundation, not only compiled the prototype volume, but also encouraged us to undertake this expansion and updating of it. As a pioneer in anthropology and alcohol studies, he has shared generously with us. During our occasional visits to the Foundation, we have enjoyed both ample hospitality and stimulating collegiality. The staff of the Library, first under Ron Hall and later under Anne Johnston, have helped to make our work there pleasant as well as fruitful. Also during our brief stays at the Foundation, working luncheons with Wolfgang Schmidt have broadened our perspectives in many other fields. The Foundation is fortunate to have Ron Hall, who combined efficiency with good humor, and flexibility with attention to detail, in editing this volume as in his multifarious other jobs. In short, he made a hard job fun. Others at ARF who assisted in putting the finishing touches on the manuscript include Library staff members Colleen Mulloy (who verified references, coded computer index forms, proofread) and Dana Tetera (who typed the final manuscript), and the staff of ARF's Computer Services.

The compilation of this volume was completed while Heath was director of a postdoctoral program of "Social Science Research Training on Alcohol" sponsored by the National Institute on Alcohol Abuse and Alcoholism, of the United States Public Health Service. However, no funds from that grant (5 T32 AA07131) were used in connection with the project, nor did any other agency, public or private, provide financial support.

CITATIONS

The following list of citations is intended to provide a fairly comprehensive guide to the diverse and scattered literature that relates to alcohol use in world cultures. For a brief discussion of the scope, format, and suggestions for using the bibliography, see the Introduction (pp. ix); criteria for inclusion, and the sequence of listing are also explained there.

Each entry is identified by a citation number (in sequence, at the beginning of the entry).

Users of this volume are invited to communicate with the compilers in order to identify any problems that may arise, and to suggest other references for inclusion in subsequent revisions.

Alcohol Use and World Cultures   Ablon, Joan

1.   Aalto, Pentii
        ALKOHOLENS STALLNING I INDIENS KLASSISKA KULTUR. [The role of
        alcohol in classical Indian culture.] [Fin]
        Alkoholpolitik, 18(2): 32-46,   1955.
        India - history, pre-1500 - prehistory   D-0100.

2.   Abad, Vicente, and Suarez, Joseph
        CROSS-CULTURAL ASPECTS OF ALCOHOLISM AMONG PUERTO RICANS.
        In: Chafetz, Morris E., ed. Research, treatment and prevention.
        Proceedings of the 4th Annual Conference of the National Institute
        on Alcohol Abuse and Alcoholism. Held June 12-14, 1974 in Washington,
        D.C. Rockville, MD: National Institute on Alcohol Abuse and
        Alcoholism (DHEW Publication No. (ADM) 76-284), pp. 282-294,   1975.
        West Indies - Puerto Rico - sex   D-0101.

3.   Ablon, Joan
        RELOCATED AMERICAN INDIANS IN THE SAN FRANCISCO BAY AREA: SOCIAL
        INTERACTION AND INDIAN IDENTITY.
        Human Organization, 23: 296-304,   1964.
        United States - Native Americans - acculturation - aggression -
        bar - stress - urbanization   D-0077.

4.   Ablon, Joan
        AMERICAN INDIAN RELOCATION: PROBLEMS OF DEPENDENCY AND
        MANAGEMENT IN THE CITY.
        Phylon, 26: 362-371,   1965.
        United States - Native Americans - dependency - stress -
        urbanization   D-0078.

5.   Ablon, Joan
        CULTURAL CONFLICT IN URBAN INDIANS.
        Mental Hygiene, 55: 199-205,   1971.
        United States - Native Americans - Dakota - acculturation - stress
        - urbanization   D-0102.

6.   Ablon, Joan
        FAMILY BEHAVIOR AND ALCOHOLISM.
        In: Everett, Michael W.; Waddell, Jack O.; and Heath, Dwight B.,
        ed. Cross-cultural approaches to the study of alcohol: An
        interdisciplinary perspective. The Hague: Mouton,
        pp. 133-160,   1976.
        family - social organization   D-0103.

7.   Ablon, Joan
        FAMILY STRUCTURE AND BEHAVIOR IN ALCOHOLISM: A REVIEW OF THE
        LITERATURE.
        In: Kissin, Benjamin, and Begleiter, Henri, ed. The biology of
        alcoholism, Volume 4: Social aspects of alcoholism. New York,
        NY: Plenum, pp. 205-242,   1976.
        family - review - social organization   D-0104.

8.   Ablon, Joan
      RESEARCH FRONTIERS FOR ANTHROPOLOGISTS IN FAMILY STUDIES: A CASE
      IN POINT, ALCOHOLISM AND THE FAMILY.
      Human Organization, 24(1): 196-200,   1979.
      family - research methods - social organization   D-1244.

9.   Abu-Laban, Baha, and Larsen, D.E.
      THE QUALITIES AND SOURCES OF NORMS AND DEFINITIONS OF ALCOHOL.
      Sociology and Social Research, 53: 34-43,   1968.
      enculturation - norms   D-0105.

10.   Ackerman, Lillian A.
      MARITAL INSTABILITY AND JUVENILE DELINQUENCY AMONG THE NEZ PERCES.
      American Anthropologist, 73(3): 595-603,   1971.
      United States - Native Americans - Nez Perce - accidents - crime
      - dysfunctions - family - religion - youth   D-0106.

11.   Adair, John
      ALCOHOLISM THROUGH NAVAJO EYES.
      Unpublished paper: American Anthropological Association,
      Washington, D.C.,   1976.
      United States - Native Americans - Navaho - attitudes -
      youth   D-1253.

12.   Adandé, A.
      LE MAIS ET SES USAGES DANS LE BAS-DAHOMEY. [Maize and its uses in
      Bas-Dahomey.] [Fre]
      Bulletin de l'Institut Français d'Afrique Noire,
      15(1): 220-282,   1953.
      Dahomey - homebrew   D-0257.

13.   Adandé, A.
      LE VIN DE PALME CHEZ LES DIOLA DE LA CASAMANCE. [Palm-wine among
      the Diola of Casamance.] [Fre]
      Notes Africaines, 61: 4-7,   1954.
      Senegal - Diola - containers - homebrew - manufacture   D-0110.

14.   Ade, George
      THE OLD-TIME SALOON: NOT WET, NOT DRY - JUST HISTORY.
      New York, NY: Ray Long and Richard R. Smith, 174 pp.,   1931.
      United States - bar - history, pre-1900   D-0083.

15.   Adler, Nathan, and Goleman, Daniel
      GAMBLING AND ALCOHOLISM: SYMPTOM SUBSTITUTION AND FUNCTIONAL
      EQUIVALENTS.
      Quarterly Journal of Studies on Alcohol, 30(3): 733-736,   1969.
      Cross-cultural - functions - gambling   D-0107.

16.   Adomakoh, C.C.
      ALCOHOLISM: THE AFRICAN SCENE.
      Annals of the New York Academy of Sciences, 273: 39-46,   1976.
      Africa - review   D-0108.

17. Adriaens, E.L., and Lozet, F.
 CONTRIBUTION A L'ETUDE DES BOISSONS FERMENTEES INDIGENES AU
 RUANDA. [Contribution to the study of indigenous fermented
 drinks in Ruanda.] [Fre]
 Bulletin Agricole du Congo Belge, 42: 933-950, 1951.
 Congo - Ruanda - homebrew - manufacture D-0111.

18. Adriaens, E.L.
 CONTRIBUTION A L'ETUDE DES VINS DE PALME AU KWANGO.
 [Contribution to the study of palm wine in Kwango.] [Fre]
 Bulletin des Séances de l'Institut Royal Colonial Belge,
 22(2): 334-350, 1951.
 Congo - Kwango - homebrew - manufacture D-0258.

19. Aguilar, German Z.
 SUSPENSION OF CONTROL: A SOCIOCULTURAL STUDY ON SPECIFIC
 DRINKING HABITS AND THEIR PSYCHIATRIC CONSEQUENCES.
 Journal of Existential Psychiatry, 4: 245-252, 1964.
 Chile - acculturation - anomie - binge - change - psychiatric
 problems - stress D-0109.

20. Ahlström-Laakso, Salme
 EUROPEAN DRINKING HABITS: A REVIEW OF RESEARCH AND SOME
 SUGGESTIONS FOR CONCEPTUAL INTEGRATION OF FINDINGS.
 In: Everett, Michael W.; Waddell, Jack O.; and Heath, Dwight
 B., ed. Cross-cultural approaches to the study of alcohol:
 An interdisciplinary perspective. The Hague: Mouton,
 pp. 119-132, 1976.
 Europe - Cross-national - review D-0112.

21. Alba, Martínez de
 THE MAGUEY AND PULQUE.
 Mexican Folkways, 2(4): 12-15, 1926.
 Mexico - homebrew - manufacture D-0113.

22. Albaugh, Bernard, and Anderson, Phillip O.
 PEYOTE IN THE TREATMENT OF ALCOHOLISM AMONG AMERICAN INDIANS.
 American Journal of Psychiatry, 131(11): 1247-1257, 1974.
 United States - Native Americans - Arapaho - Cheyenne -
 Alcoholics Anonymous - anomie - peyote - treatment D-0114.

23. Alday, Rudy K.
 ALCOHOLISM VERSUS THE SOUTHWEST AMERICAN INDIAN.
 In: Brock, Ruth, ed. Selected papers presented at the
 General Sessions, 22nd Annual Meeting. Held September 12-17,
 in Hartford, Connecticut. Washington, D.C.: Alcohol and
 Drug Problems Association of North America, pp. 23-24, 1971.
 United States - Native Americans - political -
 sociocultural D-0119.

24. Alhava, Armas
    VAKIJUOMAOLOJEN ERIKOISLUONNE LAPISSA. [Special aspects of
    the liquor situation in Lapland.] [Fin]
    Alkoholiliikkeen Aikakauskirja, 12: 35-37, 1949.
    Finland - Lapps D-0120.

25. Allardt, Erik
    ALKOHOLVANORNA PA LANDSBYGDEN I FINLAND. [Rural drinking
    habits in Finland.] [Fin]
    Alkoholpolitik, 19(3): 73-77, 1956.
    Finland D-0117.

26. Allardt, Erik
    DRINKING NORMS AND DRINKING HABITS.
    In: Allardt, Erik; Markkanen, Touko; and Takala, Martti.
    Drinking and drinkers: Three papers in behavioral sciences.
    Helsinki: Finnish Foundation for Alcohol Studies, (Volume 6),
    pp. 7-109, 1957.
    Finland - ambivalence - attitudes - norms - social
    organization D-0118.

27. Allen, H. Warner
    A HISTORY OF WINE: GREAT VINTAGE WINES FROM THE HOMERIC AGE
    TO THE PRESENT DAY.
    New York, NY: Horizon, 1961.
    history, pre-1500 - history, pre-1900 - wine D-0297.

28. Allman, Lawrence P.; Taylor, H. Augustus; and Nathan, Peter E.
    GROUP DRINKING DURING STRESS: EFFECTS ON DRINKING BEHAVIOR,
    AFFECT, AND PSYCHOPATHOLOGY.
    American Journal of Psychiatry, 129: 669-678, 1972.
    psychiatric problems - social organization - stress D-0116.

29. Almeida V., Manuel
    INVESTIGACION CLINICA SOBRE LA EVOLUCION DEL ALCOHOLISMO. UN
    ESTUDIO DE 181 CASOS DE LA CIUDAD DE LIMA. [Clinical investi-
    gation on the development of alcoholism; a study of 181 cases
    in the city of Lima.] [Spa]
    Revista de Neuro-psiquiatría, 25: 97-122, 1962.
    Peru - phases D-0121.

30. Alonso Fernández, Francisco
    FACTEURS CULTURELS ET ANTHROPOLOGIQUES DANS L'ETIOLOGIE DES
    ALCOOLISMES. [Cultural and anthropological factors in the
    etiology of alcoholism.] [Fre]
    Revue de l'Alcoolisme, 11(2): 93-104, 1965.
    alcoholism - definition - etiology - sociocultural D-0298.

31. Alonso Fernández, Francisco
    THE STATE OF ALCOHOLISM IN SPAIN COVERING ITS EPIDEMIOLOGICAL
    AND AETIOLOGICAL ASPECTS.
    British Journal of Addiction, 71: 235-242, 1976.
    Spain - alcoholism - change - customs - epidemiology - norms
    - social organization - stress D-0084.

4.

32. Amar, Ayush Morad
    SOCIAL CONTROL AS A FACTOR IN NON-MEDICAL DRUG USE.
    In: Rutledge, Barbara, and Fulton, E.Kaye, ed. International
    collaboration: Problems and opportunities. Toronto, Ont.:
    Addiction Research Foundation, pp. 113-139, 1977.
    Latin America - change - drugs - urbanization   D-0002.

33. Amark, Curt
    A STUDY IN ALCOHOLISM: CLINICAL, SOCIAL PSYCHIATRIC AND GENETIC
    INVESTIGATIONS.
    Acta Psychiatrica et Neurologica Scandinavica, Supplementum 70:
    283 pp.,   1951.
    Sweden - accidents - epidemiology - history, pre-1900 -
    temperance - treatment   D-0299.

34. Amsel, Zili; Mandel, Wallace; Matthias, Lynda; Mason, Carol;
    and Hocherman, Irit
    RELIABILITY AND VALIDITY OF SELF-REPORTED ILLEGAL ACTIVITIES AND
    DRUG USE COLLECTED FROM NARCOTIC ADDICTS.
    International Journal of the Addictions, 11(2): 325-336, 1976.
    consumption - research methods   D-0085.

35. Anderson, Barbara G.
    HOW FRENCH CHILDREN LEARN TO DRINK.
    Trans-action, 5(7): 20-22,   1968.
    France - enculturation - nutrition - youth   D-0122.

36. Anderson, R.K.; Calvo, J.; Serrano, G.; and Payne, G.
    A STUDY OF THE NUTRITIONAL STATUS AND FOOD HABITS OF OTOMI
    INDIANS IN THE MEZQUITAL VALLEY OF MEXICO.
    American Journal of Public Health, 36: 883-903,   1946.
    Mexico - Otomí - homebrew - nutrition   D-0123.

37. Ando, Haruhiko, and Hasegawa, Etsuko
    DRINKING PATTERNS AND ATTITUDES OF ALCOHOLICS AND NONALCOHOLICS
    IN JAPAN.
    Quarterly Journal of Studies on Alcohol, 31: 153-161,   1970.
    Japan - attitudes   D-0126.

38. Andorka, Rudolf; Buda, Béla; and G.-Kiss, Judith
    ALCOOLISME ET CULTURE EN HONGRIE. [Alcoholism and culture
    in Hungary.] [Fre]
    Toxicomanies, 3: 371-381,   1970.
    Hungary - etiology - enculturation - stress   D-0127.

39. András Falvy, B.
    DER ROTWEIN IN UNGARN. [Red wine in Hungary.] [Ger]
    Acta Ethnographica, 14(3-4): 227-258,   1965.
    Hungary - wine   D-0291.

40. Angrosino, Michael V.
     OUTSIDE IS DEATH: ALCOHOLISM, IDEOLOGY AND COMMUNITY
     ORGANIZATION AMONG THE EAST INDIANS OF TRINIDAD.
     Winston-Salem, NC: Wake Forest University, Overseas Research
     Center (Medical Behavioral Science Monograph),   1974.
     West Indies - Trinidad - Overseas Indians - Alcoholics
     Anonymous - caste - social organization   D-0128.

41. Angrosino, Michael V.
     ANTHROPOLOGICAL CONTRIBUTIONS TO ALCOHOLISM POLICY: LOCAL-
     LEVEL INTERACTIONS.
     Unpublished paper: American Anthropological Association,
     Houston, TX, 13 pp.,   1977.
     United States - skid row - sociocultural   D-1254.

42. Angrosino, Michael V.
     COMMUNITY RESOURCES FOR ALCOHOLISM THERAPY: AN ANTHROPOLOGICAL
     OVERVIEW.
     In: Trotter, Robert T., II, and Chavira, Juan Antonio, ed.
     El uso de alcohol: A resource book for Spanish-speaking
     communities. Atlanta, GA: Southern Area Alcohol Education
     and Training Program, pp. 46-59,   1977.
     United States - Hispanos - social organization -
     treatment   D-0129.

43. Anonymous
     EL ALCOHOL Y EL INDIO. [Alcohol and Indians.] [Spa]
     América Indígena, 14: 283-285,   1954.
     Latin America - acculturation - temperance   D-0124.

44. Anonymous
     ALCOHOL INTOXICATION IN INDIANS.
     Journal of the American Medical Association,
     156: 1375,   1954.
     "race" - review - sociocultural - stereotype   D-0570.

45. Anonymous
     THE LIQUOR PROBLEM AMONG INDIANS OF THE SOUTHWEST.
     New Mexico Association on Indian Affairs Newsletter,
     (July 1956):   1956.
     Native Americans - dysfunctions   D-1180.

46. Anonymous
     SUPPLY OF LIQUOR TO NEW GUINEA NATIVES.
     South Pacific, 8: 209-211,   1956.
     New Guinea - change   D-0906.

47. Anonymous
     NATIVE LIQUORS IN SOUTHERN RHODESIA.
     Central African Journal of Medicine, 4: 558-559,   1958.
     Rhodesia - homebrew - manufacture - moonshine   D-0320.

6.

48. Anonymous
    DRINKING AND INDIAN PROBLEMS.
    Newsletter of Southwestern Association on Indian Affairs,
    (January 1959): 1959.
    Native Americans - dysfunctions D-1181.

49. Anonymous
    ALKOHOLISME IN ZUID-AFRIKA. [Alcoholism in South Africa.]
    [Afr]
    Africa Christo, 25(4): 7-10, 1970.
    South Africa - epidemiology D-1234.

50. Anonymous
    ALCOHOLISM IN BAHRAIN.
    Drinking and Drug Practices Surveyor, 9: 8, 1974.
    Bahrein - Islam D-0125.

51. Anonymous
    DRINK PROBLEMS IN MICRONESIA.
    Pacific Islands Monthly, 45(4): 13 ff, 1974.
    Micronesia D-0761.

52. Anonymous
    SELF-HELP PROGRAMS: INDIANS AND NATIVE ALASKANS.
    Alcohol Health and Research World, (Summer): 11-16, 1974.
    United States - Aleuts - Eskimos - Native Americans
    - treatment D-0115.

53. Anonymous
    BIBLIOGRAPHY: ALCOHOL PROBLEMS AMONG AMERICAN INDIANS
    AND ESKIMOS.
    Alcohol Health and Research World, (Winter): 30-31, 1975.
    United States - Aleuts - Eskimos - Native Americans
    - bibliography D-0145.

54. Anonymous
    ALCOHOL IN THE WESTERN PACIFIC AREA.
    New Zealand Medical Journal, 84: 290, 1976.
    Oceania D-0417.

55. Anonymous
    JEWS AND ALCOHOLISM: NO CULTURAL IMMUNITY FOUND.
    Medical World News, 19(13): 20-21, 1978.
    Jews D-0720.

56. Anumonye, A.; Omoniwa, N.; and Adaranijo, H.
    EXCESSIVE ALCOHOL USE AND RELATED PROBLEMS IN NIGERIA.
    Drug and Alcohol Dependence, 2: 23-30, 1977.
    Nigeria - change - homebrew - psychiatric problems D-0130.

57. Anumonye, Amechi
    ALCOHOL AND DRUG-RELATED PROBLEMS IN NIGERIA.
    In: Rutledge, Barbara, and Fulton, E. Kaye, ed. International
    collaboration: Problems and opportunities. Toronto, Ont.:

Citations

Addiction Research Foundation, pp. 80-87, 1977.
Nigeria - change - family - homebrew - moonshine - norms   D-0003.

58. Apostle, R., and Miller, V.P.
ALCOHOL CONSUMPTION AMONG NORTH AMERICAN INDIANS.
Unpublished report: Director, Non-Medical Use of Drugs,
Ottawa, Ont., 1975.
Canada - Native Americans - consumption   D-1918.

59. Appia, M.G.
L'ALCOOLISME AU PAYS NOIR. [Alcoholism in a black
country.] [Fre]
In: VIIe Congrès International contre l'Abus des Boissons
Alcooliques, Volume 1. Paris: Social de l'Union Française
Antialcoolique, 1900.
Africa - change - prohibition   D-1127.

60. Arnold, J.P.
ORIGIN AND HISTORY OF BEER BREWING.
Chicago, IL: Alumni Association of the Wahl-Henius Institute
of Fermentology, 1911.
World survey - beer - history, pre-1500 - history, pre-1900
- homebrew - manufacture - prehistory   D-0272.

61. Askwith, G.R.
BRITISH TAVERNS: THEIR HISTORY AND LAWS.
London: Routledge and Kegan Paul, 1928.
England - bar - history, pre-1500 - history, pre-1900   D-0400.

62. Azayem, G.M.
THE PROBLEM OF ALCOHOLISM IN EGYPT.
In: Proceedings of the 25th International Congress against
Alcoholism. Lausanne: Bureau International contre
l'Alcoolisme, pp. 1-5, 1956.
Egypt - Islam   D-1128.

63. Babcock, Charlotte G.
CROSS-CULTURAL COMPARISON OF DEPENDENCY PHENOMENA.
Forest Hospital Publications, 3: 24-33, 1965.
Cross-cultural - dependency   D-0131.

64. Babor, Thomas F.; McCabe, Thomas R.; Masanes, Philippe,;
and Ferrant, Jean-Pierre
PATTERNS OF ALCOHOLISM IN FRANCE AND AMERICA: A COMPARATIVE
STUDY.
In: Chafetz, Morris, E., ed. Alcoholism: A multilevel
problem. Treatment: Organization and management. Proceedings
of the 3rd Annual Conference of the National Institute on
Alcohol Abuse and Alcoholism. Held June 20-22, 1973 in Washington, D.C.
Rockville, MD: National Institute on Alcohol Abuse and Alcoholism (DHEW
Publication No. (ADM) 75-137), pp. 113-128, 1974.
Cross-national - France - United States - epidemiology -
etiology - sociocultural   D-0135.

8.

65. Babow, Irving
    FUNCTIONS AND DYSFUNCTIONS OF ALCOHOL: A SOCIOLOGICAL
    PERSPECTIVE.
    Journal of School Health, 44: 423-427, 1974.
    United States - dysfunctions - functions - prevention   D-0132.

66. Bacon, Margaret K.; Barry, Herbert, III; Child, Irvin L.;
    and Snyder, Charles R.
    DETAILED DEFINITIONS AND DATA.
    In: Keller, M., ed. A cross-cultural study of drinking.
    New Brunswick, NJ: Center of Alcohol Studies, Rutgers
    University (Quarterly Journal of Studies on Alcohol,
    Supplement No. 3), pp. 78-111, 1965.
    Cross-cultural - research methods   D-0148.

67. Bacon, Margaret K.; Barry, Herbert, III; and Child, Irvin L.
    RELATIONS TO OTHER FEATURES OF CULTURE.
    In: Keller, M., ed. A cross-cultural study of drinking.
    New Brunswick, NJ: Center of Alcohol Studies, Rutgers
    University (Quarterly Journal of Studies on Alcohol,
    Supplement No. 3), pp. 29-48, 1965.
    Cross-cultural - World survey - dependency - enculturation
    - female - intoxication - ritual - stress - youth   D-0149.

68. Bacon, Margaret K.
    CROSS-CULTURAL STUDIES OF DRINKING.
    In: Bourne, Peter, and Fox, Ruth, ed. Alcoholism:
    Progress in research and treatment. New York, NY:
    Academic, pp. 171-192, 1973.
    Cross-cultural - sociocultural   D-0133.

69. Bacon, Margaret K.
    THE DEPENDENCY-CONFLICT HYPOTHESIS AND THE FREQUENCY OF
    DRUNKENNESS: FURTHER EVIDENCE FROM A CROSS-CULTURAL STUDY.
    Quarterly Journal of Studies on Alcohol, 35: 863-876, 1974.
    Corss-cultural - dependency - intoxication   D-0134.

70. Bacon, Margaret K.
    ALCOHOL USE IN TRIBAL SOCIETIES.
    In: Kissin, Benjamin, and Begleiter, Henri, ed. The
    biology of alcoholism, Volume 4: Social aspects of
    alcoholism. New York, NY: Plenum, pp. 1-36, 1976.
    World survey - functions - review - social organization
    - sociocultural   D-0137.

71. Bacon, Margaret K.
    CROSS-CULTURAL STUDIES OF DRINKING: INTEGRATED DRINKING
    AND SEX DIFFERENCES IN THE USE OF ALCOHOLIC BEVERAGES.
    In: Everett, Michael W.; Waddell, Jack O.; and Heath,
    Dwight B., ed. Cross-cultural approaches to the study of
    alcohol: An interdisciplinary perspective. The Hague:
    Mouton, pp. 23-33, 1976.
    Cross-cultural - World survey - female - functions -
    social organization   D-0136.

72. Bacon, Selden D.
     SOCIOLOGY AND THE PROBLEMS OF ALCOHOL: FOUNDATIONS FOR
     A SOCIOLOGICAL STUDY OF DRINKING BEHAVIOR.
     Quarterly Journal of Studies on Alcohol, 4: 399-445, 1943.
     research methods - review - sociocultural   D-0138.

73. Bacon, Selden D.
     ALCOHOL AND COMPLEX SOCIETY.
     In: Yale University, Center of Alcohol Studies. Alcohol,
     science, and society. New Haven, CT: Quarterly Journal
     of Studies on Alcohol, pp. 179-200,   1945.
     change - dysfunctions - social organization - socio-
     cultural   D-0146.

74. Bacon, Selden D.
     ALCOHOLISM AND SOCIAL ISOLATION.
     In: Bell, M., ed. Cooperation in crime control. New York,
     NY: National Probation Association, pp. 209-234,   1945.
     anomie - crime - social organization   D-0139.

75. Bacon, Selden D.
     CURRENT RESEARCH ON ALCOHOLISM: V. REPORT OF THE SECTION
     ON SOCIOLOGICAL RESEARCH.
     Quarterly Journal of Studies on Alcohol, 16: 551-564,   1955.
     research methods - review - sociocultural   D-0140.

76. Bacon, Selden D.
     ALCOHOL AND COMPLEX SOCIETY.
     In: Pittman, David J., and Snyder, Charles R., ed.
     Society, culture, and drinking patterns. New York, NY:
     John Wiley & Sons, pp. 78-93,   1962.
     change - dysfunctions - social organization -
     sociocultural   D-1243.

77. Bacon, Selden D.
     THE PROCESS OF ADDICTION TO ALCOHOL: SOCIAL ASPECTS.
     Quarterly Journal of Studies on Alcohol, 34: 1-27,   1973.
     addiction - dysfunctions - functions - intoxication -
     labeling - norms - social organization   D-0141.

78. Baddeley, Felix J.
     AFRICAN BEERHALLS.
     Thesis, University of Cape Town,   1966.
     South Africa - Bantu - bar - beer - urbanization   D-1033.

79. Badri, M.B.
     ISLAM AND ALCOHOLISM.
     Indianapolis, IN: American Trust Publications,   1976.
     Islam - history, pre-1500 - religion - prohibition   D-1034.

80. Bahr, Howard M., ed.
    DISAFFILIATED MEN: ESSAYS AND BIBLIOGRAPHY ON SKID ROW, VAGRANCY, AND OUTSIDERS.
    Toronto, Ont.: University of Toronto Press, 428 pp.,   1970.
    United States - Skid Row - anomie - bibliography - social organization   D-0087.

81. Bahr, Howard M.; Chadwick, Bruce A.; and Day, Robert C., ed.
    NATIVE AMERICANS TODAY: SOCIOLOGICAL PERSPECTIVES.
    New York, NY: Harper and Row,   1971.
    United States - Native Americans - acculturation - anomie - change - dysfunctions   D-1035.

82. Bahr, Howard M., and Caplow, Theodore
    OLD MEN DRUNK AND SOBER.
    New York, NY: New York University Press, 407 pp.,   1973.
    United States - Skid Row - anomie - social organization   B-6017.

83. Bahr, Howard M.
    SKID ROW: AN INTRODUCTION TO DISAFFILIATION.
    New York, NY: Oxford University Press, 335 pp.,   1973.
    United States - Skid Row - anomie - social organization - treatment   D-0086.

84. Bahr, Howard M., and Garrett, Gerald R.
    WOMEN ALONE: DISAFFILIATION OF URBAN FEMALES.
    Lexington, MA: Lexington (D.C. Heath),   1976.
    United States - Skid Row - anomie - female - social organization - stress   D-0401.

85. Baird, Edward G.
    THE ALCOHOL PROBLEM AND THE LAW. I. THE ANCIENTS LAWS AND CUSTOMS.
    Quarterly Journal of Studies on Alcohol, 4: 535-556,   1944.
    World survey - Classical peoples - history, pre-1500 - norms - prehistory - prevention - prohibition   D-0150.

86. Baird, Edward G.
    THE ALCOHOL PROBLEM AND THE LAW. II. THE COMMON-LAW BASES OF MODERN LIQUOR CONTROLS.
    Quarterly Journal of Studies on Alcohol, 5: 126-161,   1944.
    World survey - Classical peoples - history, pre-1500 - history, pre-1900 - norms - prehistory - prevention - prohibition   D-0151.

87. Baird, Edward G.
    THE ALCOHOL PROBLEM AND THE LAW. III. THE BEGINNINGS OF THE ALCOHOLIC-BEVERAGE CONTROL LAWS IN AMERICA. A. THE LOGICAL AND THE EMPIRICAL BASES OF THE LIQUOR-CONTROL LAWS: A METHOD OF STUDY.
    Quarterly Journal of Studies on Alcohol, 6: 335-383,   1945.
    United States -

history, pre-1900 - norms - prehistory - prevention -
prohibition   D-0152.

88.   Baird, Edward G.
      THE ALCOHOL PROBLEM AND THE LAW. III. THE BEGINNINGS OF
      THE ALCOHOLIC-BEVERAGE CONTROL LAWS IN AMERICA. D. THE
      FORMATIVE YEARS IN NEW ENGLAND: EARLY STATUTORY AND CASE
      LAW RELATING TO ALCOHOLIC BEVERAGES.
      Quarterly Journal of Studies on Alcohol, 7: 110-162, and
      271-296,   1946.
      United States - history, pre-1900 -
      norms - prehistory - prevention -
      prohibition   D-0153.

89.   Baird, Edward G.
      THE ALCOHOL PROBLEM AND THE LAW. III. THE BEGINNINGS OF
      THE ALCOHOLIC-BEVERAGE CONTROL LAWS IN AMERICA. E. THE
      FORMATIVE YEARS IN VIRGINIA: EARLY STATUTORY AND CASE
      LAW RELATING TO ALCOHOLIC BEVERAGES.
      Quarterly Journal of Studies on Alcohol, 9: 80-118,   1948.
      United States - history, pre-1900 -
      norms - prehistory - prevention -
      prohibition   D-0154.

90.   Baker, James L.
      INDIANS, ALCOHOL AND HOMICIDE.
      Journal of Social Therapy, 5: 270-275,   1959.
      United States - Native Americans - intoxication - murder   D-0142.

91.   Baker, Joan M.
      ALCOHOLISM AND THE AMERICAN INDIAN.
      In: Estes, Nada J., and Heinemann, M. Edith, ed. Alcoholism:
      Development, consequences, and interventions. Saint Louis,
      MO: C.V. Mosby, pp. 194-203,   1977.
      United States - Native Americans - history, pre-1900 -
      stereotype - treatment   D-0088.

92.   Baker, Oliver
      DRINKING VESSELS: BLACK JACKS AND LEATHER BOTTELLS.
      [no place]: [no publisher],   1921.
      England - Europe - containers - history, pre-1500 -
      history, pre-1900   D-1202.

93.   Baldus, Herbert
      BEBIDAS E NARCOTICOS DOS INDIO DO BRASIL. [Drinks and
      narcotics of indians in Brazil: Suggestions for ethnographic
      research.] [Por]
      Sociologia, 12: 161-169,   1950.
      Brazil - research methods   D-0155.

94. Bales, Robert F.
 CULTURAL DIFFERENCES IN RATES OF ALCOHOLISM.
 Quarterly Journal of Studies on Alcohol, 6: 480-499, 1946.
 Cross-ethnic - Ireland - Jews - attitudes - functions -
 norms - social organization - sociocultural - stress   D-0143.

95. Balikci, Asen
 BAD FRIENDS.
 Human Organization, 27(3): 191-199, 1968.
 Canada - Native Americans - Kutchin - aggression -
 social organization   D-0156.

96. Banay, Ralph S.
 CULTURAL INFLUENCES IN ALCOHOLISM.
 Journal of Nervous and Mental Disease, 102: 265-275, 1945.
 functions - self - sociocultural   D-0144.

97. Banks, E.
 NATIVE DRINK IN SARAWAK.
 Sarawak Museum Journal, 4: 439-447, 1937.
 Cross-ethnic - Sarawak - Dyak - Kayan - Kelabit - Kenyah -
 Murut - customs - distribution - dysfunctions - functions -
 homebrew - intoxication   D-0157.

98. Bard, Jeffrey; Mare, Christopher; Williams, Charles; and
 Wolpaw, Ivan
 EFFECTS OF INTRA-GROUP COMPETITION ON ALCOHOL CONSUMPTION
 IN PRIMITIVE CULTURES.
 Unpublished manuscript,   [ca. 1955].
 World survey - Cross-cultural - aggression - dependency   D-1255.

99. Barlett, Peggy F.
 DRINKING IN THE SAN JUAN FIESTA, OTAVALO, ECUADOR.
 Unpublished manuscript, 1976.
 Ecuador - Quechua - binge - Church - religion   D-1256.

100. Barnett, Milton L.
 ALCOHOLISM IN THE CANTONESE OF NEW YORK CITY: AN
 ANTHROPOLOGICAL STUDY.
 In: Diethelm, O., ed. Etiology of chronic alcoholism.
 Springfield, IL: Charles C. Thomas, pp. 179-227, 1955.
 United States - Overseas Chinese - attitudes - customs -
 functions - norms - ritual - social organization   D-0158.

101. Barrera Vásquez, A.
 EL PULQUE ENTRE LOS MAYAS. [Pulque among the Mayas.] [Spa]
 Cuadernos Mayas 3, Mérida, Mexico, 1941.
 Mexico - Maya - homebrew - history, pre-1500 - language -
 prehistory   D-1248.

102. Barrow, M.V.; Niswander, J.D.; and Fortuine, R.
 HEALTH AND DISEASE OF AMERICAN INDIANS NORTH OF MEXICO: A
 BIBLIOGRAPHY, 1800-1969.
 Gainesville, FL: University of Florida Press, 1972.

Canada - United States - Aleuts - Eskimos - Native Americans - alcoholism - bibliography - history, pre-1500 - history, pre-1900   D-0159.

103. Barry, Edward
      OBSERVATIONS HISTORICAL, CRITICAL, AND MEDICAL, ON THE WINES OF THE ANCIENTS...
      London: T. Cadell,   1775.
      World survey - customs - distribution - history, pre-1500 - history, pre-1900 - medical - prehistory - wine   D-0160.

104. Barry, Herbert, III; Buchwald, Charles; Child, Irvin L.; and Bacon, Margaret K.
      COMPARISONS WITH HORTON RATINGS.
      In: Keller, M., ed. A cross-cultural study of drinking. New Brunswick, NJ: Center of Alcohol Studies, Rutgers University (Quarterly Journal of Studies on Alcohol, Supplement No. 3), pp. 62-77,   1965.
      World survey - Cross-cultural - research methods   D-0162.

105. Barry, Herbert, III
      SOCIOCULTURAL ASPECTS OF ALCOHOL ADDICTION.
      In: Wikler, Abraham, ed. The addictive states. (Research Publications Association for Research in Nervous and Mental Disease, Volume 46). Baltimore, MD: Williams and Wilkins, pp. 455-471,   1968.
      dependency - norms - review - sociocultural - stress   D-0147.

106. Barry, Herbert, III
      CROSS-CULTURAL EVIDENCE THAT DEPENDENCY CONFLICT MOTIVATES DRUNKENNESS.
      In: Everett, Michael W.; Waddell, Jack O.; and Heath, Dwight B., ed. Cross-cultural approaches to the study of alcohol: An interdisciplinary perspective. The Hague: Mouton, pp. 249-263,   1976.
      World survey - Cross-cultural - dependency   D-0161.

107. Barter, E.R., and Barter, J.T.
      URBAN INDIANS AND MENTAL HEALTH PROBLEMS.
      Psychiatric Annals, 4(11): 37-43,   1974.
      United States - Native Americans - psychiatric problems - stress - urbanization   D-0163.

108. Basserman-Jordan, Friedrich v.
      DER WEINBAU DER PFALZ IM ALTERTUM. [Wine manufacture in the Palatinates of antiquity.] [Ger]
      Speyer: [no publisher],   1947.
      Europe - Near East - Classical peoples - history, pre-1500 - prehistory   D-1209.

109. Beals, Ralph L.
      THE COMPARATIVE ETHNOLOGY OF NORTHERN MEXICO BEFORE 1750.
      Berkeley, CA: University of California Press,   1932.

Cross-ethnic - Mexico - distribution - history, pre-1500 -
history, pre-1900 - prehistory - ritual   D-0164.

110. Beaubrun, Michael H.
TREATMENT OF ALCOHOLISM IN TRINIDAD AND TOBAGO, 1956-1965.
British Journal of Psychiatry, 113: 643-658,   1967.
Tobago - Trinidad - Overseas Indians - etiology - self -
sociocultural - treatment   B-3201.

111. Beaubrun, Michael H.
ALCOHOLISM AND DRINKING PRACTICES IN A JAMAICAN SUBURB.
Alcoholism, 4: 21-37,   1968.
Jamaica - Cross-ethnic - Overseas Chinese - Overseas
Indians - class - epidemiology - etiology - norms -
"race" - social organization   D-0165.

112. Beaubrun, Michael H., and Firth, Hedy
A TRANSCULTURAL ANALYSIS OF ALCOHOLICS ANONYMOUS:
TRINIDAD/LONDON.
Unpublished paper: Presented at the Joint Meeting of the
Caribbean Psychiatric Association and the American
Psychiatric Association, Ocho Rios, Jamaica, May 10-14,
1969, 29 pp.,   1969.
Cross-national - Trinidad - England - Overseas Indians -
Alcoholics Anonymous - ambivalence - family - stress   D-0173.

113. Beaubrun, Michael H.
THE INFLUENCE OF SOCIO-CULTURAL FACTORS ON THE TREATMENT
OF ALCOHOLISM IN THE WEST INDIES.
In: Kiloh, L.G., and Bell, D.S., ed. <u>29th International
Congress on Alcoholism and Drug Dependence</u>. Held February,
1970 in Sydney, Australia. Sydney: Butterworths,
pp. 525-526,   1971.
Jamaica - Trinidad - Cross-ethnic - Overseas Chinese -
class - "race" - treatment   D-0168.

114. Beaubrun, Michael H.
CANNABIS AND ALCOHOL: THE JAMAICAN EXPERIENCE.
In: Rubin, Vera, ed. <u>Cannabis and culture</u>. The Hague:
Mouton, pp. 485-494,   1975.
Jamaica - class - drugs - personality   D-0166.

115. Beaubrun, Michael H.
EPIDEMIOLOGICAL RESEARCH IN THE CARIBBEAN CONTEXT.
In: Rutledge, Barbara, and Fulton, E. Kaye, ed.
<u>International collaboration: Problems and opportunities</u>.
Toronto, Ont.: Addiction Research Foundation, pp. 36-57,   1977.
Trinidad - Tobago - accidents - consumption - economics -
epidemiology - research methods   D-0004.

116. Beckett, Jeremy
ABORIGINES, ALCOHOL, AND ASSIMILATION.
In: Reay, Marie, ed. <u>Aborigines now: New perspectives</u>

	in the study of aboriginal communities. Sydney: Angus and Robertson, pp. 32-47,
	Australia - Aborigines - acculturation - anomie - stress

                in the study of aboriginal communities. Sydney: Angus
                and Robertson, pp. 32-47, 1964.
                Australia - Aborigines - acculturation - anomie - stress D-0402.

117. Beede, Laurence I.
     TEEN-AGE INDIAN DRINKING IN SEATTLE AND KING COUNTY.
     M.A. Thesis, University of Washington, 1968.
     Cross-ethnic - Native Americans - class - crime - youth D-0169.

118. Beidelman, Thomas O.
     BEER DRINKING AND CATTLE THEFT IN UKAGURU: INTERTRIBAL
     RELATIONS IN A TANGANYIKA CHIEFDOM.
     American Anthropologist, 63: 534-549, 1961.
     Tanganyika - Cross-ethnic - Kaguru - Baraguru - bar -
     economics - history, pre-1500 - history, pre-1900 -
     political - social organization D-0167.

119. Bejarano, Jorge
     LA DERROTA DE UN VICIO: ORIGEN E HISTORIA DE LA CHICHA.
     [The story of a vice: Origin and history of chicha.] [Spa]
     Bogotá: Editorial Iqueima, 1950.
     Colombia - homebrew - history, pre-1500 - history,
     pre-1900 D-0170.

120. Bell, Michael
     RUNNING RABBITS AND TALKING SHIT: FOLKLORIC COMMUNICATIONS
     IN AN URBAN BLACK BAR.
     Ph.D. Dissertation, University of Pennsylvania, 1975.
     United States - Blacks - bar - folklore - leisure D-0171.

121. Bellmann, Herbert
     DIE DESTILLATION BEI DEN NATURVÖLKERN. [Distillation
     among primitive peoples.] [Ger]
     Wissenschaftliche Zeitschrift der Freidrich-Schiller
     Universität, 3: 179-185, 1954.
     World survey - distribution - manufacture - moonshine D-0172.

122. Belmont, François V. de
     HISTOIRE DE L'EAU-DE-VIE EN CANADA. [History of brandy
     in Canada.] [Fre]
     Québec: Société Litteraire de Québec, 1840.
     Canada - Native Americans - brandy - economics - functions -
     history, pre-1900 - intoxication D-0174.

123. Benjamin, Rommel
     RURAL BLACK FOLK AND ALCOHOL.
     In: Harper, Frederick D., ed. Alcohol abuse and Black
     America. Alexandria, VA: Douglass, pp. 49-60, 1976.
     United States - Blacks D-0175.

124. Bennett, Linda; Wolin, Steven J; and Noonan, Denise L.
     FAMILY IDENTITY AND INTERGENERATIONAL RECURRENCE OF ALCOHOLISM.
     Unpublished paper: Presented at the 6th World Congress of
     Social Psychiatry, Opatija, Yugoslavia, 10 pp., 1976.

16.

United States - enculturation - family - ritual -
social organization   D-1257.

125. Bennett, Linda; Wolin, Steven J; and Noonan, Denise L.
      INTRUSION OF ALCOHOL ON FAMILY RITUALS.
      Unpublished paper: Society for Applied Anthropology,
      Mérida, Mexico, 16 pp.,   1978.
      United States - enculturation - family - ritual   D-1258.

126. Bennion, Lynn J., and Li, Ting-Kai
      ALCOHOL METABOLISM IN AMERICAN INDIANS AND WHITES: LACK
      OF RACIAL DIFFERENCES IN METABOLIC RATE AND LIVER ALCOHOL
      DEHYDROGENASE.
      New England Journal of Medicine, 294(1): 9-13,   1976.
      Cross-ethnic - Native Americans - Whites - metabolism -
      "race"   D-0176.

127. Benos, J.
      ALKOHOLISMUS UND TRINKSITTEN; MIT BESONDERER
      BERUCKSICHTIGUNG DES ALKOHOLPROBLEM IN GRIECHENLAND.
      [Alcoholism and drinking customs; with special reference
      to problem drinking in Greece.] [Ger]
      Zeitschrift für Allgemeinmedizin, 49: 974-977,   1973.
      Greece - attitudes - customs   D-0177.

128. Berg, Carl, and Neulinger, John
      ALCOHOLICS' PERCEPTION OF LEISURE.
      Journal of Studies on Alcohol, 37: 1625-1632,   1976.
      United States - leisure   D-0178.

129. Bernier, G., and Lambrecht, A.
      ETUDE SUR LES BOISSONS INDIGENES DU KATANGA. [Study on
      indigenous drinks of Katanga.] [Fre]
      Memoires de l'Académie Royale des Sciences Coloniales,
      Classes des Sciences Naturelles et Médicales (ns),
      9(7):   1959.
      Congo - Katanga - homebrew - manufacture   D-1235.

130. Bernier, G., and Lambrecht, A.
      ETUDE SUR LES BOISSONS FERMENTEES INDIGENES DU KATANGA.
      [Study on indigenous fermented drinks of Katanga.] [Fre]
      Problèmes Sociaux Congolais, 48: 5-41,   1960.
      Congo - Katanga - economics - homebrew - manufacture -
      nutrition   D-0179.

131. Berreman, Gerald D.
      DRINKING PATTERNS OF THE ALEUTS.
      Quarterly Journal of Studies on Alcohol, 17: 503-514, 1956.
      United States - Aleuts - acculturation - anomie - binge -
      customs - history, pre-1900 - homebrew - intoxication -
      social organization - stress   D-0180.

132. Berruecos, Luis A.
PANORAMA ACTUAL DEL PROBLEMA DEL ALCOHOLISM EN MEXICO: ANTECEDENTES, ACCIONES CONCRETAS E INVESTIGACION. [Current situation of alcoholism in Mexico: Antecedents, actions and research.] [Spa]
Unpublished paper: Society for Applied Anthropology, Mérida, Mexico, 1978.
Mexico - change - epidemiology - sociocultural   D-1912.

133. Bett, W.R. [and Rogers, Webster, Dent, and Norman]
ALCOHOL AND CRIME IN CEYLON: A PRELIMINARY COMMUNICATION [and discussion].
British Journal of Inebriety, 43(2): 57-60, 1946.
Ceylon - crime - homebrew - medical - temperance   D-0181.

134. Bickerton, Yvonne J.
ALCOHOLISM AND ETHNICITY IN HAWAII.
Ph.D. Dissertation, University of Sussex, 1975.
Hawaiian Islands - Cross-ethnic   D-0184.

135. Bickerton, Yvonne J.
ETHNIC GROUP DIFFERENCES IN THE CLIENTELE OF A STATE DETOXIFICATION UNIT.
In: Seixas, Frank A., ed. Currents in alcoholism, Volume 2: Psychiatric, psychological, social and epidemiological studies. New York, NY: Grune & Stratton, pp. 357-365, 1977.
Hawaiian Islands - Cross-ethnic   D-0182.

136. Billiard, R.
LA VIGNE DANS L'ANTIQUITE. [The vine in antiquity.] [Fre]
Lyon: Lardanchet, 1913.
Europe - Near East - Classical peoples - history, pre-1500   D-0273.

137. Billings, A.G.; Weiner, S.; Kessler, M.; and Gomberg, C.A.
DRINKING BEHAVIOR IN LABORATORY AND BARROOM SETTINGS.
Journal of Studies on Alcohol, 37(1): 85-89, 1976.
United States - bar - research methods   D-0183.

138. Billings, Andrew G.; Gomberg, Christopher A.; Nash, Barbara H.; Kessler, Marc; and Weiner, Sheldon
SYNCHRONIZED SIPPING IN ALCOHOLICS AND SOCIAL DRINKERS: A PRELIMINARY INVESTIGATION.
Journal of Studies on Alcohol, 39(3): 554-559, 1978.
research methods   D-0089.

139. Bismuth, H., and Menage, C.
ALCOOLISATION DES ETATS DE LANGUE FRANCAISE DE L'AFRIQUE OCCIDENTALE. [Alcoholization of French language states in West Africa.] [Fre] ALCOOLISATION D'HAUT VOLTA. [Alcoholization in Upper Volta.] [Fre] ALCOOLISATION DU NIGER. [Alcoholization in Niger.] [Fre]

18.

ALCOOLISATION DU SENEGAL. [Alcoholization in Senegal.] [Fre] APERCU DE L'ALCOOLISATION DE LA GUINEE. [Overview of alcoholization in Guinea.] [Fre] ASPECTS DE L'ALCOOLISATION DE DAHOMEY. [Aspects of alcoholization in Dahomey.] [Fre]
Paris: Haut Comité d'Etude et d'Information sur l'Alcoolisme, 1960.
Africa - Upper Volta - Nigeria - Senegal - Guinea - Dahomey   D-1217.

140. Bismuth, H., and Menaqe, C.
LES BOISSONS ALCOOLIQUES EN A.O.F. [Alcoholic beverages in French West Africa.] [Fre]
Bulletin de l'Institute Français d'Afrique Noire, 23(1-2): 60-118,   1961.
Africa - distribution - homebrew - manufacture   D-0259.

141. Bissonette, Raymond
THE BARTENDER AS A MENTAL HEALTH SERVICE GATEKEEPER: A ROLE ANALYSIS.
Community Mental Health Journal, 13(1): 92-99,   1977.
bar - treatment   D-0090.

142. Bittker, T.E., and Metzner, R.J.
BARRIERS IN THE RELATIONSHIPS OF PHYSICIANS AND ALCOHOLIC PATIENTS IN TRANSCULTURAL SETTINGS.
Unpublished paper: Presented at the 8th Joint Meeting of the Professional Associations of the U.S. Public Health Service, Phoenix, AZ,   1973.
United States - Native Americans - attitudes - sociocultural - treatment   D-1259.

143. Bittker, Thomas E.
DILEMMAS OF MENTAL HEALTH SERVICE DELIVERY TO OFF-RESERVATION INDIANS.
Anthropological Quarterly, 46(3): 172-182,   1973.
United States - Native Americans - psychiatric problems - treatment   D-0185.

144. Blacker, Edward
SOCIOCULTURAL FACTORS IN ALCOHOLISM.
International Psychiatry Clinics, 3(2): 51-80,   1966.
World survey - ambivalence - definition - norms - review - sociocultural   D-0186.

145. Blacker, Hereth
DRINKING PRACTICES AND PROBLEMS ABROAD: 1. THE ISLE OF REUNION. 2. TAHITI.
Journal of Alcoholism, 6(2): 61-63,   1971.
Africa - Reunion - Oceania - Tahiti - accidents - aggression - crime - intoxication   D-0187.

146. Blacker, Hereth
THE ENGLISH PUB.
Journal of Alcoholism, 11(2): 56-68, 1976.
England - bar - functions - history, pre-1500 -
history, pre-1900 D-0005.

147. Blane, Howard T., and Vadnal, N. Jane
GENERATIONAL CHANGE AND DRINKING CONTEXT AMONG ITALIAN-
AMERICANS.
Unpublished paper: American Psychological Association,
Washington, D.C., 12 pp., 1976.
United States - Italian-Americans - acculturation - change -
customs D-1540.

148. Blane, Howard T.
ACCULTURATION AND DRINKING IN AN ITALIAN-AMERICAN COMMUNITY.
Journal of Studies on Alcohol, 38: 1324-1346, 1977.
United States - Italian-Americans - acculturation - change -
customs D-0188.

149. Blaney, R.
ALCOHOLISM IN IRELAND: MEDICAL AND SOCIAL ASPECTS.
Journal of the Statistical and Social Inquiry Society of
Ireland, 23(1): 108-124, 1975.
Ireland - family - social organization D-0189.

150. Blehr, Otto
SOCIAL DRINKING IN THE FAROE ISLANDS.
Ethnos: 1-4, 1974.
Denmark - Faroe Islands - customs - fighting D-0380.

151. Bleichsteiner, Robert
ZEREMONIALE TRINKSITTEN UND RAUMORDNUNG BEI TURKO-
MONGOLISCHEN NOMADER. [Ceremonial drinking customs of
Turkish-Mongolian nomads.] [Ger]
Archiv für Völkerkunde, 6-7: 181-208, 1952.
Mongolia - religion - ritual D-1064.

152. Blevans, Stephen A.
A CRITICAL REVIEW OF THE ANTHROPOLOGICAL LITERATURE ON
DRINKING, DRUNKENNESS, AND ALCOHOLISM.
M.A. Thesis, University of Washington, 1967.
review - sociocultural D-0379.

153. Blignaut, F.W.
THE PERSONALITY AND TREATMENT OF THE ALCOHOLIC IN SOUTH
AFRICA: REPORT OF THE PROJECT ALCOHOLISM (PART 1),
VOLUME 1.
Pretoria: Department of Communication, University of
South Africa, (Report No. 4 of the 1973 series of the
Department of Social Welfare and Pensions, Republic of
South Africa), 108 pp., 1971.
South Africa - epidemiology - treatment D-1103.

20.

154. Blom, Frans
ON SLOTKIN'S "FERMENTED DRINKS IN MEXICO."
American Anthropologist, 58: 185-186, 1956.
Mexico - Aztec - Maya - history, pre-1900 - history,
pre-1500 D-0190.

155. Bloom, Joseph D.
SOCIO-CULTURAL ASPECTS OF ALCOHOLISM.
Alaska Medicine, 12(3): 65-67, 1970.
anomie - economics - prevention - social organization D-0191.

156. Blum, Richard H., and Blum, Eva M.
DRINKING PRACTICES AND CONTROLS IN RURAL GREECE.
British Journal of Addiction, 60: 93-108, 1964.
Greece - attitudes - customs - functions - intoxication -
medical - nutrition - ritual D-0192.

157. Blum, Richard H., and Blum, Eva M.
A CULTURAL CASE STUDY.
In: Blum, Richard H., and Associates, ed. Society and
drugs. Drugs I: Social and cultural observations.
San Francisco, CA: Jossey-Bass, pp. 188-227, 1969.
Greece - attitudes - customs - functions - sociocultural D-0308.

158. Blum, Richard H.
A HISTORY OF ALCOHOL.
In: Blum, Richard H., and Associates, ed. Society and
drugs. Drugs I: Social and cultural observations.
San Francisco, CA: Jossey-Bass, pp. 24-42, 1969.
World survey - prehistory - review D-0307.

159. Blyth, W.
TRANSCULTURAL STUDIES IN ALCOHOLISM IN A RURAL CATCHMENT
AREA AS PERTAINING TO THREE CULTURES: WHITE AMERICANS,
AMERICAN NEGROES, AMERICAN INDIANS.
[Multigraphed], [Transcultural Psychiatric Review], 1972.
United States - Cross-ethnic - Native Americans - Blacks -
Whites D-1541.

160. Boalt, Gunnar
A SOCIOLOGICAL THEORY OF ALCOHOLISM.
Lausanne: International Bureau Against Alcoholism
(Selected Articles No. 4), 7 pp., 1961.
functions - sociocultural - stress D-0381.

161. Boatman, John F.
DRINKING AMONG INDIAN TEENAGERS.
M.A. Thesis, University of Wisconsin (Milwaukee), 1968.
United States - Native Americans - anomie - youth D-0382.

162. Bock, George E., and Bergman, Robert L.
INDIANS AND ALCOHOL.
Unpublished paper: Seminar on Indian Health, University
of Arizona, 16 pp., 1967.

United States - Native Americans - disulfiram - treatment   D-1542.

163. Bolton, Ralph
AGGRESSION AND HYPOGLYCEMIA AMONG THE QOLLA: A STUDY IN
PSYCHOBIOLOGICAL ANTHROPOLOGY.
Ethnology, 12: 227-257,   1973.
Peru - Qolla - aggression - hypoglycemia   D-0007.

164. Bonfiglio, Giovanni; Falli, Silvana; and Pacini, Antonella
ALCOHOLISM IN ITALY: AN OUTLINE HIGHLIGHTING SOME SPECIAL
FEATURES.
British Journal of Addiction, 72(1): 3-12,   1977.
Italy - change - customs   D-0091.

165. Bose, Dhirendra Krishna
WINE IN ANCIENT INDIA.
Calcutta: K.M. Connor, 51 pp.,   1922.
India - Buddhism - Hinduism - change - history, pre-1500 -
homebrew - literature - medical - norms - prohibition -
religion - temperance - wine   D-0193.

166. Botha, E.M.
ALKOHOLISME IN DIE MAATSKAPILIKEWERKPRAKTYK VAN'N
PLATTELANDSE GESINORGANISASIE. [The personality and
treatment of the alcoholic in South Africa: Report of
the Project Alcoholism, Volume 10.] [Afr]
Pretoria: Department of Social Welfare and Pensions,
Republic of South Africa,   1971.
South Africa - dysfunctions   D-1104.

167. Bourguignon, Erika E.
COMMENT ON LEACOCK'S "CEREMONIAL DRINKING IN AN AFRO-
BRAZILIAN CULT."
American Anthropologist, 66: 1393-1394,   1964.
Haiti - possession - religion   D-0194.

168. Bourguignon, Erika E., ed.
RELIGION, ALTERED STATES OF CONSCIOUSNESS AND SOCIAL CHANGE.
Columbus, OH: Ohio State University Press,   1973.
World survey - possession - religion   D-0383.

169. Bourke, John G.
PRIMITIVE DISTILLATION AMONG THE TARASCOES.
American Anthropologist (os), 6: 65-69,   1893.
Mexico - Tarascan - manufacture   D-0384.

170. Bourke, John G.
DISTILLATION BY EARLY AMERICAN INDIANS.
American Anthropologist (os), 7: 297-299,   1894.
United States - Native Americans - history, pre-1900 -
homebrew - manufacture   D-0385.

22.

171. Boyatzis, Richard E.
THE EFFECT OF ALCOHOL CONSUMPTION ON THE AGGRESSIVE
BEHAVIOR OF MEN.
Quarterly Journal of Studies on Alcohol, 35: 959-972,　　1975.
United States - aggression - intoxication　　D-0195.

172. Boyatzis, Richard E.
DRINKING AS A MANIFESTATION OF POWER CONCERNS.
In: Everett, Michael W.; Waddell, Jack O.; and Heath,
Dwight B., ed. Cross-cultural approaches to the study of
alcohol: An interdisciplinary perspective. The Hague:
Mouton, pp. 265-286,　　1976.
intoxication - power　　D-0196.

173. Boyce, George A.
ALCOHOL AND AMERICAN INDIAN STUDENTS.
Unpublished report: U.S. Department of the Interior,
Bureau of American Ethnology, Washington, D.C.,　　1965.
United States - Native Americans - sociocultural - youth　　D-1129.

174. Boyer, L. B[ryce]
PSYCHOANALYTIC INSIGHTS IN WORKING WITH ETHNIC MINORITIES.
Social Casework, 45: 519-526,　　1964.
United States - Native Americans - Apache - research
methods - sociocultural　　D-0386.

175. Boyer, L. Bryce
PSYCHOLOGICAL PROBLEMS OF A GROUP OF APACHES: ALCOHOLIC
HALLUCINOSIS AND LATENT HOMOSEXUALITY AMONG TYPICAL MEN.
In: Muensterberger, W., and Axelrad, S., ed. The
psychoanalytic study of society, Volume 3. New York, NY:
International Universities Press, pp. 203-277,　　1964.
United States - Native Americans - Apache - aggression -
ambivalence - dysfunctions - sex　　D-0387.

176. Braidwood, Robert J., et al.
SYMPOSIUM: DID MAN ONCE LIVE BY BEER ALONE?
American Anthropologist, 55: 515-526,　　1953.
Near East - prehistory - homebrew　　D-1130.

177. Branson, H.
GAY BAR.
San Francisco, CA: Pan Graphic,　　1957.
United States - bar - sex　　D-0403.

178. Brelsford, Gregg
ATHABASCAN DRINKING BEHAVIOR: A PRELIMINARY ETHNOGRAPHY.
Alaska Department of Health and Social Service Quarterly
Magazine, 34(1): 15-20,　　1977.
United States - Native Americans - Athabascan - binge -
customs - economics - intoxication　　D-0092.

179. Brettler, P.
      SORGHUM IN THE NATIVE BREWING INDUSTRY.
      Bulawayo: Rhodesia Municipal Brewery,   n.d.
      South Africa - Bantu - homebrew - manufacture   D-0389.

180. Brod, Thomas M.
      ALCOHOLISM AS A MENTAL HEALTH PROBLEM OF NATIVE AMERICANS:
      A REVIEW OF THE LITERATURE.
      Archives of General Psychiatry, 32: 1385-1391,   1975.
      Native Americans - acculturation - anomie - functions -
      psychiatric problems - review - stress   D-0197.

181. Brody, Hugh
      INDIANS ON SKID ROW.
      Ottawa, Ont.: (Northern Science Research Group, Department
      of Indian Affairs and Northern Development Publication
      No. 70-2), Information Canada, 86 pp.,   1971.
      Canada - Native Americans - Skid Row - anomie - functions -
      self - stereotype   D-0388.

182. Brown, John H.
      EARLY AMERICAN BEVERAGES.
      Rutland, VT: Charles E. Tuttle,   1966.
      United States - customs - history, pre-1900 - homebrew -
      manufacture   D-0390.

183. Brown, R. Chris; Gurunanjappa, Bale S.; Hawk, Rodney J.;
      and Bitsuie, Delphine
      THE EPIDEMIOLOGY OF ACCIDENTS AMONG THE NAVAJO INDIANS.
      Public Health Reports, 85(10): 881-888,   1970.
      United States - Native Americans - Navaho - accidents   D-0198.

184. Brown, William L.
      INEBRIETY AND ITS "CURES" AMONG THE ANCIENTS.
      Proceedings of the Society for the Study of Inebriety,
      55: 1-15,   1898.
      World survey - Classical peoples - attitudes - customs -
      disease concept - history, pre-1500 - history, pre-1900 -
      literature - treatment   D-0391.

185. Brown, William R., III
      THE DEVELOPMENT OF THE FEDERAL INDIAN LIQUOR LAWS.
      Unpublished manuscript,   1956.
      United States - Native Americans - economics - history,
      pre-1900 - political - prohibition   D-1543.

186. Brownlee, Frank
      NATIVE BEER IN SOUTH AFRICA.
      Man (os), 33: 75-76,   1933.
      South Africa - Bakoena - beer - economics - manufacture -
      medical - nutrition - political   D-0392.

187. Bruman, Henry John
 ABORIGINAL DRINK AREAS IN NEW SPAIN.
 Ph.D. Dissertation, University of California,
 243 pp., 1940.
 Mexico - distribution - history, pre-1500 - history,
 pre-1900 - homebrew D-0393.

188. Bruman, Henry J[ohn]
 ASIATIC ORIGIN OF THE HUICHOL STILL.
 Geographical Review, 34: 418-427, 1944.
 Mexico - Huichol - manufacture - prehistory D-0394.

189. Bruman, Henry J[ohn]
 EARLY COCONUT CULTURE IN WESTERN MEXICO.
 Hispanic American Historical Review, 25: 212-223, 1945.
 Mexico - distribution - history, pre-1900 - homebrew -
 moonshine D-0260.

190. Bruun, Kettil
 SIGNIFICANCE OF ROLE AND NORMS IN THE SMALL GROUP FOR
 INDIVIDUAL BEHAVIORAL CHANGES WHILE DRINKING.
 Quarterly Journal of Studies on Alcohol, 20: 53-64, 1959.
 aggression - intoxication - norms D-0199.

191. Bruun, Kettil
 DEN SOCIOKULTURELLA BACKGRUNDEN TILL ALKOHOLISMEN.
 [The sociocultural background of alcoholism.] [Fin]
 Alkoholpolitik, 22: 54-58, 1959.
 Cross-ethnic - Finland - attitudes - sociocultural -
 stress D-0395.

192. Bruun, Kettil
 DRINKING PATTERNS IN THE SCANDINAVIAN COUNTRIES.
 British Journal of Addiction, 62(3-4): 257-266, 1967.
 Denmark - Finland - Norway - Sweden - customs D-0300.

193. Bubenik, V.
 THE WORLD'S FIRST BEER BREWERS.
 New Orient, 5: 163-166, 1966.
 Near East - homebrew - manufacture - prehistory D-0093.

194. Buchanan, W.M.
 EXPERIMENTAL PRODUCTION OF "BANTU" SIDEROSIS USING
 HOME-BREWED BEER.
 South African Journal of Medical Science, 35: 15, 1970.
 South Africa - homebrew - pathology D-0301.

195. Buckland, A.W.
 ETHNOLOGICAL HINTS AFFORDED BY THE STIMULANTS IN USE
 AMONG SAVAGES AND AMONG THE ANCIENTS.
 Journal of the Royal Anthropological Institute,
 8: 239-254, 1878.
 World survey - distribution - history, pre-1500 - history,
 pre-1900 - homebrew - manufacture - prehistory D-0302.

196. Buckley, Patricia L.
A CROSS CULTURAL STUDY OF DRINKING PATTERNS IN THREE ETHNIC GROUPS: COAST SALISH INDIANS OF THE MISSION RESERVE, AND IMMIGRANT ITALIANS AND ANGLO-SAXONS OF EAST VANCOUVER.
M.A. Thesis, University of British Columbia, 1968.
Canada - Cross-ethnic - Italian-Americans - Native Americans - Salish - customs   D-0396.

197. Buehlmann, John
WHICH WAY THE MORROW?
Unpublished report: Yankton Sioux Tribe Community Alcoholism Service and Treatment Program, Greenwood, South Dakota, 41 pp., 1976.
United States - Native Americans - Sioux   D-1913.

198. Bullemer, K.
ZUR GESCHICHTE DES BERLINER BRAUWESENS: VERGANGENHEIT UND GEGENWART. [The history of the Berlin brewing industry: Past and present.] [Ger]
Bär v Berlin, 12: 60-82, 1962.
Germany - beer   D-1123.

199. Bunzel, Ruth
THE ROLE OF ALCOHOLISM IN TWO CENTRAL AMERICAN CULTURES.
Psychiatry, 3: 361-387, 1940.
Cross-ethnic - Mexico - Chamula - Guatemala - Chichicastenango - aggression - functions - intoxication - ritual - sociocultural   D-0303.

200. Bunzel, Ruth
CHAMULA AND CHICHICASTENANGO: A RE-EXAMINATION.
In: Everett, Michael W.; Waddell, Jack O.; and Heath, Dwight B., ed. Cross-cultural approaches to the study of alcohol: An interdisciplinary perspective. The Hague: Mouton, pp. 21-22, 1976.
Cross-ethnic - Mexico - Chamula - Guatemala - Chichicastenango - research methods - sociocultural   D-0304.

201. Burgstaller, E.
MET IM OBEROSTERREICHSCHEN BRAUCHTUM. [Mead in upper Austrian tradition.] [Ger]
Oberösterreichschen Heimatblätter, 10(1-2): 85-92, 1956.
Austria - customs - history, pre-1500 - history, pre-1900 - homebrew   D-0094.

202. Burns, M.; Daily, J.M.; and Moskowitz, H.
DRINKING PRACTICES AND PROBLEMS OF URBAN AMERICAN INDIANS IN LOS ANGELES. PART I: STUDY DESCRIPTION AND FINDINGS, PRELIMINARY REPORT.
Santa Monica, CA: Planning Analysis and Research Institute, 1974.
United States - Native Americans - dysfunctions - urbanization   D-0397.

26.

203. Burton-Bradley, B[urton] G.
 STONE AGE CRISIS: A PSYCHIATRIC APPRAISAL.
 Nashville, TN: Vanderbilt University Press, 128 pp., 1975.
 Papua New Guinea - change - functions - gambling -
 medical - sociocultural D-0006.

204. Burton-Bradley, B[urton] G.
 ALCOHOL DEPENDENCE IN PAPUA NEW GUINEA.
 Australian Journal of Alcoholism and Drug Dependence,
 3(4): 118-119, 1976.
 Papua New Guinea - drugs - sociocultural D-0305.

205. Busch, Carlos E.
 CONSIDERACIONES MEDICO-SOCIALES SOBRE LA CHICHA.
 [Medico-social considerations on chicha.] [Spa]
 Excelsior, 217: 25-26, 1952.
 Peru - homebrew - medical - pathology D-0306.

206. Butterfass, Theodore O.
 THE LIQUOR TRAFFIC AMONG THE INDIANS OF NEW YORK STATE
 IN THE COLONIAL PERIOD.
 M.A. Thesis, Columbia University, 1929.
 United States - Native Americans - economics -
 history, pre-1900 D-0309.

207. Butterworth, Douglas S.
 A STUDY OF THE URBANIZATION PROCESS AMONG MIXTEC MIGRANTS
 FROM TILANTONGO IN MEXICO CITY.
 In: Mangin, William, ed. Peasants in cities: Readings
 in the anthropology of urbanization. Boston, MA:
 Houghton Mifflin, pp. 99-113, 1970.
 Mexico - Mixtec - change - urbanization D-1131.

208. Cagol, A.
 A NOTE ON BAPEDI BEVERAGES.
 Primitive Man, 9: 32, 1936.
 South Africa - Bapedi - binge - homebrew D-0310.

209. Cahalan, Don; Cisin, Ira H.; and Crossley, Helen M.
 AMERICAN DRINKING PRACTICES: A NATIONAL STUDY OF
 DRINKING BEHAVIOR AND ATTITUDES.
 New Brunswick, NJ: Rutgers Center of Alcohol Studies
 (Monograph No. 6), 260 pp., 1969.
 United States - attitudes - class - consumption - customs -
 definition - disease concept - epidemiology B-6032.

210. Cahalan, Don
 PROBLEM DRINKERS: A NATIONAL SURVEY.
 San Francisco, CA: Jossey-Bass, 202 pp., 1970.
 United States - alcoholism - consumption - definition -
 disease concept - dysfunctions - epidemiology D-0311.

211. Cahalan, Don, and Room, Robin
      PROBLEM DRINKING AMONG AMERICAN MEN.
      New Brunswick, NJ: Rutgers Center of Alcohol Studies
      (Monograph No. 7), 269 pp.,   1974.
      United States - alcoholism - attitudes - class - consumption
      - customs - definition - disease concept - dysfunctions -
      epidemiology   D-0315.

212. Cahalan, Don, and Cisin, Ira H.
      EPIDEMIOLOGICAL AND SOCIAL FACTORS ASSOCIATED WITH
      DRINKING PROBLEMS.
      In: Tarter, Ralph E., and Sugerman, A. Arthur, ed.
      Alcoholism: Interdisciplinary approaches to an enduring
      problem. Reading, MA: Addison-Wesley, pp. 523-572,   1976.
      United States - class - definition - epidemiology -
      sociocultural   D-0313.

213. Cahalan, Don
      OBSERVATIONS ON METHODOLOGICAL CONSIDERATIONS FOR CROSS-
      CULTURAL ALCOHOL STUDIES.
      In: Everett, Michael W.; Waddell, Jack O.; and Heath,
      Dwight B., ed. Cross-cultural approaches to the study
      of alcohol: An interdisciplinary perspective. The Hague:
      Mouton, pp. 403-407,   1976.
      Cross-ethnic - research methods   D-0312.

214. Cahalan, Don
      IMPLICATIONS OF AMERICAN DRINKING PRACTICES AND ATTITUDES
      FOR PREVENTION AND TREATMENT OF ALCOHOLISM.
      In: Marlatt, G. Alan, and Nathan, Peter E., ed. Behavioral
      approaches to alcoholism. New Brunswick, NJ: Rutgers
      Center of Alcohol Studies, pp. 6-26,   1978.
      United States - attitudes - change - customs - norms -
      prevention - treatment   D-0095.

215. Calderón Narvaez, Guillermo
      CONSIDERACIONES ACERCA DEL ALCOHOLISMO ENTRE LOS PUEBLOS
      PRE-HISPANICOS DE MEXICO. [Observations on alcoholism
      among pre-hispanic peoples of Mexico.] [Spa]
      Revista del Instituto Nacional de Neurología,
      2(3): 5-13,   1968.
      Mexico - elderly - history, pre-1500 - manufacture -
      norms - possession - prehistory - religion   D-0398.

216. Calderón Narvaez, Guillermo
      REFLECTIONS ON ALCOHOLISM AMONG THE PREHISPANIC PEOPLES
      OF MEXICO.
      Foreign Psychiatry, 2(4): 78-92,   1974.
      Mexico - customs - history, pre-1500 - prehistory -
      religion   D-0079.

217. Calkins, Raymond
      SUBSTITUTES FOR THE SALOON: AN INVESTIGATICN MADE FOR

THE COMMITTEE OF FIFTY.
Boston, MA: Houghton Mifflin, 397 pp., 1901.
United States - bar - functions - social organization D-0096.

218. Canelos, S.P., and Cevallos, R.
MANIFESTACIONES PSICOLOGICAS Y PSIQUIATRICAS DEL
ALCOHOLISMO CRONICO DE LA POBLACION INDIGENA. [Manifesta-
tions of psychological and psychiatric chronic alcoholism
in the indigenous population.] [Spa]
Ph.D. Dissertation, Universidad de Quito, 1967.
Ecuador - dysfunctions - pathology - psychiatric
problems D-0399.

219. Caravedo Carranza, Baltazar, and Almeida Vargas, Manuel
ALCOHOLISMO Y TOXICOMANIAS: UN INFORME ACTUAL SOBRE LOS
PROBLEMAS DEL ALCOHOL, EL COQUISMO Y LAS DROGAS EN EL
PERU. [Alcoholism and addictions: A current report on
the problems of alcoholism, cocaism and drugs in Peru.]
[Spa]
Lima: Ministerio de Salud, Republica Peruana, 71 pp., 1972.
Peru - drugs - epidemiology D-1105.

220. Cardinal, Douglas J.
INDIAN ALTERNATIVE TO ALCOHOLISM.
In: Nutter, R.W., and Sinha, B.K., ed. Fifth Annual
Alberta Alcohol and Drug Research Symposium (1973).
Edmonton, Alb.: Alberta Alcohol and Drug Abuse Commission,
pp. 310-324, 1974.
Canada - Native Americans - norms - treatment D-0294.

221. Cardinal, Harold
THE UNJUST SOCIETY: THE TRAGEDY OF CANADA'S INDIANS.
Edmonton, Alb.: M.G. Hurtig, 1969.
Canada - Native Americans - acculturation - anomie -
stress D-1036.

222. Carlson, Katherine A.
RECIPROCITY IN THE MARKET PLACE: TIPPING IN THE
URBAN NIGHTCLUB.
In: Spradley, James, and McCurdy, David, ed. Conformity
and conflict: Readings in cultural anthropology. (3rd ed.)
Boston, MA: Little, Brown, pp. 337-347, 1977.
United States - bar D-1037.

223. Carpenter, Edmund S.
ALCOHOL IN THE IROQUOIS DREAM QUEST.
American Journal of Psychiatry, 116: 148-151, 1959.
Native Americans - Iroquois - attitudes - change - functions -
history, pre-1900 - possession - religion D-0316.

224. Carr, Lloyd G.
NATIVE DRINKS IN THE SOUTHEAST AND THEIR VALUES, WITH SPECIAL
EMPHASIS ON PERSIMMON BEER.
Proceedings of the Delaware County Institute of Science,

10(2): 29-43,
United States - Native Americans - homebrew

1947.
D-0317.

225. Carson, Gerald
RUM AND REFORM IN OLD NEW ENGLAND.
Sturbridge, MA: Old Sturbridge Village,
United States - attitudes - history, pre-1900 - temperance

1966.
D-1038.

226. Carstairs, G.M.
DARU AND BHANG: CULTURAL FACTORS IN THE CHOICE OF INTOXICANT.
Quarterly Journal of Studies on Alcohol, 15: 220-237,
India - Cross-ethnic - Hinduism - caste - class - drugs - occupation

1954.
D-0318.

227. Carter, William E.
RITUAL, THE AYMARA, AND THE ROLE OF ALCOHOL IN HUMAN SOCIETY.
In: du Toit, Brian M., ed. Drugs, rituals, and altered states of consciousness. Rotterdam: A.A. Halkema, pp. 101-110,
Bolivia - Peru - Aymara - functions - ritual - social organization

1977.
D-1039.

228. Cartwright, A.K., and Shaw, S.J.
A SOCIAL CULTURAL MODEL OF ALCOHOL PROBLEMS.
Unpublished paper: Presented at the 9th World Congress of Sociology, Uppsala,
dysfunctions - sociocultural

1978.
D-1544.

229. Cassava, Nicolás
LA CHICHA COMO FACTOR DEL ALCOHOLISMO EN EL PERU.
[Chicha as a factor of alcoholism in Peru.] [Spa]
Reforma Médica, 2(22):
Peru - customs - homebrew

1916.
D-1236.

230. Castetter, Edward F., and Opler, Morris E.
THE ETHNOBIOLOGY OF THE CHIRICAHUA AND MESCALERO APACHE: A. THE USE OF PLANTS FOR FOODS, BEVERAGES AND NARCOTICS.
University of New Mexico Bulletin, Biological Series, 4(5): 1-63,
United States - Native Americans - Apache - homebrew - manufacture

1936.
D-0319.

231. Cavan, Sherri
LIQUOR LICENSE: AN ETHNOGRAPHY OF BAR BEHAVIOR.
Chicago, IL: Aldine, 246 pp.,
United States - bar - functions - norms - space - stereotype

1966.
D-1040.

232. Cervantes, G.E.
EL ALCOHOLISMO, EL ASPECTO SOCIAL Y EL DESARROLLO DE LA
COMUNIDAD. [Alcoholism: Social aspects and community
development.] [Spa]
Revista Mexicana de Psicología, 5(5): 207-214, 1971.
Mexico - dysfunctions D-0008.

233. Chafetz, Morris E.
ALCOHOLISM PROBLEMS AND PROGRAMS IN CZECHOSLOVAKIA,
POLAND AND THE SOVIET UNION.
New England Journal of Medicine, 265: 68-74, 1961.
Czechoslovakia - Poland - Soviet Union D-0321.

234. Chafetz, Morris E.
CONSUMPTION OF ALCOHOL IN THE FAR AND MIDDLE EAST.
New England Journal of Medicine, 271: 297-301, 1964.
Asia - Islam - Near East D-0322.

235. Chaiaramonte, J.
MUMMING IN DEEP HARBOUR: ASPECTS OF SOCIAL ORGANIZATION
IN MUMMING AND DRINKING.
In: Halpert, H., and Storey, G.M., ed. Christmas
mumming in Newfoundland: Essays in anthropology, folk-
lore, and history. Toronto, Ont.: University of
Toronto Press, pp. 76-103, 1969.
Canada - folklore - ritual D-1237.

236. Chakravarty, Taponath
FOOD AND DRINK IN ANCIENT BENGAL.
Calcutta: P. Chakravarty, 1959.
India - Bengal - history, pre-1500 - history, pre-1900 -
Melanesia D-0404.

237. Chalfant, H.P., and Beckley, R.E.
BEGUILING AND BETRAYING: THE IMAGE OF ALCOHOL USE IN
COUNTRY MUSIC.
Journal of Studies on Alcohol, 38: 1428-1433, 1977.
United States - folklore - music D-0323.

238. Chalke, H.D.
ALCOHOL AND HISTORY.
Journal of Alcoholism, 11(4): 128-149, 1976.
World survey - Classical peoples - history, pre-1500 -
history, pre-1900 - prehistory D-0324.

239. Charest, Paul
LA CONSOMMATION DES BOISSONS ALCOOLIQUES SUR LA BASSE-
COTE-NORD DU SAINT-LAURENT. [The consumption of
alcoholic beverages on the Basse-Côte-Nord of the St.
Lawrence.] [Fre]
Toxicomanies, 3: 329-370, 1970.
Canada - Cross-ethnic - aggression - customs - history,
pre-1900 - manufacture - moonshine D-0325.

240. Chattopadhya, A.
THE ANCIENT INDIAN PRACTICE OF DRINKING WINE, WITH
REFERENCE TO KATHASAITSAGARA.
Journal of the Oriental Institute, 18: 145-152, 1969.
India - Hinduism - history, pre-1500 - wine   D-0326.

241. Chavira, Juan Antonio
RITUAL DRINKING AND DRINKING RITUALS AMONG MEXICAN
AMERICANS OF SOUTH TEXAS.
Unpublished paper: Society for Applied Anthropology,
Mérida, Mexico, 1978.
United States - Hispanos - functions - ritual   D-1545.

242. Chegwidden, M., and Flaherty, B.J.
ABORIGINAL VERSUS NON-ABORIGINAL ALCOHOLICS IN AN
ALCOHOL WITHDRAWAL UNIT.
Medical Journal of Australia, 64(1): 699-703, 1977.
Cross-ethnic - Aborigines - Australia - phases -
treatment   D-0327.

243. Cheinisse, L.
LA RACE JUIVE, JOUIT-ELLE D'UNE IMMUNITE A L'EGARD DE
L'ALCOOLISME? [Does the Jewish race enjoy immunity
from alcoholism?] [Fre]
Semaine Médicale, 28: 613-615, 1908.
Jews - anomie - ritual - social organization   D-0328.

244. Cherrington, Ernest H., ed.
STANDARD ENCYCLOPEDIA OF THE ALCOHOL PROBLEM,
VOLUMES 1-6.
Westerville, OH: American Issue, 1925-1930.
World survey - review   D-1132.

245. Chiappe, M., et al.
PSIQUIATRIA FOLKLORICA PERUANA: TRATAMIENTO DEL
ALCOHOLISMO. [Peruvian folk-psychiatry: Treatment
of alcoholism.] [Spa]
Acta Psiquiátrica y Psicológica en América Latina,
18: 385, 1972.
Peru - folklore - treatment   D-1065.

246. Child, Irvin L.; Bacon, Margaret K.; and Barry, Herbert, III
DESCRIPTIVE MEASUREMENTS OF DRINKING CUSTOMS.
In: Keller, M., ed. A cross-cultural study of drinking.
New Brunswick, NJ: Center of Alcohol Studies, Rutgers
University (Quarterly Journal of Studies on Alcohol,
Supplement No. 3), pp. 1-28, 1965.
World survey - Cross-cultural - aggression - customs -
intoxication - research methods   D-0329.

247. Child, Irvin L.; Barry, Herbert, III; and Bacon, Margaret K.
SEX DIFFERENCES.
In: Keller, M., ed. A cross-cultural study of drinking.
New Brunswick, NJ: Center of Alcohol Studies, Rutgers

	University (Quarterly Journal of Studies on Alcohol, Supplement No. 3), pp. 49-61, World survey - Cross-cultural - female	1965. B-4850.
248.	Cho, H.C., et al. DRINKING PATTERNS OF KOREANS. Neuropsychiatry, 14: 1-14, Korea - customs	1975. D-1210.
249.	Chopra, R.N.; Chopra, G.S.; and Chopra, J.C. ALCOHOLIC BEVERAGES IN INDIA. Indian Medical Gazette, 77: 224-233, 290-296, and 361-367, India - customs - homebrew	1942. D-0330.
250.	Christoffel, Karl DURCH DIE ZEITEN STROMT DER WEIN: DIE WUNDERBARE HISTORIE DES WEINES. [Wine through the ages: The wonderful history of wines.] [Ger] Hamburg: Cram, de Gruyter, 415 pp., Europe - Near East - Classical peoples - attitudes - customs - folklore - history, pre-1500 - history, pre-1900 - religion - wine	1957. D-0009.
251.	Chu, George DRINKING PATTERNS AND ATTITUDES OF ROOMING-HOUSE CHINESE IN SAN FRANCISCO. In: Keller, M., ed. Surveys of drinking and abstaining: Urban, suburban and national studies. New Brunswick, NJ: Center of Alcohol Studies, Rutgers University (Quarterly Journal of Studies on Alcohol, Supplement No. 6), pp. 58-68, United States - Overseas Chinese - gambling	1972. D-0331.
252.	Cinquemani, Dorothy K. DRINKING AND VIOLENCE AMONG MIDDLE AMERICAN INDIANS. Ph.D. Dissertation, Columbia University, Mexico - aggression - fighting - urbanization	1975. D-1041.
253.	Cisin, Ira H. COMMUNITY STUDIES OF DRINKING BEHAVIOR. Annals of the New York Academy of Sciences, 107(2): 607-612, research methods	1963. D-0332.
254.	Clairmont, Donald H. DEVIANCE AMONG INDIANS AND ESKIMOS IN AKLAVIK. Unpublished report: Northern Coordination and Research Centre, Department of Northern Affairs and National Resources, Ottawa, Ont., Canada - Eskimos - Native Americans - anomie - binge - crime - fighting - intoxication - stress	1963. D-1134.

255. Clairmont, Donald H.
NOTES ON THE DRINKING BEHAVIOUR OF THE ESKIMOS AND
INDIANS IN THE AKLAVIK AREA: A PRELIMINARY REPORT.
Unpublished report: Northern Coordination and Research
Centre, Department of Northern Affairs and National
Resources, Ottawa, Ont., 1963.
Canada - Eskimos - Native Americans - acculturation -
anomie - binge - functions - homebrew - intoxication -
responsibility - stereotype - stress   D-1133.

256. Clark, Norman H.
DELIVER US FROM EVIL: AN INTERPRETATION OF AMERICAN
PROHIBITION.
New York, NY: W.W. Norton, 246 pp.,   1976.
United States - attitudes - change - history, pre-1900 -
prohibition   D-0097.

257. Clark, Walter B.
SEX ROLES AND ALCOHOLIC BEVERAGE USAGE.
Unpublished paper: Social Research Group, School of
Public Health, University of California, Berkeley
(Working paper No. 16),   1964.
United States - female   D-1135.

258. Clark, Walter B.
NOTES ON ANOMIE: 1897-1959.
Unpublished paper: Social Research Group, School of
Public Health, University of California, Berkeley
(Working paper No. 3),   1965.
anomie - review   D-1136.

259. Clark, Walter B.
DEMOGRAPHIC CHARACTERISTICS OF TAVERN PATRONS IN
SAN FRANCISCO.
Quarterly Journal of Studies on Alcohol, 27: 316-327,   1966.
United States - bar   D-0333.

260. Clarke, Frank
THOUGHTS ON INDIAN ALCOHOLISM (PART 1 AND PART 2).
Association of American Indian Physicians Newsletter,
3(1): 3, and 3(2): 2,   1975.
Native Americans - definition - dysfunctions   D-0334.

261. Claudian, J[ean]
CHAPTER 1. HISTORY OF THE USAGE OF ALCOHOL.
In: Trémolières, J., ed. International Encyclopedia
of Pharmacology and Therapeutics, Section 20, Volume 1.
Oxford: Pergamon, pp. 3-26,   1970.
World survey - history, pre-1500 - history, pre-1900 -
medical - prehistory   D-1137.

262. Clemmesen, C.
OVERSIGT OVER ALKOHOLPROBLEMET PA GRØNLAND. [Survey of
the alcohol problem in Greenland.] [Dan]

Ugeskrift for Laeger, 120: 1374-1379, 1958.
Greenland - Eskimos - binge - change - class - homebrew   D-1042.

263. Clinard, Marshall N.
THE PUBLIC DRINKING HOUSE AND SOCIETY.
In: Pittman, David J., and Snyder, Charles R., ed.
Society, culture and drinking patterns. New York, NY:
John Wiley and Sons, pp. 270-292, 1962.
United States - bar - functions - history, pre-1900   D-0098.

264. Clinebell, Howard J., Jr.
PHILOSOPHICAL-RELIGIOUS FACTORS IN THE ETIOLOGY AND
TREATMENT OF ALCOHOLISM.
Quarterly Journal of Studies on Alcohol, 24: 477-488, 1963.
Church - etiology - religion   D-0335.

265. Cockerham, William C., Forslund, Morris A., and
Raboin, Rollard M.
DRUG USE AMONG WHITE AND AMERICAN INDIAN HIGH SCHOOL
YOUTH.
International Journal of the Addictions, 11(2): 209-220, 1976.
United States - Cross-ethnic - Native Americans - Arapaho -
Shoshone - Whites - attitudes - drugs - youth   D-0338.

266. Cockerham, William C.
DRINKING ATTITUDES AND PRACTICES AMONG WIND RIVER
RESERVATION INDIAN YOUTH.
Journal of Studies on Alcohol, 36: 321-326, 1975.
United States - Native Americans - Arapaho - Shoshone -
attitudes - youth   D-0336.

267. Cockerham, William C.
PATTERNS OF ALCOHOL AND MULTIPLE DRUG USE AMONG RURAL
WHITE AND AMERICAN INDIAN ADOLESCENTS.
International Journal of the Addictions, 12(2-3): 271-285, 1977.
United States - Cross-ethnic - Native Americans - Arapaho -
Shoshone - Whites - drugs - youth   D-0337.

268. Coffey, T[imothy] G.
BEER STREET, GIN LANE: SOME VIEWS OF 18TH-CENTURY
DRINKING.
Quarterly Journal of Studies on Alcohol, 27: 669-692, 1966.
England - change - dysfunctions - economics - history,
pre-1900 - urbanization   D-0340.

269. Coffey, T[imothy] G.
PROBLEM DRINKING AMONG AMERICAN INDIANS.
Oregon Review on Alcoholism, 8: 1-2, 1966.
Native Americans - sociocultural - treatment   D-0339.

270. Cohen, H. Hirsch
THE DRUNKENNESS OF NOAH.
University, AL: University of Alabama Press, 1974.

Near East - Jews - Biblical peoples - history, pre-1500 - semantics - symbols D-1043.

271. Cohen, Ronald
AN ANTHROPOLOGICAL SURVEY OF COMMUNITIES IN THE MACKENZIE-SLAVE LAKE REGION OF CANADA.
Unpublished report: Northern Coordination and Research Centre, Department of Northern Affairs and National Resources, Ottawa, Ont., 1962.
Canada - Native Americans D-1138.

272. Collard, J.
DRUG RESPONSES IN DIFFERENT ETHNIC GROUPS.
Journal of Neuropsychiatry, 3: 5114-5121, 1962.
Cross-ethnic - drugs - intoxication - "race" D-0341.

273. Collett, J.
HEMBRANNINGEN I SVERIGE. [Home-distilling in Sweden] [Swe]
Alkohol och Narkotika, 67: 342-346, 1973.
Sweden - moonshine D-1066.

274. Collins, Thomas
ECONOMIC CHANGE AND THE USE OF ALCOHOL AMONG AMERICAN INDIANS.
Unpublished paper: American Anthropological Association, San Diego, CA, 1970.
United States - Native Americans - change D-1546.

275. Collins, Thomas, and Dodson, John
ARAPAHOE, SHOSHONE AND UTE DRINKING BEHAVIOR: A COMPARATIVE ANALYSIS.
Unpublished paper: American Anthropological Association, Toronto, Ont., 1972.
United States - Cross-ethnic - Native Americans - Arapaho - Shoshone - Ute D-1547.

276. Collis, C.H.; Cook, P.J.; Foreman, J.K.; and Palframan, J.F.
A SEARCH FOR NITROSAMINES IN EAST AFRICAN SPIRIT SAMPLES FROM AREAS OF VARYING OESOPHAGEAL CANCER FREQUENCY.
Gut, 12: 1015-1018, 1971.
Africa - cancer - containers - distribution - homebrew - manufacture D-0342.

277. Collis, C.H.; Cook, P.J.; Foreman, J.K.; and Palframan, J.F.
CANCER OF THE OESOPHAGUS AND ALCOHOLIC DRINKS IN EAST AFRICA.
Lancet, 1: 441, 1972.
Africa - cancer - containers - distribution - homebrew - manufacture D-0343.

278. Collomb, H.; Ayats, H.; and Zwingelstein, J.
L'ALCOOLISME CHEZ L'AFRICAIN EN MILIEU HOSPITALIER: BILAN DE SIX ANNEES. [Alcoholism among Africans in a hospital

context: A six-year study.] [Fre]
Bulletin de la Société Médicale d'Afrique Noire de
Langue Française, 8(3): 313-321, 1963.
Senegal - pathology D-0010.

279. Collomb, H.; Diop, M.; and Ayats, H.
INTOXICATION PAR LE CHANVRE INDIEN AU SENEGAL.
[Marijuana intoxication in Senegal.] [Fre]
Cahiers d'Etudes Africaines, 3(9): 139-144, 1963.
Senegal - drugs - ritual D-1922.

280. Connell, K.H.
ILLICIT DISTILLATION.
In: Connell, K.H. Irish peasant society: Four
historical essays. Fair Lawn, NJ: Oxford University
Press, pp. 1-50, 1968.
Ireland - economics - history, pre-1900 - manufacture -
moonshine D-1139.

281. Connor, Walter D.
ALCOHOL PROBLEMS.
In: Connor, Walter D. Deviance in Soviet society:
Crime, delinquency, and alcoholism. New York, NY:
Columbia University Press, pp. 35-58, 1972.
Soviet Union - attitudes - dysfunctions - prevention -
treatment D-1140.

282. Connor, Walter D.
ALCOHOLISM: THERAPY AND PREVENTION.
In: Connor, Walter D. Deviance in Soviet society:
Crime, delinquency, and alcoholism. New York, NY:
Columbia University Press, pp. 59-79, 1972.
Soviet Union - attitudes - dysfunctions - prevention -
treatment D-1141.

283. Conrad, R.D., and Kahn, M.W.
AN EPIDEMIOLOGICAL STUDY OF SUICIDE AND ATTEMPTED
SUICIDE AMONG THE PAPAGO INDIANS.
American Journal of Psychiatry, 131: 69-72, 1974.
United States - Native Americans - Papago - suicide D-0344.

284. Cook, P.
CANCER OF OESOPHAGUS IN AFRICA: A SUMMARY AND EVALUATION
OF THE EVIDENCE FOR THE FREQUENCY OF OCCURRENCE, AND A
PRELIMINARY INDICATION OF THE POSSIBLE ASSOCIATION WITH
THE CONSUMPTION OF ALCOHOLIC DRINKS MADE FROM MAIZE.
British Journal of Cancer, 25: 853-880, 1971.
Africa - cancer - containers - distribution - homebrew -
manufacture D-0345.

285. Cooney, John G.
ALCOHOL AND THE IRISH.
Journal of the Irish Colleges of Physicians and Surgeons,
1(2): 51, 1971.

Ireland   D-1067.

286.   Cooper, John M.
       STIMULANTS AND NARCOTICS.
       In: Steward, Julian H., ed. Handbook of South American
       Indians, Volume 5: The comparative ethnology of South
       American Indians. Washington, D.C.: Bureau of American
       Ethnology (Bulletin 143),   1949.
       Central America - South America - West Indies - customs -
       distribution - drugs - homebrew - intoxication   D-1068.

287.   Cornwall, Edward E.
       NOTES ON THE USE OF ALCOHOL IN ANCIENT TIMES.
       Medical Times, 67: 379-380,   1939.
       Classical peoples - Egyptians, ancient - Biblical peoples -
       history, pre-1500 - prehistory   D-0346.

288.   Covington, J.W.
       THE INDIAN LIQUOR TRADE AT PEORIA, 1824.
       Journal of the Illinois State Historical Society,
       46: 142-150,   1953.
       United States - Native Americans - economics - history,
       pre-1900   D-0347.

289.   Crahan, Marcus E.
       EARLY AMERICAN INEBRIETATIS.
       Los Angeles, CA: The Zamorano Club,   1964.
       United States - attitudes - customs - history, pre-1900   D-1044.

290.   Crawfurd, J.
       ON THE HISTORY AND MIGRATION OF CULTIVATED PLANTS YIELDING
       INTOXICATING POTABLES AND OILS.
       Transactions of the Ethnological Society of London,
       7: 92-106,   1869.
       World survey - distribution - homebrew   D-0011.

291.   Crawley, A. E[rnest]
       DRINKS, DRINKING.
       In: Hastings, J., ed. Encyclopaedia of religion and
       ethics, Volume 5. New York, NY: Charles Scribner's
       Sons, pp. 72-82,   1912.
       World survey - customs - distribution - history, pre-1500 -
       history, pre-1900 - prehistory - symbols   D-1045.

292.   Crawley, [A.] Ernest
       DRINKS, DRINKERS, DRINKING.
       In: Besterman, Theodore, ed. Dress, drink, and drums.
       London: Methuen, pp. 177-232,   1931.
       World survey - customs - distribution - history, pre-1500 -
       history, pre-1900 - prehistory - symbols   D-1046.

38.

293. Cromwell, W.O.
THE TAVERN IN COMMUNITY LIFE.
Chicago, IL: Juvenile Protective Association, 1939.
United States - bar - dysfunctions - functions - social
organization D-0405.

294. Crothers, T.D.
INEBRIETY IN ANCIENT EGYPT AND CHALDEA.
Quarterly Journal of Inebriety, 25: 142-150, 1903.
Egyptians, ancient - Chaldea - history, pre-1500 -
prehistory - religion - symbols - treatment D-0348.

295. Csikszentmihalyi, Mihaly
A CROSS-CULTURAL COMPARISON OF SOME STRUCTURAL
CHARACTERISTICS OF GROUP DRINKING.
Human Development, 11: 201-216, 1968.
Cross-national - bar - customs - space D-0349.

296. Curley, Richard T.
DRINKING PATTERNS OF THE MESCALERO APACHE.
Quarterly Journal of Studies on Alcohol, 28: 116-131, 1967.
United States - Native Americans - Apache - acculturation -
anomie - binge - functions - leisure - prohibition -
responsibility - social organization D-0350.

297. Cutler, Hugh C., and Cardenas, Martin
CHICHA: A NATIVE SOUTH AMERICAN BEER.
Harvard University Botanical Museum Association Leaflet,
13: 33-60, 1947.
Bolivia - South America - homebrew - manufacture D-1047.

298. Cutler, R., and Morrison, N.
SUDDEN DEATH: A STUDY OF CHARACTERISTICS OF VICTIMS
AND EVENTS LEADING TO SUDDEN DEATH IN BRITISH COLUMBIA
WITH PRIMARY EMPHASIS ON APPARENT ALCOHOL INVOLVEMENT
AND INDIAN SUDDEN DEATH.
Vancouver, B.C.: Alcoholism Foundation of British
Columbia, 70 pp., 1971.
Canada - Native Americans - accidents - suicide D-1048.

299. Cutler, R.E., and Storm, Thomas
OBSERVATIONAL STUDY OF ALCOHOL CONSUMPTION IN NATURAL
SETTINGS: THE VANCOUVER BEER PARLOR.
Quarterly Journal of Studies on Alcohol, 36(9): 1173-1183, 1975.
Canada - bar - research methods - social organization D-0351.

300. Cutter, Henry S.G.; Key, John C.; Rothstein, Emil; and
Jones, Wyatt C.
ALCOHOL, POWER AND INHIBITION.
Quarterly Journal of Studies on Alcohol, 34: 381-389, 1973.
functions - power D-0352.

301. Cutter, Trevor, and Perkins, Neville
DRINKING PATTERNS OF ABORIGINES IN THE NORTHERN
TERRITORY.
Australian Journal of Alcoholism and Drug Dependence,
3(3): 74-76, 1976.
Australia - Aborigines - anomie - binge - stress -
treatment - youth D-0353.

302. Cuzent, Gilbert
DES BOISSONS ENVIRANTES EN USAGE CHEZ LES DIFFERENTS
PEUPLES. [Some intoxicating drinks in use among various
peoples.] [Fre]
Bulletin de la Société Académique de Brest (2nd series),
1: 141-230, 1873.
World survey - homebrew - manufacture D-1049.

303. Dabney, Joseph Earl
MOUNTAIN SPIRITS: A CHRONICLE OF CORN WHISKY FROM KING
JAMES'S ULSTER PLANTATION TO AMERICA'S APPALACHIANS AND
THE MOONSHINE LIFE.
New York, NY: Charles Scribner's Sons, 1974.
United States - economics - history, pre-1900 - manufacture -
moonshine - whiskey D-1069.

304. Dailey, Robert C.
ALCOHOL AND THE INDIANS OF ONTARIO: PAST AND PRESENT.
Toronto, Ont.: Addiction Research Foundation, Substudy
No. 1-20-64 (210), 54 pp., 1964.
Cross-ethnic - Canada - Native Americans - Algonquian -
Iroquois - aggression - anomie - change - functions -
history, pre-1900 - intoxication - leisure - possession -
"race" - religion - stereotype D-1142.

305. Dailey, Robert C.
ALCOHOL AND THE NORTH AMERICAN INDIAN: IMPLICATIONS FOR
THE MANAGEMENT OF PROBLEMS.
Toronto, Ont.: Addiction Research Foundation, Substudy
No. 2-20-66 (266), 12 pp., 1966.
Native Americans - acculturation - change - functions -
history, pre-1900 - leisure - possession - religion -
responsibility - stress D-1143.

306. Dailey, R[obert] C.
THE ROLE OF ALCOHOL AMONG NORTH AMERICAN INDIAN TRIBES
AS REPORTED IN THE JESUIT RELATIONS.
Anthropologica, 10: 45-59, 1968.
Canada - Native Americans - Iroquois - aggression - change -
customs - economics - functions - history, pre-1500 -
history, pre-1900 - possession - religion - responsibility D-1050.

307. Danielou, Jean
LES REPAS DE LA BIBLE ET LEUR SIGNIFICATION. [Meals
in the Bible and their meanings.] [Fre]

40.

	Paris: La Maison Dieu,	1949.
	Biblical peoples - history, pre-1500 - nutrition - religion - symbols	D-1051.
308.	Dann, Jeffrey L. A STUDY OF AN INDIAN TAVERN ON SKID ROAD. M.A. Thesis, University of Washington,	1967.
	United States - Native Americans - Skid Row - bar - functions - urbanization	D-1052.
309.	Da Piedade, J.; Ayats, H.; and Collomb, H. ASPECTS SOCIO-CULTURELS DE L'ALCOOLISME AU SENEGAL. [Sociocultural aspects of alcoholism in Senegal.] [Fre] Alcoholism, 7: 104-108,	1971.
	Senegal - sociocultural	D-0773.
310.	Davies, C.S. CUSTOMS GOVERNING BEER DRINKING AMONG THE AMA BOMUANA. South African Journal of Science, 24: 521-524,	1927.
	South Africa - Ama - Bomuana - customs	D-0354.
311.	Davis, William N. DRINKING: A SEARCH FOR POWER OR NURTURANCE? In: McClelland, David C.; Davis, William N.; Kalin, Rudolf; and Wanner, Eric. The drinking man. New York, NY: Free Press, pp. 198-213,	1972.
	Cross-cultural - dependency - power	D-1053.
312.	Dawson, W.R. THE LONDON COFFEE-HOUSES AND THE BEGINNINGS OF LLOYD'S. Transactions of the Royal Society, 11: 69-111,	1932.
	England - bar - history, pre-1900	D-0099.
313.	Defer, B. VARIATIONS EPIDEMIOLOGIQUES DE TOXICOMANIES ASSOCIEES A DES CONTACTS DE CULTURE. [Epidemiological variation in addictions as related to cultural contacts.] [Fre] Toxicomanies, 2: 9-18,	1969.
	Cross-ethnic - Morocco - acculturation - drugs - epidemiology - occupation	D-0355.
314.	De la Fuente, Ramón, and Campillo-Serrano, Carlos ALCOHOLISM AND DRUG ABUSE IN MEXICO. In: Rutledge, Barbara, and Fulton, E. Kaye, ed. International collaboration: Problems and opportunities. Toronto, Ont.: Addiction Research Foundation, pp. 88-102,	1977.
	Mexico - epidemiology	D-0016.
315.	De Lejarza, Fidel LAS BORRACHERAS Y EL PROBLEMA DE LAS CONVERSIONES EN INDIAS. [Drunken binges and the problem of conversion in the Indies.] [Spa] Archivo Ibero-Americano, 1: 111-142, and 3: 229-269,	1941.

	Latin America - acculturation - binge - Church - customs - dysfunctions - religion - prohibition	D-1168.
316.	De Lint, Jan THE EPIDEMIOLOGY OF ALCOHOLISM, WITH SPECIAL REFERENCE TO SOCIOCULTURAL FACTORS. In: Everett, Michael W.; Waddell, Jack O.; and Heath, Dwight B., ed. <u>Cross-cultural approaches to the study of alcohol: An interdisciplinary perspective.</u> The Hague: Mouton, pp. 323-339, epidemiology - prevention - sociocultural	1976. D-0646.
317.	Demerdash, Adel PRELIMINARY PSYCHIATRIC STUDY OF HOSPITAL POPULATION OF ALCOHOL AND DRUG DEPENDENT PATIENTS IN KUWAIT. Journal of the Kuwaiti Medical Association, 10: 3-6, Kuwait - Islam	1976. D-0200.
318.	Dennis, Philip A. THE ROLE OF THE DRUNK IN A OAXACAN VILLAGE. American Anthropologist, 77(4): 856-863, Mexico - Zapotec - functions - responsibility	1975. D-0356.
319.	De Rios, Marlene Dobkin, and Feldman, Daniel J. AN ANTHROPOLOGICAL APPROACH TO THE STUDY OF MINORITY GROUP DRINKING PATTERNS. Newsletter of the California Society for the Treatment of Alcoholism and Other Drug Dependencies, 3(3): 5-6, research methods - sociocultural	1976. D-0815.
320.	De Rios, Marlene Dobkin, and Feldman, Daniel J. SOUTHERN CALIFORNIAN MEXICAN AMERICAN DRINKING PATTERNS: SOME PRELIMINARY OBSERVATIONS. Journal of Psychedelic Drugs, 9(2): 151-158, United States - Hispanos - acculturation - bar - functions - responsibility - social organization - stress	1977. D-0054.
321.	Desai, A.V. AN EXPLORATORY SURVEY OF DRINKING IN SURAF AND BULSAR COMMUNITY. Unpublished paper: Department of Psychology, S.B. Garda College, Navsari, India, 54 pp., India - Bulsar - Suraf - attitudes - moonshine - prohibition - stress	1965. D-1238.
322.	[Dessirier, R.] <u>ALCOOL EN OCEANIE.</u> [Alcohol in Oceania.] [Fre] Paris: Senlis, Oceania - change - history, pre-1900 - temperance	1956. D-1211.

323. Dettori, Renato G.
WEINE UND LIKORE AUS ITALIEN. [Wine and liquor in Italy.] [Ger]
Rome: Aussenhandelsinstitut, 1953.
Italy - consumption - customs - wine   D-0274.

324. Devenyi, Paul
SOCIOCULTURAL FACTORS IN DRINKING AND ALCOHOLISM.
Toronto, Ont.: Addiction Research Foundation, (Clinical)
Substudy No. 17-1967, 7 pp., 1967.
Cross-ethnic - ambivalence - review - sociocultural   D-1144.

325. Devereux, George
THE FUNCTION OF ALCOHOL IN MOHAVE SOCIETY.
Quarterly Journal of Studies on Alcohol, 9: 207-251, 1948.
United States - Native Americans - Mohave - customs -
functions - history, pre-1900 - sex - sociocultural   D-0357.

326. Devereux, George
MOHAVE ETHNOPSYCHIATRY AND SUICIDE: THE PSYCHIATRIC KNOWLEDGE AND THE PSYCHIC DISTURBANCES OF AN INDIAN TRIBE.
Washington, D.C.: Bureau of American Ethnology (Bulletin 175), 1961.
United States - Native Americans - Mohave - functions -
responsibility - rape - sex - suicide   D-1070.

327. Dewar, Robert, and Sommer, Robert
ALCOHOL CONSUMPTION IN PRAIRIEVILLE: EFFECT OF CHANGE IN TYPE OF OUTLET ON DRINKING IN A SMALL TOWN.
Quarterly Journal of Studies on Alcohol, 25(2): 300-313, 1964.
United States - bar - change - customs - social
organization   D-0201.

328. Dight, Susan E.
SCOTTISH DRINKING HABITS: A SURVEY OF SCOTTISH DRINKING HABITS AND ATTITUDES TOWARDS ALCOHOL CARRIED OUT IN 1972 FOR THE SCOTTISH HOME AND HEALTH DEPARTMENT.
London: Her Majesty's Stationery Office, 315 pp., 1976.
Scotland - consumption - customs - epidemiology   D-1194.

329. Dinitz, Simon
THE RELATION OF THE TAVERN TO THE DRINKING PHASES OF ALCOHOLICS.
Ph.D. Dissertation, University of Wisconsin, 1951.
United States - bar - functions - phases   D-0406.

330. Disselhoff, H.D.
TRINK- UND TRINKOPFER- BRAUCHE IM LAND DER INKA. [Drinking and drink-offering practices in the land of the Incas.] [Ger]
Jahrbuch der Gesellschaft für Geschichte und Bibliographie
des Brauwesens, (1961): 28-54, 1961.
Peru - Quechua   D-1218.

331.   Djenda, M.
        DESTILLATION VON ALKOHOL BEI DEN MPYEMO. [Distillation
        among the Mpyemo.] [Ger]
        Mitteilungen Anthropologische Gesellschaft in Wien,
        96-97: 312-313,   1967.
        homebrew   D-1923.

332.   Dobyns, Henry F.
        DRINKING PATTERNS IN LATIN AMERICA: A REVIEW.
        Unpublished paper: American Association for the
        Advancement of Science, Berkeley, CA,   1965.
        Latin America - review   D-1548.

333.   Dodson, John W.
        SOCIOECONOMIC ASPECTS OF DRINKING PATTERNS ON THE WIND
        RIVER RESERVATION.
        M.A. Thesis, University of Utah,   1972.
        United States - Native Americans - Arapaho - Shoshone -
        economics   D-1054.

334.   Donnelly, Joseph P.
        THE LIQUOR TRAFFIC AMONG THE ABORIGINES OF THE NEW
        NORTHWEST: 1800-1860.
        Ph.D. Dissertation, St. Louis University,   1940.
        United States - Native Americans - economics - history,
        pre-1900   D-1055.

335.   Dosman, Edgar J.
        INDIANS: THE URBAN DILEMMA.
        Toronto, Ont.: McClelland and Stewart, 192 pp.,   1972.
        Canada - Native Americans - Métis - anomie - Skid Row -
        urbanization   D-1071.

336.   Doughty, Paul L.
        THE SOCIAL USES OF ALCOHOLIC BEVERAGES IN A PERUVIAN
        COMMUNITY.
        Human Organization, 30: 187-197,   1971.
        Peru - Quechua - economics - functions - social
        organization   D-0358.

337.   Douyon, E.
        ALCOOLISME ET TOXICOMANIE EN HAITI. [Alcoholism and
        addiction in Haiti.] [Fre]
        Toxicomanies, 2: 31-38,   1969.
        West Indies - Haiti - ritual   D-0359.

338.   Doxat, John
        DRINKS AND DRINKING: AN INTERNATIONAL DISTILLATION.
        London: Ward Lock, 256 pp.,   1971.
        World survey - beer - brandy - distribution - history,
        pre-1500 - history, pre-1900 - homebrew - manufacture -
        whiskey - wine   D-1072.

339. Dozier, Edward P.
 PROBLEM DRINKING AMONG AMERICAN INDIANS: THE ROLE
 OF SOCIOCULTURAL DEPRIVATION.
 Quarterly Journal of Studies on Alcohol, 27: 72-87, 1966.
 United States - Native Americans - acculturation -
 anomie - conversion - dysfunctions - prevention - stress   D-0360.

340. Drilling, V[ernon]
 PROBLEMS WITH ALCOHOL AMONG URBAN INDIANS IN
 MINNEAPOLIS.
 Washington, D.C.: U.S. Office of Education, 1970.
 United States - Native Americans - review - urbanization   D-1073.

341. Driver, Harold E.
 ALCOHOLIC BEVERAGES IN NATIVE NORTH AMERICA.
 Proceedings of the Indiana Academy of Science, 64:
 50-51, 1955.
 Latin America - Native Americans - distribution - history,
 pre-1500 - homebrew - prehistory   D-0012.

342. Driver, Harold E.
 ALCOHOLIC BEVERAGES.
 In: Driver, Harold E. Indians of North America.
 Chicago, IL: University of Chicago Press, pp. 109-111, 1969.
 Cross-ethnic - Native Americans - customs - distribution -
 history, pre-1500 - history, pre-1900 - homebrew -
 manufacture   D-1074.

343. Drower, E.S.
 WATER INTO WINE: A STUDY OF RITUAL IDIOM IN THE MIDDLE
 EAST.
 London: John Murray, 273 pp., 1956.
 Cross-ethnic - Near East - Biblical peoples - Church -
 customs - religion - ritual - symbols - wine   D-1075.

344. Duennebier, Stephen A.
 DRINKING AND SOCIAL RELATIONS IN A SHETLAND ISLAND
 COMMUNITY.
 A.B. Thesis, Trinity College, Wesleyan University, 1974.
 Scotland - social organization   D-1056.

345. Duka, N.
 ODBYT ALKOHOLICKYCH NAPOJOV NA SLOVENSKU V MINULOSTI:
 OBCHOD, VYVOZ, DOVOZ V STRADOVEKU. [Consumption of
 alcoholic beverages in Slovakia in the past: Trade,
 export, and import in the Middle Ages.] [Cze]
 Proti Alcoholický Obzor, 5: 51-55, 1970.
 Slovakia - consumption - economics - history, pre-1500 -
 wine   D-1106.

346.   Dumett, Raymond E.
        THE SOCIAL IMPACT OF THE EUROPEAN LIQUOR TRADE ON THE
        AKAN OF GHANA (GOLD COAST AND ASANTE), 1875-1910.
        Journal of Inter-Disciplinary History, 5: 69-101,   1974.
        Africa - Akan - acculturation - economics - history,
        pre-1900   D-1057.

347.   Dumont, Matthew P.
        TAVERN CULTURE: THE SUSTENANCE OF HOMELESS MEN.
        American Journal of Orthopsychiatry, 37: 938-945,   1967.
        United States - Skid Row - bar - functions   D-0361.

348.   Duncan, Earl, and Eyolfson, Connie
        NATIVES AND ALCOHOL: A COMPLEX CONCEPT, A SIMPLE TASK.
        Unpublished paper: Canadian Foundation on Alcohol and
        Drug Dependencies, Winnipeg, Man.,   1977.
        Canada - Native Americans   D-1549.

349.   Durand, Douglas
        EFFECTS OF DRINKING ON THE POWER AND AFFILIATION NEEDS
        OF MIDDLE-AGED FEMALES.
        Journal of Clinical Psychology, 31: 549-553,   1975.
        female - power   D-0202.

350.   Durand, Loyal
        MOUNTAIN MOONSHINING IN EAST TENNESSEE.
        Geographical Review, 46:   1956.
        United States - manufacture - moonshine   D-1145.

351.   Durgin, Edward
        BREWING AND BOOZING: A STUDY OF DRINKING HABITS AMONG
        THE HARE INDIANS.
        Ph.D. Dissertation, University of Oregon,   1974.
        United States - Native Americans - Hare - acculturation -
        anomie - customs - homebrew - norms - sociocultural   D-1058.

352.   Du Toit, Brian M.
        SUBSTITUTION: A PROCESS IN CULTURE CHANGE.
        Human Organization, 23: 16-23,   1964.
        Native Americans - Klamath - binge - change - norms -
        social organization   D-1102.

353.   Dwyer, Ellen
        THE RHETORIC OF REFORM: A STUDY OF VERBAL PERSUASION
        AND BELIEF SYSTEMS IN THE ANTI-MASONIC AND TEMPERANCE
        MOVEMENTS, 1825-1860.
        Ph.D. Dissertation, Yale University, 293 pp.,   1977.
        United States - attitudes - Church - history, pre-1900 -
        political - semantics - temperance   D-1059.

354. Eddy, Richard
ALCOHOL IN HISTORY, AN ACCOUNT OF INTEMPERANCE IN ALL
AGES: TOGETHER WITH A HISTORY OF THE VARIOUS METHODS
EMPLOYED FOR ITS REMOVAL.
New York, NY: National Temperance Society and
Publication House, 481 pp., 1887.
World survey - Classical peoples - customs - economics -
history, pre-1500 - history, pre-1900 - prehistory -
prevention - temperance D-1076.

355. Edgerton, Robert B.
ANTHROPOLOGY AND ALCOHOL: IN SEARCH OF A NEW PARADIGM.
Reviews in Anthropology, 2: 407-415, 1975.
review - sociocultural D-1060.

356. Edzard, D.O.
BRAUEREI, BIERKONSUM UND TRINKBRAUCHE IM ALTEN
MESOPOTAMIEN. [Brewing, beer consumption and drinking
customs in ancient Mesopotamia.] [Ger]
Jahrbuch der Gesellschaft für Geschichte und Biblio-
graphie des Brauwesens, (1966): 9-21, 1966.
Near East - Mesopotamia - Biblical peoples - customs -
history, pre-1500 - homebrew - manufacture - prehistory D-1219.

357. Efron, Vera
THE TAVERN AND THE SALOON IN OLD RUSSIA: AN ANALYSIS
OF I.G. PRYZHOV'S HISTORICAL SKETCH.
Quarterly Journal of Studies on Alcohol, 16: 484-503, 1955.
Soviet Union - bar - change - history, pre-1500 -
history, pre-1900 D-0362.

358. Efron, Vera
SOCIOLOGICAL AND CULTURAL FACTORS IN ALCOHOL ABUSE.
In: Popham, Robert E., ed. Alcohol and alcoholism.
Toronto, Ont.: University of Toronto Press, pp. 290-293, 1970.
Cross-ethnic - sociocultural D-1061.

359. Eguchi, Paul Kazuhisa
BEER DRINKING AND FESTIVALS AMONG THE HIDE.
Kyoto University African Studies, 9: 69-90, 1975.
Africa - Hide - customs - economics - functions - ritual D-1062.

360. Eis, G.
ALTDEUTSCHE HAUSMITTEL GEGEN TRUNKENHEIT UND TRUNKSUCHT.
[Old German household remedies for drunkenness and
alcoholism.] [Ger]
Medizinische Monatsschrift, 15: 269-271, 1961.
Germany - folklore - history, pre-1500 - history, pre-1900 -
medical A-0661.

361. Eldar, P.
AN ISRAELI EXPERIMENT IN THE TREATMENT OF ALCOHOLISM,
EDITED BY A. LAVINE.
Unpublished report: State of Israel, Ministry of Social

	Welfare, Department of International Relations, Jerusalem, 20 pp.,	1976.
	Israel - Jews - acculturation - class - treatment	D-1909.
362.	Elwin, Verrier THE CAUSES OF CRIME: ALCOHOL. In: Maria murder and suicide. Bombay: Oxford University Press, pp. 131-142,	1943.
	India - Gond - folklore - homebrew - manufacture - murder	D-1146.
363.	Emboden, William DIONYSUS AS SHAMAN AND WINE AS A MAGICAL DRUG. - Journal of Psychedelic Drugs, 9(3): 187-192, Classical peoples - folklore - history, pre-1500 - manufacture - prehistory - religion - responsibility - symbols - wine	1977. D-0363.
364.	Emerson, Edward R. BEVERAGES PAST AND PRESENT: AN HISTORICAL SKETCH OF THEIR PRODUCTION, TOGETHER WITH A STUDY OF THE CUSTOMS CONNECTED WITH THEIR USE, VOLUMES 1 AND 2. New York, NY: G. Putnam's Sons, World survey - Classical peoples - customs - distribution - folklore - history, pre-1500 - history, pre-1900 - homebrew - prehistory - religion	1908. D-1147.
365.	Eriksson, K., and Kärkkäinen, K. PULLO-JA TOLKKIJATTEEN KASAANTRIMINEN LUONTOON SUOMESSA UVONNA 1970. [The accumulation of waste bottles and jars in the environment in Finland in 1970.] [Fin] Alkoholipolitiika, 36: 175-186, Finland - containers - research methods	1971. D-1063.
366.	Erlich, Vera S. COMMENT ON D. MANDELBAUM'S "ALCOHOL AND CULTURE." Current Anthropology, 6: 288-289, Yugoslavia - customs	1965. D-1077.
367.	Ervin, A.M. NEW NORTHERN TOWNSMEN IN INUVIK. Unpublished report: Department of Indian Affairs and Northern Development, (Mackenzie Delta River Project 5), Ottawa, Ont., Canada - Eskimos - anomie - attitudes - bar - dysfunctions - economics - fighting - urbanization	(ca. 1971). D-1148.
368.	Evangelista, Alfredo E. TEMPERED INTEMPERANCE: TUBA-DRINKING IN A TAGALOG COMMUNITY. Philippine Sociological Review, 21(1): 5-28, Philippines - Tagalog - customs - homebrew	1973. D-0364.

369. Everett, Michael W.; Baha, Carla J.; Declay, Edwin; Endfield, Marilyn R.; and Selby, Karen
ANTHROPOLOGICAL EXPERTISE AND THE "REALITIES" OF WHITE MOUNTAIN APACHE ADOLESCENT DRINKING.
Unpublished paper: Society for Applied Anthropology, Tucson, AZ, 43 pp.,
United States - Native Americans - Apache - research methods - youth
1973.
D-1550.

370. Everett, Michael W.; Waddell, Jack O.; and Heath, Dwight B.
CROSS-CULTURAL APPROACHES TO THE STUDY OF ALCOHOL: AN INTERDISCIPLINARY PERSPECTIVE, INTRODUCTION - ALCOHOL STUDIES AND ANTHROPOLOGY.
Alcoholism, 11(2): 143-151,
sociocultural
1975.
D-1079.

371. Everett, Michael W.; Waddell, Jack O.; and Heath, Dwight B.
CROSS-CULTURAL APPROACHES TO THE STUDY OF ALCOHOL: AN INTERDISCIPLINARY PERSPECTIVE.
The Hague: Mouton, 432 pp.,
Cross-ethnic - research methods - review - sociocultural
1976.
D-1078.

372. Ewing, John A.; Rouse, Beatrice A.; and Pellizzari, E.D.
ALCOHOL SENSITIVITY AND ETHNIC BACKGROUND.
American Journal of Psychiatry, 131(2): 206-210,
Cross-ethnic - metabolism - "race"
1974.
D-0365.

373. Ezell, Paul H.
A COMPARISON OF DRINKING PATTERNS IN THREE HISPANIC CITIES.
Unpublished paper: American Association for the Advancement of Science, Berkeley, CA, 21 pp.,
Cross-national - Bolivia - Mexico - Mestizos - class
1965.
D-1551.

374. F., H.
CHIKARANGA COCKTAILS.
Nada, 11: 116-117,
Rhodesia - homebrew - manufacture
1933.
D-1080.

375. Fairbanks, Robert A.
THE CHEYENNE-ARAPAHO AND ALCOHOLISM: DOES THE TRIBE HAVE A LEGAL RIGHT TO A MEDICAL REMEDY?
American Indian Law Review, 1(1): 55-77,
United States - Native Americans - Arapaho - Cheyenne - acculturation - history, pre-1900 - treatment
1973.
D-1081.

376. Fallding, Harold
THE SOURCE AND BURDEN OF CIVILIZATION, ILLUSTRATED IN THE USE OF ALCOHOL.
Quarterly Journal of Studies on Alcohol, 25: 714-724,
dysfunctions - functions - social organization - symbols
1964.
D-0366.

377. Farris, John J., and Jones, Ben Morgan
       ETHANOL METABOLISM AND MEMORY IMPAIRMENT IN AMERICAN
       INDIANS AND CAUCASIANS.
       Alcohol Technical Reports, 6: 1-4,   1977.
       Cross-ethnic - Native Americans - Whites - metabolism -
       "race"   D-1082.

378. Farris, John J., and Jones, Ben Morgan
       ETHANOL METABOLISM IN MALE AMERICAN INDIANS AND WHITES.
       Alcoholism: Clinical and Experimental Research,
       2: 77-82,   1978.
       Cross-ethnic - Native Americans - Whites - metabolism -
       "race"   D-0367.

379. Favre, Henri
       NOTAS SOBRE EL HOMICIDIO ENTRE LOS CHAMULAS. [Notes on
       homicide among the Chamula.] [Spa]
       Estudios de Cultura Maya, 4(1964): 318,   1964.
       Mexico - Chamula - murder - responsibility   D-1083.

380. Fazey, C[indy]
       THE AETIOLOGY OF PSYCHOACTIVE SUBSTANCE USE: A REPORT
       AND CRITICALLY ANNOTATED BIBLIOGRAPHY ON RESEARCH INTO
       THE AETIOLOGY OF ALCOHOL, NICOTINE, OPIATE AND OTHER
       PSYCHOACTIVE SUBSTANCE USE.
       Paris: United Nations Educational, Scientific and
       Cultural Organization, 226 pp.,   1977.
       bibliography   D-0013.

381. Feldman, W.M.
       RACIAL ASPECTS OF ALCOHOLISM.
       British Journal of Inebriety, 21: 1-15,   1923.
       Cross-ethnic - "race"   D-0368.

382. Feldman, W.M.
       ALCOHOL IN ANCIENT JEWISH LITERATURE.
       British Journal of Inebriety, 24: 121-124,   1927.
       Jews - Biblical peoples - history, pre-1500 - literature -
       norms - religion   D-0369.

383. Feldstein, Aaron
       THE METABOLISM OF ALCOHOL: ON THE VALIDITY OF THE
       WIDMARK EQUATIONS, IN OBESITY, AND IN RACIAL AND ETHNIC
       GROUPS.
       Journal of Studies on Alcohol, 39(5): 926-932,   1978.
       metabolism - "race"   D-0203.

384. Felice, Ph. de
       POISONS SACRES, IVRESSES DIVINES. [Sacred potions,
       divine ecstasy.]
       Paris: Albin Michel,   1936.
       possession - religion - ritual   D-1084.

385. Feliciano, R.T.
ILLICIT BEVERAGES.
Philippine Journal of Science, 29: 465-474, 1926.
Philippines - manufacture - moonshine - prohibition   D-1085.

386. Fenasse, J.M.
LA BIBLE ET L'USAGE DU VIN. [The Bible and uses of wine.] [Fre]
Alcool ou Santé, 63: 17-28, 1964.
Biblical peoples - customs - history, pre-1500 - symbols - wine   D-0370.

387. Fenna, D.; Mix, L,; Schaefer, O.; and Gilbert, J.A.L.
ETHANOL METABOLISM IN VARIOUS RACIAL GROUPS.
Canadian Medical Association Journal, 105: 472-475, 1971.
Cross-ethnic - Eskimos - Native Americans - Whites - metabolism - "race"   D-0371.

388. Ferguson, Frances N.
NAVAHO DRINKING: SOME TENTATIVE HYPOTHESES.
Human Organization, 27: 159-167, 1968.
United States - Native Americans - Navaho - acculturation - anomie - crime - disulfiram - leisure - stress - treatment   D-0372.

389. Ferguson, Frances N.
A TREATMENT PROGRAM FOR NAVAHO ALCOHOLICS: RESULTS AFTER FOUR YEARS.
Quarterly Journal of Studies on Alcohol, 31: 898-919, 1970.
United States - Native Americans - Navaho - acculturation - anomie - crime - disulfiram - stress - treatment   B-3950.

390. Ferguson, Frances N.
CHANGE FROM WITHOUT AND WITHIN: NAVAJO INDIANS' RESPONSE TO AN ALCOHOLISM TREATMENT PROGRAM IN TERMS OF SOCIAL STAKE.
In: Atti del XL Congresso Internazionale Degli Americanisti, Volume 2. Rome-Genova: pp. 557-566, 1974.
United States - Native Americans - Navaho - acculturation - anomie - norms - stress - treatment   D-1149.

391. Ferguson, Frances N.
SIMILARITIES AND DIFFERENCES AMONG A HEAVILY-ARRESTED GROUP OF NAVAJO INDIAN DRINKERS IN A SOUTHWESTERN AMERICAN TOWN.
In: Everett, Michael W.; Waddell, Jack O.; and Heath, Dwight B., ed. Cross-cultural approaches to the study of alcohol: An interdisciplinary perspective. The Hague: Mouton, pp. 161-171, 1976.
United States - Native Americans - Navaho - acculturation - anomie - crime - stress   D-0373.

392. Ferguson, Frances N.
STAKE THEORY AS AN EXPLANATORY DEVICE IN NAVAJO
ALCOHOLISM TREATMENT RESPONSE.
Human Organization, 35(1): 65-78, 1976.
United States - Native Americans - Navaho - acculturation
- anomie - norms - stress - treatment D-0374.

393. Ferreira, A.G.
ALCOHOLISM IN PORTUGAL.
International Journal on Mental Health, 5(1): 63-73, 1976.
Portugal - attitudes - bar - consumption - customs -
economics - treatment - sociocultural - urbanization D-0204.

394. Field, Peter B.
A NEW CROSS-CULTURAL STUDY OF DRUNKENNESS.
In: Pittman, David J., and Snyder, Charles R., ed.
Society, culture and drinking patterns. New York, NY:
John Wiley and Sons, pp. 48-74, 1962.
World survey - Cross-cultural - functions - social
organization D-0375.

395. Figueroa-Rosales, R.
EL ALCOHOLISMO Y SU RELACION CON EL ASPECTO SOCIAL Y
EL DESARROLLO DE LA COMUNIDAD. [Alcoholism and its
relationship with aspects of social and community
development.] [Spa]
Revista Mexicana de Psicología, 6(6): 244-250, 1971.
Mexico - dysfunctions D-0014.

396. Finkler, H.W.
ALCOHOL ABUSE AND ITS CRIMINOGENIC ROLE IN FROBISHER
BAY, N.W.T.
Unpublished paper: Presented at the 3rd International
Symposium on Circumpolar Health, Yellowknife, N.W.T.
July 8-11, 1974.
Canada - Eskimos - crime - norms D-1910.

397. Finney, F.F.
THE OSAGE INDIANS AND THE LIQUOR PROBLEM BEFORE STATEHOOD.
Chronicles of Oklahoma, 34: 456-464, 1956.
United States - Native Americans - Osage - economics -
history, pre-1900 D-1086.

398. Firebaugh, W.C.
THE INNS OF THE MIDDLE AGES.
Chicago, IL.: Pascal Covici, 274 pp., 1924.
Europe - bar - functions - history, pre-1500 D-0205.

399. Firebaugh, W.C.
THE INNS OF GREECE AND ROME: AND A HISTORY OF HOSPITALITY
FROM THE DAWN OF TIME TO THE MIDDLE AGES.
Chicago, IL: Pascal Covici, 271 pp., 1928.

52.

Alcohol Use and World Cultures		Frederikson, Otto F.

	Asia - Europe - Biblical peoples - Classical peoples -
	Greeks, ancient - Romans, ancient - bar - functions -
	history, pre-1500 - prehistory - sociocultural	D-0206.

400.	Fiume, S.
	GLI ASPETTI SOCIO-CULTURALI DELL'ALCOOLISMO IN ITALIA.
	[Sociocultural aspects of alcoholism in Italy.] [Ita]
	Anali Bolnice "Dr. Mladen Stojanović", 5(2): 368-372,	1966.
	Italy - sociocultural	D-1087.

401.	Fort, Joel
	CULTURAL ASPECTS OF ALCOHOL (AND DRUG) PROBLEMS.
	In: Selected Papers presented at the 27th International
	Congress on Alcohol and Alcoholism, Volume I: Alcohol as
	a cultural question. Held September 6-12, 1964 in
	Frankfurt-am-Main, West Germany. Lausanne: International
	Council on Alcohol and Alcoholism, pp. 27-36,	1965.
	Cross-ethnic - prevention - review - sociocultural	D-1150.

402.	Foulks, Edward F., and Katz, Solomon H.
	THE MENTAL HEALTH OF ALASKAN NATIVES.
	Acta Psychiatrica Scandinavica, 49: 91-96,	1973.
	Aleuts - Eskimos - Native Americans - acculturation -
	economics - psychiatric problems - stress - urbanization	D-0376.

403.	Fouquet, Pierre
	ALCOOL ET RELIGIONS. [Alcohol and religions.] [Fre]
	Revue de l'Alcoolisme, 11: 81-92,	1965.
	Europe - Near East - folklore - history, pre-1500 -
	possession - prehistory - religion - ritual - symbols	D-0377.

404.	Frake, Charles O.
	HOW TO ASK FOR A DRINK IN SUBANUN.
	American Anthropologist, 66(6, pt. 2): 127-132,	1964.
	Philippines - Subanun - semantics	D-0378.

405.	Frederick, Calvin J.
	SUICIDE, HOMICIDE, AND ALCOHOLISM AMONG AMERICAN INDIANS:
	GUIDELINES FOR HELP.
	Washington, D.C.: U.S. Government Printing Office
	(DHEW Publication (HSM) 73-9124), 36 pp.,	1973.
	United States - Native Americans - murder - prevention -
	suicide	D-0015.

406.	Frederikson, Otto F.
	THE LIQUOR QUESTION AMONG THE INDIAN TRIBES IN KANSAS,
	1804-1881.
	Bulletin of the University of Kansas, 33, 8,	1932.
	United States - Native Americans - acculturation -
	aggression - anomie - dysfunctions - economics - history,
	pre-1900 - prohibition	D-1151.

407.   French, Richard Valpy
        NINETEEN CENTURIES OF DRINK IN ENGLAND.
        London: Longmans, Green, 398 pp.,   1884.
        England - customs - history, pre-1500 - history, pre-1900 -
        prehistory   D-0429.

408.   Freund, Paul, and Marshall, Mac
        RESEARCH BIBLIOGRAPHY OF ALCOHOL AND KAVA STUDIES IN
        OCEANIA: UPDATE AND ADDITIONAL ITEMS.
        Micronesia, 13(2): 313-317,   1977.
        Oceania - bibliography - kava   D-0430.

409.   Fritz, W.B.
        PSYCHIATRIC DISORDERS AMONG NATIVES AND NON-NATIVES IN
        SASKATCHEWAN.
        Canadian Psychiatric Association Journal, 21(6): 393-400, 1976.
        Canada - Native Americans - psychiatric problems   D-0261.

410.   Frøland, Bjarke
        DRINKING PATTERNS IN ZAMBIZA (PICHINCHA).
        In: Maynard, Eileen; Frøland, B.; and Rasmussen, Christian,
        ed. Drinking patterns in Highland Ecuador. Ithaca, NY:
        Cornell University, pp. 10-17,   1965.
        Ecuador - Quechua - aggression - economics - intoxication -
        ritual   D-1203.

411.   Fromm, Erich, and Maccoby, Michael
        ALCOHOLISM.
        In: Social character in a Mexican village: A
        sociopsychoanalytic study. Englewood Cliffs, NJ: Prentice-
        Hall, pp. 156-178,   1970.
        Mexico - Mestizos - aggression - conversion - dysfunctions -
        economics - family - psychiatric problems - sociocultural D-0431.

412.   Fukui, Katsuyoshi
        ALCOHOLIC DRINKS OF THE IRAQU: BREWING METHODS AND
        SOCIAL FUNCTIONS.
        Kyoto University African Studies, 5: 125-148,   1970.
        Tanganyika - Iraqu - functions - homebrew - manufacture -
        social organization   D-0432.

413.   Fukui, M., and Wakasugi, C.
        LIVER ALCOHOL DEHYDROGENASE IN A JAPANESE POPULATION.
        Japanese Journal of Legal Medicine, 26: 46-51,   1972.
        Japan - liver - "race"   D-0433.

414.   Gabe, Ruth C.; Phelps, Graham H.; and Ruck, James A.
        AN EXPLORATORY STUDY OF THE INCIDENCE OF ALCOHOL-RELATED
        ARRESTS AMONG AMERICAN INDIANS OF ONONDAGA COUNTY, N.Y.
        M.S.W. Thesis, Syracuse University,   1968.
        United States - Cross-ethnic - Native Americans - Blacks -
        Whites - crime   D-0434.

415. Gadourek, I.
RISKANTE GEWOONTEN EN ZORG VOOR EIGEN WELZIJN: EEN STRUCTUREEL-SOCIOLOGISCHE ANALYSE VAN HET ROKEN EN HET DRINKEN ALSMEDE... [Hazardous habits and human well-being: A structural-sociological analysis of smoking and drinking habits...] [Dut]
Groningen: J.B. Wolters, 1963.
Netherlands - attitudes - class - customs - drugs - economics - epidemiology - sociocultural D-0407.

416. Gai, B.M.
WINE IN THE ORIENT AND ITS PROHIBITION.
Indo-Iranica, 9(3): 31-46, 1956.
Iran - Islam - Persians, ancient - history, pre-1500 - literature - medical - prohibition - religion - wine D-0017.

417. Galan, Fernando Javier
CHICANO DRINKING: A CULTURE-CONFLICT MODEL.
Unpublished paper: Society for Applied Anthropology, Mérida, Mexico, 1978.
United States - Hispanos - anomie - class - stress D-1552.

418. Galang, Ricardo C.
PANGASI: THE BUKIDNON WINE.
Philippine Magazine, 31: 540, 1934.
Philippines - Bukidnon - homebrew - manufacture D-0435.

419. Gallagher, Orvoell R.
DRINKING PROBLEMS OF THE TRIBAL BIHAR.
Quarterly Journal of Studies on Alcohol, 26: 617-628, 1965.
India - Oraon - change - customs - economics - homebrew - leisure - moonshine - stereotype D-0436.

420. García Alcaraz, Agustín
EL MAGUEY Y EL PULQUE EN TEPETLAOXTOC. [Maguey and pulque in Tepetlaoxtoc.] [Spa]
Comunidad, 7(38): 461-474, 1972.
Mexico - homebrew - manufacture D-0437.

421. Gardner, R.E.
THE ROLE OF A PAN-INDIAN CHURCH IN URBAN INDIAN LIFE.
Anthropology UCLA, 1(1): 14-26, 1969.
Native Americans - bar - Church - functions - urbanization D-0438.

422. Garland, M.A., and Talman, J.J.
PIONEER DRINKING HABITS AND THE RISE OF TEMPERANCE AGITATION IN UPPER CANADA PRIOR TO 1840.
Ontario History, 27: 341-363, 1931.
Canada - change - customs - history, pre-1900 - temperance D-0207.

423.   Gayre, G.R.
       <u>WASSAIL! IN MAZERS OF MEAD: AN ACCOUNT OF MEAD,
       METHEGLIN, SACK AND OTHER ANCIENT LIQUORS, AND OF THE
       MAZER CUPS OUT OF WHICH THEY WERE DRUNK, WITH SOME
       COMMENT UPON THE DRINKING CUSTOMS OF OUR FOREBEARS.</u>
       London: Phillimore, 176 pp.,   1948.
       Europe - beer - containers - folklore - history, pre-1500 -
       homebrew - manufacture   D-0018.

424.   Geertz, Clifford
       DROUGHT, DEATH AND ALCOHOL IN FIVE SOUTHWESTERN CULTURES.
       Unpublished manuscript: Department of Social Relations,
       Harvard University, Cambridge, MA,   1951.
       United States - Cross-ethnic - Mormon - Navaho - Hispanos -
       Whites - Zuni - attitudes - customs   D-1553.

425.   Gelfand, Michael
       ALCOHOLISM IN CONTEMPORARY AFRICAN SOCIETY.
       Central African Journal of Medicine, 12: 12-13,   1966.
       Africa - dysfunctions - pathology   D-0439.

426.   Gelfand, M[ichael]
       THE EXTENT OF ALCOHOL CONSUMPTION BY AFRICANS: THE
       SIGNIFICANCE OF THE WEAPONS AT BEER DRINKS.
       Journal of Forensic Medicine, 18: 53-64,   1971.
       Rhodesia - crime - fighting - murder - responsibility   D-0440.

427.   Geralin, H.
       LE PROBLEME DE L'ALCOOLISME DANS LES TERRITOIRES D'OUTRE-
       MER. [The problem of alcoholism in the overseas terri-
       tories.] [Fre]
       Population, 8: 291-310,   1953.
       World survey - change - accidents - dysfunctions -
       prevention - psychiatric problems - temperance   D-0019.

428.   Ghosh, Samir K.
       ALCOHOL AND ALCOHOLISM IN THE NORTH-EAST FRONTIER AREA.
       Unpublished paper: International Congress of Anthropol-
       ogical and Ethnological Sciences, Chicago, IL,   1973.
       India - Cross-ethnic   D-1554.

429.   Giesbrecht, N[orman]; Giffen, P.J.; Lambert, S.; and
       Oki, G.
       CHANGES IN THE SOCIAL CONTROL OF "SKID ROW" INEBRIATES:
       THE VIEWS OF POLICEMEN, ADMINISTRATORS OF SERVICES AND
       "SKID ROW" INEBRIATES.
       Toronto, Ont.: Addiction Research Foundation, Substudy
       No. 763, 94 pp.,   1976.
       Canada - Skid Row - attitudes - change - crime   D-0210.

430. Giesbrecht, Norman; Brown, Joe; de Lint, Jan; and
Lambert, Sylvia
ALCOHOL PROBLEMS IN NORTHWESTERN ONTARIO - PRELIMINARY
REPORT: CONSUMPTION PATTERNS, AND PUBLIC ORDER AND
PUBLIC HEALTH PROBLEMS.
Toronto, Ont.: Addiction Research Foundation, Substudy
No. 872, 328 pp., 1977.
Canada - Native Americans - Eskimos - acculturation -
anomie - change - economics - prevention - sociocultural   D-0209.

431. Giesbrecht, Norman
ALCOHOL CONSUMPTION, ALCOHOL PROBLEMS AND ECONOMIC
DEVELOPMENT IN NORTHERN ONTARIO.
Toronto, Ont.: Addiction Research Foundation, Substudy
No. 945, 69 pp., 1978.
Canada - Native Americans - Eskimos - accidents -
acculturation - change - customs - epidemiology -
prevention   D-0208.

432. Gilbert, J.A.L., and Schaefer, O.
METABOLISM OF ETHANOL IN DIFFERENT RACIAL GROUPS.
Canadian Medical Association Journal, 116(5): 476, 1977.
Cross-ethnic - metabolism - "race"   D-0441.

433. Gilbert, M. Jean
A FIVE-WEEK ALCOHOLISM ETHNOGRAPHY CONDUCTED IN THREE
SPANISH-SPEAKING COMMUNITIES.
Unpublished paper: American Anthropological Association,
Houston, TX, 12 pp., 1977.
United States - Hispanos - research methods   D-1914.

434. Gilder, D.D.
DRINK IN THE SCRIPTURES OF THE NATIONS.
Anthropological Society of Bombay, 12: 172-189, 1921.
World survey - Biblical peoples - Hinduism - Islam -
history, pre-1500 - literature - norms - religion -
symbols   D-0442.

435. Gill, Mary
PATTERNS OF ALCOHOL USE AMONG WOMEN CHARACTERS IN
MEXICAN FICTION.
Unpublished paper: Society for Applied Anthropology,
Mérida, Mexico, 1978.
Mexico - female - folklore   D-1555.

436. Gillin, John
ACQUIRED DRIVES IN CULTURE CONTACT.
American Anthropologist, 44: 545-554, 1942.
United States - Native Americans - Chippewa -
acculturation - anomie - stress   D-0020.

437.   Gillis, L.S.; Lewis, J.; and Slabbert, M.
        ALCOHOLISM AMONG THE CAPE COLOUREDS.
        South African Medical Journal, 47(30): 1374-1382,   1973.
        South Africa - Cape Coloured - class - psychiatric
        problems - social organization   D-0443.

438.   Girard, G.
        A PROPOS DE L'ALCOOLISME OUTRE-MER. [Concerning
        alcoholism overseas.] [Fre]
        Bulletin de la Société de Pathologie Exotique et de
        ses Filiales, 48: 121-125,   1955.
        World survey - accidents - dysfunctions - economics -
        prevention   D-0021.

439.   Girouard, Mark
        VICTORIAN PUBS.
        London: Studio Vista, 223 pp.,   1975.
        England - bar - history, pre-1900   D-0022.

440.   Glad, D.D.
        ATTITUDES AND EXPERIENCES OF AMERICAN-JEWISH AND
        AMERICAN-IRISH MALE YOUTH AS RELATED TO DIFFERENCES IN
        ADULT RATES OF INEBRIETY.
        Quarterly Journal of Studies on Alcohol, 8: 406-472,   1947.
        United States - Irish-Americans - Jews - attitudes -
        etiology - norms - youth   D-0444.

441.   Glatt, M.M.
        HISTORICAL NOTE - HASHISH AND ALCOHOL "SCENES" IN FRANCE
        AND GREAT BRITAIN 120 YEARS AGO.
        British Journal of Addiction, 64: 99-108,   1969.
        England - France - change - class - drugs - history,
        pre-1900 - literature   D-0445.

442.   Glatt, M.M.
        ALCOHOLISM AND DRUG DEPENDENCE AMONGST JEWS.
        British Journal of Addiction, 64: 297-304,   1970.
        Jews - change - drugs   D-0446.

443.   Glatt, M.M.
        THE ENGLISH DRINK PROBLEM THROUGH THE AGES.
        Proceedings of the Royal Society of Medicine, 70:
        202-206,   1977.
        England - change - customs - history, pre-1500 -
        history, pre-1900 - temperance   D-0447.

444.   Glick, Carl
        DRINKS ON THE HOUSE.
        In: Glick, Carl. Shake hands with the dragon.
        New York, NY: McGraw-Hill, pp. 176-193,   1971.
        China - wine   D-1088.

445. Glover, Edward
COMMON PROBLEMS IN PSYCHO-ANALYSIS AND ANTHROPOLOGY:
DRUG RITUAL AND ADDICTION.
British Journal of Medical Psychology, 12: 109-131, 1932.
drugs - possession - ritual D-0448.

446. Gluckman, L.K.
ALCOHOL AND THE MAORI IN HISTORIC PERSPECTIVE.
New Zealand Medical Journal, 79: 553-555, 1974.
New Zealand - Maori - acculturation - history, pre-1500 -
history, pre-1900 D-0449.

447. Goffman, Erving
ENGAGEMENTS AMONG THE UNACQUAINTED.
In: Goffman, Erving. Behavior in public places: Notes on the social organization of gatherings. New York, NY: Free Press, pp. 124-148, 1963.
United States - bar - social organization D-0080.

448. Gold, Robert S.; Zimmerli, William H.; and Austin, Winnifred K.
COMPREHENSIVE BIBLIOGRAPHY OF EXISTING LITERATURE ON ALCOHOL: 1969 to 1974.
Dubuque, IA: Kendall/Hunt, 470 pp., 1975.
bibliography D-0450.

449. Goldman, Irving
THE DRINKING PARTY.
In: The Cubeo: Indians of the Northwest Amazon.
Urbana, IL: Illinois Studies in Anthropology 2, 1963.
Brazil - Cubeo - binge - functions - social organization D-1152.

450. Gómez Huamán, Nilo
IMPORTANCIA SOCIAL DE LA CHICHA COMO BEBIDA POPULAR EN HUAMANGA. [Social importance of chicha as a folk beverage in Huamanga.] [Spa]
Wamani, 1(1): 33-57, 1966.
Peru - customs - functions - homebrew - medical -
sociocultural D-0451.

451. Gonçalves de Lima, Oswaldo
EL MAGUEY Y EL PULQUE EN LOS CODICES MEXICANOS. [Maguey and pulque in the Mexican codices.] [Spa]
México: Fondo de Culture Económica, (ca. 1956).
Mexico - history, pre-1500 - homebrew - literature -
prehistory - religion D-1556.

452. Gonçalves de Lima, Oswaldo; de Mello, J.F.; D'Albuquerque, I.L.; Delle Monache, F.; Marini-Bettolo, G.B.; and Sousa, M.
CONTRIBUTION TO THE KNOWLEDGE OF THE MAYA RITUAL WINE: BALCHE.
Lloydia: The Journal of Natural Products, 40(2): 195-200, 1977.

Maya - history, pre-1500 - homebrew - prehistory - religion - ritual   D-0452.

453.   Goodenough, Erwin R.
        JEWISH SYMBOLS IN THE GRECO-ROMAN PERIOD, VOLUMES 5-6:
        FISH, BREAD, AND WINE.
        Princeton, NJ: Princeton University Press,   1956.
        Jews - Near East - Biblical peoples - history, pre-1500 -
        literature - norms - religion - symbols - wine   D-1089.

454.   Goodwin, Donald W.; Johnson, James; Maher, Chauncey;
        Rappaport, Allan; and Guze, Samuel B.
        WHY PEOPLE DO NOT DRINK: A STUDY OF TEETOTALERS.
        Comprehensive Psychiatry, 10(3): 209-214,   1969.
        United States - Protestants - abstainers - attitudes -
        religion   D-0211.

455.   Gorad, Stephen L.; McCourt, William F.; and Cobb, Jeremy C.
        A COMMUNICATIONS APPROACH TO ALCOHOLISM.
        Quarterly Journal of Studies on Alcohol, 32(3): 651-668, 1971.
        functions - intoxication - responsibility - stereotype D-0453.

456.   Gordon, Andrew J., ed.
        ETHNICITY AND ALCOHOL USE.
        Medical Anthropology, 2(4): 155 pp.,   1978.
        United States - Cross-ethnic - Hispanos - Irish-Americans -
        Native Americans - bar - change - female - functions -
        sociocultural   D-0425.

457.   Gordon, Andrew J.
        HISPANIC DRINKING AFTER MIGRATION: THE CASE OF DOMINICANS.
        Medical Anthropology, 2(4): 61-84,   1978.
        United States - Hispanos - Dominican Republic - change -
        norms   D-0427.

458.   Górski, Jan
        ALKOHOL U KULTURZE I OBYCZAJU. [Alcohol in culture and
        custom.] [Pol]
        Problemy Alkoholizmu, 17(7-8): 10-11,   1969.
        Poland - customs - folklore - history, pre-1500 -
        history, pre-1900   D-0454.

459.   Goshen, Charles E.
        THE DRINKING CULTURE AND DRINKING PATTERNS.
        In: Goshen, Charles E. Drinks, drugs, and do-gooders.
        New York, NY: Free Press, pp. 79-101,   1973.
        United States - attitudes - change - customs - history,
        pre-1900   D-0212.

460.   Gottleib, David
        THE NEIGHBORHOOD TAVERN AND THE COCKTAIL LOUNGE: A STUDY
        OF CLASS DIFFERENCES.
        American Journal of Sociology, 62: 559-562,   1957.

60.

	United States - bar - class	D-0455.
461.	Gould, Lewis L. PROGRESSIVES AND PROHIBITIONISTS: TEXAS DEMOCRATS IN THE WILSON ERA. Austin, TX: University of Texas Press, United States - attitudes - change - political - prohibition	1973. D-1220.
462.	Grace, V. WINE JARS. Classical Journal, 42: 443-452, Classical peoples - containers - history, pre-1500 - research methods	1947. D-0456.
463.	Gracia, M.F. ANALYSIS OF INCIDENCE OF ALCOHOLIC INTAKE BY INDIAN POPULATION IN ONE STATE OF U.S.A. (MONTANA). Unpublished paper: International Congress of Anthropological and Ethnological Sciences, Chicago, IL, United States - Native Americans - consumption	1973. D-1557.
464.	Grandoit, G. UNE BOISSON POPULAIRE: LE MABI. [A popular drink: Mabi.] [Fre] Bulletin du Bureau d'Ethnologie, 3(28): 43-55, customs	1962. D-0213.
465.	Graves, Theodore D. ACCULTURATION, ACCESS, AND ALCOHOL IN A TRI-ETHNIC COMMUNITY. American Anthropologist, 69: 306-321, United States - Cross-ethnic - Hispanos - Native Americans - Ute - Whites - acculturation - anomie - norms - sociocultural	1967. D-0457.
466.	Graves, Theodore D. THE PERSONAL ADJUSTMENT OF NAVAJO INDIAN MIGRANTS TO DENVER, COLORADO. American Anthropologist, 72: 35-54, United States - Native Americans - Navaho - class - stress - urbanization	1970. D-0458.
467.	Graves, Theodore D. DRINKING AND DRUNKENNESS AMONG URBAN INDIANS. In: Waddell, Jack O., and Watson, O.M., ed. The American Indian in urban society. Boston, MA: Little, Brown, pp. 274-311, United States - Native Americans - Navaho - anomie - crime - norms - stress - urbanization	1971. D-0459.

468. Gray, James H.
      BOOZE: THE IMPACT OF WHISKEY ON THE PRAIRIE WEST.
      Toronto, Ont.: Macmillan, 243 pp.,   1972.
      Canada - attitudes - change - history, pre-1900 -
      temperance - prohibition - whiskey   D-0461.

469. Greeley, Andrew M., and McCready, William C.
      A PRELIMINARY RECONNAISSANCE INTO THE PERSISTENCE AND
      EXPLANATION OF ETHNIC SUBCULTURAL DRINKING PATTERNS.
      Medical Anthropology, 2(4): 31-51,   1978.
      United States - Cross-ethnic - enculturation   D-0428.

470. Gregory, D.
      RACIAL DIFFERENCES IN THE INCIDENCE AND PREVALENCE
      OF ALCOHOL ABUSE IN OKLAHOMA.
      Alcohol Technical Reports, 4: 37-41,   1975.
      United States - Cross-ethnic - Native Americans - Blacks -
      Whites - crime - epidemiology - "race"   D-0462.

471. Gregson, Ronald E.
      BEER, LEADERSHIP, AND THE EFFICIENCY OF COMMUNAL LABOR.
      Unpublished paper: American Anthropological Association,
      New Orleans, LA, 8 pp.,   1969.
      Malawi - Henga - economics - functions - social
      organization   D-1558.

472. Grmek, Mirko Dražen
      OPOJNA PICA I OTROVI ANTIKNIH ILIRA. [Intoxicating
      beverages and poisons in ancient Illyria.] [Ser-Cro]
      Farmaceutski Glasnik, 6: 33-38,   1950.
      Yugoslavia - Illyria - Classical peoples - customs -
      history, pre-1500 - homebrew - medical - wine   D-1090.

473. Groff, J.
      THE GOLDEN AGE OF COCAINE WINE.
      High Times, 5: 31-34,   1975.
      wine   D-0214.

474. Guiart, Jean
      UN SIECLE ET DEMI DE CONTACTS CULTURELS A TANNA,
      NOUVELLES HEBRIDES. [A century and a half of cultural
      contacts in Tanna, New Hebrides.] [Fre]
      Paris: Publications de la Société des Océanistes 5,   1956.
      Oceania - New Hebrides - acculturation - change - Church -
      history, pre-1900 - religion - temperance   D-1153.

475. Gunson, Niel
      ON THE INCIDENCE OF ALCOHOLISM AND INTEMPERANCE IN EARLY
      PACIFIC MISSIONS.
      Journal of Pacific History, 1: 43-62,   1966.
      Oceania - change - history, pre-1900   D-0463.

62.

476. Gusfield, Joseph
THE PREVENTION OF DRINKING PROBLEMS.
In: Filstead, William J.; Rossi, Jean J.; and Keller, Mark, ed. Alcohol and alcohol problems: New thinking and new directions. Cambridge, MA: Ballinger, pp. 267-291, 1976.
prevention - review - sociocultural
D-0023.

477. Gusfield, Joseph R.
SYMBOLIC CRUSADE: STATUS POLITICS AND THE AMERICAN TEMPERANCE MOVEMENT.
Urbana, IL: University of Illinois Press, 198 pp., 1963.
United States - economics - history, pre-1900 - political - temperance
D-0464.

478. Haavio-Manilla, Elina
ALKOHELENS ROLL VID BYSLAGSMALEN I FINLAND. [The role of alcohol in village fights in Finland.] [Fin]
Alkoholpolitik, 22: 16-18, 1959.
Finland - fighting - folklore - history, pre-1900 - social organization - stereotype
D-0465.

479. Hackenberg, Robert A., and Gallagher, Mary M.
THE COSTS OF CULTURAL CHANGE: ACCIDENTAL INJURY AND MODERNIZATION AMONG THE PAPAGO INDIANS.
Human Organization, 31(2): 211-226, 1972.
United States - Native Americans - Papago - accidents - acculturation - stress - urbanization
D-0024.

480. Hackwood, Frederick W.
INNS, ALES AND DRINKING CUSTOMS OF OLD ENGLAND.
London: T. Fisher Unwin, 1909.
England - bar - change - containers - customs - history, pre-1500 - history, pre-1900
D-0467.

481. Hagaman, Barbara L.
ECONOMIC POWER AND SOCIAL STATUS OF WOMEN IN A WEST AFRICAN CULTURE: BEER AND DOUBLE DESCENT.
Ph.D. Dissertation, Northeastern University, (ca. 1975).
Africa - economics - family - female - homebrew - social organization
D-1154.

482. Hage, Per
MUNCHNER BEER CATEGORIES.
In: Spradley, James P., ed.
Culture and cognition: Rules, maps and plans. San Francisco, CA: Chandler, pp. 263-278, 1972.
Austria - beer - customs - semantics
D-0468.

483. Hahn, D.S.
ALCOHOLISM IN KOREA: KOREAN PATTERN OF DRINKING.
Korean Medical Association Journal, 14: 833-838, 1971.
Korea - customs - epidemiology
D-0025.

484. Hamer, John H.
ACCULTURATION STRESS AND THE FUNCTIONS OF ALCOHOL AMONG
THE FOREST POTAWATOMI.
Quarterly Journal of Studies on Alcohol, 26: 285-302, 1965.
United States - Native Americans - Potawatomi -
acculturation - anomie - change - customs - economics -
functions - history, pre-1900 - responsibility - social
organization - stress   D-0470.

485. Hamer, John H.
GUARDIAN SPIRITS, ALCOHOL, AND CULTURAL DEFENSE MECHANISMS.
Anthropologica, 11: 215-241, 1969.
United States - Native Americans - Potawatomi - dependency -
functions - possession   D-0471.

486. Hanna, Joel M.
ETHNIC GROUPS, HUMAN VARIATION, AND ALCOHOL USE.
In: Everett, Michael W.; Waddell, Jack O.; and Heath,
Dwight B., ed. Cross-cultural approaches to the study of
alcohol: An interdisciplinary perspective. The Hague:
Mouton, pp. 235-242, 1976.
Cross-ethnic - "race" - review   D-0472.

487. Hanna, Joel M.
METABOLIC RESPONSES OF CHINESE, JAPANESE AND EUROPEANS
TO ALCOHOL.
Alcoholism: Clinical and Experimental Research,
2(1): 89-92, 1978.
Cross-ethnic - metabolism - "race"   D-0473.

488. Hansen, Edward C.
FROM POLITICAL ASSOCIATION TO PUBLIC TAVERN: TWO PHASES
OF URBANIZATION IN RURAL CATALONIA.
Annals of the New York Academy of Sciences,
220(6): 509-521, 1974.
Spain - Catalonia - bar - political - social organization   D-0474.

489. Hansen, Edward C.
DRINKING TO PROSPERITY: THE ROLE OF BAR CULTURE AND
COALITION FORMATION IN THE MODERNIZATION OF THE ALTO
PANADES.
Queens College Papers in Anthropology, 2: 42-51, 1976.
Spain - Catalonia - bar - economics - social organization   D-0475.

490. Harding, Wayne M., and Zinberg, Norman E.
THE EFFECTIVENESS OF THE SUBCULTURE IN DEVELOPING RITUALS
AND SOCIAL SANCTIONS FOR CONTROLLED DRUG USE.
In: du Toit, Brian M., ed. Drugs, rituals and altered
states of consciousness. Rotterdam: A.A. Balkema,
pp. 111-133, 1977.
United States - enculturation - norms - ritual -
sociocultural   D-0476.

491. Harford, Charles F.
DRINKING HABITS OF UNCIVILIZED AND SEMI-CIVILIZED RACES.
British Journal of Inebriety, 2: 92-103, 1905.
Africa - India - dysfunctions - homebrew - manufacture   D-0477.

492. Harford, Thomas C.; Dorman, Nancy; and Feinhandler, Sherwin
ALCOHOL CONSUMPTION IN BARS: VALIDATION OF SELF-REPORTS AGAINST OBSERVED BEHAVIOR.
Drinking and Drug Practices Surveyor, 11: 13-15, 1976.
United States - bar - consumption - research methods   D-0478.

493. Harford-Battersby, [C.F.]
LE TRAFIC DES SPIRITUEUX ET LES RACES INDIGENES. [The liquor traffic and native peoples.] [Fre]
In: VIIe Congres International contre l'Abus des Boissons Alcooliques, Vol. 1. Paris: A. Coueslant, pp. 355-359, 1900.
Africa - economics - prohibition   D-0215.

494. Harper, Frederick D., ed.
ALCOHOL ABUSE AND BLACK AMERICA.
Alexandria, VA: Douglass, 229 pp., 1976.
United States - Blacks   D-1221.

495. Harper, Frederick D.
ALCOHOL USE AMONG NORTH AMERICAN BLACKS.
In: Israel, Yedy; Glaser, Frederick B.; Kalant, Harold; Popham, Robert E.; Schmidt, Wolfgang; and Smart, Reginald G., ed. Research advances in alcohol and drug problems, Volume 4. New York, NY: Plenum, pp. 349-364, 1978.
United States - Blacks   D-0216.

496. Harrison, Brian
DRINK AND THE VICTORIANS: THE TEMPERANCE QUESTION IN ENGLAND, 1815-1872.
London: Faber and Faber, 510 pp., 1971.
England - attitudes - change - history, pre-1900 - temperance   D-0480.

497. Harrison, B[rian] H., and Trinder, B.
DRINK AND SOBRIETY IN AN EARLY VICTORIAN COUNTRY TOWN: BANBURY, 1830-1869.
English Historical Review Supplement, 4: 1-72, 1969.
England - change - history, pre-1900 - temperance   D-0479.

498. Hartman, Louis Francis, and Oppenheim, A. Leo
BEER AND BREWING TECHNIQUES IN ANCIENT MESOPOTAMIA ACCORDING TO THE XXIIIrd TABLET OF THE SERIES HAR RA-HUBULLU.
New Haven, CT: American Oriental Society, 1950.
Mesopotamia - history, pre-1500 - homebrew - manufacture - prehistory   D-0481.

499. Hartmann, Günther
ALKOHOLISCHE GETRANKE BEI DEN NATURVOLKERN SUDAMERIKAS.
[Alcoholic beverages among the native peoples of South
America.] [Ger]
Ph.D. Dissertation, Freien Universitat Berlin, 341 pp.,   1958.
South America - customs - distribution - homebrew -
manufacture   D-0482.

500. Hartmann, Günther
GEGORENE GETRANKE BEI DEN NATURVOLKERN SUDAMERIKAS.
[Fermented drinks among South American native peoples.]
[Ger]
Jahrbuch der Gesellschaft für Geschichte und Bibliographie
des Brauwesens, (1960): 77-91,   1960.
South America - distribution - homebrew   D-1222.

501. Hartmann, Günther
DESTILLIERANLAGEN BEI SUDAMERIKANISCHEN NATURVOLKERN.
[Distillation among the native peoples of South America.]
[Ger]
Zeitschrift für Ethnologie, 93: 225-232,   1968.
South America - distribution - manufacture   D-0483.

502. Hartocollis, P.
ALCOHOLISM IN CONTEMPORARY GREECE.
Quarterly Journal of Studies on Alcohol, 27: 721-727,   1966.
Greece - bar - change - customs - history, pre-1500 -
history, pre-1900 - temperance - treatment   D-0484.

503. Harwood, Alan
BEER DRINKING AND FAMINE IN A SAFWA VILLAGE: A CASE OF
ADAPTATION IN A TIME OF CRISIS.
Unpublished paper: East African Institute of Social
Research, Kampala, 10 pp.,   1964.
Tanganyika - Safwa - economics - functions - homebrew   D-1559.

504. Hasan, Khwaja A.
DRINKS, DRUGS AND DISEASE IN A NORTH INDIAN VILLAGE.
Eastern Anthropologist, 17: 1-9,   1964.
India - caste - drugs - homebrew - medical - moonshine   D-0485.

505. Hasan, Khwaja A.
COMMENT ON D. MANDELBAUM'S "ALCOHOL AND CULTURE."
Current Anthropology, 6: 289,   1965.
India - ambivalence - customs - drugs   D-0486.

506. Hatcher, E[lizabeth] R.
ALCOHOLICS ANONYMOUS: THE SOBRIETY SUBCULTURE.
Alcoholism, 11(2): 102-109,   1975.
Alcoholics Anonymous - folklore - functions   D-0487.

507. Hauser, S[ol] Frederick
       A STUDY OF ALCOHOLISM IN AN AMERICAN INDIAN TRIBE.
       M.A. Thesis, Columbia University,   1942.
       United States - Native Americans - Pomo - customs   D-0488.

508. Havard, V[alery]
       DRINK PLANTS OF THE NORTH AMERICAN INDIANS.
       Bulletin of the Torrey Botanical Club, 23: 33-46,   1896.
       Native Americans - distribution - manufacture   D-0489.

509. Hawthorn, Harry, B.; Belshaw, Cyril S.; and Jamieson, S.M.
       THE INDIANS OF BRITISH COLUMBIA AND ALCOHOL.
       Alcoholism Review, 2(3): 10-14,   1957.
       Canada - Native Americans - acculturation - anomie   D-0490.

510. Hays, Terence E.
       SAN CARLOS APACHE DRINKING GROUPS: INSTITUTIONAL
       DEVIANCE AS A FACTOR IN COMMUNITY DISORGANIZATION.
       Unpublished paper: American Anthropological Association,
       Seattle, 6 pp.,   1968.
       United States - Native Americans - Apache - anomie -
       norms - responsibility - social organization   D-1560.

511. Heaston, Michael D.
       WHISKEY REGULATIONS AND INDIAN LAND TITLES IN NEW MEXICO
       TERRITORY, 1851-1861.
       Journal of the West, 10(3): 474-483,   1971.
       United States - Native Americans - economics - history,
       pre-1900 - stress   D-0491.

512. Heath, Dwight B.
       ALCOHOL IN A NAVAJO COMMUNITY.
       A.B. Thesis (Social Relations), Harvard University, 94 pp.,   1952.
       United States - Native Americans - Navaho - attitudes -
       customs - functions - norms - social organization -
       sociocultural   D-0492.

513. Heath, Dwight B.
       DRINKING PATTERNS OF THE BOLIVIAN CAMBA.
       Quarterly Journal of Studies on Alcohol, 19: 491-508,   1958.
       Bolivia - Camba - Mestizos - attitudes - binge -
       conversion - customs - functions - norms - ritual -
       social organization - sociocultural   D-0493.

514. Heath, Dwight B.
       DRINKING PATTERNS OF THE BOLIVIAN CAMBA.
       In: Pittman, David J., and Snyder, Charles R., ed.
       Society, culture, and drinking patterns. New York, NY:
       John Wiley and Sons, pp. 22-36,   1962.
       Bolivia - Camba - Mestizos - attitudes - binge -
       conversion - customs - functions - norms - ritual -
       social organization - sociocultural   D-0494.

515. Heath, Dwight B.
      PROHIBITION AND POST-REPEAL DRINKING PATTERNS AMONG
      THE NAVAHO.
      Quarterly Journal of Studies on Alcohol, 25: 119-135,   1964.
      United States - Native Americans - Navaho - change -
      customs - functions - prohibition - social organization-
      sociocultural   D-0495.

516. Heath, Dwight B.
      COMMENT ON D. MANDELBAUM'S "ALCOHOL AND CULTURE."
      Current Anthropology, 6: 289-290,   1965.
      Bolivia - Camba - change - functions - social organization -
      sociocultural   D-0496.

517. Heath, Dwight B.
      PEASANTS, REVOLUTION, AND DRINKING: INTERETHNIC DRINKING
      PATTERNS IN TWO BOLIVIAN COMMUNITIES.
      Human Organization, 30: 179-186,   1971.
      Cross-ethnic - Bolivia - Aymara - Camba - Mestizos -
      change - functions - social organization - sociocultural   D-0497.

518. Heath, D[wight] B.
      ANTHROPOLOGICAL APPROACHES TO ALCOHOL: A REVIEW.
      Alcoholism, 10(1-2): 24-42,   1974.
      review - sociocultural   D-0499.

519. Heath, Dwight B.
      PERSPECTIVAS SOCIOCULTURALES DEL ALCOHOL EN AMERICA
      LATINA. [Socio-cultural perspectives of alcohol in
      Latin America.] [Spa]
      Acta Psiquiátrica y Psicológica de América Latina,
      20(2): 99-111,   1974.
      Latin America - review - sociocultural   D-0498.

520. Heath, Dwight B.
      A CRITICAL REVIEW OF ETHNOGRAPHIC STUDIES OF ALCOHOL USE.
      In: Gibbins, R.J.; Israel, Y.; Kalant, H.; Popham, R.E.;
      Schmidt, W.; and Smart, R., ed. Research advances in
      alcohol and drug problems, Volume 2. New York, NY:
      John Wiley and Sons, pp. 1-92,   1975.
      World survey - norms - research methods - review -
      sociocultural   D-0500.

521. Heath, Dwight B.
      ANTHROPOLOGICAL PERSPECTIVES ON ALCOHOL: AN HISTORICAL
      REVIEW.
      In: Everett, Michael W.; Waddell, Jack O.; and Heath,
      Dwight B., ed. Cross-cultural approaches to the study
      of alcohol: An interdisciplinary perspective. The Hague:
      Mouton, pp. 41-101,   1976.
      history, pre-1900 - research methods - review -
      sociocultural   D-0501.

522. Heath, Dwight B.
ANTHROPOLOGICAL PERSPECTIVES ON THE SOCIAL BIOLOGY OF
ALCOHOL: AN INTRODUCTION TO THE LITERATURE.
In: Kissin, Benjamin, and Begleiter, Henri, ed.
The biology of alcoholism, Volume 4: Social aspects
of alcoholism. New York, NY: Plenum, pp. 37-76, 1976.
World survey - norms - "race" - research methods - review -
sociocultural D-0505.

523. Heath, Dwight B.
OBSERVATIONAL STUDIES INTO ALCOHOL-RELATED PROBLEMS.
World Health Organization Project on Community Response
to Alcohol-related Problems, Background document, Geneva,
37 pp., 1977.
Cross-national - research methods - review - sociocultural D-1561.

524. Heath, Dwight B.
THE SOCIOCULTURAL MODEL OF ALCOHOL USE: PROBLEMS AND
PROSPECTS.
Journal of Operational Psychiatry, 9(1): 55-66, 1978.
sociocultural D-0506.

525. Heath, Dwight B.
OVERVIEW OF EPIDEMIOLOGY.
In: Galanter, Marc, ed. Currents in alcoholism, Volume 6:
Treatment and rehabilitation and epidemiology. New York,
NY: Grune & Stratton, pp. 179-195, 1979.
review - sociocultural - epidemiology D-1973.

526. Heidenreich, C. Adrian, ed.
ALCOHOLISM EDUCATION, TREATMENT, AND PREVENTION AMONG
INDIANS IN MONTANA: PROCEEDINGS OF A CONFERENCE.
Unpublished paper: Presented at the Center for Indian
Studies, Rocky Mountain College, Billings, Montana, 1971.
Native Americans - epidemiology - prevention - treatment D-1155.

527. Heidenreich, C. Adrian
ALCOHOL AND DRUG USE AND ABUSE AMONG INDIAN-AMERICANS:
A REVIEW OF ISSUES AND SOURCES.
Journal of Drug Issues, 6(3): 256-272, 1976.
Native Americans - customs - drugs - dysfunctions -
functions - review - sociocultural D-0507.

528. Helgason, T.
EPIDEMIOLOGY OF MENTAL DISORDERS IN ICELAND: A
PSYCHIATRIC AND DEMOGRAPHIC INVESTIGATION OF 5,395
ICELANDERS.
Acta Psychiatrica Scandinavica, 40(Supplement 173):
1 ff, 1964.
Iceland - epidemiology D-1921.

529.   Helgason, Thomas, and Asmundsson, Gylfi
       BEHAVIOR AND SOCIAL CHARACTERISTICS OF YOUNG ASOCIAL
       ALCOHOL ABUSERS.
       Neuropsychobiology, 1: 109-120,   1975.
       Iceland - crime - youth   D-0217.

530.   Hellman, Ellen
       THE IMPORTANCE OF BEER-BREWING IN AN URBAN NATIVE YARD.
       Bantu Studies, 8: 38-60,   1934.
       South Africa - Bantu - bar - dysfunctions - economics -
       fighting - functions - homebrew - leisure - manufacture -
       prohibition - sociocultural - social organization -
       urbanization   D-0508.

531.   Helmick, Edward F.; McClure, William Thomas; and
       Mitchell, Patricia M.
       A PROJECT TO ANALYZE RISK TO ALCOHOL ABUSE AMONG ALASKAN
       NATIVE STUDENTS.
       In: Seixas, Frank A. ed. Currents in alcoholism: Volume 2:
       Psychiatric, psychological, social and epidemiological
       studies. New York, NY: Grune & Stratton, pp. 367-376,   1977.
       Native Americans - etiology - youth   D-0509.

532.   Helwig, R.
       BAUERN- UND BURGERBIER: BRAUEN UND TRINKEN ZWISCHEN
       WEICHSEL UND MEMEL IN TAUSEND JAHREN. [Peasant- and
       citizen-beer: A thousand years of brewing between Weichsel
       and Memel.] [Ger]
       Jahrbuch der Gesellschaft für Geschichte und Bibliographie
       des Brauwesens, (1965): 9-159,   1965.
       Germany - beer - history, pre-1900 - history, pre-1500 -
       homebrew   D-1223.

533.   Henderson, Norman B.
       CROSS-CULTURAL ACTION RESEARCH: SOME LIMITATIONS,
       ADVANTAGES AND PROBLEMS.
       Journal of Social Psychology, 73: 61-70,   1967.
       United States - Cross-ethnic - Native Americans - Navaho -
       Zuni - crime - research methods - sociocultural -
       stereotype - treatment   D-0510.

534.   Henderson, Norman B.
       INDIAN PROBLEM DRINKING: STEREOTYPE OR REALITY? A
       STUDY OF NAVAJO PROBLEM DRINKING.
       Unpublished paper: American Psychological Association,
       Honolulu, HI, 15 pp.,   1972.
       United States - Native Americans - Navaho - crime -
       dysfunctions - self - stereotype   D-1562.

535.   Henk, M.L.
       TREATMENT PROGRAM FOR THE NAVAJO ALCOHOLIC.
       Unpublished paper: Presented at the 4th Joint Meeting of
       the Clinical Society and the Commissioned Officers Association

of the U.S. Public Health Service, 4 pp., 1969.
United States - Native Americans - Navaho - treatment D-1563.

536. Hentig, H. von
THE DELINQUENCY OF THE AMERICAN INDIAN.
Journal of Criminal Law and Criminology, 36: 75-84, 1945.
Native Americans - crime - homebrew - stereotype D-0511.

537. Herick, F.A.
ACCULTURATION AND DRINKING IN ALASKA.
Rehabilitation Record, 11: 13-17, 1970.
Native Americans - Eskimos - binge - customs - fighting - functions - medical - norms - social organization - stress - youth D-0512.

538. Herrero, Miguel
LAS VINAS Y LOS VINOS DEL PERU. [Wines and vintners of Peru.] [Spa]
Revista de Indias, 1(2): 111-116, 1940.
Peru - dysfunctions - economics - history, pre-1900 - wine D-0513.

539. Hes, J.P.
DRINKING IN A YEMENITE RURAL SETTLEMENT IN ISRAEL.
British Journal of Addiction, 65: 293-296, 1970.
Israel - Yemenites - acculturation - change - drugs - ritual D-0514.

540. Hill, Thomas W.
FROM HELL-RAISER TO FAMILY MAN.
In: Spradley, James P., and McCurdy, David M., ed. Conformity and conflict: Readings in cultural anthropology. (2nd ed.)
Boston, MA: Little, Brown, pp. 186-200, 1974.
United States - Native Americans - norms - responsibility - urbanization - youth D-0515.

541. Hill, Thomas W.
"FEELING GOOD" AND "GETTING HIGH": ALCOHOL USE OF URBAN INDIANS.
Ph.D. Dissertation, University of Pennsylvania, 1976.
United States - Native Americans - Santee - Winnebago - norms - responsibility - sociocultural - urbanization - youth D-0516.

542. Hippler, Arthur E.
AN ALASKAN ATHABASCAN TECHNIQUE FOR OVERCOMING ALCOHOL ABUSE.
Arctic, 27(1): 53-67, 1974.
United States - Native Americans - Athabascan - conversion - norms - treatment D-0517.

543.   Hirsch, Joseph
       HISTORICAL PERSPECTIVES ON THE PROBLEM OF ALCOHOLISM.
       Bulletin of the New York Academy of Medicine,
       29: 961-971,   1953.
       Near East - Biblical peoples - Classical peoples -
       attitudes - customs - history, pre-1500 - medical - norms -
       religion - symbols   D-0518.

544.   Hirvonen, K.
       ANTIIKIN ALKOHOLIJUOMAT.   [Alcoholic beverages in
       antiquity.]   [Fin]
       Alkoholipolitiikka, 34: 138-142, 191-194, 244-248, and
       300-305,   1969.
       Europe - Near East - Classical peoples - history, pre-1500
       - prehistory   D-0519.

545.   Hittman, Michael
       GHOST DANCES, DISILLUSIONMENT AND OPIATE ADDICTION: AN
       ETHNOHISTORY OF SMITH AND MASON VALLEY PAIUTES.
       Ph.D. Dissertation, University of New Mexico,   1973.
       United States - Native Americans - Paiute - acculturation -
       change - conversion - drugs - history, pre-1900 - norms -
       religion - stress   D-0520.

546.   Hitz, Danielle
       DRUNKEN SAILORS AND OTHERS: DRINKING PROBLEMS IN SPECIFIC
       OCCUPATIONS.
       Quarterly Journal of Studies on Alcohol, 34(2): 496-505,   1973.
       occupation - sociocultural   D-0521.

547.   Hocking, R.B.
       PROBLEMS ARISING FROM ALCOHOL IN THE NEW HEBRIDES.
       Medical Journal of Australia, 2: 908-910,   1970.
       Oceania - New Hebrides - change - crime - kava   D-0522.

548.   Hoff, Ebbe C.
       CULTURAL ASPECTS OF THE USE OF ALCOHOLIC BEVERAGES.
       Concord, NH: New Hampshire State Department of Health
       (Division on Alcoholism Publication No. 22),   1958.
       sociocultural   D-1156.

549.   Hoffman, M.
       5000 JAHRE BIER.   [5000 years of beer.]   [Ger]
       Berlin: Alfred Metzner, 180 pp.,   1956.
       World survey - attitudes - beer - change - customs -
       folklore - history, pre-1500 - history, pre-1900 -
       literature - manufacture - prehistory   D-0525.

550.   Hoffmann, Helmut, and Jackson, Douglas N.
       COMPARISON OF MEASURED PSYCHOPATHOLOGY IN INDIAN AND NON-
       INDIAN ALCOHOLICS.
       Psychological Reports, 33(3): 793-794,   1973.

United States - Cross-ethnic - Native Americans - Whites -
personality - psychiatric problems - sociocultural   D-0523.

551. Hoffmann, Helmut, and Jackson, Douglas N.
HOSPITALIZED MINNESOTA INDIANS: THEIR SOCIAL PSYCHIATRIC
HISTORY, PSYCHOPATHOLOGY AND MOTIVATION.
Unpublished report: University of Western Ontario
(Research Bulletin 255), London, Ont.,   1973.
United States - Native Americans - alcoholism - personality
- psychiatric problems   D-1157.

552. Hoffmann, Helmut, and Noem, Avis A.
ADJUSTMENT OF CHIPPEWA INDIAN ALCOHOLICS TO A PREDOMINANTLY
WHITE TREATMENT PROGRAM.
Psychological Reports, 37: 1284-1286,   1975.
United States - Cross-ethnic - Chippewa - Whites -
Alcoholics Anonymous - treatment   D-0524.

553. Hoffmann, Helmut, and Noem, Avis A.
ALCOHOLISM AND ABSTINENCE AMONG RELATIVES OF AMERICAN
INDIAN ALCOHOLICS.
Journal of Studies on Alcohol, 36(1): 165,   1975.
United States - Native Americans - abstainers -
enculturation - family - stress   D-0081.

554. Holloway, Robert
DRINKING AMONG INDIAN YOUTH: A STUDY OF THE DRINKING
BEHAVIOUR, ATTITUDES AND BELIEFS OF INDIAN AND METIS
YOUNG PEOPLE IN MANITOBA.
Winnipeg, Man.: Alcohol Education Service, 124 pp.,   1966.
Canada - Métis - Native Americans - attitudes - youth   D-0526.

555. Holmberg, Allan R.
THE RHYTHMS OF DRINKING IN A PERUVIAN COASTAL MESTIZO
COMMUNITY.
Human Organization, 30: 198-202,   1971.
Peru - Mestizos - customs - functions - homebrew -
religion - social organization - sociocultural   D-0527.

556. Honigmann, John J., and Honigmann, Irma
DRINKING IN AN INDIAN-WHITE COMMUNITY.
Quarterly Journal of Studies on Alcohol, 5: 575-619,   1945.
Cross-ethnic - Canada - Native Americans - Whites -
aggression - binge - functions - homebrew - moonshine -
prohibition - sex - sociocultural   D-0532.

557. Honigmann, John J.
DYNAMICS OF DRINKING IN AN AUSTRIAN VILLAGE.
Ethnology, 2: 157-169,   1963.
Austria - attitudes - bar - customs - functions -
medical - sociocultural   D-0528.

558.   Honigmann, John J.
        SURVIVAL OF A CULTURE FOCUS.
        In: Goodenough, Ward H., ed. Explorations in cultural
        anthropology: Essays in honor of George P. Murdock.
        New York, NY: McGraw-Hill, pp. 277-292,   1964.
        Austria - attitudes - bar - customs - functions -
        sociocultural   D-0529.

559.   Honigmann, John J.
        COMMENT ON D. MANDELBAUM'S "ALCOHOL AND CULTURE."
        Current Anthropology, 6: 290-291,   1965.
        Eskimos - class - economics   D-0530.

560.   Honigmann, John J., and Honigmann, Irma
        HOW BAFFIN ISLAND ESKIMO HAVE LEARNED TO USE ALCOHOL.
        Social Forces, 44: 73-83,   1965.
        Canada - Eskimos - aggression - ambivalence - change -
        class - crime - dysfunctions - enculturation - socio-
        cultural   D-0533.

561.   Honigmann, John J.
        SOCIAL DISINTEGRATION IN FIVE NORTHERN CANADIAN
        COMMUNITIES.
        Canadian Review of Sociology and Anthropology, 2(4):
        199-213,   1966.
        Canada - Eskimos - Native Americans - social organization   D-0531.

562.   Honigmann, John J., and Honigmann, Irma
        ALCOHOL IN A CANADIAN NORTHERN TOWN.
        Unpublished report: Institute for Research in Social
        Science, University of North Carolina, Chapel Hill, NC,   1968.
        Cross-ethnic - Canada - Eskimos - Native Americans -
        Whites - ambivalence - crime - consumption - socio-
        cultural   D-1158.

563.   Honigmann, John J., and Honigmann, Irma
        ARCTIC TOWNSMEN: ETHNIC BACKGROUNDS AND MODERNIZATION.
        Ottawa, Ont.: Canadian Research Centre for Anthropology,
        Saint Paul University,   1970.
        Cross-ethnic - Canada - Eskimos - Native Americans -
        Whites - ambivalence - crime - consumption - sociocultural
        - urbanization   D-1159.

564.   Honigmann, John J.
        ALCOHOL IN ITS CULTURAL CONTEXT.
        In: Chafetz, Morris E., ed. Research on alcoholism:
        Clinical problems and special populations. Proceedings
        of the First Annual Alcoholism Conference of the National
        Institute on Alcohol Abuse and Alcoholism. Held June
        25-26, 1971 in Washington, D.C. Washington, D.C.:
        U.S. Government Printing Office, pp. 252-257,   1973.
        functions - sociocultural - stereotype   D-0026.

74.

565. Horton, Donald J.
THE FUNCTIONS OF ALCOHOL IN PRIMITIVE SOCIETIES:
A CROSS-CULTURAL STUDY.
Quarterly Journal of Studies on Alcohol, 4: 199-320, 1943.
World survey - acculturation - aggression - Cross-cultural -
dysfunctions - economics - functions - research methods -
stress
D-0534.

566. Horwitz, José; Marconi, Juan; and Adis Castro, Gonzalo, ed.
BASES PARA UNA EPIDEMIOLOGIA DEL ALCOHOLISMO EN AMERICA
LATINA. [Bases for an epidemiology of alcoholism in
Latin America.] [Spa]
Buenos Aires: Fondo para la Salud Mental, 1967.
Cross-national - Latin America - epidemiology
D-0536.

567. Horwitz, J[osé], and Marconi, J[uan]
STUDIES OF THE DRINKING PATTERNS, THE "PROBLEMS OF
ALCOHOL" AND ALCOHOLISM IN LATIN AMERICA.
Alcoholism, 3(1): 3-12, 1967.
Cross-national - Latin America - epidemiology -
sociocultural
D-0535.

568. Houlett, W.
RUM TRADING IN THE AMERICAN COLONIES BEFORE 1793.
Journal of American History, 28(3): 129-152, 1934.
United States - economics - history, pre-1900 - moonshine
D-1928.

569. Howard-Craft, A.
THE NATIVE AMERICAN MALE ALCOHOLIC.
MPH Thesis, University of California (Berkeley), 1975.
Native Americans - Alcoholics Anonymous - treatment -
urbanization
D-0537.

570. Howay, F.W.
THE INTRODUCTION OF INTOXICATING LIQUOR AMONGST THE
INDIANS OF THE NORTHWEST COAST.
British Columbia Historical Quarterly, 6: 157-169, 1942.
Canada - Native Americans - acculturation - change -
economics - history, pre-1900
D-0538.

571. Howland, Richard W., and Howland, Joe W.
200 YEARS OF DRINKING IN THE UNITED STATES: EVOLUTION
OF THE DISEASE CONCEPT.
In: Ewing, John A., and Rouse, Beatrice A., ed.
Drinking: Alcohol in American society - Issues and
current research. Chicago, IL: Nelson-Hall, pp. 39-60, 1978.
United States - attitudes - change - disease concept -
history, pre-1900 - temperance - prohibition
D-0218.

572. Hrdlička, A[les]
METHOD OF PREPARING TESVINO AMONG THE WHITE RIVER APACHES.
American Anthropologist, 6: 190-191, 1904.

United States - Native Americans - Apache - aggression -
history, pre-1900 - homebrew - manufacture D-0539.

573. Hsien Rin
THE ALCOHOLISM PROBLEM IN NAN-SHIH AMI PEOPLE.
Studia Taiwanica, 2: 1957.
Taiwan - Ami - dysfunctions D-1212.

574. Hudolin, Vladimir
ALCOHOLISM IN CROATIA.
International Journal of Social Psychiatry, 15(2): 85-91, 1969.
Yugoslavia - Croatia - epidemiology - treatment D-0027.

575. Hunt, George M., and Azrin, N.H.
A COMMUNITY-REINFORCEMENT APPROACH TO ALCOHOLISM.
Behavior Research and Therapy, 14: 91-104, 1973.
etiology - family - norms - sociocultural D-0540.

576. Hunt, H.J.
ALCOHOLISM AMONG ABORIGINAL PEOPLE AND TREATMENT ASPECTS.
In: Proceedings of the Alcohol and Drug Dependence
Multidisciplinary Institute. Held August 31-September 4,
1975 at Burgmann College, Canberra. Australian Foundation
on Alcoholism and Drug Dependence, pp. 125-126, 1975.
Australia - Aborigines - stereotype - treatment D-1160.

577. Hurt, Wesley R.
THE URBANIZATION OF THE YANKTON INDIANS.
Human Organization, 20(4): 226-231, 1961-1962.
United States - Native Americans - Sioux - leisure - social
organization - urbanization D-0541.

578. Hurt, Wesley R., and Brown, Richard M.
SOCIAL DRINKING PATTERNS OF THE YANKTON SIOUX.
Human Organization, 24: 222-230, 1965.
United States - Native Americans - Sioux - class - customs -
history, pre-1900 - leisure - social organization D-0542.

579. Hutchinson, Bertram
ALCOHOL AS A CONTRIBUTING FACTOR IN SOCIAL DISORGANIZATION:
THE SOUTH AFRICAN BANTU IN THE NINETEENTH CENTURY.
Revista de Antropologia, 9: 1-13, 1961.
South Africa - Bantu - acculturation - attitudes - change -
history, pre-1900 - norms - social organization - symbols D-0543.

580. Hutchison, H.
THE "DRUNKEN INDIAN": AN AMERICAN CASUALTY.
In: Blair, Brenda; Pawlak, Victor; Tongue, Eva; and
Zwicky, Claude, ed. Proceedings of the 31st International
Congress on Alcoholism and Drug Dependence, Volume 2.
Held February 23-28, 1975 in Bangkok, Thailand. Lausanne:
International Council on Alcohol and Addictions, pp. 185-186, 1975.
Native Americans - norms - stereotype D-0295.

76.

Alcohol Use and World Cultures   Jackson, Charles

581. Indian Brotherhood of the Northwest Territories
      REPORT ON ALCOHOL WORKSHOPS.
      Unpublished manuscript,   (ca. 1974).
      Canada - Native Americans - treatment   D-1564.

582. Indian Health Service Task Force on Alcoholism
      ALCOHOLISM: A HIGH PRIORITY HEALTH PROBLEM.
      Washington, D.C.: Public Health Service Publication
      (HSA) 77-1001,   (ca. 1977).
      Aleuts - Eskimos - Native Americans - dysfunctions -
      pathology - treatment   D-1161.

583. International Labor Office
      ALCOHOLISM AND THE MASTICATION OF COCA IN SOUTH AMERICA.
      In: Indigenous populations. Geneva: International
      Labor Office,   1953.
      South America - dysfunctions - pathology   D-1162.

584. Irgens-Jensen, Olav
      THE USE OF ALCOHOL IN AN ISOLATED AREA OF NORTHERN NORWAY.
      British Journal of Addiction, 65: 181-185,   1970.
      Norway - consumption - social organization - stress   D-0544.

585. Irgens-Jensen, Olav
      RUSMEDLENS SOCIALA OCH PSYKOLOGISKA FUNKTIONER I OLIKA
      KULTURER. [Social and psychological functions of
      intoxicants in various cultures.] [Swe]
      Alkohol och Narkotika, 68: 339-344,   1974.
      Cross-cultural - functions - sociocultural   D-0545.

586. Ivey, Thomas
      ALCOHOL EDUCATION IN SCHOOLS ON THE NORTHERN CHEYENNE
      RESERVATION: TEACHERS MANUAL.
      Lame Deer, MT: Northern Cheyenne Council on Alcoholism, 1967.
      United States - Native Americans - Cheyenne - prevention D-0408.

587. Jabour, C.
      MEDICAL ASPECTS: EPIDEMIOLOGICAL APPROACH TO ALCOHOLISM
      IN THE REPUBLIC OF SOUTH AFRICA. THE PERSONALITY AND
      TREATMENT OF THE ALCOHOLIC IN SOUTH AFRICA: REPORT OF
      THE PROJECT ALCOHOLISM, VOLUME 5.
      Pretoria: Department of Social Welfare and Pensions,
      Republic of South Africa,   1971.
      South Africa - epidemiology - pathology   D-1107.

588. Jackson, Charles
      SOME SITUATIONAL AND PSYCHOLOGICAL CORRELATES OF DRINKING
      BEHAVIOR IN DOMINICA, W.I.
      Unpublished paper: American Anthropological Association,
      San Diego, CA,   1970.
      West Indies - Dominica   D-1565.

589. Jackson, Michael
       THE ENGLISH PUB.
       Toronto, Ont.: Fitzhenry and Whiteside, 170 pp.,   1976.
       England - bar - change - history, pre-1500 - history,
       pre-1900   D-0546.

590. Jacobs, Rosevelt
       A STUDY OF DRINKING BEHAVIOR AND PERSONALITY CHARACTERISTICS
       OF THREE ETHNIC GROUPS.
       Ph.D. Dissertation, California School of Professional
       Psychology,   1975.
       United States - Cross-ethnic - Blacks - Hispanos - Whites D-0409.

591. Jacobs, Wilbur R.
       DIPLOMACY AND INDIAN GIFTS: ANGLO AND FRENCH RIVALRY
       ALONG THE OHIO AND NORTHWEST FRONTIERS, 1748-63.
       Stanford, CA: Stanford University Press,   1950.
       Native Americans - economics - history, pre-1900 -
       political   D-0547.

592. Jacobsen, Erik
       ALKOHOL ALS SOZIALES PROBLEM. [Alcohol as a social
       problem.] [Ger]
       In: Møller, K.O., ed. Rauschgifte und Genussmittel.
       Basel: Benno Schwabe, pp. 231-268,   1951.
       Scandinavia - attitudes - change - consumption - dysfunctions
       - history, pre-1900 - stress - temperance   D-0548.

593. James, Bernard J.
       SOCIAL-PSYCHOLOGICAL DIMENSIONS OF OJIBWA ACCULTURATION.
       American Anthropologist, 63: 721-746,   1961.
       United States - Native Americans - Ojibwa - acculturation -
       aggression - responsibility - stereotype   D-0028.

594. Jansen, G.H.
       TRANSLATION OF "THE TAVERN: A NEGLECTED TOPIC OF
       SOCIOLOGICAL IMPORTANCE."
       Toronto, Ont.: Addiction Research Foundation, Substudy
       No. 1-10 & 2-63 (179), 22 pp.,   1963.
       bar - functions - sociocultural   D-0029.

595. Jarvis, D.H.
       REPORT OF THE CRUISE OF THE U.S. REVENUE CUTTER BEAR, AND
       THE OVERLAND EXPEDITION FOR THE RELIEF OF THE WHALERS IN
       THE ARCTIC OCEAN.
       Washington, D.C.: U.S. Government Printing Office (House
       Document 511 - 56th Congress, 2nd Session, Volume 93),   1899.
       Eskimos - moonshine   D-1163.

596. Jastrow, Morris, Jr.
       WINE IN THE PENTATEUCHAL CODES.
       Journal of the American Oriental Society, 33: 180-192,   1913.

Jews - Biblical peoples - history, pre-1500 - literature - norms - religion - wine   D-0549.

597. Jay, Edward J.
RELIGIOUS AND CONVIVIAL USES OF ALCOHOL IN A GOND VILLAGE OF MIDDLE INDIA.
Quarterly Journal of Studies on Alcohol, 27: 88-96,   1966.
India - Gond - attitudes - functions - homebrew - moonshine - religion - sociocultural   D-0550.

598. Jay, Maurice
L'EVOLUTION DE L'ALCOOLISME A LA REUNION. [The evolution of alcoholism on Reunion.] [Fre]
Alcool ou Santé, 104: 32-38,   1971.
Africa - Reunion - change   D-0551.

599. Jeanselme, E.
LE VIN, LA VIGNE, ET L'ALCOOLISME DANS LES GAULES A L'EPOQUE DE L'ETABLISSEMENT DES BARBARES ($v^e - x^e$ siècle). [Wine, vine and alcoholism among the Gauls during the period of the barbarian occupation (5th - 10th century).] [Fre]
Bulletin de la Société Français d'Histoire de la Médecine et de ses Filiales, 14: 264-291,   1920.
France - history, pre-1500 - wine   D-0030.

600. Jeffreys, M.D.W.
PALM WINE AMONG THE IBIBIO.
Nigerian Field, 22: 40-45,   1937.
Nigeria - Ibibio - folklore - homebrew - manufacture - nutrition   D-0552.

601. Jellinek, E.M.
ALKOHOLBRUKET SASOM EN FOLKSED. [Drinking as a folkway.] [Fin]
Alkoholpolitik, 15: 36-40,   1952.
World survey - power - symbols   D-0553.

602. Jellinek, E.M.
THE WORLD AND ITS BOTTLE.
World Health, 10(4): 4-6,   1957.
Cross-national - alcoholism - attitudes - customs - definition - dysfunctions   D-0554.

603. Jellinek, E.M.
THE DISEASE CONCEPT OF ALCOHOLISM.
New Haven, CT: Hillhouse Press, 246 pp.,   1960.
Cross-national - alcoholism - customs - definition - disease concept - etiology - sociocultural   D-0555.

604. Jellinek, E.M.
DRINKERS AND ALCOHOLICS IN ANCIENT ROME.
Journal of Studies on Alcohol, 37: 1718-1741, 1976.
Romans, ancient - Classical peoples - attitudes - change -
customs - economics - history, pre-1500 - wine   D-0556.

605. Jellinek, E.M.
THE SYMBOLISM OF DRINKING: A CULTURE-HISTORICAL APPROACH.
Journal of Studies on Alcohol, 38: 849-866, 1977.
World survey - Classical peoples - attitudes - history,
pre-1500 - prehistory - religion - symbols   D-0557.

606. Jepson, William W.
INDIANS, ALCOHOL, AND VIOLENT DEATH.
Minnesota Medicine, 56(8): 697, 1973.
United States - Native Americans - Chippewa - accidents -
aggression   D-0558.

607. Jessor, Richard; Graves, Theodore D.; Hanson, Robert C.;
and Jessor, Shirley L.
SOCIETY, PERSONALITY AND DEVIANT BEHAVIOR: A STUDY OF A
TRI-ETHNIC COMMUNITY.
New York, NY: Holt, Rinehart and Winston, 500 pp., 1968.
Cross-ethnic - United States - Hispanos - Native Americans -
Ute - Whites - customs - dysfunctions - functions - norms -
research methods - sociocultural   D-0559.

608. Jessor, Richard, and Jessor, Shirley L.
PROBLEM BEHAVIOR AND PSYCHOSOCIAL DEVELOPMENT: A
LONGITUDINAL STUDY OF YOUTH.
New York, NY: Academic, 281 pp., 1977.
Cross-ethnic - United States - Hispanos - Native Americans -
Ute - Whites - dysfunctions - functions - norms -
sociocultural - youth   D-0560.

609. Jilek, W.G.
INDIAN HEALING POWER: INDIGENOUS THERAPEUTIC PRACTICES
IN THE PACIFIC NORTHWEST.
Psychiatric Annals, 4(11): 13-21, 1974.
Native Americans - Salish - possession - prohibition -
treatment   D-0562.

610. Jilek, W.G.
SALISH INDIAN MENTAL HEALTH AND CULTURE CHANGE.
New York, NY: Holt, Rinehart and Winston, 1974.
Canada - Native Americans - Salish - acculturation -
anomie - psychiatric problems - stress   D-0561.

611. Jilek-Aal, Louise
ALCOHOL AND THE INDIAN-WHITE RELATIONSHIP: THE FUNCTION
OF ALCOHOLICS ANONYMOUS IN COAST SALISH SOCIETY.
M.A. Thesis, University of British Columbia, 1972.

Alcohol Use and World Cultures   Johnston, T.F.

       Native Americans - Salish - Alcoholics Anonymous -
       acculturation - functions - stress   D-0563.

612.   Jilek-Aal, Louise
       PSYCHOSOCIAL ASPECTS OF DRINKING AMONG COAST SALISH
       INDIANS.
       Canadian Psychiatric Association Journal,
       19(4): 357-361,   1974.
       Native Americans - Salish - Alcoholics Anonymous -
       possession - power - self - stereotype - stress - symbols D-0564.

613.   Jochelson, Waldemar
       KUMISS FESTIVALS OF THE YAKUT AND THE DECORATION OF
       KUMISS VESSELS.
       In: Laufer, B. ed. Boas Anniversary Volume. New York, NY:
       Stechert,   1906.
       Soviet Union - Yakut - containers - customs - homebrew -
       manufacture - nutrition - religion   D-0565.

614.   Johannsen, E., and Purchase, I.F.H.
       KAFFIRCORN MALTING AND BREWING STUDIES, XXI: THE EFFECT
       OF THE FUSEL OILS OF BANTU BEER ON RAT LIVER.
       South African Medical Journal, 43: 326,   1969.
       South Africa - Bantu - homebrew - manufacture   D-0566.

615.   Johnson, L.V., and Matre, Marc
       ANOMIE AND ALCOHOL USE: DRINKING PATTERNS IN MEXICAN
       AMERICAN AND ANGLO NEIGHBORHOODS.
       Journal of Studies on Alcohol, 39: 894-902,   1978.
       United States - Hispanos - anomie - customs   D-0567.

616.   Johnston, Thomas F.
       THE CULTURAL ROLE OF TSONGA BEER-DRINK MUSIC.
       In: Haywood, Charles, ed. International Folk Music
       Council 1973 Yearbook. Kingston, Ont.: Queens University,
       Department of Music,   1973.
       Congo - Tsonga - binge - folklore - music   D-0568.

617.   Johnston, T.F.
       DAGGA USE AMONG THE SHANGANA-TSONGA OF MOZAMBIQUE AND
       THE NORTHERN TRANSVAAL.
       Zeitschrift fur Ethnologie, 98: 277-286,   1973.
       Mozambique - Transvaal - Tsonga - binge - drugs - ritual   D-0220.

618.   Johnston, T.F.
       A SOCIAL EXPLANATION OF TSONGA SONG-TEXTS MAKING
       REFERENCE TO FOOD AND DRINK.
       Ethnologische Zeitschrift, 2: 21-35,   1973.
       Mozambique - Tsonga - folklore - music   D-0219.

619.   Johnston, T.F.
       THE CULTURAL ROLE OF TSONGA BEER-DRINK MUSIC.
       Yearbook of the International Folk Music Council,

5: 132-155, 1974.
Mozambique - Tsonga - binge - folklore - music D-0221.

620. Jones, A.D.
CANNABIS AND ALCOHOL USAGE AMONG THE PLATEAU TONGA:
AN OBSERVATIONAL REPORT OF THE EFFECTS OF CULTURAL
EXPECTATION.
Psychological Record, 25: 329-332, 1975.
South Africa - Thonga - binge - drugs - intoxication -
sociocultural D-0222.

621. Jorgensen, Joseph G.
ON ETHICS AND ANTHROPOLOGY.
Current Anthropology, 12(3): 321-334, 1971.
research methods - sociocultural D-0569.

622. Joyce, K.
ALCOHOL AND THE INDIANS.
Medical Times, 103(6): 124 ff, 1975.
Native Americans - "race" - stereotype D-0571.

623. Juhász, P.
PATHOGENIC FACTORS ELICITING NEUROSIS IN THE INHABITANTS
OF A HUNGARIAN VILLAGE IN THE YEAR FOLLOWING THE FORMATION
OF AGRICULTURAL CO-OPERATIVES.
International Journal of Social Psychiatry, 19: 173-179, 1973.
Hungary - bar - change - economics - leisure - political -
psychiatric problems - social organization D-0572.

624. Jupp, G. [Alex]
THE ROLE AND FUNCTION OF THE TAVERN IN MONTREAL.
M.A. Thesis, University of Alberta, 1969.
Canada - bar - functions D-0573.

625. Jupp, G. Alex
SOCIAL-CULTURAL INFLUENCES ON DRINKING PRACTICES.
Brewers Digest, 46: 76 ff, 1971.
sociocultural D-0574.

626. Kahn, M.W., and Delk, J.L.
DEVELOPING A COMMUNITY MENTAL HEALTH CLINIC ON AN
INDIAN RESERVATION.
International Journal of Social Psychiatry, 19: 299-306, 1973.
United States - Native Americans - treatment D-0262.

627. Kaiser, W., and Piechochi, W.
VERSUCHE EINER BEKAMPFUNG DES ALKOHOLABUSUS IM
SPATMITTELATTERLICHEN UND BAROCKEN HALLE. [Attempts
to combat inebriety in late medieval and baroque Halle.]
[Ger]
Protialkoholický Obzor, 7: 55-60, 1972.
Germany - change - Church - class - economics - history,
pre-1500 - temperance D-0575.

628. Kalin, Rudolf; Davis, William N.; and McClelland, David C.
THE RELATIONSHIP BETWEEN USE OF ALCOHOL AND THEMATIC CONTENT OF FOLKTALES IN PRIMITIVE SOCIETIES.
In: Stone, P.J.; Dunphy, D.C.; Smith, M.A.; and Ogilvie, D.M., ed. The general inquirer. Cambridge, MA: M.I.T. Press, 1966.
Cross-cultural - folklore - power - research methods   D-0576.

629. Kamien, Max
ABORIGINES AND ALCOHOL: INTAKE, EFFECTS AND SOCIAL IMPLICATIONS IN A RURAL COMMUNITY IN WESTERN NEW SOUTH WALES.
Medical Journal of Australia, 1(10): 291-298, 1975.
Australia - Aborigines - aggression - dysfunctions - economics - epidemiology - responsibility - stress   D-0578.

630. Kamien, Max
A SURVEY OF DRUG USE IN A PART-ABORIGINAL COMMUNITY.
Medical Journal of Australia, 1(9): 261-264, 1975.
Australia - Aborigines - binge - drugs - stress   D-0577.

631. Kamien, M[ax]
PSYCHIATRIC DISORDERS IN BOURKE ABORIGINAL ADULTS.
Medical Journal of Australia, 63(2, Supplement): 11-16, 1976.
Australia - Aborigines - aggression - dysfunctions - psychiatric problems - stress   D-0579.

632. Kane, Stephen L.
A STUDY OF RELATED PROBLEMS OF NEVADA INDIANS RESULTING FROM THE MISUSE OF ALCOHOL.
Unpublished report: Inter-Tribal Council Alcoholism Program, Carson City, NV, 1972.
United States - Native Americans - dysfunctions   D-1566.

633. Kant, Immanuel
ANTHROPOLOGY FROM A PRAGMATIC POINT OF VIEW. (Original: Anthropologie in pragmatischer Hinsicht. Koenigsberg: F. Nicolovius, 1798.)
Rudnick, Hans H., ed. Carbondale, IL: Southern Illinois University Press, 1978.
sociocultural   D-1164.

634. Kaplan, Bert
THE SOCIAL FUNCTIONS OF NAVAHO "HEAVY DRINKING".
Unpublished paper: Society for Applied Anthropology, Kansas City, KS, 7 pp., 1962.
United States - Native Americans - Navaho - aggression - norms - responsibility - self - suicide   D-1567.

635. Karayannis, Alexander D., and Kelepouris, Michael B.
IMPRESSIONS OF THE DRINKING HABITS AND ALCOHOLIC PROBLEMS IN MODERN GREECE.

	British Journal of Addiction, 62: 71-73, Greece - attitudes - medical - norms - religion	1967. D-0031.
636.	Karp, Ivan BEER-DRINKING AMONG THE ITESO. Unpublished paper: Institute for Development Studies, Discussion Paper No. 9, University College, Nairobi, 17 pp., Kenya - Iteso - customs - functions - social organization	1970. D-1568.
637.	Kearney, Michael DRUNKENNESS AND RELIGIOUS CONVERSION IN A MEXICAN VILLAGE. Quarterly Journal of Studies on Alcohol, 31: 132-152, Mexico - Zapotec - attitudes - binge - conversion - economics - functions - norms - religion	1970. D-0580.
638.	Keast, Horace THE CHURCH AND THE PUBLIC HOUSE. London: Church Literature Association, England - bar - religion	1936. D-1924.
639.	Keehn, J.D. TRANSLATING BEHAVIORAL RESEARCH INTO PRACTICAL TERMS FOR ALCOHOLISM. Canadian Psychologist, 10: 438-446, stereotype - treatment	1969. D-0581.
640.	Keehn, J.D. REINFORCEMENT OF ALCOHOLISM: SCHEDULE CONTROL OF SOLITARY DRINKING. Quarterly Journal of Studies on Alcohol, 31: 28-39, functions - social organization - treatment	1970. D-0582.
641.	Kelbert, M., and Hale, L. THE INTRODUCTION OF ALCOHOL INTO IROQUOIS SOCIETY. Toronto, Ont.: Addiction Research Foundation, Substudy No. 1-K & H-65 (243), 37 pp., Native Americans - Iroquois - change - history, pre-1900 - research methods - stress	1965. D-1091.
642.	Keller, Mark BEER AND WINE IN ANCIENT MEDICINE. Quarterly Journal of Studies on Alcohol, 19: 153-154, Near East - beer - history, pre-1500 - medical - prehistory - wine	1958. D-0583.
643.	Keller, Mark ALCOHOL IN HEALTH AND DISEASE: SOME HISTORICAL PERSPECTIVES. Annals of the New York Academy of Sciences, 113: 820-827, World survey - history, pre-1500 - history, pre-1900 - medical - prehistory	1966. D-0584.

84.

644. Keller, Mark, ed.
INTERNATIONAL BIBLIOGRAPHY OF STUDIES ON ALCOHOL,
VOLUMES I AND II.
New Brunswick, NJ: Rutgers Center of Alcohol Studies, 1966-68.
bibliography D-1165.

645. Keller, Mark
THE GREAT JEWISH DRINK MYSTERY.
British Journal of Addiction, 64: 287-296, 1970.
Jews - Near East - functions - history, pre-1500 -
religion - social organization - temperance D-0585.

646. Keller, Mark
A DOCUMENTATION RESOURCE FOR CROSS-CULTURAL STUDIES ON
ALCOHOL.
In: Everett, Michael W.; Waddell, Jack O.; and Heath,
Dwight B., ed. Cross-cultural approaches to the study
of alcohol: An interdisciplinary perspective. The Hague:
Mouton, pp. 409-410, 1976.
bibliography - research methods D-0586.

647. Keller, Mark
PROBLEMS WITH ALCOHOL: A HISTORICAL PERSPECTIVE.
In: Filstead, William J.; Rossi, Jean J.; and Keller,
Mark, ed. Alcohol and alcohol problems: New thinking
and new directions. Cambridge, MA: Ballinger, pp. 5-28, 1976.
history, pre-1500 - history, pre-1900 - prehistory -
review D-0032.

648. Kellner, Esther
MOONSHINE: ITS HISTORY AND FOLKLORE.
Indianapolis, IN: Bobbs-Merrill, 1971.
United States - manufacture - moonshine D-0292.

649. Kelly, Roger E., and Cramer, John O.
AMERICAN INDIANS IN SMALL CITIES: A SURVEY OF URBAN
ACCULTURATION IN TWO NORTHERN ARIZONA COMMUNITIES.
Flagstaff, AZ: Northern Arizona University (Rehabilitation
Monograph 1), 1966.
United States - Native Americans - Navaho - crime -
leisure - urbanization D-1092.

650. Kemnitzer, Luis S.
THE STRUCTURE OF COUNTRY DRINKING PARTIES ON THE PINE
RIDGE RESERVATION, SOUTH DAKOTA.
Plains Anthropologist, 17: 134-142, 1972.
United States - Native Americans - Sioux - binge -
functions - history, pre-1900 - social organization D-0587.

651. Kennedy, E., and Whop, J.
THE ABORIGINAL ALCOHOL PROBLEM IN TOWNSVILLE.
Australian Journal of Alcoholism and Drug Dependence,
4(2): 56-58, 1977.

Australia - Aborigines - dysfunctions   D-0588.

652.   Kennedy, John G.
       TESGUINO COMPLEX: THE ROLE OF BEER IN TARAHUMARA
       CULTURE.
       American Anthropologist, 65: 620-640,   1963.
       Mexico - Tarahumara - accidents - economics - functions -
       homebrew - norms - religion - ritual - social organization -
       sociocultural   D-0589.

653.   Kennedy, John G.
       THE TARAHUMARA OF THE SIERRA MADRE: BEER, ECOLOGY, AND
       SOCIAL ORGANIZATION.
       Arlington Heights, IL: AMH Publishing,   1978.
       Mexico - Tarahumara - economics - functions - homebrew -
       religion - ritual - social organization - sociocultural D-0590.

654.   Kerketta, Kushal
       RICE BEER AND THE ORAON CULTURE: A PRELIMINARY OBSERVATION.
       Journal of Social Research, 3: 62-67,   1960.
       India - Oraon - economics - functions - homebrew -
       religion - ritual - social organization - sociocultural D-0591.

655.   Kermorgant, A.
       L'ALCOOLISME DANS IES COLONIES FRANCAISES. [Alcoholism
       in the French colonies.] [Fre]
       Bulletin de la Société de Pathologie Exotique et de Ses
       Filiales, 2: 330-340,   1909.
       World survey - functions   D-0592.

656.   Kessler, Marc, and Gomberg, Christopher
       OBSERVATIONS OF BARROOM DRINKING: METHODOLOGY AND
       PRELIMINARY RESULTS.
       Quarterly Journal of Studies on Alcohol, 35: 1392-1396, 1974.
       Scotland - bar - research methods   D-0593.

657.   Kim, Sil D.
       THE NIGHT CLUBS OF SEOUL, KOREA: PLURALITY AND SYNTHESIS
       OF TRADITIONAL AND MODERN VALUES IN ORGANIZATIONAL
       STRUCTURE.
       Urban Life and Culture, 2: 314-329,   1973.
       Korea - acculturation - bar - norms   D-0594.

658.   Kim, Yong
       A STUDY OF ALCOHOL CONSUMPTION AND ALCOHOLISM AMONG
       SASKATCHEWAN INDIANS: SOCIAL AND CULTURAL VIEWPOINTS.
       Regina, Sask.: Alcoholism Commission of Saskatchewan,
       61 pp.,   1972.
       Canada - Native Americans - crime - customs - functions -
       dysfunctions - homebrew - leisure - sociocultural - stress D-0595.

659. Kim, Y.S., and Lee, C.K.
DRINKING PATTERNS OF RURAL MALE RESIDENTS IN KOREA.
Neuropsychiatry, 124: 376-388,
Korea - customs
1975.
D-0033.

660. King, Frank A.
BEER HAS A HISTORY.
London: Hutchinson's Scientific and Technical Publications, 173 pp.,
United Kingdom - bar - change - economics - history, pre-1500 - history, pre-1900 - manufacture
1947.
D-0275.

661. Kingsdale, Jon M.
THE "POOR MAN'S CLUB": SOCIAL FUNCTIONS OF THE URBAN WORKING-CLASS SALOON.
American Quarterly, 25: 472-490,
United States - bar - class - functions
1973.
D-0596.

662. Kircher, Karl
DIE SAKRALE BEDEUTUNG DES WEINES IM ALTERUM. [The sacred meanings of wines in antiquity.] [Ger]
Religionsgeschichtliche Versuche und Vorarbeiten, 9: 2,
Classical peoples - customs - history, pre-1500 - prehistory - religion - ritual - symbols - wine
1910.
D-0597.

663. Kissin, Benjamin, and Begleiter, Henri, ed.
THE BIOLOGY OF ALCOHOLISM, VOLUME 4: SOCIAL ASPECTS OF ALCOHOLISM.
New York, NY: Plenum, 643 pp.,
review - sociocultural
1976.
D-0598.

664. Klatsky, Arthur L.; Friedman, Gary D.; Siegelaub, Abraham; and Gerard, Marie J.
ALCOHOL CONSUMPTION AMONG WHITE, BLACK, OR ORIENTAL MEN AND WOMEN: KAISER-PERMANENTE MULTIPHASIC HEALTH EXAMINATION DATA.
American Journal of Epidemiology, 105: 311-323,
United States - Cross-ethnic - Blacks - Orientals - Whites - consumption - pathology - research methods
1977.
D-0223.

665. Klausner, Samuel Z.
SACRED AND PROFANE MEANINGS OF BLOOD AND ALCOHOL.
Journal of Social Psychology, 64: 27-43,
World survey - Cross-cultural - religion - ritual - symbols
1964.
D-0600.

666. Kmet, J., and Mahboubi, E.
ESOPHAGEAL CANCER IN THE CASPIAN LITTORAL OF IRAN: INITIAL STUDIES.
Science, 175: 846-853,
Iran - moonshine - pathology
1972.
D-0263.

667.   Knisley, E.R.
        NATIVE ALASKAN INDIANS, ESKIMOS AND ALEUTS, AND THEIR
        DRINKING HABITS.
        Unpublished paper: Presented at the 30th International
        Congress on Alcoholism and Drug Dependence. Held
        September 4-9, 1972 in Amsterdam.   1972.
        United States - Aleuts - Eskimos - Native Americans -
        acculturation - anomie - stress   D-1920.

668.   Knupfer, Genevieve
        USE OF ALCOHOLIC BEVERAGES BY SOCIETY AND ITS CULTURAL
        IMPLICATIONS.
        California's Health, 18: 9-13,   1960.
        ambivalence - sociocultural   D-0601.

669.   Knupfer, Genevieve, and Room, Robin
        DRINKING PATTERNS AND ATTITUDES OF IRISH, JEWISH AND
        WHITE PROTESTANT AMERICAN MEN.
        Quarterly Journal of Studies on Alcohol, 28: 676-699,   1967.
        United States - Cross-ethnic - Irish-Americans - Jews -
        Protestants - attitudes - Church - epidemiology - norms   D-0602.

670.   Köbben, A.J.
        NEW WAYS OF PRESENTING AN OLD IDEA: THE STATISTICAL
        METHOD IN SOCIAL ANTHROPOLOGY.
        Journal of the Royal Anthropological Institute,
        82: 129-146,   1952.
        World survey - Cross-cultural - research methods   D-0034.

671.   Koolage, William W., Jr.
        DIFFERENTIAL ADAPTATIONS OF ATHABASKANS AND OTHER NATIVE
        ETHNIC GROUPS TO A NORTHERN TOWN.
        Arctic Anthropology, 13(1): 70-83,   1976.
        Cross-ethnic - Canada - Native Americans - Chipewyan -
        Eskimos - acculturation - urbanization   D-0603.

672.   Koplowitz, Isidore
        MIDRASH YAYIN VESHECHOR: TALMUDIC AND MIDRASHIC
        EXEGETICS ON WINE AND STRONG DRINK.
        Detroit, MI: [no publisher],   1923.
        Jews - Biblical peoples - history, pre-1500 - history,
        pre-1900 - prohibition - religion   D-1204.

673.   Kotarba, J.A.
        THE SERIOUS NATURE OF TAVERN SOCIABILITY.
        Unpublished paper: Society for the Study of Social
        Problems, Chicago, IL, 15 pp.,   1977.
        United States - bar - crime - enculturation - functions   D-1915.

674.   Krasilowsky, D.; Halpern, B.; and Gutman, J.
        THE PROBLEM OF ALCOHOLISM IN ISRAEL.
        Israel Annals of Psychiatry and Related Disciplines,
        3(2): 249-258,   1965.

	Israel - Jews - acculturation - change - stress	D-0035.
675.	Kraus, Robert PATTERNS OF MENTAL ILLNESS, ALCOHOL ABUSE, AND DRUG ABUSE AMONG ALASKAN NATIVES. Unpublished report: Alaska Federation of Natives, Anchorage, 40 pp., United States - Aleuts - Eskimos - Native Americans - accidents - pathology - psychiatric problems - suicide	(n.d.) D-1916.
676.	Krause, Marilyn L. A STUDY OF DRINKING ON A PLATEAU INDIAN RESERVATION. M.A. Thesis, University of Washington, United States - Native Americans - Yakima - customs - functions - social organization - sociocultural - stereotype	1969. D-0604.
677.	Kriek, J.J. KLINIESE-SIELKUNDIGE ASPEKTE VAN ALKOHOLISME. THE PERSONALITY AND TREATMENT OF THE ALCOHOLIC IN SOUTH AFRICA: REPORT OF THE PROJECT ALCOHOLISM, VOLUME 8. [Afr] Pretoria: Department of Social Welfare and Pensions, Republic of South Africa, South Africa - psychiatric problems	1971. D-1108.
678.	Krige, Eileen J. THE SOCIAL SIGNIFICANCE OF BEER AMONG THE BALOBEDU. Bantu Studies, 6: 343-357, South Africa - Balobedu - economics - functions - homebrew - manufacture - nutrition - religion - ritual - social organization - sociocultural	1932. D-0605.
679.	Kruger, J.J. DIE BEHANDELING VAN BLANKE ALKOHOLISTE IN STAATS-TOEVLUGTE. THE PERSONALITY AND TREATMENT OF THE ALCOHOLIC IN SOUTH AFRICA: REPORT OF THE PROJECT ALCOHOLISM, VOLUME 11. [Afr] Pretoria: Department of Social Welfare and Pensions, Republic of South Africa, South Africa - Whites	1971. D-1109.
680.	Kubodera, I. [see also 967] AINU NO KOZOKU, SAKE NO JOZO OYOBI SONO SAIGI. [On the practice and ritual of brewing among the Ainu.] [Jap] Minozokugaku Kenkyū, 1: 501-532, Japan - Ainu - homebrew - manufacture	1935. D-0504.
681.	Kunitz, Stephen J.; Levy, Jerrold E.; and Everett, Michael W. ALCOHOLIC CIRRHOSIS AMONG THE NAVAHO. Quarterly Journal of Studies on Alcohol, 30: 672-685, United States - Native Americans - Navaho - epidemiology - liver	1969. D-0608.

682.   Kunitz, Stephen J.
       NAVAJO DRINKING PATTERNS.
       Ph.D. Dissertation, Yale University,   1970.
       United States - Native Americans - Navaho - acculturation -
       customs - functions - norms - research methods - social
       organization - sociocultural - youth   D-0606.

683.   Kunitz, Stephen J.; Levy, Jerrold E.; Odoroff, C.L.;
       and Bollinger, J.
       THE EPIDEMIOLOGY OF ALCOHOLIC CIRRHOSIS IN TWO SOUTH-
       WESTERN INDIAN TRIBES.
       Quarterly Journal of Studies on Alcohol, 32: 706-720,   1971.
       United States - Cross-ethnic - Native Americans - Hopi -
       Navaho - customs - epidemiology - liver - norms   D-0609.

684.   Kunitz, Stephen J., and Levy, Jerrold E.
       CHANGING IDEAS OF ALCOHOL USE AMONG NAVAHO INDIANS.
       Quarterly Journal of Studies on Alcohol, 35: 243-259,   1974.
       United States - Native Americans - Navaho - attitudes -
       change - history, pre-1900 - labeling   D-0607.

685.   Kuttner, Robert E., and Lorincz, Albert B.
       ALCOHOLISM AND ADDICTION IN URBANIZED SIOUX INDIANS.
       Mental Hygiene, 51(4): 530-542,   1967.
       United States - Cross-ethnic - Native Americans - Omaha -
       Ponca - Sioux - Skid Row - Winnebago - bar - customs -
       economics - etiology - enculturation - family - functions -
       urbanization   D-0611.

686.   Kuttner, Robert E.
       POVERTY AND SEX: RELATIONSHIPS IN A "SKID ROW" SLUM.
       Sexual Behavior, 1(7): 55-63,   1971.
       United States - Native Americans - Skid Row - sex -
       urbanization   D-0610.

687.   Kylmälä, Timo
       FRANSMAN VID GLASET. [Wine among the French.]   [Fin]
       Alkoholpolitik, 19(3): 78-80,   1956.
       France - customs - wine   D-0036.

688.   La Barre, Weston
       NATIVE AMERICAN BEERS.
       American Anthropologist, 40: 224-234,   1938.
       Latin America - Native Americans - distribution - homebrew -
       manufacture   D-0612.

689.   La Barre, Weston
       A CULTIST DRUG-ADDICTION IN AN INDIAN ALCOHOLIC.
       Bulletin of the Menninger Clinic, 5: 40-46,   1941.
       United States - Native Americans - Osage - peyote   D-0037.

90.

690. La Barre, Weston
SOME OBSERVATIONS ON CHARACTER STRUCTURE IN THE
ORIENT: II. THE CHINESE, PART 2.
Psychiatry, 9: 375-395, 1946.
China - customs - functions - social organization   D-0613.

691. La Barre, Weston
PROFESSOR WIDJOJO GOES TO A KOKTEL PARTI.
New York Times Magazine, (Dec. 9, 1956): 17 et seq., 1956.
United States - customs - ritual   D-0614.

692. Laforest, Lucien
FORCE ET FAIBLESSE DE LA THEORIE DE L'ANOMIE COMME
SOURCE EXPLICATIVE DE LA DEVIANCE ALCOOLIQUE. [Strength
and weakness of the theory of anomia as an explanation of
alcoholic deviance.] [Fre]
Toxicomanies, 8: 219-238, 1975.
Canada - anomie - class - economics   D-0615.

693. La Gravière, Emmanuel
THE PROBLEM OF ALCOHOLISM IN THE COUNTRIES AND TERRITORIES
SOUTH OF THE SAHARA.
International Review of Missions, 46(183): 290-298, 1957.
Africa - prevention   D-0460.

694. Lane, Edward W.
ARABIAN SOCIETY IN THE MIDDLE AGES.
London: Chatto and Windus, 1883.
Islam - customs - history, pre-1500 - religion - wine   D-0616.

695. Lang, Gretchen M.
ADAPTIVE STRATEGIES OF URBAN INDIAN DRINKERS.
Ph.D. Dissertation, University of Missouri (Columbia), 1974.
United States - Native Americans - Chippewa - economics -
social organization - treatment   D-0617.

696. Langness, L[ew] L., and Hennigh, Laurence
AMERICAN INDIAN DRINKING: ALCOHOLISM OR INSOBRIETY?
Unpublished paper: Mental Health Research Meeting,
Fort Steilacoom, Washington, D.C., 16 pp., 1964.
Cross-ethnic - Native Americans - dysfunctions - functions -
sociocultural   D-1569.

697. Larkins, John R.
ALCOHOL AND THE NEGRO: EXPLOSIVE ISSUES.
Zebulon, NC: Record, 251 pp., 1965.
United States - Blacks - change - customs - economics -
history, pre-1900 - political - religion - sociocultural   D-0224.

698. Larni, M.
KINESISKA DRYCKESSEDER. [Chinese drinking customs.] [Fin]
Alkoholpolitik, 23: 116-118, 1960.
China - customs   D-0618.

699.   Latronico, N.
        I VINI MEDICINALI. [Medicinal wines.]   [Ita]
        Milano: Ulrico Holpi,   1947.
        medical - wine   D-0410.

700.   Laubach, F.D.
        THE SOCIAL VALUE OF THE NEW YORK SALOON.
        M.A. Thesis, Columbia University,   1911.
        United States - bar - functions   D-0411.

701.   Leacock, Seth
        CEREMONIAL DRINKING IN AN AFRO-BRAZILIAN CULT.
        American Anthropologist, 66: 344-354,   1964.
        Brazil - Batuque - possession - religion   D-0619.

702.   Lechnyr, R.J.
        A THEORY OF THE EFFECTS OF IDENTIFICATION OF ALCOHOLISM
        AMONG HOPI INDIAN MALES.
        Unpublished report: Indian Health Service, Window Rock,
        AZ   1970.
        United States - Native Americans - Hopi - self   D-1570.

703.   Ledermann, Sully
        ALCOOL, ALCOOLISME, ALCOOLISATION: DONEES SCIENTIFIQUE
        DE CARACTERE PHYSIOLOGIQUE, ECONOMIQUE ET SOCIAL. [Alcohol,
        alcoholism, and alcoholization: Scientific data on
        physiological, economic and social characteristics.] [Fre]
        Paris: Presses Universitaires de France (Institut National
        d'Etudes Démographiques, Travaux et Documents, Cahier 29),
        314 pp.,   1956.
        Cross-national - accidents - consumption - definition -
        economics - epidemiology - pathology - review   D-1166.

704.   Ledermann, Sully
        ALCOOL, ALCOOLISME, ALCOOLISATION: MORTALITE, MORBIDITE,
        ACCIDENTS DU TRAVAIL. [Alcohol, alcoholism, and alcoholization:
        Mortality, morbidity, work accidents.] [Fre]
        Paris: Presses Universitaires de France (Institut National
        d'Etudes Démographiques, Travaux et Documents, Cahier 41),
        613 pp.,   1964.
        Cross-national - accidents - consumption - definition -
        economics - epidemiology - pathology - review   D-1167.

705.   Legnaro, Aldo
        SOZIOLOGISCHE ASPEKTE DES ALKOHOLISMUS. [Sociological
        aspects of alcoholism.] [Ger]
        Kölner Zeitschrift für Soziologie und Sozialpsychologie,
        25(2): 403-419,   1973.
        Cross-national - Europe - dysfunctions - labeling - norms   D-0038.

706. Leibowitz, J.O.
 ACUTE ALCOHOLISM IN ANCIENT GREEK AND ROMAN MEDICINE.
 British Journal of Addiction, 62: 83-86, 1967.
 Classical peoples - Greeks, ancient - Romans, ancient -
 alcoholism - diagnosis - history, pre-1500 - psychiatric
 problems D-0620.

707. Leis, Philip E.
 PALM OIL, ILLICIT GIN, AND THE MORAL ORDER OF THE IJAW.
 American Anthropologist, 66: 828-838, 1964.
 Nigeria - Ijaw - change - economics - moonshine - norms D-0621.

708. Leland, Joy [Hanson]
 FIREWATER MYTHS: NORTH AMERICAN INDIAN DRINKING AND
 ALCOHOL ADDICTION.
 New Brunswick, NJ: Rutgers Center of Alcohol Studies
 (Monograph No. 11), 158 pp., 1976.
 Cross-cultural - Native Americans - alcoholism -
 definition - diagnosis - "race" - stereotype D-0623.

709. Leland, Joy [Hanson]
 NORTH AMERICAN INDIAN DRINKING AND ALCOHOL ABUSE: A REVIEW.
 Unpublished manuscript, 145 pp., 1977.
 Native Americans - review - sociocultural D-1571.

710. Leland, Joy Hanson
 DRINKING STYLES IN AN INDIAN SETTLEMENT: A NUMERICAL
 FOLK TAXONOMY.
 Ph.D. Dissertation, University of California (Irvine), 1975.
 Native Americans - attitudes - customs - research methods -
 semantics D-0622.

711. Leland, Joy Hanson
 WOMEN AND ALCOHOL IN AN INDIAN SETTLEMENT.
 Medical Anthropology, 2(4): 85-119, 1978.
 United States - Native Americans - consumption - female -
 language D-0284.

712. LeMasters, E.E.
 SOCIAL LIFE IN A WORKING-CLASS TAVERN.
 Urban Life and Culture, 2: 27-52, 1973.
 United States - bar - class - functions D-0225.

713. LeMasters, E.E.
 BLUE-COLLAR ARISTOCRATS: LIFE STYLES AT A WORKING-CLASS
 TAVERN.
 Madison, WI: University of Wisconsin Press, 218 pp., 1975.
 United States - bar - attitudes - class - customs -
 norms D-0624.

714. Lemert, Edwin M.
 ALCOHOL AND THE NORTHWEST COAST INDIANS.
 University of California Publications in Culture and

Society, 2: 303-406, 1954.
Cross-ethnic - Native Americans - Haida - Kwakiutl -
Nootka - Salish - Tsimshian - acculturation - binge -
customs - dysfunctions - functions - history, pre-1900 -
norms - social organization - sociocultural D-0625.

715. Lemert, Edwin M.
ALCOHOLISM AND THE SOCIOCULTURAL SITUATION.
Quarterly Journal of Studies on Alcohol, 17: 306-317, 1956.
norms - sociocultural D-0626.

716. Lemert, Edwin M.
THE USE OF ALCOHOL IN THREE SALISH TRIBES.
Quarterly Journal of Studies on Alcohol, 19: 90-107, 1958.
Cross-ethnic - Native Americans - Salish - aggression -
crime - dysfunctions - functions - homebrew - intoxication
- social organization - sociocultural - stereotype D-0627.

717. Lemert, Edwin M.
ALCOHOL USE IN POLYNESIA.
Tropical and Geographical Medicine, 14: 183-191, 1962.
Cross-ethnic - Polynesia - Cook Islands - Samoa - Society
Islands - acculturation - aggression - anomie - functions -
history, pre-1900 - homebrew - ritual - social organization
- sociocultural D-0628.

718. Lemert, Edwin M.
ALCOHOL, VALUES, AND SOCIAL CONTROL.
In: Pittman, David J., and Snyder, Charles R., ed.
Society, culture, and drinking patterns. New York, NY:
John Wiley and Sons, pp. 553-571, 1962.
intoxication - norms - sociocultural D-1093.

719. Lemert, Edwin M.
DRINKING IN HAWAIIAN PLANTATION SOCIETY.
Quarterly Journal of Studies on Alcohol, 25: 689-713, 1964.
Cross-ethnic - Hawaiian Islands - change - customs -
occupation D-0630.

720. Lemert, Edwin M.
FORMS AND PATHOLOGY OF DRINKING IN THREE POLYNESIAN
SOCIETIES.
American Anthropologist, 66: 361-374, 1964.
Cross-ethnic - Polynesia - Cook Islands - Samoa - Society
Islands - dysfunctions - functions - homebrew - norms -
social organization - sociocultural D-0629.

721. Lemert, Edwin M.
COMMENT ON D. MANDELBAUM'S "ALCOHOL AND CULTURE."
Current Anthropology, 6: 291, 1965.
norms - social organization D-0631.

722. Lemert, Edwin M.
SOCIO-CULTURAL RESEARCH ON DRINKING.
In: Keller, Mark, and Coffey, Timothy G., ed. *Proceedings of the 28th International Congress on Alcohol and Alcoholism, Volume 2*. Held September 15-20, 1968 in Washington, D.C. Highland Park, NJ: Hillhouse Press, pp. 56-64, 1969.
research methods - review - sociocultural
D-0632.

723. Lemert, Edwin M.
KONI, KONA, KAVA: ORANGE-BEER CULTURE OF THE COOK ISLANDS.
Journal of Studies on Alcohol, 37(5): 565-585, 1976.
Oceania - Cook Islands - change - customs - homebrew - kava
D-0633.

724. Lender, Mark [Edward]
DRUNKENNESS AS AN OFFENSE IN EARLY NEW ENGLAND: A STUDY OF "PURITAN" ATTITUDES.
Quarterly Journal of Studies on Alcohol, 34: 353-366, 1973.
United States - Protestants - Church - history, pre-1900 - norms
D-0634.

725. Lender, Mark Edward
THE ROLE OF HISTORY IN EARLY ALCOHOL EDUCATION: THE IMPACT OF THE TEMPERANCE MOVEMENT.
Journal of Alcohol and Drug Education, 23(1): 56-62, 1977.
history, pre-1500 - history, pre-1900 - prevention - temperance
D-0226.

726. Lenoir, Raymond
LES FETES DE BOISSON. [Drinking festivals.] [Fre]
In: *Compte-Rendue de la 21 Congrés Internationale des Américanistes, Pt. 2*. Göteborg: Museum, 1925.
Cross-ethnic - South America - functions - social organization
D-1169.

727. Levine, Harry G.
THE DISCOVERY OF ADDICTION: CHANGING CONCEPTIONS OF HABITUAL DRUNKENNESS IN AMERICAN HISTORY.
Journal of Studies on Alcohol, 39(1): 143-174, 1978.
United States - addiction - attitudes - customs - definition - diagnosis - disease concept - history, pre-1900 - sociocultural
D-1252.

728. Levy, Hermann
DRINK: AN ECONOMIC AND SOCIAL STUDY.
London: Routledge and Kegan Paul, 256 pp., 1951.
World survey - economics - political - religion - sociocultural
D-0264.

729. Levy, Jerrold E.; Kunitz, Stephen J.; and Everett, Michael W.
NAVAJO CRIMINAL HOMICIDE.
Southwestern Journal of Anthropology, 25: 124-152, 1969.
United States - Native Americans - Navaho - history, pre-1900 - murder
D-0638.

730   Citations

730.   Levy, Jerrold E., and Kunitz, Stephen J.
        INDIAN RESERVATIONS, ANOMIE, AND SOCIAL PATHOLOGIES.
        Southwestern Journal of Anthropology, 27: 97-128,   1971.
        United States - Native Americans - Hopi - Navaho -
        anomie - history, pre-1900 - liver - murder - norms -
        sociocultural - suicide   D-0635.

731.   Levy, Jerrold E., and Kunitz, Stephen J.
        INDIAN DRINKING: PROBLEMS OF DATA COLLECTION AND
        INTERPRETATION.
        In: Chafetz, Morris E., ed. Proceedings of the 1st
        Annual Alcoholism Conference of the National Institute
        on Alcohol Abuse and Alcoholism. Held June 25-26, 1971
        in Washington, D.C. Washington, D.C.: U.S. Government
        Printing Office, pp. 217-236,   1973.
        Native Americans - research methods - review   D-0636.

732.   Levy, Jerrold E., and Kunitz, Stephen J.
        INDIAN DRINKING: NAVAJO PRACTICES AND ANGLO-AMERICAN
        THEORIES.
        Toronto, Ont.: John Wiley and Sons, 257 pp.,   1974.
        United States - Native Americans - Cross-ethnic - Apache -
        Hopi - Navaho - etiology - history, pre-1900 - liver -
        norms - social organization   D-0637.

733.   Levy, Jerrold E., and Kunitz, Stephen J.
        UTILIZING BASIC RESEARCH FINDINGS IN INDIAN ALCOHOL
        TREATMENT PROGRAMS: PROBLEMS AND PROSPECTS.
        Unpublished paper: American Anthropological Association,
        Houston, TX, 20 pp.,   1977.
        United States - Native Americans - Cross-ethnic - Hopi -
        Navaho - Shoshone - economics - research methods -
        treatment   D-1572.

734.   Levy, Robert I.
        MA'OHI DRINKING PATTERNS IN THE SOCIETY ISLANDS.
        Journal of the Polynesian Society, 75: 304-320,   1966.
        Oceania - Society Islands - Maohi - ambivalence - change -
        customs - functions - homebrew - leisure   D-0639.

735.   Lewis, Hylan
        BLACKWAYS OF KENT.
        New Haven, CT: College and University Press, 337 pp.,   1955.
        United States - Blacks   D-0640.

736.   Lewis, Robert Gene
        AN ANALYSIS OF ALCOHOL DRINKING PATTERNS AMONG FOUR ETHNIC
        GROUPS.
        Ph.D. Dissertation, University of Denver,   1974.
        United States - Cross-ethnic - Native Americans - Blacks -
        Hispanos - Whites   D-0641.

96.

737. Leyburn, J.G.
NATIVE FARM LABOR IN SOUTH AFRICA.
Social Forces, 23: 133-140, 1944.
South Africa - homebrew - leisure - nutrition   D-0642.

738. Lickiss, J. Norelle
ALCOHOL AND ABORIGINES IN CROSS-CULTURAL SITUATIONS.
Australian Journal of Social Issues, 6: 210-216, 1971.
Australia - Aborigines - acculturation - anomie - bar -
dependency - economics - functions   D-0643.

739. Liebenau, Th[eodor] von
DAS GASTHOF- UND WIRTSHAUSWESEN DER SCHWEIZ IN ALTERER ZEIT. [The character of inns and pubs of Switzerland in days of old.] [Ger]
Zurich: J.A. Preuss, [cf. p. 43]   1891.
Switzerland - bar - history, pre-1900   D-1224.

740. Lieber, Charles S.
METABOLISM OF ETHANOL AND ALCOHOLISM: RACIAL AND ACQUIRED FACTORS.
Annals of Internal Medicine, 76(2): 326-327, 1972.
metabolism - "race" - review   D-0644.

741. Lindner, Paul
EL SECRETO DEL "SOMA", BEBIDA DE LOS ANTIGUOS INDIOS Y PERSAS. [The secret of "Soma", drink of the ancient Indians and Persians.] [Spa]
Investigación y Progreso, 7: 272-274, 1933.
India - Persians, ancient - history, pre-1500 - homebrew   D-0645.

742. Listiak, Alan
"LEGITIMATE DEVIANCE" AND SOCIAL CLASS: BAR BEHAVIOR DURING GREY CUP WEEK.
Sociological Focus, 7(3): 13-44, 1974.
Canada - Whites - bar - responsibility   D-0647.

743. Little, Michael A.
EFFECTS OF ALCOHOL AND COCA ON FOOT TEMPERATURE RESPONSES OF HIGHLAND PERUVIANS DURING A LOCALIZED COLD EXPOSURE.
American Journal of Physical Anthropology, 32: 233-242, 1970.
Peru - Quechua - "race"   D-0648.

744. Littman, Gerard
SOME OBSERVATIONS ON DRINKING AMONG AMERICAN INDIANS IN CHICAGO.
In: Selected Papers presented at the 27th International Congress on Alcohol and Alcoholism, Volume 1: Alcohol as a cultural question. Held September 6-12, 1964 in Frankfurt-am-Main, West Germany. Lausanne: International Council on Alcohol and Alcoholism, pp. 67-78, 1965.
Native Americans - Skid Row - Alcoholics Anonymous - anomie - attitudes - urbanization   D-1170.

745. Littman, Gerard
ALCOHOLISM, ILLNESS AND SOCIAL PATHOLOGY AMONG AMERICAN
INDIANS IN TRANSITION.
American Journal of Public Health, 60: 1769-1787, 1970.
Native Americans - acculturation - anomie - customs -
disulfiram - functions - review - sociocultural -
urbanization   D-0649.

746. Lobban, Mary C.
CULTURAL PROBLEMS AND DRUNKENNESS IN AN ARCTIC POPULATION.
British Medical Journal, 1: 344, 1971.
Canada - Eskimos - acculturation   D-0650.

747. Lockhard, R.
SCOTCH: THE WHISKY OF SCOTLAND IN FACT AND STORY.
London: Putnam, 1971.
Scotland - history, pre-1900 - manufacture - moonshine -
whiskey   D-0412.

748. Locklear, Herbert H.
AMERICAN INDIAN ALCOHOLISM: PROGRAM FOR TREATMENT.
Social Work, 22(3): 202-207, 1977.
Native Americans - treatment   D-0651.

749. Loeb, Edwin M.
PRIMITIVE INTOXICANTS.
Quarterly Journal of Studies on Alcohol, 4: 387-398, 1943.
World survey - distribution - functions - history, pre-1500 -
prehistory - religion - social organization - symbols   D-0652.

750. Loeb, Edwin M.
WINE, WOMEN AND SONG: ROOT PLANTING AND HEAD-HUNTING IN
SOUTHEAST ASIA.
In: Diamond, Stanley, ed. Culture and history. New York,
NY: Columbia University Press, pp. 302-316, 1960.
distribution - drugs   D-0653.

751. Loedolff, J.F.
SOSIOLOGIESE ASPEKTE: DIE OUERHUIS VAN DIE ALCOHOLIS.
THE PERSONALITY AND TREATMENT OF THE ALCOHOLIC IN SOUTH
AFRICA: REPORT OF THE PROJECT ALCOHOLISM, VOLUME 3. [Afr]
Pretoria: Department of Social Welfare and Pensions,
Republic of South Africa, 1971.
South Africa - class - social organization   D-1110.

752. Lolli, Giorgio; Serianni, Emidio; Golder, Grace M.; and
Luzzatto-Fegiz, Pierpaolo
ALCOHOL IN ITALIAN CULTURE: FOOD AND WINE IN RELATION TO
SOBRIETY AMONG ITALIANS AND ITALIAN AMERICANS.
Glencoe, IL: Free Press (Monographs of the Yale Center
of Alcohol Studies, No. 3), 132 pp., 1958.
United States - Italian-Americans - Italy - customs -
research methods - norms - sociocultural   D-0654.

753. Lolli, Giorgio
THE COCKTAIL HOUR: PHYSIOLOGICAL, PSYCHOLOGICAL, AND
SOCIAL ASPECTS.
In: Lucia, Salvatore Pablo, ed. Alcohol and civilization.
New York, NY: McGraw-Hill, pp. 183-199, 1963.
United States - customs - responsibility D-0039.

754. Lomnitz, Larissa
FUNCION DEL ALCOHOL EN LA SOCIEDAD MAPUCHE. [The function
of alcohol in Mapuche society.] [Spa]
Acta Psiquiátrica y Psicológica de América Latina,
15: 157-167, 1969.
Chile - Mapuche - customs - economics - functions -
ritual - social organization - urbanization D-0656.

755. Lomnitz, Larissa
PATTERNS OF ALCOHOL CONSUMPTION AMONG THE MAPUCHE.
Human Organization, 28: 287-296, 1969.
Chile - Mapuche - binge - economics - functions - homebrew -
social organization - sociocultural - youth D-0655.

756. Lomnitz, Larissa
INFLUENCIA DE LOS CAMBIOS POLITICOS Y ECONOMICOS EN LA
INGESTION DEL ALCOHOL: EL CASO MAPUCHE. [The influence
of political and economic changes on alcohol use: The
Mapuche case.] [Spa]
América Indígena, 33: 133-150, 1973.
Chile - Mapuche - change - economics - history, pre-1900 -
political D-0657.

757. Lomnitz, Larissa
ALCOHOL AND CULTURE: THE HISTORICAL EVOLUTION OF DRINKING
PATTERNS AMONG THE MAPUCHE.
In: Everett, Michael W.; Waddell, Jack O.; and Heath, Dwight
B., ed. Cross-cultural approaches to the study of alcohol:
An interdisciplinary perspective. The Hague: Mouton,
pp. 177-198, 1976.
Chile - Mapuche - change - economics - history, pre-1900 -
political D-0658.

758. Lookout, M.
ALCOHOL AND THE NATIVE AMERICAN.
Alcohol Technical Reports, 4: 30-37, 1975.
Native Americans D-0659.

759. Lorenzo, A.M.
THE DRINK PROBLEM IN URBAN BOMBAY: AN INQUIRY INTO THE
SOCIAL AND ECONOMIC ASPECTS OF DRINKING IN URBAN CENTRES
OF BOMBAY STATE.
Bombay: Government Central Press, 1953.
India - customs - economics - research methods -
urbanization D-0660.

760.   Lotterhos, Jerry F.
       HISTORICAL AND SOCIOLOGICAL PERSPECTIVES OF ALCOHOL-
       RELATED PROBLEMS.
       In: Williams, Richard L., and Moffat, Gene H., ed.
       Occupational Alcoholism Programs. Springfield, IL:
       Charles C. Thomas, pp. 3-39,   1975.
       United States - history, pre-1900 - occupation -
       sociocultural   D-0227.

761.   Lovald, K.A.
       HOBOHEMIA TO SKID ROW: THE CHANGING COMMUNITY OF THE
       HOMELESS MAN.
       Ph.D. Dissertation, University of Minnesota,   1960.
       United States - Skid Row - economics - social organization   D-0276.

762.   Lubart, J.M.
       FIELD STUDY OF THE PROBLEMS OF ADAPTATION CF MACKENZIE
       DELTA ESKIMOS TO SOCIAL AND ECONOMIC CHANGE.
       Psychiatry, 32: 447-458,   1969.
       Canada - Eskimos - acculturation - bar - homebrew -
       stress   D-0661.

763.   Lucia, Salvatore P.
       WINE AS FOOD AND MEDICINE.
       New York, NY: Blakiston, 120 pp.,   1954.
       World survey - history, pre-1500 - history, pre-1900 -
       medical - nutrition - review - wine   D-0228.

764.   Lucia, Salvatore P.
       A HISTORY OF WINE AS THERAPY.
       Philadelphia, PA: J.B. Lippincott, 234 pp.,   1963.
       World survey - history, pre-1500 - history, pre-1900 -
       medical - review - wine   D-0229.

765.   Lucia, Salvatore Pablo
       THE ANTIQUITY OF ALCOHOL IN DIET AND MEDICINE.
       In: Lucia, Salvatore Pablo, ed. Alcohol and civilization.
       New York, NY: McGraw-Hill, pp. 151-166,   1963.
       World survey - functions - history, pre-1500 - medical -
       prehistory   D-0040.

766.   Ludovici, A.M.
       MAN'S DESCENT FROM THE GODS, OR: THE CASE AGAINST
       PROHIBITION.
       London: Heinemann,   1921.
       World survey - customs - functions - prohibition   D-0277.

767.   Lumsden, D. Paul
       TOWARDS A SYSTEM MODEL OF STRESS: FEEDBACK FROM AN
       ANTHROPOLOGICAL STUDY OF THE IMPACT OF GHANA'S VOLTA
       RIVER PROJECT.
       In: Sarason, I., and Spielberger, C., ed. Stress and
       Anxiety, Volume 2. Washington, D.C.: Hemisphere,   1975.

100.

	Ghana - fighting - stress	D-0662.
768.	Lurie, Nancy O. THE WORLD'S OLDEST ON-GOING PROTEST DEMONSTRATION: NORTH AMERICAN INDIAN DRINKING PATTERNS. Pacific Historical Review, 40: 311-332, Native Americans - functions - sociocultural - stereotype	1971. D-0663.
769.	Lurie, Nancy O. INDIAN DRINKING PATTERNS. American Journal of Orthopsychiatry, 42: 554, Native Americans - functions - sociocultural - stereotype	1972. D-0664.
770.	Lutes, Steven V. ALCOHOL USE AMONG THE YAQUI INDIANS OF POTAM, SONORA, MEXICO. Ph.D. Dissertation, University of Kansas, Mexico	1977. D-1245.
771.	Lutz, H.F. VITICULTURE AND BREWING IN THE ANCIENT ORIENT. Leipzig: J.C. Heinrichs, Near East - history, pre-1500 - homebrew - manufacture - prehistory - wine	1922. D-0665.
772.	Lynge, Inge ALCOHOL PROBLEMS IN WESTERN GREENLAND. In: Shephard, Roy J., and Itoh, S., ed. Circumpolar Health. Toronto, Ont.: University of Toronto Press, pp. 543-547, Denmark - Greenland - Eskimos - psychiatric problems	1976. D-0041.
773.	MacAndrew, Craig, and Edgerton, Robert B. DRUNKEN COMPORTMENT: A SOCIAL EXPLANATION. Chicago, IL: Aldine, 197 pp., Native Americans - acculturation - change - history, pre-1900 - intoxication - responsibility - review - stereotype	1969. D-0666.
774.	Maccoby, Michael ALCOHOLISM IN A MEXICAN VILLAGE. In: McClelland, David C.; Davis, William N.; Kalin, Rudolf; and Wanner, Eric. The drinking man. New York, NY: Free Press, pp. 232-260, Mexico - customs - functions - psychiatric problems	1972. D-1171.
775.	MacLeod, William Christie HOW THE INDIAN TRIED PROHIBITION BUT DRANK TOO MUCH. In: MacLeod, W.C. The American Indian Frontier. New York, NY: Alfred A. Knopf, Native Americans - acculturation - change - dysfunctions - history, pre-1900 - prohibition	1928. D-0687.

776. MacLeod, W[illiam] C[hristie]
ALCOHOL: HISTORICAL ASPECTS.
In: Seligman, E.R.A., and Johnson, A., ed. Encyclopaedia of the Social Sciences, Volume 1. New York, NY: Macmillan, pp. 619-620, 1930.
World survey - history, pre-1500 - history, pre-1900 - prehistory - review
D-0688.

777. Macrory, Boyd E.
THE TAVERN AND THE COMMUNITY.
Quarterly Journal of Studies on Alcohol, 13: 609-637, 1952.
United States - bar - functions
D-0689.

778. Madsen, William
THE ALCOHOLIC AGRINGADO.
American Anthropologist, 66: 355-361, 1964.
United States - Hispanos - acculturation - anomie - sociocultural - stress - treatment
D-0690.

779. Madsen, William
COMMENT ON D. MANDELBAUM'S "ALCOHOL AND CULTURE".
Current Anthropology, 6: 291-292, 1965.
Mexico - acculturation - change - history, pre-1900
D-0691.

780. Madsen, William, and Madsen, Claudia
THE CULTURAL STRUCTURE OF MEXICAN DRINKING BEHAVIOR.
Quarterly Journal of Studies on Alcohol, 30: 701-718, 1969.
Cross-ethnic - Mexico - Mexica - Mestizos - customs - norms - sociocultural
D-0693.

781. Madsen, William
ALCOHOLICS ANONYMOUS AS A CRISIS CULT.
In: Chafetz, Morris E., ed. Alcoholism: A multi-level problem. Treatment: Organization and management. Proceedings of the 3rd Annual Conference of the National Institute on Alcohol Abuse and Alcoholism. Held June 20-22, 1973 in Washington, D.C. Rockville, MD: National Institute on Alcohol Abuse and Alcoholism (DHEW Publication No. (ADM) 75-137), pp. 158-174, 1974.
Alcoholics Anonymous - conversion - religion
D-1173.

782. Madsen, William
THE AMERICAN ALCOHOLIC: THE NATURE-NURTURE CONTROVERSY IN ALCOHOL RESEARCH AND THERAPY.
Springfield, IL: Charles C. Thomas, 248 pp., 1974.
United States - Alcoholics Anonymous - disease concept - functions - pathology - psychiatric problems - research methods - review
D-1172.

783. Madsen, William
BODY, MIND AND BOOZE.
In: Everett, Michael W.; Waddell, Jack O.; and Heath, Dwight B., ed. Cross-cultural approaches to the study of alcohol: An interdisciplinary perspective. The Hague:

102.

	Mouton, pp. 217-225, functions - dysfunctions - research methods - review	1976. D-0692.
784.	Mahoney, F.B. SOCIAL AND CULTURAL FACTORS RELATING TO THE CAUSE AND CONTROL OF ALCOHOL ABUSE AMONG MICRONESIAN YOUTH. Unpublished report: James R. Leonard Associates, to Government of the Trust Territory of the Pacific Islands, Washington, D.C., 85 pp., Micronesia - youth	1974. D-1574.
785.	Mail, Patricia D. THE USE AND INFLUENCE OF ALCOHOL IN THE SAN CARLOS APACHE: AN INTERIM REPORT. Unpublished report: Phoenix Area Indian Health Service, Research Advisory Committee, San Carlos, AZ, United States - Native Americans - Apache - crime - suicide	1966. D-1575.
786.	Mail, Patricia D. THE PREVALENCE OF PROBLEM DRINKING IN THE SAN CARLOS APACHE. M.P.H. Thesis, Yale University Medical School, 126 pp., United States - Native Americans - Apache - customs - epidemiology - prevention	1967. D-0694.
787.	Mail, Patricia D., and McDonald, David R. NATIVE AMERICANS AND ALCOHOL: A PRELIMINARY ANNOTATED BIBLIOGRAPHY. Behavior Science Research, 12(3): 169-196, Native Americans - bibliography	1977. D-0695.
788.	Mäkelä, Klaus CONSUMPTION LEVEL AND CULTURAL DRINKING PATTERNS AS DETERMINANTS OF ALCOHOL PROBLEMS. Journal of Drug Issues, 5(4): 344-357, World survey - consumption - prevention - research methods - review	1975. D-0696.
789.	Mäkelä, Klaus LEVEL OF CONSUMPTION AND SOCIAL CONSEQUENCES OF DRINKING. In: Israel, Yedy; Glaser, Frederick B.; Kalant, Harold; Popham, Robert E.; Schmidt, Wolfgang; and Smart, Reginald G., ed. Research advances in alcohol and drug problems, Volume 4. New York, NY: Plenum, pp. 303-348, consumption - epidemiology - prevention - sociocultural	1978. D-0231.
790.	Malik, M.O.A., and Sawi, O. A PROFILE OF HOMICIDE IN THE SUDAN. Forensic Science, 7: 141-150, moonshine - murder	1976. D-0042.

791.   Mandelbaum, David C. [and others]
        ALCOHOL AND CULTURE [with comments].
        Current Anthropology, 6: 281-294,   1965.
        World survey - change - distribution - review -
        sociocultural   D-1174.

792.   Mangin, William
        DRINKING AMONG ANDEAN INDIANS.
        Quarterly Journal of Studies on Alcohol, 18: 55-66,   1957.
        Peru - Quechua - binge - customs - functions - homebrew -
        political - sociocultural   D-0697.

793.   Mann, Brenda
        BAR TALK.
        In: Spradley, James P., and McCurdy, David W., ed.
        Conformity and conflict: Readings in cultural anthropology.(2nd ed.)
        Boston, MA: Little, Brown, pp. 101-111,   1974.
        United States - bar - semantics - social organization   D-0698.

794.   Mann, Brenda
        THE ETHICS OF FIELDWORK IN AN URBAN BAR.
        In: Rynkiewich, Michael A., and Spradley, James P., ed.
        Ethics and anthropology: Dilemmas in fieldwork. New York, NY:
        John Wiley and Sons, pp. 95-109,   1976.
        bar - research methods   D-0699.

795.   Manning, Frank E.
        BLACK CLUBS IN BERMUDA: ETHNOGRAPHY OF A PLAY WORLD.
        Ithaca, NY: Cornell University Press,   1973.
        West Indies - Bermuda - Blacks - bar - leisure   D-0414.

796.   Manning, Frank E.
        THE SALVATION OF A DRUNK.
        American Ethnologist, 4: 397-412,   1977.
        Bermuda - Protestants - Church - possession   D-0700.

797.   Manning, Frank E.
        TRAMPS, PISSTANKS, AND GOPHERS: THE DRINKING PROBLEM AT
        SEA.
        Canadian Ethnological Society Proceedings, 4: 99-126,   1977.
        Canada - occupation - social organization   D-1249.

798.   Marconi, Juan
        BARRERAS CULTURALES EN LA COMUNICACION QUE AFECTAN EL
        DESARROLLO DE PROGRAMAS DE CONTROL Y PREVENCION DEL
        ALCOHOLISMO. [Cultural barriers in communication that
        affect the development of programs of control and
        prevention of alcoholism.] [Spa]
        Acta Psiquiátrica y Psicológica de América Latina,
        15: 351-355,   1969.
        Chile - Mapuche - sociocultural   D-0701.

104.

799. Mariani, C.
ALCOHOLISMO Y GIROS FOLKLORICOS CHILENOS. [Alcoholism and Chilean folklore.] [Spa]
In: Seguín, C.A., and Rios, C.R., ed. Anales de Tercer Congreso Latino-americano de Psiquiatría. Lima: Villanueva, 1964.
Chile - folklore   D-0702.

800. Mariátegui, Javier
INGESTION DE ALCOHOL Y FACTORES SOCIOCULTURALES. [Alcohol consumption and sociocultural factors.] [Spa]
In: Horwitz, José; Marconi, Juan; and Adis, Gonzalo, ed. Bases para una epidemiología del alcoholismo en América Latina. Buenos Aires: Acta, pp. 24-31, 1967.
Latin America - consumption - sociocultural   D-0703.

801. Maril, Robert Lee, and Zavaleta, Anthony
DRINKING PATTERNS OF LOW-INCOME MEXICAN AMERICAN WOMEN.
Journal of Studies on Alcohol, 40(5): 480-484, 1979.
United States - Hispanos   D-1250.

802. Marinovich, N.; Larsson, O.; and Barber, K.
COMPARATIVE METABOLISM RATES OF ETHANOL IN ADULTS OF ABORIGINAL AND EUROPEAN DESCENT.
Medical Journal of Australia, 7(1, Special Supplement): 44-46, 1976.
Cross-ethnic - Australia - Aborigines - Whites - metabolism - "race"   D-0704.

803. Maritz, F.A.
KOMUNIKASIE EN INLIGTING: MASSAKOMMUNIKASIE EN DIE WANGEBRUIK VAN ALKOHOLIESE DRANK. THE PERSONALITY AND TREATMENT OF THE ALCOHOLIC IN SOUTH AFRICA: REPORT OF THE PROJECT ALCOHOLISM, VOLUME 14, HOOFSTUK 1. [Afr]
Pretoria: Department of Social Welfare and Pensions, Republic of South Africa, 1971.
South Africa - prevention   D-1111.

804. Marlatt, G. Alan
BEHAVIORAL ASSESSMENT OF SOCIAL DRINKING AND ALCOHOLISM.
In: Marlatt, G. Alan, and Nathan, Peter E., ed. Behavioral approaches to alcoholism. New Brunswick, NJ: Rutgers Center of Alcohol Studies, pp. 35-57, 1978.
consumption - research methods   D-0232.

805. Marrison, L.W.
WINES AND SPIRITS.
Harmondsworth: Penguin, 320 pp., 1958.
World survey - beer - brandy - distribution - history, pre-1500 - history, pre-1900 - homebrew - manufacture - review - whiskey - wine   D-0415.

806. Marroquín, José
ALCOHOLISMO ENTRE LOS ABORIGENES PERUANOS. [Alcoholism among Peruvian Indians.] [Spa]
Crónica Médica, 60: 226-231, 1943.
Peru - customs - dysfunctions - history, pre-1500 - history, pre-1900 - homebrew - prohibition - symbols   D-0705.

807. Marrus, Michael R.
SOCIAL DRINKING IN THE BELLE EPOQUE.
Journal of Social History, 7: 115-141, 1974.
France - bar - change - functions - history, pre-1900   D-0706.

808. Marshall, Mac
RESEARCH BIBLIOGRAPHY OF ALCOHOL AND KAVA STUDIES IN OCEANIA.
Micronesica, 10(2): 299-306, 1974.
Oceania - bibliography - kava   D-0707.

809. Marshall, Mac, and Marshall, Leslie B.
OPENING PANDORA'S BOTTLE: RECONSTRUCTING MICRONESIANS' EARLY CONTACTS WITH ALCOHOLIC BEVERAGES.
Journal of the Polynesian Society, 84(4): 441-465, 1975.
Cross-ethnic - Micronesia - change - distribution - history, pre-1900   D-0710.

810. Marshall, Mac
THE POLITICS OF PROHIBITION ON NAMOLUK ATOLL.
Journal of Studies on Alcohol, 36(5): 597-610, 1975.
Micronesia - Truk - change - political - prohibition - responsibility - social organization   D-0708.

811. Marshall, Mac, and Marshall, Leslie B.
HOLY AND UNHOLY SPIRITS: THE EFFECTS OF MISSIONIZATION ON ALCOHOL USE IN EASTERN MICRONESIA.
Journal of Pacific History, 11(3-4): 135-166, 1976.
Cross-ethnic - Micronesia - change - class - economics - history, pre-1900 - homebrew - occupation - prohibition - social organization   D-0711.

812. Marshall, Mac
A REVIEW AND APPRAISAL OF ALCOHOL AND KAVA STUDIES IN OCEANIA.
In: Everett, Michael W.; Waddell, Jack O.; and Heath, Dwight B., ed. Cross-cultural approaches to the study of alcohol: An interdisciplinary perspective. The Hague: Mouton, pp. 103-118, 1976.
Oceania - kava - review   D-0709.

813. Marshall, Mac
BELIEFS, BEHAVIORS, AND ALCOHOLIC BEVERAGES: A CROSS-CULTURAL SURVEY.
Minneapolis, MN: University of Minnesota Press, 1979.
World survey - review   D-1247.

814. Marshall, Mac
WEEKEND WARRIORS: ALCOHOL IN A MICRONESIAN CULTURE.
Palo Alto, CA: Mayfield, 1979.
Micronesia - Truk - accultturation - change - customs -
sociocultural D-1246.

815. Marshall, William E.
SUICIDE AND ALCOHOL: A DISCUSSION OF THE DIRECT CAUSE
EFFECT THEORY AS APPLIED TO NORTH BRITISH COLUMBIA.
Unpublished paper: Presented at the International
Arctic Rim Conference on Alcohol Problems. Anchorage,
Alas.: National Council on Alcoholism, Alaska Region, 1978.
Canada - Eskimos - Native Americans - acculturation -
anomie - drugs - sociocultural - suicide - stress D-1226.

816. Martín del Campo, Rafael
EL PULQUE EN MEXICO PRECORTESIANO. [Pulque in pre-
hispanic Mexico.] [Spa]
Universidad Nacional Autónoma de México, Anales del
Instituto de Biología, 9: 5-23, 1938.
Mexico - history, pre-1500 - homebrew - prehistory D-0712.

817. Massicotte, E.Z.
L'INDUSTRIE HOTELIERE ET LES PREMIERS AUBERGISTES DU
REGIME ANGLAIS. [The hotel industry and the first inn-
keepers of the English period.] [Fre]
Bulletin des Recherches Historiques, 36: 203-206, 1930.
France - bar - history, pre-1900 D-0233.

818. Mass Observation
THE PUB AND THE PEOPLE: A WORK TOWN STUDY.
London: Victor Gollancz, 350 pp., 1943.
England - bar - research methods D-1094.

819. Maurizio, A.
GESCHICHTE DER GEGORENEN GETRANKE. [History of fermented
spirits.] [Ger]
Berlin: Paul Parey, 1933.
Germany D-1227.

820. May, J[oan]
SURVEY OF THE URBAN AFRICAN DRINKING PATTERNS IN THE
BULAWAYO MUNICIPAL TOWNSHIP.
Unpublished report: Department of Sociology, Alcoholism
Research Unit, University of Rhodesia, Salisbury, 54 pp., 1970.
Rhodesia - urbanization D-1576.

821. May, J[oan]
DRINKING IN A RHODESIAN AFRICAN TOWNSHIP.
Unpublished paper: Institute of Social Research, Department
of Sociology, University of Rhodesia (Occasional Paper
No. 8), Salisbury, 94 pp., 1973.
Rhodesia - change - customs - functions - dysfunctions -
urbanization D-1577.

822. May, Joan
       DRINKING IN HARARE.
       Unpublished report: Institute of Social Research,
       Department of Sociology, University of Rhodesia,
       Salisbury,   1973.
       Rhodesia - customs - urbanization   D-1578.

823. May, Philip A.
       ARRESTS, ALCOHOL, AND ALCOHOL LEGALIZATION AMONG AN
       AMERICAN INDIAN TRIBE.
       Plains Anthropologist, 20: 129-134,   1975.
       United States - Native Americans - change - crime -
       prohibition   D-0713.

824. May, Philip A.
       ALCOHOL LEGALIZATION AND NATIVE AMERICANS: A SOCIOLOGICAL
       INQUIRY.
       Ph.D. Dissertation, University of Montana,   1976.
       United States - Cross-ethnic - Native Americans - Blackfeet
       - Crow - Cheyenne - accidents - change - crime - liver -
       murder - prohibition - suicide   D-0714.

825. May, Philip A.
       EXPLANATIONS OF NATIVE AMERICAN DRINKING: A LITERATURE
       REVIEW.
       Plains Anthropologist, 22: 223-232,   1977.
       Native Americans - etiology - functions - review   D-0715.

826. Maynard, Eileen; Frøland, Bjarke; and Rasmussen, Christian, ed.
       DRINKING PATTERNS IN HIGHLAND ECUADOR.
       Ithaca, NY: Cornell University (Andean Indian Community
       Research and Development Program),   1965.
       Ecuador - Quechua   D-0718.

827. Maynard, Eileen
       DRINKING PATTERNS IN THE COLTA LAKE ZONE (CHIMBORAZO).
       In: Maynard, E.; Frøland, B.; and Rasmussen, C., ed. Drinking
       patterns in Highland Ecuador. Ithaca, NY: Cornell
       University,   1965.
       Ecuador - Quechua - customs - functions - dysfunctions -
       economics - sociocultural   D-0716.

828. Maynard, Eileen, and Twiss, Gayla
       DRINKING.
       In: That these people may live: Conditions among the
       Oglala Sioux of the Pine Ridge Reservation. Pine Ridge,
       SD: U.S. Public Health Service Community Mental Health
       Program, pp. 161-166,   1969.
       United States - Native Americans - Sioux - dysfunctions -
       economics - functions - sociocultural   D-0719.

829. Maynard, Eileen
DRINKING AS PART OF AN ADJUSTMENT SYNDROME AMONG THE OGLALA SIOUX.
Pine Ridge Reservation Bulletin, 9: 35-51, 1969.
United States - Native Americans - Sioux - acculturation - economics - functions - stress
D-0717.

830. McBeth, Kate C., and Crawford, Mazie
THE RISE AND FALL OF "KING ALCOHOL" IN THE NEZ PERCE COUNTRY.
The Red Man, 6: 259-265, 1914.
United States - Native Americans - Nez Perce - change - history, pre-1900
D-0667.

831. McCarthy, Robert G., ed.
DRINKING AND INTOXICATION: SELECTED READINGS IN SOCIAL ATTITUDES AND CONTROLS.
Glencoe, IL: Free Press, 446 pp., 1959.
World survey - customs - norms - review
D-0668.

832. McClelland, David C.; Davis, William; Wanner, Eric; and Kalin, Rudolf
A CROSS-CULTURAL STUDY OF FOLK-TALE CONTENT AND DRINKING.
Sociometry, 29: 308-333, 1966.
Cross-cultural - folklore - functions - power
D-0670.

833. McClelland, David C.; Davis, William N.; Wanner, Eric; and Kalin, Rudolf
A CROSS-CULTURAL STUDY OF FOLK-TALE CONTENT AND DRINKING.
In: McClelland, David C.; Davis, William N.; Kalin, Rudolf; and Wanner, Eric. The drinking man. New York, NY: Free Press, pp. 48-72, 1972.
Cross-cultural - folklore - functions - power
D-1947.

834. McClelland, David C.; Davis, William N.; Kalin, Rudolf; and Wanner, Eric
THE DRINKING MAN.
New York, NY: Free Press, 402 pp., 1972.
functions - power - social organization
D-0669.

835. McFarland, Kathy
HAUSER'S PLACE: AN ETHNOGRAPHY OF A BUSINESSMEN'S BAR.
M.A. Thesis, University of Houston, 1974.
bar - space
D-0671.

836. McGlashan, N.D.
OESOPHAGEAL CANCER AND ALCOHOLIC SPIRITS IN CENTRAL AFRICA.
Gut, 10: 643-650, 1969.
Africa - cancer - containers - distribution - homebrew - manufacture - moonshine - sociocultural
D-0672.

837. McGonegal, J.
THE ROLE OF SANCTION IN DRINKING BEHAVIOR.
Quarterly Journal of Studies on Alcohol, 33: 692-697, 1972.
Jews - enculturation - family - norms   D-0673.

838. McGoodwin, James R.
ETHNOSEMANTIC ANALYSIS OF COGNITION IN THE ALCOHOLIC PATIENT.
International Journal of the Addictions, 11(4): 619-628, 1976.
language - research methods   D-0230.

839. McGregor, H.G.
ALCOHOL AND ALCOHOLISM.
Journal of the Royal Institute of Public Health,
11: 266-283,   1948.
England - economics - history, pre-1500 - history, pre-1900
- homebrew - medical - pathology   D-0674.

840. McGunigle, E.
PROBLEM DRINKING AMONG AMERICAN INDIANS, AND A NEW LOOK
AT ITS CAUSE.
Unpublished paper: Southwest Studies Summer Institute,
Colorado College, Colorado Springs, CO (US, NCALI
accession # NCAI 016893),   1973.
Native Americans - acculturation - etiology - history,
pre-1900 - "race"   D-1573.

841. McKinlay, Arthur P[atch]
THE "INDULGENT" DIONYSIUS.
Transactions of the American Philosophical Association,
70: 51-61,   1939.
Romans, ancient - history, pre-1500 - religion   D-0675.

842. McKinlay, Arthur P[atch]
HOW THE ATHENIANS HANDLED THE DRINK PROBLEM AMONG THEIR
SLAVES.
Classical Weekly, 37: 127-128,   1944.
Greeks, ancient - caste - history, pre-1500   D-0676.

843. McKinlay, Arthur Patch
THE ROMAN ATTITUDE TOWARD WOMEN'S DRINKING.
Classical Bulletin, 22: 14-15,   1945.
Romans, ancient - female - history, pre-1500   D-0677.

844. McKinlay, Arthur Patch
ANCIENT EXPERIENCE WITH INTOXICATING DRINKS: NON-CLASSICAL
PEOPLES.
Quarterly Journal of Studies on Alcohol, 9(3): 388-414, 1948.
World survey - history, pre-1500 - review   D-0680.

845. McKinlay, Arthur Patch
EARLY ROMAN SOBRIETY.
Classical Bulletin, 24: 52,   1948.
Romans, ancient - history, pre-1500 - temperance   D-0679.

846. McKinlay, Arthur P[atch]
TEMPERATE ROMANS.
Classical Weekly, 41: 146-149, 1948.
Romans, ancient - history, pre-1500 - temperance   D-0678.

847. McKinlay, Arthur Patch
ANCIENT EXPERIENCE WITH INTOXICATING DRINKS: NON-ATTIC GREEK STATES.
Quarterly Journal of Studies on Alcohol, 10(2): 289-315, 1949.
World survey - history, pre-1500 - review   D-0681.

848. McKinlay, Arthur Patch
ROMAN SOBRIETY IN THE LATER REPUBLIC.
Classical Bulletin, 25: 27-28, 1949.
Romans, ancient - history, pre-1500 - temperance   D-0682.

849. McKinlay, Arthur P[atch]
BACCHUS AS HEALTH-GIVER.
Quarterly Journal of Studies on Alcohol, 11: 230-246, 1950.
Classical peoples - history, pre-1500 - homebrew -
medical - wine   D-0683.

850. McKinlay, Arthur Patch
ROMAN SOBRIETY IN THE COMEDIES.
Classical Outlook, 27(5): 56-57, 1950.
Romans, ancient - literature - norms   D-0044.

851. McKinlay, Arthur Patch
ROMAN SOBRIETY IN THE EARLY EMPIRE.
Classical Bulletin, 26: 31-36, 1950.
Romans, ancient - history, pre-1500 - literature   D-0684.

852. McKinlay, Arthur Patch
ATTIC TEMPERANCE.
Quarterly Journal of Studies on Alcohol, 12: 61-102, 1951.
Greeks, ancient - history, pre-1500 - temperance   D-0685.

853. McKinlay, Arthur P[atch]
NEW LIGHT ON THE QUESTION OF HOMERIC TEMPERANCE.
Quarterly Journal of Studies on Alcohol, 14: 78-93, 1953.
Greeks, ancient - history, pre-1500 - literature   D-0686.

854. McLaughlin, D.; Carter, C.; and Rashad, M.H.
RELATIVE RATES OF ALCOHOLISM AMONGST RACIAL GROUPS IN HAWAII.
American Journal of Human Genetics, 27: 634 ff, 1975.
Hawaiian Islands - Cross-ethnic - epidemiology - "race"   D-1225.

855. McNair, Crawford N.
DRINKING PATTERNS AND DEVIANCE IN A MULTI-RACIAL COMMUNITY IN NORTHERN CANADA.
Toronto, Ont.: Addiction Research Foundation, (Clinical)
Substudy No. 32-1969, 17 pp., 1969.

Cross-ethnic - Canada - Native Americans - Kaska - Métis -
Tahltan - Whites - aggression - anomie - bar - customs -
functions - "race" - sex - stereotype - stress   D-1205.

856. McNeill, F.M.
      THE SCOTS CELLAR: ITS TRADITION AND LORE.
      Edinburgh: Paterson,   1956.
      Scotland - customs - history, pre-1900   D-0413.

857. Mears, A.R.R.
      PELLAGRA IN TSOLO DISTRICT.
      South African Medical Journal, 16: 385-387,   1942.
      South Africa - Cross-ethnic - Fingo - Pondomi - Xosa -
      homebrew - nutrition - pathology   D-0314.

858. Medical Practitioner, A
      NOTICES RESPECTING DRUNKENNESS, AND OF THE VARIOUS MEANS
      WHICH HAVE BEEN EMPLOYED IN DIFFERENT COUNTRIES FOR
      RESTRAINING THE PROGRESS OF THAT EVIL.
      Glasgow: William Collins,   1830.
      World survey - norms - pathology - prohibition - religion -
      temperance   D-1175.

859. Medina C., and Marconi, J.
      PREVALENCIA DE DISTINTOS TIPOS DE BEBEDORES EN ADULTOS
      MAPUCHES DE ZONA RURAL EN CAUTIN. [Prevalence of distinct
      types of drinkers among Mapuche adults in rural Cautin.]
      [Spa]
      Acta Psiquiátrica y Psicológica de América Latina,
      16: 273-285,   1970.
      Chile - Mapuche - occupation - urbanization   D-0721.

860. Mendelsohn, Oscar A.
      DRINKING WITH PEPYS.
      London: Macmillan, 125 pp.,   1963.
      England - customs - history, pre-1900 - literature   D-0043.

861. Metzger, Duane G.
      INTERPRETATIONS OF DRINKING PERFORMANCES IN AGUACATENANGO,
      [MEXICO].
      Ph.D. Dissertation, University of Chicago,   1964.
      Mexico - Tojolabal - intoxication - semantics -
      sociocultural   D-0722.

862. Meza Y Posada, Samuel Arturo
      HISTORIA DEL ALCOHOL Y DEL ALCOHOLISMO EN EUROPA Y EN
      AMERICA. [History of alcohol and alcoholism in Europe
      and America.] [Spa]
      Orientaciones Médicas, 8: 107-113,   1959.
      World survey - history, pre-1500 - history, pre-1900   D-0723.

863. Micev, M.
TRANSKULTURELNI ASPEKTI ALKOHOLIZMA SUPTARSKE ALBANESKE
NACIONALNE MANJINE U.S.R. MAKEDONIJI. [Transcultural
aspects of alcoholism among Albanians in the Socialist
Republic of Macedonia.] [Ser-Cro]
Anali Bolnice "Dr. Mladen Stojanović", 6(2-3): 145-148, 1967.
Yugoslavia - Albanians - customs D-1095.

864. Midgley, J.
DRINKING AND ATTITUDE TOWARD DRINK IN A MUSLIM COMMUNITY.
Quarterly Journal of Studies on Alcohol, 32: 148-158, 1971.
South Africa - Islam - attitudes - customs D-0724.

865. Miles, J.D.
THE DRINKING PATTERNS OF BANTU IN SOUTH AFRICA.
Unpublished report: National Bureau of Education and
Social Research Series 18, Department of Education, Arts
and Sciences (Johannesburg), 1965.
South Africa - Bantu - customs D-1579.

866. Millar, L.L.
ROLE OF THE DEPARTMENT OF INDIAN AFFAIRS IN COMBINING
ALCOHOLISM AND DRUG DEPENDENCE AMONGST THE INDIAN COMMUNITY.
Unpublished report: South African National Council on
Alcoholism and Drug Dependence, Information Bulletin,
Bellville, 1973.
South Africa - Overseas Indians D-1176.

867. Mitra, Bábu Rájendralála
SPIRITUOUS DRINKS IN ANCIENT INDIA.
Journal of the Asiatic Society, 43: 1-23, 1873.
India - Hinduism - change - history, pre-1500 - homebrew -
manufacture - norms - religion D-0725.

868. Mizruchi, Ephraim H., and Perrucci, Robert
NORM QUALITIES AND DIFFERENTIAL EFFECTS OF DEVIANT
BEHAVIOR: AN EXPLORATORY ANALYSIS.
American Sociological Review, 27: 391-399, 1962.
Cross-ethnic - Jews - Protestants - dysfunctions -
enculturation - norms D-0726.

869. Modi, Jivanji Jamshedji
WINE AMONG THE ANCIENT PERSIANS.
Bombay: Bombay Gazette Steam Press, 16 pp., 1888.
Classical peoples - Near East - Persians, ancient -
history, pre-1500 - medical - political - religion - wine D-0727.

870. Mohatt, Gerald
THE SACRED WATER: THE QUEST FOR PERSONAL POWER THROUGH
DRINKING AMONG THE TETON SIOUX.
In: McClelland, David C.; Davis, William N.; Kalin, Rudolf;
and Wanner, Eric. The drinking man. New York, NY: Free
Press, pp. 261-275, 1972.

| | United States - Native Americans - Sioux - history, pre-1900 - power - stress - symbols | D-0728. |

871. Monckton, H.A.
ENGLISH ALE AND BEER IN SHAKESPEARE'S TIME.
History Today, 17: 828-834, 1967.
England - beer - economics - history, pre-1500 - history, pre-1900 - homebrew - manufacture   D-0729.

872. Montell, G[osta]
DISTILLING IN MONGOLIA.
Ethnos, 2: 321-332, 1937.
Mongolia - class - customs - functions - manufacture   D-0730.

873. Montoya y F., J.B.
EL ALCOHOLISMO ENTRE LOS ABORIGENES DE ANTIOQUIA.
[Alcoholism among the Indians of Antioquia.] [Spa]
Anales de la Academia de Medicina, 12: 132, 1903.
Colombia   D-0731.

874. Moore, E.C.
THE SOCIAL VALUE OF THE SALOON.
American Journal of Sociology, 3: 4, 1897.
United States - bar - economics - functions - social organization   D-0732.

875. Moore, Merrill
CHINESE WINE: SOME NOTES ON ITS SOCIAL USE.
Quarterly Journal of Studies on Alcohol, 9: 270-279, 1948.
China - attitudes - customs - history, pre-1500 - literature - responsibility - wine   D-0733.

876. Mora de Jaramillo, V.
CHICHAS DE UNA REGION RURAL DE LA COSTA ATLANTICA COLOMBIANA.
[Chichas of a rural region on the Atlantic Colombian coast.] [Spa]
Revista Colombiana Folclórica, 3: 233-242, 1962.
Colombia - homebrew - manufacture   D-0234.

877. Morewood, Samuel
A PHILOSOPHICAL AND STATISTICAL HISTORY OF THE INVENTION AND CUSTOMS OF ANCIENT AND MODERN NATIONS IN THE MANUFACTURE AND USE OF INEBRIATING LIQUORS.
Dublin: William Curry Jun. and Company and William Carson, 745 pp., 1838.
World survey - distribution - history, pre-1500 - history, pre-1900 - manufacture - review   D-1096.

878. Morgan, John P., and Tulloss, Thomas C.
THE JAKE-WALK BLUES: A TOXICOLOGIC TRAGEDY MIRRORED IN AMERICAN POPULAR MUSIC.
Annals of Internal Medicine, 85: 804-808, 1976.
United States - folklore - moonshine - music - prohibition   D-0734.

114.

879. Morice, R.D.
WOMEN DANCING DREAMING: PSYCHOSOCIAL BENEFITS OF THE
ABORIGINAL OUTSTATION MOVEMENT.
Medical Journal of Australia, 63(2): 939-942,   1976.
Australia - Aborigines - conversion - prohibition   D-0735.

880. Morote Best, Efraín
CHICHA.
Impulso, 1(3): 1-6,   1952.
Peru - homebrew - manufacture   D-0736.

881. Morris, Joan, and Ebrahimi, Fred
AMERICAN INDIAN ALCOHOLISM EVALUATION - MONITORING -
DESIGN PROJECT: FINAL REPORT.
Unpublished report: Tribal American Training Consultants
Associated, Glendale, CA,   1974.
Native Americans - treatment   D-1580.

882. Moser, Joy
COMMUNITY RESPONSE TO ALCOHOL-RELATED PROBLEMS: A WHO
RESEARCH PROPOSAL.
Alcoholism: Clinical and Experimental Research,
1: 267-270,   1977.
Cross-national - Canada - Mexico - Scotland - Zambia -
sociocultural   D-0737.

883. Mosher, J.F.
LIQUOR LEGISLATION AND NATIVE AMERICANS: HISTORY AND
PERSPECTIVE.
Unpublished paper: University of California, Berkeley,
Boalt Hall School of Law,   1975.
Native Americans - acculturation - change - history,
pre-1900 - prohibition   D-1177.

884. Moss, F.E.
PROPOSED ALCOHOLISM PROJECT FOR THE UINTAH-OURAY INDIAN
RESERVATION.
In: An Indian alcoholism training project. Salt Lake
City: University of Utah, Bureau of Indian Services,   1968.
United States - Native Americans - Ute - prevention -
treatment   D-1178.

885. Mossman, Beal M., and Zamora, Mario D.
CULTURE-SPECIFIC TREATMENT FOR ALCOHOLISM.
Unpublished paper: International Congress of Anthropological
and Ethnological Sciences, Chicago, IL,   1973.
sociocultural - treatment   D-1581.

886. Muelle, Jorge C.
LA CHICHA EN EL DISTRITO DE SAN SEBASTIAN. [Chicha in
the San Sebastian district.] [Spa]
Revista del Museo Nacional, 14: 144-152,   1945.
Peru - Quechua - bar - homebrew - manufacture   D-0738.

887. Murcia Valcarcel, E.
ALCOHOLISMO EN TARRASCA. [Alcoholism in Tarrasca.] [Spa]
Boletín Informativo del Instituto de Medicina Psicológica,
4:   1963.
Spain - Catalonia - epidemiology   D-1925.

888. Murphy, H.B.M.
ALCOHOLISM AND SCHIZOPHRENIA IN THE IRISH: A REVIEW.
Transcultural Psychiatric Research Review, 12: 116-139,   1975.
Ireland - Irish-Americans - review - psychiatric problems -
social organization - sociocultural   D-0739.

889. Murray, R.F., Jr., and Price, P.H.
ONTOGENETIC, POLYMORPHIC AND INTERETHNIC VARIATION IN THE
ISOENZYMES OF HUMAN ALCOHOL DEHYDROGENASE.
Annals of the New York Academy of Sciences, 197: 68-72,   1972.
Cross-ethnic - metabolism - "race"   D-0740.

890. Myerson, Abraham
ALCOHOL: A STUDY OF SOCIAL AMBIVALENCE.
Quarterly Journal of Studies on Alcohol, 1: 13-20,   1940.
United States - ambivalence - enculturation - history,
pre-1900 - norms   D-0741.

891. Myerson, Abraham
THE SOCIAL PSYCHOLOGY OF ALCOHOLISM.
Diseases of the Nervous System, 1: 43-50,   1940.
Jews - ambivalence - enculturation - female - norms   D-0742.

892. Nagler, Mark
INDIANS IN THE CITY: A STUDY OF THE URBANIZATION OF
INDIANS IN TORONTO.
Ottawa, Ont.: Canadian Research Centre for Anthropology,
107 pp.,   1970.
Canada - Native Americans - change - functions - leisure -
stress - urbanization   D-0743.

893. Naroll, Raoul
DATA QUALITY CONTROL: A NEW RESEARCH TECHNIQUE -
PROLEGOMENA TO A CROSS-CULTURAL STUDY OF CULTURE STRESS.
New York, NY: Free Press,   1962.
World survey - Cross-cultural - research methods - stress   D-0416.

894. Nason, James D.
SARDINES AND OTHER FRIED FISH: THE CONSUMPTION OF
ALCOHOLIC BEVERAGES ON A MICRONESIAN ISLAND.
Journal of Studies on Alcohol, 36: 611-625,   1975.
Micronesia - binge - change - functions - norms - social
organization   D-0744.

895. Nastrucci, M.
PREPARAZIONE DELLE BEIANDE, ALCOOLICHE ABISSINE NELL'HARAR.
[Preparation of beiande, alcoholic drink of the Ethiopian

Harar.] [Ita]
L'Agricoltura Coloniale, 34(10): 408-425, 1940.
Abyssinia - homebrew - manufacture D-0265.

896. National Institute on Alcohol Abuse and Alcoholism
SELECTED PUBLICATIONS ON SOCIOCULTURAL ASPECTS OF
ALCOHOL USE AND ALCOHOLISM.
Washington, D.C.: U.S. Government Printing Office,
Department of Health, Education and Welfare, Grouped
Interest Guide 1-5 (Cumulative), 1976.
bibliography D-1179.

897. Negrete, Juan Carlos
CULTURAL INFLUENCES AND SOCIAL PERFORMANCE OF ALCOHOLICS.
Quarterly Journal of Studies on Alcohol, 34: 905-916, 1973.
attitudes - norms - sociocultural D-0235.

898. Negrete, Juan Carlos
FACTORES CULTURALES EN ESTUDIOS EPIDEMIOLOGICOS SOBRE
ALCOHOLISMO. [Cultural factors in epidemiological studies
of alcoholism.] [Spa]
Acta Psiquiátrica y Psicológica de América Latina,
20: 112-120, 1974.
Latin America - epidemiology - sociocultural D-0745.

899. Negrete, J[uan] C[arlos]
EL ALCOHOL Y LAS DROGAS COMO PROBLEMAS DE SALUD EN
AMERICA LATINA. [Alcohol and drugs as health problems
in Latin America.] [Spa]
Boletín de la Oficina Sanitaria Panamericana, 81: 158-175, 1976.
Latin America - drugs - epidemiology D-0746.

900. Negrete, J[uan] C[arlos]
ALCOHOLISM IN LATIN AMERICA.
Annals of the New York Academy of Sciences, 273: 9-23, 1976.
Latin America - review D-0747.

901. Nelson, G.K.; Novellie, L; Reader, D.H.; Reuning, H.;
and Sachs, H.
PSYCHOLOGICAL, NUTRITIONAL, AND SOCIOLOGICAL STUDIES OF
KAFFIR BEER.
Unpublished report: Johannesburg Kaffir Beer Research
Project, South African Council for Scientific and Industrial
Research, Pretoria, 54 pp., 1964.
South Africa - customs - functions - homebrew -
nutrition D-1582.

902. Nelson, Leonard
ALCOHOLISM IN ZUNI, NEW MEXICO.
Preventive Medicine, 6: 152-166, 1977.
United States - Native Americans - Zuni - change - customs -
dysfunctions - economics - family - prevention -
responsibility - treatment D-0748.

903. Netting, Robert McC.
BEER AS A LOCUS OF VALUE AMONG THE WEST AFRICAN KOFYAR.
American Anthropologist, 66: 375-384, 1964.
Nigeria - Kofyar - binge - change - economics - functions -
nutrition - ritual - social organization - sociocultural   D-0749.

904. Nicholson, G. Edward
CHICHA MAIZE TYPES AND CHICHA MANUFACTURE IN PERU.
Economic Botany, 14(4): 290-299, 1960.
Peru - homebrew - manufacture   D-0266.

905. Nickerson, Gifford
ALCOHOL AND NATIVE NORTH AMERICANS: A CROSS-DISCIPLINARY
BIBLIOGRAPHY OF RELEVANT STUDIES AND SOURCE MATERIALS.
Unpublished manuscript, 31 pp., 1977.
Native Americans - bibliography   D-1583.

906. Nida, Eugene A.
DRUNKENNESS IN INDIGENOUS RELIGIOUS RITES.
Practical Anthropology, 6: 20-23, 1959.
possession   D-0750.

907. Nightingale, K.W.
HEALTH PROBLEMS OF A SOUTH AFRICAN TRIBAL HOMELAND.
New Zealand Medical Journal, 85: 18-21, 1977.
South Africa - homebrew - nutrition - pathology   D-0751.

908. Niiniluoto, Yrjö
OM ENGELSMANNENS DRYCKESSEDER. [On English drinking customs.]
[Fin]
Alkoholpolitik, 17(1): 20-22, 1954.
England - customs - history, pre-1900 - literature   D-0045.

909. Nordland, O.
BREWING AND BEER TRADITION IN NORWAY: THE SOCIAL
ANTHROPOLOGICAL BACKGROUND OF THE BREWING INDUSTRY.
Oslo: Universitetsforlaget, 1970.
Norway - beer - customs - homebrew - manufacture   D-0418.

910. Nordland, O.
TRADITIONAL BEER IN SCANDINAVIA AND SOME REFLECTIONS
ON TASTE.
Ethnologia Scandinavica, 1: 166-171, 1971.
Scandinavia - beer - customs - homebrew - manufacture   D-1926.

911. Norelle Lickiss, F.
HEALTH PROBLEMS OF URBAN ABORIGINES: WITH SPECIAL
REFERENCE TO THE ABORIGINAL PEOPLE OF SYDNEY.
Social Science and Medicine, 9: 313-318, 1975.
Australia - Aborigines - acculturation - stress -
urbanization   D-0267.

912. Norick, Frank A.
ACCULTURATION AND DRINKING IN ALASKA.
Rehabilitation Record, 11(5): 13-17, 1970.
Eskimos - Native Americans - acculturation - aggression -
anomie - leisure - medical - norms - sex - stress -
youth   D-0752.

913. Norman, A.J.
ALCOHOL: ITS USE AND ABUSE AMONG TWO CULTURES IN
RHODESIA.
Central African Journal of Medicine, 20(2): 62-64,   1974.
Rhodesia   D-0753.

914. Novellie, L.
KAFFIR BEER BREWING: ANCIENT AND MODERN INDUSTRY.
Wallerstein Laboratory Communications, 31(104): 17-32, 1968.
South Africa - homebrew - manufacture   D-0268.

915. Obayemi, Ade M.U.
ALCOHOL USAGE IN AN AFRICAN SOCIETY.
In: Everett, Michael W.; Waddell, Jack O.; and Heath,
Dwight B., ed. Cross-cultural approaches to the study
of alcohol: An interdisciplinary perspective. The Hague:
Mouton, pp. 199-208,   1976.
Nigeria - Yoruba - customs - functions - sociocultural   D-0754.

916. O'Connor, Joyce
CULTURAL INFLUENCES AND DRINKING BEHAVIOUR: DRINKING IN
IRELAND AND ENGLAND: A TRI-ETHNIC STUDY OF DRINKING
AMONG YOUNG PEOPLE AND THEIR PARENTS.
Journal of Alcoholism, 10(3): 94-121,   1975.
Cross-national - England - Ireland - change - customs -
enculturation - norms - youth   D-0755.

917. O'Connor, Joyce
SOCIAL AND CULTURAL FACTORS INFLUENCING DRINKING BEHAVIOUR.
Irish Journal of Medical Science, (Supplement): 65-71, 1975.
review - sociocultural   D-0756.

918. Ogan, Eugene
DRINKING BEHAVIOR AND RACE RELATIONS.
American Anthropologist, 68: 181-187,   1966.
Melanesia - Nasioi - anomie - binge - change - class -
functions - prohibition - stereotype - youth   D-0757.

919. O'Meara, James E.
THE CONTROL OF LIQUOR TRAFFIC AMONG THE INDIANS OF NEW
FRANCE, AND THE WORK OF THE CHURCH IN SUPPRESSING IT.
M.A. Thesis, John Carroll University,   1933.
Canada - Native Americans - Church - economics - history,
pre-1900   D-0758.

920. Ossenberg, R.J.
SOCIAL CLASS AND BAR BEHAVIOR DURING AN URBAN FESTIVAL.
Human Organization, 28(1): 29-34, 1969.
Cross-ethnic - Canada - Native Americans - Whites - bar -
class - responsibility D-0759.

921. Otélé, Achille
LES BOISSONS FERMENTEES DE L'OUBANGUI-CHARI. [Fermented
beverages of the Ubangi-Chari.] [Fre]
Liaison, 67: 34-42, 1959.
Congo - Ubangi-Chari - homebrew - manufacture - nutrition D-0760.

922. Otsyula, Walter, and Aldo, P.
SOCIAL AND PSYCHIATRIC PROBLEMS CAUSED BY EXCESSIVE ALCOHOL
DRINKING IN KENYA.
In: The use and abuse of drugs and chemicals in tropical
Africa. Nairobi: East African Literature Bureau,
pp. 523-524, 1974.
Kenya - dysfunctions - epidemiology D-0278.

923. Pagés Larraya, Fernando
MODOS CULTURALES DEL BEBER EN LOS ABORIGINES DEL CHACO.
[Drinking patterns of the Indians of the Chaco.] [Spa]
Acta Psiquiátrica y Psicológica de América Latina,
22(1): 21-45, 1976.
Cross-ethnic - Chaco - Argentina - Bolivia - Paraguay -
acculturation - anomie - change - functions - history,
pre-1900 - possession - review D-0762.

924. Pan, Lynn
ALCOHOL IN COLONIAL AFRICA.
Helsinki: Finnish Foundation for Alcohol Studies, 121 pp., 1975.
Africa - cross-ethnic - economics - history, pre-1900 -
review - sociocultural D-0763.

925. Paredes, Alfonso; West, Louis Jolyon; and Snow, Clyde
Collins
BIOSOCIAL ADAPTATION AND CORRELATES OF ACCULTURATION IN
THE TARAHUMARA ECOSYSTEM.
International Journal of Social Psychiatry, 16: 163-174, 1970.
Mexico - Tarahumara - economics - social organization D-0765.

926. Paredes, Alfonso
SOCIAL CONTROL OF DRINKING AMONG THE AZTEC INDIANS OF
MESOAMERICA.
Quarterly Journal of Studies on Alcohol, 36(9): 1139-1153, 1975.
Mexico - Aztec - history, pre-1500 - norms - possession -
religion D-0764.

927. Parker, Douglas A., and Harman, Marsha S.
THE DISTRIBUTION OF CONSUMPTION MODEL OF PREVENTION OF
ALCOHOL PROBLEMS: A CRITICAL ASSESSMENT.
Journal of Studies on Alcohol, 39(3): 377-399, 1978.

120.

consumption - epidemiology - prevention - research methods - sociocultural
D-0236.

928. Parkin, David J.
PALMS, WINE, AND WITNESSES: PUBLIC SPIRIT AND PRIVATE GAIN IN AN AFRICAN FARMING COMMUNITY.
San Francisco, CA: Chandler, 1972.
Kenya - Giriama - change - economics - homebrew - ritual - social organization
D-0766.

929. Pascarosa, Paul, and Futterman, Sanford
ETHNOPSYCHEDELIC THERAPY FOR ALCOHOLICS: OBSERVATIONS ON THE PEYOTE RITUAL OF THE NATIVE AMERICAN CHURCH.
Journal of Psychedelic Drugs, 8(3): 215-221, 1976.
United States - Native Americans - Arapaho - Church - peyote - treatment
D-0046.

930. Pascarosa, Paul; Futterman, Sanford; and Halsweig, Mark
OBSERVATIONS OF ALCOHOLICS IN THE PEYOTE RITUAL: A PILOT STUDY.
Annals of the New York Academy of Sciences, 273: 518-524, 1976.
Native Americans - Church - peyote - treatment
D-0767.

931. Patnaik, Nityananda
OUTCASTING AMONG OILMEN FOR DRINKING WINE.
Man in India, 40: 1-7, 1960.
India - caste - norms - occupation - social organization
D-0768.

932. Patrick, Clarence H.
ALCOHOL, CULTURE AND SOCIETY.
Durham, NC: Duke University Press (Sociological Series No. 8), 176 pp., 1952.
World survey - review - sociocultural
D-0769.

933. Patton, William
BIBLE WINES: OR, THE LAWS OF FERMENTATION AND WINES OF THE ANCIENTS.
Little Rock, AR: Central Baptist Church Publications, 133 pp., 1872.
Near East - Biblical peoples - Classical peoples - history, pre-1500 - wine
D-0279.

934. Peeke, Hewson L.
AMERICAN EBRIETATIS: THE FAVORITE TIPPLE OF OUR FOREFATHERS AND THE LAWS AND CUSTOMS RELATING THERETO.
New York, NY: [no publisher], 1917.
United States - change - history, pre-1900
D-1183.

935. Pelto, Pertti J.
ALCOHOL USE IN SKOLT LAPP SOCIETY.
Unpublished paper: American Ethnological Society, Stanford, CA, 1960.
Finland - Lapps - aggression - functions - social organization
D-1584.

936.   Pendered, Arthur
       KUBIKA WAWA: BEER MAKING.
       Nada, 9: 30,   1931.
       Rhodesia - homebrew - manufacture   D-0770.

937.   Perisse, Julien; Adrian, Jean; Rerat, Alain; and
       Le Berre, Simone
       BILAN NUTRITIF DE LA TRANSFORMATION DU SORGHO EN BIERE:
       PREPARATION, COMPOSITION, CONSOMMATION D'UNE BIERE DU
       TOGO. [Nutritional loss in the transformation of sorghum
       to beer: Preparation, composition, and consumption of
       a Togo mead.] [Fre]
       Annales de la Nutrition et de L'Alimentation, 13: 1-15,   1959.
       Togo - Moba - economics - homebrew - manufacture   D-0771.

938.   Pertold, O.
       THE LITURGICAL USE OF MAHUDA LIQUOR BY BHILS.
       Archiv Orientálni, 3: 400-407,   1931.
       India - Bhils - Hinduism - folklore - manufacture -
       moonshine - ritual   D-0772.

939.   Peterson, William Jack
       THE CULTURE OF THE SKID ROW WINO.
       M.A. Thesis, State College of Washington,   1955.
       United States - customs - Skid Row - semantics - social
       organization - sociocultural   D-0280.

940.   Peterson, William Jack, and Maxwell, Milton
       THE SKID ROW "WINO".
       Social Problems, 5: 308-316,   1958.
       United States - Skid Row - class   D-0047.

941.   Pfautz, Harold W.
       THE IMAGE OF ALCOHOL IN POPULAR FICTION: 1900-1904 AND
       1946-1950.
       Quarterly Journal of Studies on Alcohol, 23(1): 131-146,   1962.
       United States - folklore - literature - norms   D-0048.

942.   Piga Pascual, Antonio
       INFLUENCIA DEL USO DE LAS BEBIDAS FERMENTADAS EN LA
       PRIMITIVA CIVILIZACION EGIPCIA. [Influence of the use
       of fermented beverages on primitive Egyptian civilization.]
       [Spa]
       Actas y Memorias de la Sociedad Española de Antropología,
       Etnografía, y Prehistoria, 17: 61-86,   1942.
       Egyptians, ancient - dysfunctions - history, pre-1500 -
       stress   D-0774.

943.   Piga Pascual, Antonio
       LA LUCHA ANTIALCOHOLICA DE LOS ESPANOLES EN LA EPOCA
       COLONIAL. [The anti-alcoholic struggle of the Spaniards
       in the colonial era.] [Spa]
       Revista de Indias, 3: 711-742,   1942.

Latin America - acculturation - Church - customs -
history, pre-1900 - temperance   D-0775.

944. Pilgrim, K.
UBER GETRANKE UND TRINKSITTEN IN DEN NIEDERLANDEN IM
WANDEL DER ZEITEN. [On drinks and drinking customs
in the Netherlands in changing times.] [Ger]
Jahrbuch der Gesellschaft für Geschichte und Bibliographie
des Brauwesens, (1966): 185-205,   1966.
Netherlands - change - consumption - customs - stress   D-1228.

945. Pinto, Leonard J.
ALCOHOL AND DRUG ABUSE AMONG NATIVE AMERICAN YOUTH ON
RESERVATIONS: A GROWING CRISIS.
In: National Commission on Marihuana and Drug Abuse.
Drug use in America: Problem in perspective - The
Technical Papers of the Second Report of the National
Commission on Marihuana and Drug Abuse. Appendix,
Volume I: Patterns and consequences of drug use.
Washington, D.C.: U.S. Government Printing Office,
pp. 1157-1178,   1973.
Native Americans - drugs - dysfunctions - functions -
review - stress - youth   D-1184.

946. Pitt, Peter
ALCOHOLISM IN NEPAL.
Journal of Alcoholism, 6: 15-19,   1971.
Nepal - aggression - homebrew - manufacture - medical -
pathology   D-0776.

947. Pittman, David J., and Snyder, Charles R., ed.
SOCIETY, CULTURE AND DRINKING PATTERNS.
New York, NY: John Wiley and Sons, 616 pp.,   1962.
review - sociocultural   D-0777.

948. Pittman, David J.
SOCIAL AND CULTURAL FACTORS IN DRINKING PATTERNS,
PATHOLOGICAL AND NONPATHOLOGICAL.
In: Selected Papers presented at the 27th International
Congress on Alcohol and Alcoholism, Volume 1: Alcohol as
a cultural question. Held September 6-12, 1964 in
Frankfurt-am-Main, West Germany. Lausanne: International
Council on Alcohol and Alcoholism, pp. 1-13,   1965.
World survey - functions - norms - review - sociocultural   D-1185.

949. Pittman, David J.
PART III. SOME SOCIO-CULTURAL ASPECTS OF ALCOHOLISM.
In: Pittman, David J., ed. Alcoholism. New York, NY:
Harper and Row, pp. 55-128,   1967.
review - sociocultural   D-1186.

950.   Pittman, David J.
        TRANSCULTURAL ASPECTS OF DRINKING AND DRUG USAGE.
        In: Kiloh, L.G., and Bell, D.S., ed. Proceedings of
        the 29th International Congress on Alcoholism and Drug
        Dependence. Held February, 1970 in Sydney, Australia.
        Australia: Butterworths, pp. 56-68,   1971.
        review - sociocultural   D-1187.

951.   Pittman, David J.
        CROSS-CULTURAL INFLUENCES ON IDEAS ABOUT ALCOHOL.
        In: Tongue, Archer, and Tongue, Eva, ed. Proceedings
        of the 30th International Congress on Alcoholism and Drug
        Dependence: Man and his mind-changers. Held September
        4-9, 1972 in Amsterdam. Lausanne: International Council
        on Alcohol and Addictions, pp. 67-73,   1972.
        review - sociocultural   D-1188.

952.   Pittman, David J.
        SOCIAL AND CULTURAL FACTORS IN ALCOHOL AND DRUG DEPENDENCY:
        AN INTERNATIONAL OVERVIEW.
        In: Blair, Brenda; Pawlak, Victor; Tongue, Eva; and
        Zwicky, Claude, ed. Proceedings of the 31st International
        Congress on Alcoholism and Drug Dependence, Volume 2,
        Part 1. Held February 23-28, 1975 in Bangkok, Thailand.
        Lausanne: International Council on Alcohol and Addictions,
        pp. 32-38,   1975.
        World survey - drugs - review - sociocultural   D-1189.

953.   Plant, Martin A.; Kreitman, Norman; Miller, Tiiu-Imbi;
        and Duffy, John
        OBSERVING PUBLIC DRINKING.
        Journal of Studies on Alcohol, 38: 867-880,   1977.
        Scotland - bar - research methods   D-0778.

954.   Platt, B.S.
        SOME TRADITIONAL ALCOHOLIC BEVERAGES AND THEIR IMPORTANCE
        IN INDIGENOUS AFRICAN COMMUNITIES.
        Proceedings of the Nutritional Society, 14: 115-124,   1955.
        South Africa - customs - economics - homebrew - manufacture -
        nutrition - social organization   D-0779.

955.   Plaut, Thomas F.A.
        ALCOHOL PROBLEMS: A REPORT TO THE NATION BY THE COOPERATIVE
        COMMISSION ON THE STUDY OF ALCOHOLISM.
        New York, NY: Oxford University Press, 200 pp.,   1967.
        United States - alcoholism - definition - dysfunctions -
        prevention - treatment   D-0780.

956.   Podlewski, Henry; and Catanzaro, Ronald J.
        TREATMENT OF ALCOHOLISM IN THE BAHAMA ISLANDS.
        In: Catanzaro, R.J., ed. Alcoholism: The total treatment
        approach. Springfield, IL: Charles C. Thomas, pp. 494-501, 1968.

West Indies - Bahama Islands - epidemiology - treatment   D-0781.

957.   Poikolainen, Kari
       FATAL ALCOHOL POISONINGS IN CULTURAL CONTEXT.
       Helsinki: Social Research Institute of Alcohol Studies
       (Report No. 86), 12 pp.,   1975.
       Cross-national - Denmark - Finland - Sweden - accidents -
       norms   D-0281.

958.   Poirier, Jean
       A. PRESENTATION D'UN PROGRAME DE RECHERCHE: ETHNOLOGIE
       ET SOCIOLOGIE DES ALCOOLISME A MADAGASCAR (1966-1969).
       B. RAPPORT PRELIMINAIRE SUR LA CONSOMMATION DE L'ALCOOL
       A MADAGASCAR. [A. Proposal for a research project:
       Ethnology and sociology of alcoholism in Madagascar (1966-
       1969). B. Preliminary report on the consumption of
       alcohol in Madagascar.] [Fre]
       Unpublished report: Centre International d'Alcoologie,
       Lausanne, 14 pp.,   1966.
       Cross-ethnic - Madagascar - Malagache - Overseas Chinese -
       Islam - Overseas Indians - acculturation - caste - change -
       economics - functions - dysfunctions - homebrew -
       responsibility - stress   D-1241.

959.   Poirier, Jean
       L'ALCOOLISME A MADAGASCAR: DONNEES STATISTIQUES ET
       PROBLEMES PSYCHOSOCIOLOGIQUES. [Alcoholism in Madagascar:
       Statistical data and psycho-sociological problems.] [Fre]
       Toxicomanies, 2: 57-77,   1969.
       Cross-ethnic - Madagascar - dysfunctions - epidemiology D-0782.

960.   Pollnac, Robert B., and Robbins, Michael C.
       GRATIFICATION PATTERNS AND MODERNIZATION IN RURAL BUGANDA.
       Human Organization, 31: 63-72,   1972.
       Uganda - Buganda - acculturation - change - functions   D-0783.

961.   Polovina, H.; Milaković, I.; and Resavac, S.
       THE DEEP PSYHOLOGICAL [SIC] BACKGROUND IN THE POEMS
       ABOUT ALCOHOLISM IN BOSNIA AND HERZEGOVINA.
       Alcoholism, 12(2): 141-143,   1976.
       Yugoslavia - Bosnia - Herzegovina - ambivalence - folklore -
       literature   D-0049.

962.   Poot, A.
       LE "MUNKOYO" BOISSON DES INDIGENES BAPENDE (KATANGA).
       ["Munkuyo" drink of the Bapende of Katanga.] [Fre]
       Bulletin des Séances de l'Institut Royal Colonial Belge,
       25: 386-389,   1954.
       Congo - Bapende - homebrew - manufacture - nutrition   D-0784.

963.   Popham, H.E.
       THE TAVERNS IN THE TOWN.
       London: Robert Hale, 221 pp.,   1937.

England - bar - functions - history, pre-1500 - history,
pre-1900 - social organization   D-0237.

964.   Popham, Robert E.
       SOME PROBLEMS OF ALCOHOL RESEARCH FROM A SOCIAL ANTHRO-
       POLOGIST'S POINT OF VIEW.
       Alcoholism, 6(2): 19-24,   1959.
       research methods - review - sociocultural   D-0785.

965.   Popham, Robert E.
       SOME SOCIAL AND CULTURAL ASPECTS OF ALCOHOLISM.
       Canadian Psychiatric Association Journal, 4: 222-229,   1959.
       definition - labeling - sociocultural   D-0786.

966.   Popham, Robert E.
       THE URBAN TAVERN: SOME PRELIMINARY REMARKS.
       Addictions, 9(2): 16-28,   1962.
       bar - functions   D-0787.

967.   Popham, R[obert] E., and Yawney, C.[D.]
       TRANSLATION OF "ON THE PRACTICE AND RITUAL OF BREWING
       AMONG THE AINU" BY I. KUBODERA.
       Toronto, Ont.: Addiction Research Foundation, Substudy
       No. 1-2 & Y-65 (217), 30 pp.,   1965.
       Japan - Ainu - homebrew - manufacture   D-0296.

968.   Popham, Robert E., and Yawney, Carole D.
       CULTURE AND ALCOHOL USE: A BIBLIOGRAPHY OF ANTHROPOLOGICAL
       STUDIES. (2nd ed.)
       Toronto, Ont.: Addiction Research Foundation (A.R.F.
       Bibliographic Series No. 1), 52 pp.,   1967.
       bibliography   D-0792.

969.   Popham, Robert E.
       THE PRACTICAL RELEVANCE OF TRANSCULTURAL STUDIES.
       Toronto, Ont.: Addiction Research Foundation, Substudy
       No. 9-2-70 (356), 5 pp.,   1970.
       sociocultural   D-1097.

970.   Popham, Robert E.
       AN EXAMPLE OF PSYCHOCULTURAL BARRIERS TO SUCCESSFUL THERAPY.
       Toronto, Ont.: Addiction Research Foundation, Substudy
       No. 756, 26 pp.,   1976.
       Canada - Native Americans - sociocultural - treatment   D-0788.

971.   Popham, Robert E., ed.
       JELLINEK WORKING PAPERS ON DRINKING PATTERNS AND ALCOHOL
       PROBLEMS.
       Toronto, Ont.: Addiction Research Foundation, Substudy
       No. 804, 208 pp.,   1976.
       Cross-national - sociocultural   D-0789.

Alcohol Use and World Cultures   Preller, A.C.N.

972. Popham, Robert E., ed.
      JELLINEK'S INTERNATIONAL SURVEY OF DRINKING CUSTOMS.
      Toronto, Ont.: Addiction Research Foundation, Substudy
      No. 805, 85 pp.,   1976.
      Cross-national - World survey - research methods -
      sociocultural   D-0791.

973. Popham, Robert E.
      WORKING PAPERS ON THE TAVERN, 1: SOCIAL HISTORY OF THE
      TAVERN.
      Toronto, Ont.: Addiction Research Foundation, Substudy
      No. 808, 66 pp.,   1976.
      World survey - bar - economics - history, pre-1500 -
      history, pre-1900 - political   D-0790.

974. Popham, Robert E.
      THE SOCIAL HISTORY OF THE TAVERN.
      In: Israel, Yedy; Glaser, Frederick B.; Kalant, Harold;
      Popham, Robert E.; Schmidt, Wolfgang; and Smart, Reginald
      E., ed. Research advances in alcohol and drug problems,
      Volume 4. New York, NY: Plenum, pp. 225-302,   1978.
      World survey - Cross-cultural - bar - customs - functions -
      history, pre-1500 - history, pre-1900 - political -
      prehistory - review - social organization - sociocultural D-0238.

975. Pozas Arciniegas, Ricardo
      EL ALCOHOLISMO Y LA ORGANIZACION SOCIAL. [Alcoholism
      and social organization.] [Spa]
      La Palabra y el Hombre, 1: 19-26,   1957.
      Mexico - Chamula - functions - medical - religion -
      ritual - social organization   D-0793.

976. Poznanski, Andrew
      OUR DRINKING HERITAGE.
      McGill Medical Journal, 25: 35-41,   1956.
      World survey - Biblical peoples - Classical peoples -
      history, pre-1500 - history, pre-1900 - medical   D-0794.

977. Prakash, Om
      FOOD AND DRINKS IN ANCIENT INDIA: FROM EARLIEST TIMES
      TO c. 1200 A.D.
      Delhi: Munshi Ram Manohar Lal, 341 pp.,   1961.
      India - Hinduism - history, pre-1500 - prehistory -
      review   D-0795.

978. Preller, A.C.N.
      DIE SENTRUMBEHANDELING VAN DIE ALKOHOLIS. THE PERSONALITY
      AND TREATMENT OF THE ALCOHOLIC IN SOUTH AFRICA: REPORT OF
      THE PROJECT ALCOHOLISM, VOLUME 6. [Afr]
      Pretoria: Department of Social Welfare and Pensions,
      Republic of South Africa,   1971.
      South Africa   D-1112.

979.   Prestan Simon, Arnulfo
        EL USO DE LA CHICHA Y LA SOCIEDAD KUNA. [The use of
        chicha in Cuna society.] [Spa]
        Mexico: Instituto Indigenista Interamericano (Edición
        Especial 72),   1975.
        Panama - Cuna - functions - homebrew - social organization
        - sociocultural   D-0796.

980.   Preuss, K. Th.
        DAS FEST DES ERWACHENS (WEINFEST) BEI DEN CORA-INDIANERN.
        [The Feast of Awakening (Winefestival) of the Cora
        Indians.] [Ger]
        In: Verhandlungen des XVI Internationalen Amerikanisten
        - Kongresses (bd.2). Wien: A. Hartleben, pp. 489-512,   1910.
        Mexico - Cora - folklore - music - religion - ritual   D-1098.

981.   Price, John A.
        AN APPLIED ANALYSIS OF NORTH AMERICAN INDIAN DRINKING
        PATTERNS.
        Human Organization, 34(1): 17-26,   1975.
        Native Americans - dysfunctions - norms - prevention -
        stress   D-0797.

982.   Price, John A.
        U.S. AND CANADIAN INDIAN URBAN ETHNIC INSTITUTIONS.
        Urban Anthropology, 4(1): 35-52,   1975.
        Cross-national - Canada - United States - Native Americans -
        bar - urbanization   D-0798.

983.   Prins, S.J.
        PASTORALE SORG AAN DIE ALKOHOLIS. THE PERSONALITY AND
        TREATMENT OF THE ALCOHOLIC IN SOUTH AFRICA: REPORT OF
        THE PROJECT ALCOHOLISM, VOLUME 12. [Afr]
        Pretoria: Department of Social Welfare and Pensions,
        Republic of South Africa,   1971.
        South Africa - dysfunctions - norms   D-1113.

984.   Quichaud, J.
        PROBLEMES MEDICO-SOCIAUX D'OUTRE-MER: L'ALCOOLISME EN
        GUINEE. [Medico-social problems overseas: Alcoholism
        in Guinea.] [Fre]
        Semaine Médicale Professionelle et Médico-Sociale,
        31: 574-575,   1955.
        Guinea - Islam - change   D-0799.

985.   Radke, G.
        GERSTENBRAU IN DER ANTIKE. [Barley-brewing in antiquity.]
        [Ger]
        Jahrbuch der Gesellschaft für Geschichte und Bibliographie
        des Brauwesens, (1963-1964): 26-45,   1963-1964.
        Near East - history, pre-1500 - homebrew - manufacture   D-1229.

986. Radović, Bosiljka
 PECHENJE RAJIJE V NASHEM NARODU. [Brandy distilling
 in our country.] [Ser-Cro]
 Glasnik Ethnograficheskog Muzea, 55: 69-112, 1937.
 Yugoslavia - Serbia - brandy - history, pre-1500 -
 history, pre-1900 - manufacture - moonshine D-1099.

987. Raman, A.C.
 CULTURAL FACTORS IN ALCOHOLISM.
 Unpublished paper: International Congress of Mental
 Health, London, 4 pp., 1968.
 Africa - Cross-ethnic - Hinduism - Islam - norms -
 psychiatric problems - religion D-1585.

988. Rao, Satyanarayana S.V.V., and Rao, C.R. Prasad
 DRINKING IN THE TRIBAL WORLD: A CROSS-CULTURAL STUDY
 IN "CULTURE THEME" APPROACH.
 Man in India, 57: 97-102, 1977.
 India - Cross-ethnic - attitudes - customs - norms -
 sociocultural D-0239.

989. Rasmussen, Christian
 DRINKING PATTERNS IN PEGUCHE (IMBABURA).
 In: Maynard, E.; Frøland, B.; and Rasmussen, C., ed.
 Drinking patterns in highland Ecuador. Ithaca, NY:
 Cornell University, 1965.
 Ecuador - Quechua - functions - ritual D-0800.

990. Ravi Varma, L.A.
 ALCOHOLISM IN AYURVEDA.
 Quarterly Journal of Studies on Alcohol, 11: 484-491, 1950.
 Indian - diagnosis - history, pre-1500 - medical D-0801.

991. Ray, Rai Bahadur Joges-Chandra
 HINDU METHOD OF MANUFACTURING SPIRIT FROM RICE.
 Journal of the Asiatic Society of Bengal (ns), 2(4): 1906.
 India - manufacture - moonshine D-1190.

992. Ray, Rai Bahadur Joges-Chandra
 FOOD AND DRINK IN ANCIENT INDIA.
 Man in India, 13(4): 217-239, 1933.
 India - history, pre-1500 - prehistory D-0050.

993. Ray, Rai Bahadur Joges-Chandra
 FOOD AND DRINK IN ANCIENT INDIA.
 Man in India, 14(1): 15-37, 1933.
 India - history, pre-1500 - prehistory D-0502.

994. Raymond, Irving W.
 THE TEACHING OF THE EARLY CHURCH ON THE USE OF WINE
 AND STRONG DRINK.
 New York, NY: Columbia University (Studies in History,
 Economics, and Public Law 286), 1927.

	Cross-national - Church - history, pre-1500 - norms - religion	D-1191.
995.	Reader, D.H. ALCOHOLISM AND EXCESSIVE DRINKING: A SOCIOLOGICAL REVIEW. Johannesburg: National Institute for Personnel Research (Psychologia Africana Monograph, Supplement 3), 69 pp., World survey - alcoholism - ambivalence - definition - functions - review - sociocultural	1967. D-1192.
996.	Reader, D.H., and May, Joan DRINKING PATTERNS IN RHODESIA: HIGHFIELD AFRICAN TOWNSHIP, SALISBURY. Unpublished paper: University of Rhodesia, Department of Sociology (Occasional Paper No. 5), Salisbury, Rhodesia - customs - functions - urbanization	1971. D-1586.
997.	Redding, Cyrus A HISTORY AND DESCRIPTION OF MODERN WINES. (3rd ed.) London: Henry G. Bohn, World survey - history, pre-1500 - history, pre-1900 - manufacture - wine	1860. D-0802.
998.	Reed, R.E. THE PROBLEM OF ADDICTIVE DRINKING, 1: BEVERAGE ALCOHOL IN SIMPLE AND COMPLEX SOCIETIES. North Carolina Medical Journal, 14: 101-105, Cross-ethnic - sociocultural	1953. D-0803.
999.	Reed, T. Edward; Kalant, Harold; and Gibbins, Robert J. ETHNIC AND SEX DIFFERENCES IN RESPONSES TO ALCOHOL. Behavioral Genetics, 3: 413, Cross-ethnic - Objibwa - Orientals - Whites - metabolism - "race"	1973. D-0806.
1000.	Reed, T. Edward; Kalant, Harold; Gibbins, Robert J.; Kapur, Bushan M.; and Rankin, James G. ALCOHOL AND ACETALDEHYDE METABOLISM IN CAUCASIANS, CHINESE AND AMERINDS. Canadian Medical Association Journal, 115: 851-855, Cross-ethnic - Ojibwa - Orientals - Whites - metabolism - "race"	1976. D-0807.
1001.	Reed, T. E[dward], and Kalant, Harold METABOLISM OF ETHANOL IN DIFFERENT RACIAL GROUPS. Canadian Medical Association Journal, 116: 476, metabolism - "race" - research methods - review	1977. D-0805.
1002.	Reed, T. Edward RACIAL COMPARISONS OF ALCOHOL METABOLISM: BACKGROUND, PROBLEMS AND RESULTS. Alcoholism: Clinical and Experimental Research, 2: 83-88, metabolism - "race" - research methods - review	1978. D-0804.

130.

1003.   Regier, M.C.
        THE DETOXIFICATION OF SKID ROW: A FIELD INVESTIGATION
        INTO THE IMPLEMENTATION OF THE UNIFORM ALCOHOLISM AND
        INTOXICATION TREATMENT ACT.
        Ph.D. Dissertation, Brandeis University,   1977.
        United States - Skid Row - change   D-0808.

1004.   Reiche C., Carlos Enrique
        ESTUDIO SOBRE EL PATRON DE EMBRIAGUEZ EN LA REGION RURAL
        ALTAVERAPACENSE. [Study of patterned drunkenness in
        the rural region of Alto Verapaz.] [Spa]
        Guatemala Indígena, 5: 103-127,   1970.
        Guatemala - functions - responsibility   D-0809.

1005.   Reid, John B.
        STUDY OF DRINKING IN NATURAL SETTINGS.
        In: Marlatt, G. Alan, and Nathan, Peter E., ed.
        Behavioral approaches to alcoholism. New Brunswick,
        NJ: Rutgers Center of Alcohol Studies, pp. 58-76,   1978.
        research methods - review   D-0240.

1006.   Reid, J.C., and Mununggurr, D.
        WE ARE LOSING OUR BROTHERS: SORCERY AND ALCOHOL IN
        AN ABORIGINAL COMMUNITY.
        Medical Journal of Australia (Special Supplement, 2):
        1-5,   1977.
        Australia - Aborigines - bar - change - norms -
        sociocultural   D-0051.

1007.   Reilly, C., and McGlashan, N.D.
        ZINC AND COPPER CONTAMINATION IN ZAMBIAN ALCOHOLIC
        DRINKS.
        South African Journal of Medical Sciences, 34: 43-48,   1969.
        Zambia - containers - homebrew - manufacture - moonshine -
        sociocultural   D-0052.

1008.   Reilly, Joseph
        THE AMERICAN BAR AND THE IRISH PUB: A STUDY OF
        COMPARISONS AND CONTROLS.
        Journal of Popular Culture, 2: 571-578,   1977.
        Cross-national - Ireland - United States - bar   D-0810.

1009.   Reuband, Karl-Heinz
        THE PATHOLOGICAL AND THE SUBCULTURAL MODEL OF DRUG USE
        - A TEST OF TWO CONTRASTING EXPLANATIONS.
        In: Madden, J.S.; Walker, Robin; and Kenyon, W.H., ed.
        Alcoholism and drug dependence: A multidisciplinary
        approach. New York, NY: Plenum, pp. 151-169,   1977.
        enculturation - sociocultural   D-0811.

1010.   Rhuneaud, G.
        SPRACHLICHES VOM BIER. [Sayings about beer.] [Ger]
        Jahrbuch der Gesellschaft für Geschichte und Bibliographie
        des Brauwesens, (1965): 169-197,   1965.
        Germany - beer - folklore - homebrew - language   D-1230.

1011.   Ribstein, M.; Certhoux, A.; and Lavenaire, A.
        ALCOOLISME AU RHUM: ETUDE DE LA SYMPTOMATOLOGIE ET
        ANALYSE DE LA PERSONALITE DE L'HOMME MARTINIQUAIS
        ALCOOLIQUE AU RHUM. [Rum-alcoholism: Study of the
        symptomatology and personality analysis of the male
        rum-alcoholic in Martinique.] [Fre]
        Annales Médico-Psychologiques, 125: 537-548,   1967.
        West Indies - Martinique - functions - psychiatric
        problems   D-0812.

1012.   Richard-Molard, J.
        LE PROGRES DE L'ALCOOLISME EN AFRIQUE NOIRE FRANCAISE.
        [The spread of alcoholism in French Black Africa.] [Fre]
        Bulletin de l'Institute Français d'Afrique Noire,
        12: 841-844,   1950.
        Africa - dysfunctions - prohibition   D-0053.

1013.   Richard[-Molard, J.]
        L'ALCOOLISME DANS QUELQUES TERRITOIRES DU CONTINENT
        AFRICAIN. [Alcoholism in some territories of the African
        continent.] [Fre]
        Bulletin de l'Academie Nationale de Médicine,
        139: 124-126,   1955.
        Africa - dysfunctions - stereotype - temperance   D-0282.

1014.   Richards, Cara E.
        CITY TAVERNS.
        Human Organization, 22: 260-268,   1964.
        United States - bar - functions   D-0813.

1015.   Riches, D.
        ALCOHOL ABUSE AND THE PROBLEMS OF SOCIAL CONTROL IN A
        MODERN ESKIMO SETTLEMENT.
        In: Holý, Ladislav, ed. Knowledge and behaviour.
        Belfast: Queen's University (Papers in Social Anthropology
        1),   1976.
        Canada - Eskimos - acculturation - norms - stress   D-1193.

1016.   Riffenburgh, Arthur S.
        CULTURAL INFLUENCES AND CRIME AMONG INDIAN-AMERICANS OF
        THE SOUTHWEST.
        Federal Probation, 28(3): 38-46,   1964.
        Native Americans - change - crime   D-0814.

132.

1017. Rip, C.M.
SOCIOLOGICAL ASPECTS: THE ALCOHOLIC IN THE FAMILY OF PROCREATION. THE PERSONALITY AND TREATMENT OF THE ALCOHOLIC IN SOUTH AFRICA: REPORT OF THE PROJECT ALCOHOLISM, VOLUME 2.
Pretoria: Department of Social Welfare and Pensions, Republic of South Africa, 1971.
South Africa - enculturation - family   D-1114.

1018. Robbins, Michael C., and Pollnac, Richard B.
DRINKING PATTERNS AND ACCULTURATION IN RURAL BUGANDA.
American Anthropologist, 71: 276-284, 1969.
Uganda - Buganda - acculturation - change - homebrew - research methods - sociocultural   D-0817.

1019. Robbins, Michael C.
PROBLEM-DRINKING AND THE INTEGRATION OF ALCOHOL IN RURAL BUGANDA.
Medical Anthropology, 1(3): 1-24, 1977.
Uganda - Buganda - functions - homebrew - moonshine - nutrition - social organization - sociocultural   D-0816.

1020. Robbins, Richard H.
ROLE REINFORCEMENT AND RITUAL DEPRIVATION: DRINKING BEHAVIOR IN A NASKAPI VILLAGE.
Papers on the Social Sciences, 1: 1-7, 1969.
Canada - Native Americans - Naskapi - functions - intoxication - responsibility - social organization   D-0818.

1021. Robbins, Richard H.
DRINKING BEHAVIOR AND IDENTITY RESOLUTION.
Ph.D. Dissertation, University of North Carolina (Chapel Hill), 1970.
Canada - Native Americans - Naskapi - acculturation - economics - self - social organization   D-0819.

1022. Robbins, Richard H.
ALCOHOL AND THE IDENTITY STRUGGLE: SOME EFFECTS OF ECONOMIC CHANGE ON INTERPERSONAL RELATIONS.
American Anthropologist, 75: 99-122, 1973.
Canada - Native Americans - Naskapi - acculturation - economics - self - social organization   D-0820.

1023. Robinson, David
FROM DRINKING TO ALCOHOLISM: A SOCIOLOGICAL COMMENTARY.
New York, NY: John Wiley and Sons, 211 pp., 1976.
England - diagnosis - dysfunctions - sociocultural   D-0821.

1024. Roca W., Demetrio
APUNTES SOBRE LA CHICHA. [Notes on chicha.] [Spa]
La Verdad, 42(2004): 3, 1953.
Peru - homebrew   D-0822.

1025.   Rodríguez Sandoval, Leonidas
        DRINKING MOTIVATIONS AMONG THE INDIANS OF THE ECUADOREAN
        SIERRA.
        Primitive Man, 18: 39-46,   1945.
        Ecuador - Quechua - economics - functions - homebrew -
        medical - power - ritual - social organization   D-0823.

1026.   Roebuck, Julian B., and Spray, S. Lee
        THE COCKTAIL LOUNGE: A STUDY OF HETEROSEXUAL RELATIONS
        IN A PUBLIC ORGANIZATION.
        American Journal of Sociology, 72: 386-396,   1967.
        United States - bar - class - sex   D-0826.

1027.   Roebuck, Julian B., and Frese, Wolfgang
        THE AFTER-HOURS CLUB: AN ILLEGAL SOCIAL ORGANIZATION
        AND ITS CLIENT SYSTEM.
        Urban Life, 5(2): 131-164,   1976.
        United States - bar - functions - social organization D-0824.

1028.   Roebuck, Julian B., and Frese, Wolfgang
        THE RENDEZVOUS: A CASE STUDY OF AN AFTER-HOURS CLUB.
        New York, NY: Free Press, 278 pp.,   1976.
        United States - bar - functions - social organization -
        space   D-0825.

1029.   Rohner, R.P., and Rohner, E.C.
        DRINKING AND SOCIAL INTERACTION.
        In: Rohner, R.P., and Rohner, E.C., ed. The Kwakiutl
        Indians of British Columbia. New York, NY: Holt, Rinehart
        and Winston, pp. 46-52,   1970.
        Canada - Native Americans - Kwakiutl - economics -
        functions - social organization - sociocultural   D-0827.

1030.   Rohrmann, Charles A.
        DRINKING AND VIOLENCE: A CROSS CULTURAL SURVEY.
        Unpublished manuscript, 15 pp.,   (ca. 1972).
        World survey - Cross-cultural - aggression - sociocultural -
        stress   D-1587.

1031.   Rojas, Ulises
        LA LUCHA CONTRA LAS BEBIDAS ALCOHOLICAS EN LA EPOCA DE
        LA COLONIA. [The fight against alcoholic beverages in
        the colonial period.] [Spa]
        Repertorio Boyacense, 46: 877,   1960.
        Latin America - Church - history, pre-1900 - prohibition D-0829.

1032.   Rojas González, Francisco
        ESTUDIO HISTORICO-ETNOGRAFICO DEL ALCOHOLISMO ENTRE LOS
        INDIOS DE MEXICO. [Ethnohistoric study of alcohol among
        the Indians of Mexico.] [Spa]
        Revista Mexicana de Sociología, 4: 111-125,   1942.
        Mexico - acculturation - anomie - change - history, pre-1500
        - history, pre-1900 - prehistory   D-0055.

134.

1033. Rojas-Mackenzie, R., and Rios-Osorio, J. de los
HABITOS DE INGESTION DE BEBIDAS ALCOHOLICAS EN UNA
COMUNIDAD RURAL DE ANTIOQUIA, COLOMBIA. [Drinking
patterns in a rural community of Antioquia, Colombia.]
[Spa]
Boletín de la Oficina Sanitaria Panamericana,
83: 148-162, 1977.
Colombia - customs - functions - social organization D-0830.

1034. Rolleston, J.D.
ALCOHOLISM IN CLASSICAL ANTIQUITY.
British Journal of Inebriety, 24: 101-120, 1927.
Europe - Classical peoples - Greeks, ancient - Romans,
ancient - history, pre-1500 - medical - religion D-0832.

1035. Rolleston, J.D.
ALCOHOLISM IN MEDIAEVAL ENGLAND.
British Journal of Inebriety, 31: 33-49, 1933.
England - history, pre-1500 D-0831.

1036. Rolleston, J.D.
THE FOLKLORE OF ALCOHOLISM.
British Journal of Inebriety, 39: 30-36, 1941.
Europe - folklore - treatment A-2213.

1037. Room, Robin
CULTURAL CONTINGENCIES OF ALCOHOLISM: VARIATIONS
BETWEEN AND WITHIN NINETEENTH-CENTURY URBAN ETHNIC
GROUPS IN ALCOHOL-RELATED DEATH RATES.
Journal of Health and Social Behavior, 9: 99-113, 1968.
United States - Cross-ethnic - Irish-Americans -
Italian-Americans - Jews - epidemiology - history, pre-1900
- pathology - social organization D-0833.

1038. Room, Robin
A LIST OF REFERENCES ON CROSS-NATIONAL AND CROSS-CULTURAL
STUDIES WITH STATISTICAL DATA.
Unpublished report: University of California, Social
Research Group, Berkeley, 1971.
World survey - Cross-cultural - Cross-national -
bibliography D-0283.

1039. Room, Robin
NOTES ON TAVERNS AND SOCIABILITY.
Unpublished paper: Social Research Group Working
Paper F25, University of California, Berkeley, 37 pp., 1972.
bar - functions D-1588.

1040. Room, Robin
SOME PROPOSITIONS ON THE ANALYSIS OF CROSS-CULTURAL DATA
ON ALCOHOL.
Drinking and Drug Practices Surveyor, 6: 2 ff, 1972.
Cross-ethnic - research methods D-0834.

1041. Room, Robin
NORMATIVE PERSPECTIVES ON ALCOHOL USE AND PROBLEMS.
Journal of Drug Issues, 5: 358-368, 1975.
United States - norms D-0835.

1042. Room, Robin
AMBIVALENCE AS A SOCIOLOGICAL EXPLANATION: THE CASE OF
CULTURAL EXPLANATIONS OF ALCOHOL PROBLEMS.
American Sociological Review, 41: 1047-1065, 1976.
ambivalence - norms - sociocultural D-0836.

1043. Room, Robin
A NOTE ON OBSERVATIONAL STUDIES OF DRINKING AND COMMUNITY
RESPONSE.
Drinking and Drug Practices Surveyor, 13: 17-22, 1977.
research methods D-0837.

1044. Rooney, James F.
GROUP PROCESSES AMONG SKID ROW WINOS: A RE-EVALUATION OF
THE UNDERSOCIALIZATION HYPOTHESIS.
Quarterly Journal of Studies on Alcohol, 22: 444-460, 1961.
United States - Skid Row - economics - functions -
social organization D-0056.

1045. Rorabaugh, W.J.
THE ALCOHOLIC REPUBLIC: AMERICA, 1790-1840.
Ph.D. Dissertation, University of California (Berkeley), 1976.
United States - change - history, pre-1900 D-0838.

1046. Roth, Walter E.
ON THE NATIVE DRINKS OF THE GUIANESE INDIAN.
Timehri Demerara (series 3), 2: 128-134, 1912.
Guiana - homebrew - manufacture D-0839.

1047. Rotman, Arthur E.
NAVAHO INDIAN PROBLEM DRINKING: AN ANALYSIS OF FIVE
LIFE-HISTORIES.
M.A. Thesis, California State University (San Francisco), 1969.
United States - Native Americans - Navaho - phases D-0840.

1048. Rotter, H.
DIE BEDEUTUNG DES ALKOHOLISCHEN MILIEUS FUR DEN ALKOHOLISMUS.
[The significance of the drinking milieu in alcoholism.]
[Ger]
Wiener Medizinische Wochenschrift, 107: 236-239, 1957.
norms D-0841.

1049. Roueché, Berton
I. THE CHRISTIAN DIVERSION.
In: Roueché, Berton. The neutral spirit: A portrait
of alcohol. Boston, MA: Little, Brown, pp. 3-43, 1960.
World survey - history, pre-1500 - history, pre-1900 -
prehistory D-0842.

1050.   Roueché, Berton
        ALCOHOL IN HUMAN CULTURE.
        In: Lucia, Salvatore Pablo, ed. Alcohol and
        civilization. New York, NY: McGraw-Hill, pp. 167-182,   1963.
        review - sociocultural   D-0057.

1051.   Roueché, Berton
        CULTURAL FACTORS AND DRINKING PATTERNS.
        Annals of the New York Academy of Sciences,
        133: 846-855,   1966.
        World survey - history, pre-1500 - history, pre-1900 -
        prehistory   D-0843.

1052.   Roufs, Timothy G., and Bregenzer, John M.
        SOME ASPECTS OF THE PRODUCTION OF PULQUE.
        In: Miller, Frank, and Pelto, Pertti, ed. Social and
        cultural aspects of modernization in Mexico. Minneapolis,
        MN: University of Minnesota (Department of Anthropology), 1968.
        Mexico - economics - homebrew - manufacture   D-0844.

1053.   Rubington, Earl
        THE BOTTLE GANG.
        Quarterly Journal of Studies on Alcohol, 29: 943-955,   1968.
        United States - Skid Row - economics - social
        organization   D-0845.

1054.   Rubington, Earl
        THE LANGUAGE OF "DRUNKS".
        Quarterly Journal of Studies on Alcohol, 32: 721-740,   1971.
        United States - Skid Row - research methods - semantics   D-0846.

1055.   Rubington, Earl
        VARIATIONS IN BOTTLE-GANG CONTROLS.
        In: Rubington, Earl, and Weinberg, Martin S., ed.
        Deviance, the interactionist perspective: Text and
        readings in the sociology of deviance. (2nd ed.)
        New York, NY: Macmillan, pp. 338-347,   1973.
        United States - Skid Row - norms - social organization   D-0847.

1056.   Rudas, N., and Mulas, L.
        ASPETTI SOCIO CULTURALI E DINAMICA MOTIVAZIONALE IN
        UN GRUPPO DE ETILISTI SARDI. [Sociocultural aspects
        and motivational dynamics in a group of Sardinian
        alcoholics.] [Ita]
        Acta Neurologica, 20: 56-59,   1965.
        Italy - norms - sociocultural   D-0058.

1057.   Rüden, E.
        DER ALKOHOL IN LEBENSPROZESS DER RASSE. [Alcohol in
        the life-process of the race.] [Ger]
        Internationale Monatsschrift zur Erforschung des
        Alkoholismus und Bekämpfung der Trinksitten, 13: 374-379, 1903.
        "race"   D-0848.

1058. Rühmland, R., and Rühmland, U.
       ESSEN UND TRINKEN IN DEUTSCHEN LANDEN. [Food and drink
       in German areas.] [Ger]
       Bonn: Grenzland, 1969.
       Germany - customs - history, pre-1500 - history, pre-1900   D-0419.

1059. Ruiz Moreno, Aníbal
       LA LUCHA ANTIALCOHOLICA DE LOS JESUITAS EN LA EPOCA
       COLONIAL. [The anti-alcoholic struggle of the Jesuits
       in the colonial era.] [Spa]
       Estudios, 62: 339-352, and 423-446, 1939.
       Paraguay - acculturation - change - Church - dysfunctions -
       history, pre-1900 - homebrew - temperance   D-0849.

1060. Sadler, Patricia
       THE "CRISIS CULT" AS A VOLUNTARY ASSOCIATION: AN
       INTERACTIONAL APPROACH TO ALCOHOLICS ANONYMOUS.
       Human Organization, 36(2): 207-210, 1977.
       Alcoholics Anonymous - conversion - social organization   D-0850.

1061. Sadoun, Roland; Lolli, Giorgio; and Silverman, Milton
       DRINKING IN FRENCH CULTURE.
       New Brunswick, NJ: Rutgers Center of Alcohol Studies
       (Monograph 5), 133 pp., 1965.
       France - customs - enculturation - functions - liver -
       social organization   D-0851.

1062. Saint, Eric G.
       BACCHUS TRANSPORTED: PURPORTING TO BE AN HISTORICAL
       IMPRESSION OF ALCOHOLISM IN AUSTRALIA.
       Medical Journal of Australia, 2: 548-551, 1970.
       Australia - customs - history, pre-1900   D-0852.

1063. Salo, Kalle
       "HAVE A DRINK..." - ENGELSKA ALKOHOLVANOR. ["Have a
       drink..." - English drinking customs.] [Fin]
       Alkoholpolitik, 25(4): 167-169, 1962.
       England - bar - customs   D-0059.

1064. Salone, Emile
       LES SAUVAGES DU CANADA ET LES MALADIES IMPORTEES DE
       FRANCE AU XVIIe ET AU XVIIIe SIECLE: LA PICOTE ET
       L'ALCOOLISME. [The natives of Canada and the diseases
       imported from France in the 17th and 18th centuries:
       Smallpox and alcoholism.] [Fre]
       Journal de la Société des Américanistes de Paris (ns):
       4: 7-20, 1907.
       Canada - Native Americans - acculturation - change -
       history, pre-1900   D-0853.

1065. Salonen, Armas
       KORANEN OCH RUSDRYCKERNA. [Intoxicating beverages in
       the Koran.] [Fin]

	Alkoholpolitik, 20(3): 81-83, Islam - economics - history, pre-1500 - prohibition - religion - wine	1957. D-0060.
1066.	Salonen, Armas DRYCKESSEDER FORE OCH EFTER MUHAMMED. [Drinking customs before and after Mohammed.] [Fin] Alkoholpolitik, 21: 50-52, Near East - Biblical peoples - Islam - change - customs - fighting - gambling - literature - prohibition - sex - wine	1958. D-0854.
1067.	Sams, G. Kenneth BEER IN THE CITY OF MIDAS. Archaeology, 30(2): 108-115, Near East - homebrew - prehistory	1977. D-0855.
1068.	Samuelson, James THE HISTORY OF DRINK: A REVIEW, SOCIAL, SCIENTIFIC AND POLITICAL. London: Trübner, World survey - change - customs - economics - history, pre-1500 - history, pre-1900 - manufacture - political	1878. D-0285.
1069.	Sangree, Walter H. THE SOCIAL FUNCTIONS OF BEER DRINKING IN BANTU TIRIKI. In: Pittman, David J., and Snyder, Charles R., ed. Society, culture, and drinking patterns. New York, NY: John Wiley and Sons, pp. 6-21, South Africa - Tiriki - change - customs - elderly - functions - homebrew - religion - ritual - social organization - sociocultural	1962. D-0856.
1070.	Sapper, Karl SPEISE UND TRANK DER KEKCHI-INDIANER. [Food and drink of the Kekchi Indians.] [Ger] Globus, 80: 259-263, Guatemala - Kekchi - homebrew	1901. D-0857.
1071.	Sargent, Margaret J. CHANGES IN JAPANESE DRINKING PATTERNS. Quarterly Journal of Studies on Alcohol, 28: 709-722, Japan - ambivalence - change - functions - ritual - social organization - stress	1967. D-0858.
1072.	Sargent, Margaret J. A CROSS-CULTURAL STUDY OF ATTITUDES AND BEHAVIOUR TOWARDS ALCOHOL AND DRUGS. British Journal of Sociology, 22: 83-96, Cross-ethnic - Australia - Japan - Jews - Overseas Chinese - attitudes - customs - drugs - functions - norms	1971. D-0859.

1073.   Sargent, Margaret J.
        THEORY IN ALCOHOL STUDIES.
        In: Everett, Michael W.; Waddell, Jack O.; and Heath,
        Dwight B., ed. Cross-cultural approaches to the study
        of alcohol: An interdisciplinary perspective. The Hague:
        Mouton, pp. 341-352,   1976.
        attitudes - research methods - review   D-0860.

1074.   Sariola, Sakari
        LAPPI JA VAKIJUOMAT. [Lapland and liquor.] [Fin]
        Helsinki: Väkijuomakysymyksen Tutkimussäätiö,   1954.
        Finland - Lapps - binge - customs - social organization   D-0503.

1075.   Sariola, Sakari
        DRINKING PATTERNS IN FINNISH LAPLAND.
        Helsinki: Finnish Foundation for Alcohol Studies, 88 pp.,   1956.
        Finland - Lapps - binge - customs - social organization   D-0286.

1076.   Sariola, Sakari
        INDIANER OCH ALKOHOL. [Indians and alcohol.] [Fin]
        Alkoholpolitik, 19: 39-43,   1956.
        Bolivia - binge - customs - possession - religion -
        social organization - stress   D-0861.

1077.   Sariola, Sakari
        [DRINKING CUSTOMS IN RURAL COLOMBIA.]
        Alkoholpolitik, 24: 162-166,   1961.
        Colombia - Mestizos - economics - homebrew - murder   D-0862.

1078.   Sasaki, T.
        RESEARCH ON BANSHAKU: A CHARACTERISTIC DRINKING CUSTOM
        OF JAPAN.
        Japanese Journal of Studies on Alcohol, 12: 67-79,   1977.
        Japan - ritual   D-0863.

1079.   Savard, Robert J.
        CULTURAL STRESS AND ALCOHOLISM: A STUDY OF THEIR
        RELATIONSHIP AMONG NAVAJO ALCOHOLIC MEN.
        Ph.D. Dissertation, University of Minnesota,   1968.
        Native Americans - Navaho - aggression - customs -
        prohibition - stress   D-0864.

1080.   Savard, Robert J.
        EFFECTS OF DISULFIRAM THERAPY ON RELATIONSHIPS WITHIN
        THE NAVAJO DRINKING GROUP.
        Quarterly Journal of Studies on Alcohol, 29: 909-916,   1968.
        Native Americans - Navaho - disulfiram - social
        organization - treatment   B-3899.

1081.   Savishinsky, Joel S.
        MOBILITY AS AN ASPECT OF STRESS IN AN ARCTIC COMMUNITY.
        American Anthropologist, 73(3): 604-618,   1971.

Native Americans - Hare - acculturation - binge - functions - leisure - social organization - stress D-0865.

1082. Savishinsky, Joel S.
A THEMATIC ANALYSIS OF DRINKING BEHAVIOR IN A HARE INDIAN COMMUNITY.
Papers in Anthropology, 18(2): 43-59, 1977.
Native Americans - Hare - acculturation - functions - norms - stress D-0866.

1083. Sayres, William C.
RITUAL DRINKING, ETHNIC STATUS AND INEBRIETY IN RURAL COLOMBIA.
Quarterly Journal of Studies on Alcohol, 17: 53-62, 1956.
Colombia - Cross-ethnic - Mestizos - Quechua - customs - functions - medical - religion - ritual - social organization - sociocultural - stress D-0867.

1084. Schaefer, James M.
DRUNKENNESS AND CULTURE STRESS: A HOLOCULTURAL TEST.
In: Everett, Michael W.; Waddell, Jack O.; and Heath, Dwight B., ed. <u>Cross-cultural approaches to the study of alcohol: An interdisciplinary perspective</u>. The Hague: Mouton, pp. 287-321, 1976.
World survey - Cross-cultural - research methods - stress D-0868.

1085. Schaefer, James M.
ALCOHOL METABOLISM AND SENSITIVITY REACTIONS AMONG THE REDDIS OF SOUTH INDIA.
Alcoholism: Clinical and Experimental Research, 2: 61-70, 1978.
India - Reddi - metabolism - "race" D-0869.

1086. Scheper-Hughes, Nancy
<u>INHERITANCE OF THE MEEK: ANOMIC THEMES IN RURAL IRELAND</u>.
Ph.D. Dissertation, University of California (Berkeley), 1976.
Ireland - anomie - psychiatric problems - social organization D-0870.

1087. Schmidt, Wolfgang, and Popham, Robert E.
<u>SOME HYPOTHESES AND PRELIMINARY OBSERVATIONS CONCERNING ALCOHOLISM AMONG JEWS</u>.
Toronto, Ont.: Addiction Research Foundation, Substudy No. 114, 10 pp., 1961.
Canada - Jews D-0871.

1088. Schmidt, Wolfgang, and Popham, Robert E.
IMPRESSIONS OF JEWISH ALCOHOLICS.
Journal of Studies on Alcohol, 37(7): 931-939, 1976.
Canada - Jews D-0872.

1089. Schmidt, Wolfgang, and Popham, Robert E.
       THE SINGLE DISTRIBUTION THEORY OF ALCOHOL CONSUMPTION:
       A REJOINDER TO THE CRITIQUE OF PARKER AND HARMAN.
       Journal of Studies on Alcohol, 39(3): 400-419,   1978.
       consumption - epidemiology - prevention - research
       methods   D-0241.

1090. Schmitt, N.; Hole, L.W.; and Barclay, W.S.
       ACCIDENTAL DEATHS AMONG BRITISH COLUMBIA INDIANS.
       Canadian Medical Association Journal, 94(5): 228-234,   1966.
       Canada - Native Americans - accidents - binge   D-0061.

1091. Schmitthenner, E., and Schmitthenner, H.
       SPEISE UND TRANK IN EUROPA. [Food and drink in Europe.]
       [Ger]
       Wissenschaftliche Veröffentlichungen des Deutschen
       Institut für Länderkunde, 17-18: 109-166,   1959.
       Europe - customs   D-1124.

1092. Schreiber, Georg
       DER WEIN UND DIE VOLKSTUMSFORSCHUNG: ZUR SAKRALKULTUR
       UND ZUM GENOSSENRECHT. [Wine and folklore research:
       Contributions to the understanding of religious culture.]
       [Ger]
       Rheinisches Jahrbuch für Volkskunde, 9: 207-243,   1958.
       Germany - customs - folklore - history, pre-1500 -
       history, pre-1900 - norms - religion - wine   D-0873.

1093. Schreiber, G.
       DER WEIN ALS HEILTRANK: ZUR VOLKSKUNDE, MEDIZINGESCHICHTE,
       KULTURGESCHICHTE. [Wine as a healing beverage: Folklore,
       medical history, and cultural history.] [Ger]
       Rheinisch-Westfälische Zeitschrift für Volkskunde,
       9: 39-55,   1962.
       Germany - customs - folklore - history, pre-1500 -
       history, pre-1900 - medical - wine   D-1125.

1094. Schultze, Rudolf
       GESCHICHTE DES WEINES UND DER TRINKGELAGE. [History of
       wines and drinking bouts.] [Ger]
       Berlin: Nicolai,   1867.
       Europe - binge - history, pre-1500 - history, pre-1900 -
       homebrew - prehistory - wine   D-0287.

1095. Schwartz, Theodore, and Romanucci-Ross, Lola
       DRINKING AND INEBRIATE BEHAVIOR IN THE ADMIRALTY ISLANDS,
       MELANESIA.
       Ethos, 2(3): 213-231,   1974.
       Melanesia - Manus - change - class - intoxication -
       prohibition - stereotype   D-0874.

1096. Sclare, A.B.
       DRINKING HABITS IN SCOTLAND.
       International Journal of Offender Therapy, 19: 241-249,   1976.

142.

Scotland D-0875.

1097. Seekirchner, A.
DER ALKOHOL IN AFRIKA. [Alcohol in Africa.] [Ger]
In: Frobenius, L., and von Wilm, R., ed. Atlas
Africanus, Volume 8. Berlin: W. de Gruyter,
pp. 44-47, 1931.
Africa - distribution - history, pre-1900 - homebrew D-0876.

1098. Segal, Boris M.
DRINKING PATTERNS AND ALCOHOLISM IN SOVIET AND AMERICAN
SOCIETIES: A MULTIDISCIPLINARY COMPARISON.
In: Corson, Samuel A., and Corson, Elizabeth O'Leary,
ed. Psychiatry and psychology in the USSR. New York,
NY: Plenum, 1976.
Cross-national - United States - Soviet Union - customs -
dysfunctions - epidemiology - functions D-0288.

1099. S[elby], H[enry]
NON-DRINKING SOCIETIES.
Unpublished paper: [Institute for the Study of Human
Problems, Stanford, CA], Manuscript No. 46, 11 pp., 1963.
World survey - abstainers - conversion - distribution -
norms - prohibition D-1239.

1100. Selby, Henry
REVIEW OF ANTHROPOLOGICAL LITERATURE ON DRINKING
BEHAVIOR.
Unpublished report: Institute for the Study of Human
Problems, Cooperative Commission on the Study of
Alcoholism, Stanford, CA, 5 pp., 1965.
review - sociocultural D-1195.

1101. Selley, E.
THE ENGLISH PUBLIC HOUSE AS IT IS.
London: Longmans, Green, 184 pp., 1927.
England - bar - functions D-0242.

1102. Seltman, Charles
WINE IN THE ANCIENT WORLD.
London: Routledge and Kegan Paul, 196 pp., 1957.
Europe - Near East - Classical peoples - history,
pre-1500 - wine D-0877.

1103. Semple, B.M., and Yarrow, A.
HEALTH EDUCATION, ALCOHOL, AND ALCOHOLISM IN SCOTLAND.
Health Bulletin, 32: 31-34, 1974.
Scotland - epidemiology - prevention D-0243.

1104. Serebro, Boris
TOTAL ALCOHOL CONSUMPTION AS AN INDEX OF ANXIETY AMONG
URBANIZED AFRICANS.
British Journal of Addiction, 67: 251-254, 1972.

	South Africa - Bantu - consumption - epidemiology - stress	D-0878.
1105.	Setälä, V. ISLAM OCH RUSHDRYCKERNA. [Islam and intoxicating beverages.] [Fin] Tidskrift för Alkoholpolitik, [1950] (3): 74-77, Islam - norms - religion	1950. D-1115.
1106.	Seto, A.; Tricomi, S.; Goodwin, D.W.; Kolodney, R.; and Sullivan, T. BIOCHEMICAL CORRELATES OF ETHANOL-INDUCED FLUSHING IN ORIENTALS. Journal of Studies on Alcohol, 39: 1-11, Orientals - metabolism - "race"	1978. D-0879.
1107.	Shadwell, A. DRINK IN 1914-1922: A LESSON IN CONTROL. London: Longmans, Green, 245 pp., England - change - prohibition	1923. D-0244.
1108.	Shalloo, Jeremiah P. SOME CULTURAL FACTORS IN THE ETIOLOGY OF ALCOHOLISM. Quarterly Journal of Studies on Alcohol, 2: 464-478, Cross-ethnic - United States - etiology - sociocultural	1941. D-0880.
1109.	Sheen, James R. WINE AND OTHER FERMENTED LIQUORS: FROM THE EARLIEST AGES TO THE PRESENT TIME. London: Robert Hardwicke, World survey - customs - history, pre-1500 - history, pre-1900 - homebrew - prehistory - wine	1864. D-0881.
1110.	Sheldon, Mary, and Sparling, Russell, ed. WOMAN AND ALCOHOL: CULTURAL PERSPECTIVES AND PUBLIC RESPONSIBILITIES. Unpublished report: Amarillo College, (Amarillo, TX), Cross-ethnic - United States - female	1977. D-1589.
1111.	Sheldon, Mary, and Stuart, Claudio CHICANAS, ALCOHOLISM AND ANOMIE. Unpublished paper: Society for Applied Anthropology, Mérida, Mexico, United States - Hispanos - anomie - female - norms	1978. D-1590.
1112.	Shore, James H., and von Fumetti, Billee THREE ALCOHOL PROGRAMS FOR AMERICAN INDIANS. American Journal of Psychiatry, 128: 1450-1454, Cross-ethnic - Native Americans - Apache - Ute - prevention - treatment - youth	1972. D-0882.

1113.   Shore, J.H.; Kinzie, J.D.; and Hampson, J.L.
        PSYCHIATRY EPIDEMIOLOGY OF AN INDIAN VILLAGE.
        Psychiatry, 36(1): 70-81,   1973.
        Native Americans - alcoholism - epidemiology - pathology -
        psychiatric problems - social organization   D-0883.

1114.   Shuval, R., and Krasilowsky, D.
        A STUDY OF HOSPITALIZED MALE ALCOHOLICS.
        Israel Annals of Psychiatry and Related Disciplines,
        1(2): 277-292,   1963.
        Cross-ethnic - Israel - Jews - Near East - acculturation -
        stress   A-2029.

1115.   Siegel, Harvey A.; Peterson, David M.; and Chambers,
        Carl D.
        THE EMERGING SKID ROW: ETHNOGRAPHIC AND SOCIAL NOTES
        ON A CHANGING SCENE.
        Journal of Drug Issues, 5: 160-166,   1975.
        United States - Skid Row - economics   D-0885.

1116.   Siegel, Harvey Alan
        OUTPOSTS OF THE FORGOTTEN: SOCIALLY TERMINAL PEOPLE
        IN SLUM HOTELS AND SINGLE ROOM OCCUPANCY TENEMENTS.
        New Brunswick, NJ: Transactions,   1978.
        United States - Skid Row - economics - social
        organization   D-0884.

1117.   Sievers, Maurice L.
        CIGARETTE AND ALCOHOL USAGE BY SOUTHWESTERN AMERICAN
        INDIANS.
        American Journal of Public Health, 58: 71-82,   1968.
        Cross-ethnic - Native Americans - drugs - liver   D-0886.

1118.   Siliceo Pauer, Paul
        EL PULQUE. [Pulque.]   [Spa]
        Ethnos, 2: 60-63,   1920.
        Mexico - homebrew - manufacture - medical - nutrition   D-0887.

1119.   Simboli, Ben J.
        ACCULTURATED DRINKING PRACTICES AND PROBLEM DRINKING
        AMONG THREE GENERATIONS OF ITALIANS IN AMERICA.
        D.P.H. Dissertation, University of California
        (San Francisco),   1976.
        United States - Italian-Americans - acculturation -
        change   D-0888.

1120.   Simeone, Carolynn M.
        THE TAKE OVER CYCLE.
        Unpublished paper: Presented at the International
        Arctic Rim Conference on Alcohol Problems. Anchorage,
        Alas: National Council on Alcoholism, Alaska Region,   1978.
        United States - Native Americans - Athabascan - binge -
        economics - functions - ritual - social organization -
        sociocultural - stereotype   D-1231.

1121.   Simmons, Ozzie G.
        DRINKING PATTERNS AND INTERPERSONAL PERFORMANCE IN
        A PERUVIAN MESTIZO COMMUNITY.
        Quarterly Journal of Studies on Alcohol, 20: 103-111,   1959.
        Peru - Mestizos - customs - economics - functions -
        ritual - social organization - sociocultural   D-0889.

1122.   Simmons, Ozzie G.
        AMBIVALENCE AND THE LEARNING OF DRINKING BEHAVIOR IN
        A PERUVIAN COMMUNITY.
        American Anthropologist, 62: 1018-1027,   1960.
        Peru - Mestizos - ambivalence - enculturation - functions -
        norms - social organization - sociocultural   D-0890.

1123.   Simmons, Ozzie G.
        THE SOCIOCULTURAL INTEGRATION OF ALCOHOL USE: A PERUVIAN
        STUDY.
        Quarterly Journal of Studies on Alcohol, 29: 152-171,   1968.
        Peru - Mestizos - customs - economics - functions - ritual -
        social organization - sociocultural   D-0891.

1124.   Singer, K.
        DRINKING PATTERNS AND ALCOHOLISM IN THE CHINESE.
        British Journal of Addiction, 67: 3-14,   1972.
        Hong Kong - Overseas Chinese - attitudes - customs -
        functions - medical - norms - social organization   D-0892.

1125.   Singer, K., and Wong, M.
        ALCOHOLIC PSYCHOSES AND ALCOHOLISM IN THE CHINESE.
        Quarterly Journal of Studies on Alcohol, 34: 878-886,   1973.
        Hong Kong - Overseas Chinese - alcoholism - psychiatric
        problems   D-0894.

1126.   Singer, K.
        THE CHOICE OF INTOXICANT AMONG THE CHINESE.
        British Journal of Addiction, 69: 257-268,   1974.
        Hong Kong - Overseas Chinese - customs - drugs   D-0893.

1127.   Singh, Sarabit
        PREPARATION OF BEER BY THE LOI-MANIPURIS OF SEKAMI.
        Man in India, 17: 80,   1937.
        India - Loi-Manipuri - moonshine - manufacture   D-0895.

1128.   Sišnik, L.
        O ZGANJEKUHI V BREZNICI POD LUBNIKOM. [Brandy distillation
        in Breznica.] [Yug]
        Slovenski Etnograf, 11: 167-178,   1958.
        Czechoslovakia - brandy - customs - moonshine   D-0245.

1129.   Siverts, Henning, ed.
        DRINKING PATTERNS IN HIGHLAND CHIAPAS.
        Bergen: Universitetsforlaget,   1972.

Cross-ethnic - Mexico - Maya - customs - functions -
research methods - semantics - sociocultural   D-0897.

1130. Siverts, Henning
OXCHUC CEREMONIAL DRINKING: A PRELIMINARY SURVEY OF
RESPONSES TO 120 QUERY FRAMES.
In: Siverts, Henning, ed. Drinking patterns in
Highland Chiapas. Bergen: Universitetsforlaget,
pp. 147-176,   1972.
Mexico - Oxchuc - research methods - semantics   D-0896.

1131. Skirrow, Jan
THE NORTH AMERICAN INDIAN AND ALCOHOL: A BIBLIOGRAPHY.
Edmonton, Alb.: Alberta Alcoholism and Drug Abuse
Commission,   1971.
Native Americans - bibliography   D-1100.

1132. Skolnik, Jerome H.
RELIGIOUS AFFILIATION AND DRINKING BEHAVIOR.
Quarterly Journal of Studies on Alcohol, 19: 453-470,   1958.
Cross-ethnic - United States - Jews - Protestants -
Church - consumption   D-0898.

1133. Skorzyski, L.
L'ALCOOL CHEZ LES PEUPLES PRIMITIFS DE RUSSIE. [Alcohol
among the primitive peoples of Russia.] [Fre]
In: Congrés Internationale contre l'Abus des Boissons
Alcooliques. Paris,   1889.
Cross-ethnic - Soviet Union   D-1196.

1134. Slater, Arthur D., and Albrecht, Stan L.
THE EXTENT AND COSTS OF EXCESSIVE DRINKING AMONG THE
UINTAH-OURAY INDIANS.
In: Bahr. H.M., et al., ed. Native Americans today:
Sociological perspectives. New York, NY: Harper
and Row, pp. 358-366,   1971.
Native Americans - dysfunctions - economics - epidemiology -
stress   D-1197.

1135. Slotkin, Jerome S.
FERMENTED DRINKS IN MEXICO.
American Anthropologist, 56: 1089-1090,   1954.
Mexico - distribution - history, pre-1500 - history,
pre-1900 - homebrew - manufacture - prehistory   D-0899.

1136. Smythe, Dallas W.
ALCOHOL AS A SYMPTOM OF SOCIAL DISORDER: AN ECOLOGICAL
VIEW.
Social Psychiatry, 1: 144-151,   1966.
dysfunctions - social organization - stress   D-0900.

1137.   Snyder, Charles R.
        ALCOHOL AND THE JEWS: A CULTURAL STUDY OF DRINKING
        AND SOBRIETY.
        Glencoe, IL: Free Press (Yale Center of Alcohol Studies
        Monograph No. 1), 226 pp.,   1958.
        United States - Jews - attitudes - customs - enculturation -
        medical - norms - religion - ritual - sociocultural   D-0901.

1138.   Snyder, Charles R.
        CULTURE AND JEWISH SOBRIETY: THE INGROUP-OUTGROUP FACTOR.
        In: Sklare, M., ed. The Jews: Social patterns of an
        American group. Glencoe, IL: Free Press, pp. 560-594,   1958.
        Jews - customs - norms - ritual - social organization -
        sociocultural   D-0902.

1139.   Snyder, Charles R.
        INEBRIETY, ALCOHOLISM, AND ANOMIE.
        In: Clinard, Marshall B., ed. Anomie and deviant
        behavior: A discussion and a critique. Glencoe, IL:
        Free Press, pp. 189-212,   1964.
        anomie - review - sociocultural   D-0903.

1140.   Snyder, Charles R., and Pittman, David J.
        DRINKING AND ALCOHOLISM: SOCIAL ASPECTS.
        In: Sills, D.E., ed. International encyclopedia of
        the Social Sciences, Volume 4. New York, NY: Macmillan,
        pp. 268-275,   1968.
        World survey - review - sociocultural   D-1198.

1141.   Snyder, Charles R.
        THE RARITY OF ALCOHOLISM AMONG JEWS. IS IT BIOLOGICALLY
        OR SOCIO-CULTURALLY DETERMINED?
        Unpublished paper: Presented at the 1st International
        Symposium on Genetic Diseases among Ashkenazi Jews,   1977.
        Jews - review - sociocultural   D-1591.

1142.   Sølling, Leif
        ALKOHOLKONSUMTIONEN PA GRØNLAND. [Alcohol consumption
        in Greenland.] [Dan]
        Alkohol och Narkotika, 67: 285-293,   1973.
        Denmark - Greenland - Eskimos - change - economics -
        female - history, pre-1900   D-0904.

1143.   Sølling, Leif
        ALCOHOL AND THE SUBJECTIVE EXPERIENCE OF POWER.
        Unpublished paper: Presented at the 3rd International
        Symposium on Circumpolar Health. Held July 8-11, in
        Yellowknife, N.W.T., 5 pp.,   1974.
        functions - power   D-1242.

1144.   Sølling, Leif
        ALKOHOLFORBRUGET I GRØNLAND. [Alcohol consumption in
        Greenland.] [Dan]

148.

[Copenhagen: Danish National Institute of Social Research,] 198 pp., 1974.
Denmark - Greenland - consumption   D-0289.

1145. Solms, H.
SOZIO-KULTURELLE UND WIRTSCHAFTLICHE BEDINGUNGEN DER GIFTSUCHTEN, DES MEDIKAMENTENMISSBRAUCHES UND DES CHRONISCHEN ALKOHOLISMUS. [Socio-cultural and economic pre-conditions of drug addiction, drug abuse, and chronic alcoholism.] [Ger]
Hippokrates, 37: 184-192, 1966.
sociocultural   D-0905.

1146. Sommer, Robert
THE ISOLATED DRINKER IN THE EDMONTON BEER PARLOR.
Quarterly Journal of Studies on Alcohol, 26: 95-110, 1965.
Canada - bar - research methods   D-0269.

1147. Sommer, Robert
DESIGNED FOR DRINKING.
In: Sommer, Robert. Personal space: The behavioral basis of design. Englewood Cliffs, NJ: Prentice-Hall, pp. 120-131, 1969.
bar - space   D-0270.

1148. Sommerschield, F.E.
MJOD- OCH OLBRYGD I NORDEN FOR 450 AR SEDAN. [Mead- and beer-brewing in Nordic countries 450 years ago.] [Fin]
Alkoholpolitik, 20(2): 56-60, 1957.
Scandinavia - history, pre-1500 - homebrew - manufacture   D-0062.

1149. Spaulding, Philip
THE SOCIAL INTEGRATION OF A NORTHERN COMMUNITY: WHITE MYTHOLOGY AND METIS REALITY.
In: Davis, A.K., ed. A northern dilemma: Reference papers. Bellingham, WA: Western Washington State College, 1966.
Cross-ethnic - Canada - Métis - anomie - stereotype   D-0907.

1150. Specht, F.A.
GASTMAHLER UND TRINKGELAGE DER DEUTSCHEN. [Banquets and drinking bouts of the Germans.] [Ger]
Stuttgart: [no publisher], 1887.
Germany - binge - customs - folklore - history, pre-1500 - history, pre-1900   D-1213.

1151. Spencer, Edward
THE FLOWING BOWL: A TREATISE ON DRINKS OF ALL KINDS AND OF ALL PERIODS, INTERSPERSED WITH SUNDRY ANECDOTES AND REMINISCENCES.
London: Grant Richards, 243 pp., 1903.
World survey - history, pre-1500 - history, pre-1900 - manufacture - review   D-0063.

1152. Spiller, B.
THE STORY OF BEER.
Geographical Magazine, 28: 86-94, 143-154, and 169-181,   1955.
beer - distribution - homebrew   D-0064.

1153. Spindler, George D.
ALCOHOL SYMPOSIUM: EDITORIAL PREVIEW.
American Anthropologist, 66: 341-343,   1964.
sociocultural   D-0908.

1154. Spitulnik, Karen
THE INN CROWD: THE AMERICAN INN, 1730-1830.
Pennsylvania Folklife, 22(2): 25-41,   1972.
United States - bar - functions - history, pre-1900 -
social organization   D-0246.

1155. Spradley, James P.
YOU OWE YOURSELF A DRUNK: AN ETHNOGRAPHY OF URBAN NOMADS.
Boston, MA: Little, Brown, 310 pp.,   1970.
United States - Skid Row - customs - functions - semantics -
social organization - sociocultural   D-0909.

1156. Spradley, James P.
BEATING THE DRUNK CHARGE.
In: Spradley, James P., and McCurdy, David W., ed.
Conformity and conflict: Readings in cultural anthropology.
Boston, MA: Little, Brown, pp. 377-384,   1974.
United States - Skid Row - crime - stereotype   D-0910.

1157. Spradley, James P., and Mann, Brenda J.
THE COCKTAIL WAITRESS: WOMAN'S WORK IN A MAN'S WORLD.
New York, NY: John Wiley and Sons, 154 pp.,   1975.
United States - bar - economics - occupation - social
organization - space   D-0912.

1158. Spradley, James P.
TROUBLE IN THE TANK.
In: Rynkiewich, Michael A., and Spradley, James P., ed.
Ethics and anthropology: Dilemmas in fieldwork. New York,
NY: John Wiley and Sons, pp. 17-31,   1976.
United States - Skid Row - crime - research methods   D-0911.

1159. Stage, T.B., and Keast, T.J.
A PSYCHIATRIC SERVICE FOR PLAINS INDIANS.
Hospital and Community Psychiatry, 17(3): 74-76,   1966.
Native Americans - treatment   D-0065.

1160. Stamatoyannopoulous, George; Chen, Shi-Han; and Fukui,
Miyoshi
LIVER ALCOHOL DEHYDROGENASE IN JAPANESE: HIGH POPULATION
FREQUENCY OF ATYPICAL FORM AND ITS POSSIBLE ROLE IN ALCOHOL
SENSITIVITY.
American Journal of Human Genetics, 27(6): 789-796,   1975.
Japan - metabolism - "race"   D-0913.

150.

1161. Stanbury, W.T.
SUCCESS AND FAILURE: INDIANS IN URBAN SOCIETY.
[Vancouver, B.C.]: University of British Columbia
Press, 1975.
Canada - Native Americans - anomie - suicide -
urbanization D-0914.

1162. Stanislawski, Dan
LANDSCAPES OF BACCHUS: THE VINE IN PORTUGAL.
Austin, TX: University of Texas Press, 1969.
Portugal - distribution - economics - manufacture -
wine D-0420.

1163. Stanley, G.F.G.
THE INDIANS AND THE BRANDY TRADE DURING THE ANCIEN REGIME.
Revue d'Histoire de l'Amérique Française, 6: 489-505, 1953.
Canada - Native Americans - brandy - economics -
history, pre-1900 D-0915.

1164. Steffenhagen, R.A.
MOTIVATION FOR DRUG AND ALCOHOL USE: A SOCIAL PERSPECTIVE.
In: Goodstadt, Michael, ed. Research on methods and programs of drug education. Toronto, Ont.: Addiction Research Foundation, pp. 85-95, 1974.
United States - attitudes - drugs - functions - stress -
youth D-0916.

1165. Steigelmann, W.
DER WEIN IN DER BIBEL. [Wine in the Bible.] [Ger]
Neustadt: Meininger, 1962.
Near East - Biblical peoples - customs - history, pre-1500
- wine D-0421.

1166. Steinbring, Jack
ACCULTURATIONAL PHENOMENA AMONG THE LAKE WINNIPEG
OJIBWAS OF CANADA.
In: Verhandlungen des XXVIII Internationalen
Amerikanistenkongresses, (bd. iii). München: Klaus
Renner, pp. 179-188, 1972.
Canada - Native Americans - Ojibwa - acculturation -
Alcoholics Anonymous - conversion - social organization D-1101.

1167. Sterne, Muriel A., and Pittman, David J.
DRINKING PATTERNS IN THE GHETTO, VOLUMES 1 AND 2.
Unpublished report: Social Science Institute, Washington
University, St. Louis, MO, 713 pp., 1972.
Cross-ethnic - United States - Blacks - Whites - attitudes -
bar - class - customs - dysfunctions - functions -
youth D-1199.

1168.   Stevens, Joyce A.
        SOCIAL AND CULTURAL FACTORS RELATED TO DRINKING
        PATTERNS AMONG THE BLACKFEET.
        M.A. Thesis, University of Montana,   1969.
        United States - Native Americans - Blackfeet -
        sociocultural   D-0917.

1169.   Stewart, Eugene R.
        THE LIQUOR TRAFFIC AMONG THE SOUTHERN PLAINS INDIANS,
        1835-1875.
        M.A. Thesis, University of Oklahoma,   1936.
        United States - Native Americans - economics - history,
        pre-1900 - prohibition   D-0918.

1170.   Stewart, Omer C.
        THEORY FOR UNDERSTANDING THE USE OF ALCOHOLIC BEVERAGES.
        Unpublished paper: American Anthropological Association,
        Minneapolis, MN,   1960.
        abstainers - functions   D-1592.

1171.   Stewart, Omer C.
        QUESTIONS REGARDING AMERICAN INDIAN CRIMINALITY.
        Human Organization, 23: 61-66,   1964.
        Native Americans - crime   D-0919.

1172.   Stivers, Richard [A.]
        CULTURE AND ALCOHOLISM.
        In: Tarter, Ralph E., and Sugerman, A. Arthur, ed.
        Alcoholism: Interdisciplinary approaches to an enduring
        problem. Reading, MA: Addison-Wesley, pp. 573-602,   1976.
        review - sociocultural   D-0293.

1173.   Stivers, Richard [A.]
        IRISH ETHNICITY AND ALCOHOL USE.
        Medical Anthropology, 2(4): 121-135,   1978.
        United States - Irish-Americans - acculturation - change -
        customs - economics - political - stereotype   D-0469.

1174.   Stivers, Richard A.
        THE BACHELOR GROUP ETHIC AND IRISH DRINKING.
        Ph. D. Dissertation, Southern Illinois University
        (Carbondale),   1971.
        Ireland - customs - norms - social organization   D-0920.

1175.   Stivers, Richard A.
        A HAIR OF THE DOG: IRISH DRINKING AND AMERICAN STEREOTYPE.
        University Park, PA: Pennsylvania State University Press,
        197 pp.,   1976.
        Cross-national - Ireland - United States - Irish-Americans -
        change - class - customs - economics - history, pre-1900 -
        political - stereotype - temperance   D-0921.

1176.   Stolte, Edward
        THE URBAN BEER TAVERN: A STUDY OF PSEUDONYMITY.

Studies in Sociology, 2(2): 6-11, 1938.
United States - bar - social organization D-0922.

1177. Stratton, John
COPS AND DRUNKS: POLICE ATTITUDES AND ACTIONS IN
DEALING WITH INDIAN DRUNKS.
International Journal of the Addictions, 8: 613-621, 1973.
Native Americans - Navaho - attitudes - crime D-0923.

1178. Stratton, R[ay]; Zeiner, A[rthur]; and Paredes, A[lfonso]
TRIBAL AFFILIATION AND PREVALENCE OF ALCOHOL PROBLEMS.
Journal of Studies on Alcohol, 39(7): 1166-1177, 1978.
Cross-ethnic - Native Americans - accidents - crime -
epidemiology - liver - murder - suicide - urbanization D-1200.

1179. Straus, Robert, and McCarthy, Raymond G.
NONADDICTIVE PATHOLOGICAL DRINKING PATTERNS OF HOMELESS
MEN.
Quarterly Journal of Studies on Alcohol, 12: 601-611, 1951.
United States - Skid Row - alcoholism - definition -
economics - functions - social organization - stress D-0925.

1180. Straus, Robert
ALCOHOL AND SOCIETY.
Psychiatric Annals, 3(10): 43-55, 1973.
review - sociocultural D-0924.

1181. Straus, Robert
PROBLEM DRINKING IN THE PERSPECTIVE OF SOCIAL CHANGE,
1940-1973.
In: Filstead, William J.; Rossi, Jean J.; and Keller,
Mark, ed. Alcohol and alcohol problems: New thinking
and new directions. Cambridge, MA: Ballinger,
pp. 29-56, 1976.
United States - change - leisure - phases - research
methods - stress D-0066.

1182. Street, Pamela B.; Wood, Ronald C.; and Chowenhill,
Rita C., ed.
ALCOHOL USE AMONG NATIVE AMERICANS: A SELECTIVE
ANNOTATED BIBLIOGRAPHY. (Based substantially on the
unpublished work of Patricia Mail and Victoria Sears.)
Berkeley, CA: Social Research Group, School of Public
Health, University of California, 115 pp., 1976.
Native Americans - bibliography D-0926.

1183. Streit, Fred, and Nicolich, Mark J.
MYTHS VERSUS DATA ON AMERICAN INDIAN DRUG ABUSE.
Journal of Drug Education, 7(2): 117-122, 1977.
Native Americans - drugs - stereotype D-0927.

1184. Strübing, E.
VOM WEIN ALS GENUSS- UND HEILMITTEL IM ALTERUM MIT
PLINIUS UND ASKLEPIADES. [On wine as a means of
pleasure and healing in antiquity, following Pliny
and Asclepiades.] [Ger]
Ernährungsforschung, 5: 572-594, 1960.
Cross-ethnic - Classical peoples - Egyptians, ancient -
Greeks, ancient - folklore - functions - history, pre-1500 -
medical - wine D-0928.

1185. Stull, Donald D.
MODERNIZATION AND SYMPTOMS OF STRESS: ATTITUDES,
ACCIDENTS, AND ALCOHOL USE AMONG URBAN PAPAGO INDIANS.
Ph.D. Dissertation, University of Colorado, 1973.
United States - Native Americans - Papago - accidents -
acculturation - occupation - stress D-0929.

1186. Stull, Donald D.
HOLOGEISTIC STUDIES OF DRINKING: A CRITIQUE.
Drinking and Drug Practices Surveyor, 10: 4 ff , 1975.
Cross-cultural - research methods D-0930.

1187. Súkeník, L.
ZHISTORIE NAVYKOVYCH DROG: ALKOHOLICKE - VINO, PIVO,
MEDOVINA. [History of addictive drugs: Alcoholic
beverages - wine, beer, mead.] [Cze]
Protialkoholický Obzor, 12: 239-256, 1977.
World survey - beer - customs - history, pre-1500 -
history, pre-1900 - homebrew - review D-0424.

1188. Suolahti, Jaakko
DE GAMLA ROMARNAS ALKOHOLVANOR. [Drinking customs of
the ancient Romans.] [Fin]
Alkoholpolitik, 17(2): 47-52, 1954.
Romans, ancient - change - customs - history, pre-1500 D-0067.

1189. Suolahti, Jaakko
ALKOHOLMISSBRUKET UNDER ANTIKEN. [Alcohol abuse in
antiquity.] [Fin]
Alkoholpolitik, 18: 77-79, 1955.
Romans, ancient - Classical peoples - Greeks, ancient -
history, pre-1500 - temperance D-0931.

1190. Suolahti, Jaakko
STATLIG ALKOHOLPOLITIK I ROM UNDER KEJSARTIDENS SLUTSKEDE.
[Government alcohol policy in Rome toward the end of
the Empire.] [Fin]
Alkoholpolitik, 20: 5-11, 1956.
Romans, ancient - economics - history, pre-1500 -
political D-0932.

1191. Suolahti, Jaakko
COCKTAIL OCH VERMUT HOS ANTIKENS ROMARE. [Cocktails and cordials of the ancient Romans.] [Fin]
Alkoholpolitik, 25(4): 158-162, 1962.
Romans, ancient - history, pre-1500 - homebrew - manufacture - wine
D-0068.

1192. Suuronen, Kerttu
TRADITIONAL FESTIVE DRINKING IN FINLAND ACCORDING TO RESPONSES TO AN ETHNOLOGICAL QUESTIONNAIRE A18/73.
Helsinki: Social Research Institute of Alcohol Studies (Report 76), 53 pp., 1973.
Finland - change - customs - economics - folklore - history, pre-1900 - homebrew - moonshine - norms - ritual - social organization - sociocultural
D-0933.

1193. Swanson, David W.; Bratrude, Amos P.; and Brown, Edward M.
ALCOHOL ABUSE IN A POPULATION OF INDIAN CHILDREN.
Diseases of the Nervous System, 32: 835-842, 1971.
Native Americans - Salish - dependency - leisure - stress - youth
D-0934.

1194. Szuter, C.F., and Saiki, J.H.
USE OF DISULFIRAM IN TREATMENT OF ALCOHOLIC PROBLEMS IN AN AMERICAN INDIAN POPULATION.
Unpublished paper: New Mexico Regional Meeting of the American College of Physicians, Albuquerque, 1964.
United States - Native Americans - disulfiram - treatment
D-1911.

1195. Szwed, John F.
GOSSIP, DRINKING AND SOCIAL CONTROL: CONSENSUS AND COMMUNICATION IN A NEWFOUNDLAND PARISH.
Ethnology, 5: 343-441, 1966.
Canada - norms - sociocultural
D-0935.

1196. Tadesse, Eshete
PREPARATION OF TAG AMONG THE AMHARA OF SAWA.
Bulletin of Addis Ababa University College in Ethnology and Sociology, 8: 101-109, 1958.
Ethiopia - Amhara - change - folklore - homebrew - manufacture - medical - power
D-0936.

1197. Tapia, Isabel; Gaete, Jorge; Muñoz, Carlos; Sescovitch, Sonia; Miranda, Isabel; Minguell, Jorge; Pérez, Gilberto; and Orellana, Gastón
PATRONES SOCIO-CULTURALES DE LA INGESTION DE ALCOHOL EN CHILOE: INFORME PRELIMINAR, ALGUNOS PROBLEMAS METODOLOGICOS. [Sociocultural patterns of alcohol use in Chiloé: Preliminary report, some methodological problems.] [Spa]
Acta Psiquiátrica y Psicológica de América Latina,

	12: 232-240, Chile - research methods - sociocultural	1966. D-0937.
1198.	Taussig, Charles William RUM, ROMANCE AND REBELLION. New York, NY: Minton, Balch, 289 pp., United States - customs - economics - history, pre-1900 - political	1928. D-0938.
1199.	Taylor, William B. DRINKING, HOMICIDE AND REBELLION IN COLONIAL MEXICAN VILLAGES. Stanford, CA: Stanford University Press, Mexico - change - crime - history, pre-1900 - murder - responsibility	1979. D-1251.
1200.	Termansen, P.E., and Ryan, J. HEALTH AND DISEASE IN A BRITISH COLUMBIAN INDIAN COMMUNITY. Canadian Psychiatric Association Journal, 15(2): 121-127, Canada - Native Americans - psychiatric problems	1970. D-0939.
1201.	Theron, J.S. ALKOHOLISME UIT DIE OOGPUNT VAN DIE MAATSKAPLIKE WERK. THE PERSONALITY AND TREATMENT OF THE ALCOHOLIC IN SOUTH AFRICA: REPORT OF THE PROJECT ALCOHOLISM, VOLUME 9. [Afr] Pretoria: Department of Social Welfare and Pensions, Republic of South Africa, South Africa - treatment	1971. D-1117.
1202.	Theron, J.S. KOMUNIKASIE EN INLIGTING: ENKELA PRAKTIES-ORGANISATORIESE ASPEKTE VAN INLIGTINGSVERSKAFFING. THE PERSONALITY AND TREATMENT OF THE ALCOHOLIC IN SOUTH AFRICA: REPORT OF THE PROJECT ALCOHOLISM, VOLUME 14, HOOFSTUK 2. [Afr] Pretoria: Department of Social Welfare and Pensions, Republic of South Africa, South Africa - treatment	1971. D-1116.
1203.	Thomas, Anthony E. CLASS AND SOCIABILITY AMONG URBAN WORKERS: A STUDY OF THE BAR AS SOCIAL CLUB. Medical Anthropology, 2(4): 9-30, United States - bar - functions - social organization	1978. D-0426.
1204.	Thorner, I. ASCETIC PROTESTANTISM AND ALCOHOLISM. Psychiatry, 16: 167-176, abstainers - Protestants - Church - norms - religion	1953. D-0940.
1205.	Thudichum, G. TRAUBE UND WEIN IN DER KULTURGESCHICHTE. [Grape and wine in cultural history.] [Ger] Tübingen: [no publisher],	1881.

156.

	World survey - history, pre-1500 - history, pre-1900 - prehistory - wine	D-1214.

1206. Thune, Carl E.
ALCOHOLISM AND THE ARCHETYPAL PAST: A PHENOMENOLOGICAL PERSPECTIVE ON ALCOHOLICS ANONYMOUS.
Journal of Studies on Alcohol, 38: 75-88, 1977.
Alcoholics Anonymous - self - treatment   D-0941.

1207. Tihon, L.
A PROPOS DE QUELQUES BOISSONS FERMENTEES INDIGENES.
[On some fermented indigenous drinks.] [Fre]
Bulletin Agricole du Congo Belge, 25: 128-134, 1934.
Congo - homebrew - manufacture   D-0942.

1208. Tillhagen, C.-H.
FOOD AND DRINK AMONG THE SWEDISH KALDERASA GYPSIES.
Journal of the Gypsy Lore Society, 36: 25-52, 1957.
Sweden - Gypsies - change - customs   D-0943.

1209. Timberlake, J.
PROHIBITION AND THE PROGRESSIVE MOVEMENT: 1900-1920.
New York, NY: Atheneum,   1970.
United States - history, pre-1900 - political - prohibition   D-0944.

1210. Toerian, I.
MEDIESE BEHANDELING VAN DIE ALKOHOLIS IN 'N SANRA-KLINIEK.
THE PERSONALITY AND TREATMENT OF THE ALCOHOLIC IN SOUTH AFRICA: REPORT OF THE PROJECT ALCOHOLISM, VOLUME 7, HOOFSTUK 2. [Afr]
Pretoria: Department of Social Welfare and Pensions, Republic of South Africa,   1971.
South Africa - treatment   D-1118.

1211. Tongue, Archer
5,000 YEARS OF DRINKING.
In: Ewing, John A., and Rouse, Beatrice A., ed. DRINKING: ALCOHOL IN AMERICAN SOCIETY - ISSUES AND CURRENT RESEARCH. Chicago, IL: Nelson-Hall, pp. 31-38, 1978.
World survey - customs - history, pre-1500 - history, pre-1900 - prehistory - sociocultural   D-0247.

1212. Topper, Martin D.
DRINKING PATTERNS, CULTURE CHANGE, SOCIABILITY, AND NAVAJO "ADOLESCENTS".
Addictive Diseases, 1(1): 97-116, 1974.
United States - Native Americans - Navaho - change - customs - economics - social organization - youth   D-0945.

1213. Topper, Martin D.
THE CULTURAL APPROACH, VERBAL PLANS, AND ALCOHOL RESEARCH.
In: Everett, Michael W.; Waddell, Jack O.; and

	Heath, Dwight B., ed. <u>Cross-cultural approaches to the study of alcohol: An interdisciplinary perspective</u>. The Hague: Mouton, pp. 379-402, United States - Native Americans - Navaho - research methods - semantics	1976. D-0946.
1214.	Torres, Martha, and Martin, David PATTERNS OF ALCOHOL CONSUMPTION AMONG MEXICAN AMERICAN FEMALES. Unpublished paper: Society for Applied Anthropology, Mérida, Mexico, United States - Hispanos - female	1978. D-1593.
1215.	Toulouse, Julian H. HIGH ON THE HAWG, OR HOW THE WESTERN MINER LIVED, AS TOLD BY THE BOTTLES HE LEFT BEHIND. Great Plains Journal, 4: 59-69, United States - containers - history, pre-1900 - occupation - research methods	1970. D-0947.
1216.	Towle, Leland H. ALCOHOLISM TREATMENT OUTCOMES IN DIFFERENT POPULATIONS. In: Chafetz, Morris E., ed. <u>Research, treatment and prevention. Proceedings of the 4th Annual Alcoholism Conference of the National Institute on Alcohol Abuse and Alcoholism.</u> Held June 12-14, 1974 in Washington, D.C. Rockville, MD: National Institute on Alcohol Abuse and Alcoholism (DHEW Publication No. (ADM) 76-284), pp. 112-133, 1975. United States - Native Americans - treatment	D-1517.
1217.	Treiman, Beatrice R.; Shanks, Patricia; Street, Pamela B.; and Hyman, Edward, comp. <u>ALCOHOL USE AMONG THE SPANISH-SPEAKING: A SELECTIVE ANNOTATED BIBLIOGRAPHY</u>. Berkeley, CA: Social Research Group, School of Public Health, University of California, 47 pp., United States - Hispanos - bibliography	1976. D-0422.
1218.	Treviño M. Elsa MACHISMO ALCOHOLISM: MEXICAN-AMERICAN MACHISMO DRINKING. In: Chafetz, Morris E., ed. <u>Research, treatment and prevention: Proceedings of the 4th Annual Alcoholism Conference of the National Institute on Alcohol Abuse and Alcoholism.</u> Held June 12-14, 1974 in Washington, D.C. Rockville, MD: National Institute on Alcohol Abuse and Alcoholism (DHEW Publication No. (ADM) 76-284), pp. 295-302, 1975. United States - Hispanos - norms - prevention	D-0948.
1219.	Trice, Harrison M., and Pittman, David J. SOCIAL ORGANIZATION AND ALCOHOLISM: A REVIEW OF SIGNIFICANT RESEARCH SINCE 1940. Social Problems, 5: 294-306,	1958.

158.

	research methods - review - social organization - sociocultural	D-0949.
1220.	Trotter, Robert T., II CULTURAL PERSPECTIVES ON ALCOHOLISM. In: Sheldon, Mary, and Sparling, Russell, ed. <u>Women and alcohol: Public responsibilities.</u> [Amarillo, TX]: Amarillo College, pp. 34-39, sociocultural	1977. D-0950.
1221.	Trotter, Robert T., II, and Chavira, Juan Antonio, ed. <u>EL USO DEL ALCOHOL: A RESOURCE BOOK FOR SPANISH SPEAKING COMMUNITIES.</u> Atlanta, GA: Southern Area Alcohol Education and Training Program, United States - Hispanos - bibliography - review	1977. D-0951.
1222.	Trudell, John ALCOHOL AND NATIVE PEOPLES. Akwesasne Notes, 7(4): 38-39, Native Americans - dysfunctions	1975. D-0952.
1223.	Turner, E.S. THE PROUD AND AWFUL ANNALS OF THE PEERLESS BRITISH PUB. In: McGill, A., ed. <u>Pub: A celebration.</u> London: Longmans, Green, England - bar - functions - social organization	1969. D-1232.
1224.	Tzu-ch^{c}ing, H., and Yiin-Ts^{c}ung, C. THE PREPARATION OF FERMENTS AND WINES BY CHIA SSU-HSIEH OF THE LATER WEI DYNASTY. Harvard Journal of Asiatic Studies, 9: 22-24, China - history, pre-1500 - homebrew - manufacture - wine	1945. D-1119.
1225.	Udvalget for Samfundsforskning i Grønland ALKOHOLSITUATIONEN I VESTGRØNLAND. [The alcohol situation in West Greenland.] [Dan] Copenhagen: Dansk Bibliografisk Kontor, Denmark - Greenland - Eskimos	1961. D-0953.
1226.	Uecker, Albert E., and Boutilier, L.R. KNOWLEDGE OF ALCOHOLISM, INITIAL ATTITUDES AND ATTITUDE CHANGE: INDIANS VS. WHITE ALCOHOLICS. Newsletter for Research in Mental Health and Behavioral Sciences, 17(1): 13-16, Cross-ethnic - Native Americans - Whites - attitudes	1975. D-0954.
1227.	Ullman, Albert D. SOCIOCULTURAL BACKGROUNDS OF ALCOHOLISM. Annals of the American Academy of Political and Social Science, 315: 48-54, ambivalence - attitudes - norms - sociocultural	1958. D-0955.

1228. Umunna, Ifekandu
THE DRINKING CULTURE OF A NIGERIAN COMMUNITY: ONITSHA.
Quarterly Journal of Studies on Alcohol, 28: 529-537, 1967.
Nigeria - binge - customs - economics - functions -
homebrew - ritual - social organization   D-0956.

1229. United States, Department of Health, Education and Welfare
HISTORY, PATTERNS AND PROBLEMS OF INDIAN DRINKING.
Unpublished report: Department of Health, Education
and Welfare, Washington, D.C., 11 pp., 1971.
Native Americans - change - dysfunctions - history,
pre-1900   D-1595.

1230. United States, Department of Health, Education and Welfare,
Indian Health Service
ALCOHOLISM - A HIGH PRIORITY HEALTH PROBLEM: A REPORT OF
THE INDIAN HEALTH SERVICE TASK FORCE ON ALCOHOLISM.
Washington, D.C.: U.S. Government Printing Office, 1970.
Native Americans - dysfunctions - pathology - prevention -
psychiatric problems - treatment   D-0957.

1231. United States, Department of the Interior, Bureau of
Indian Affairs
REPORT [OF THE COMMISSION TO STUDY ALCOHOLISM AMONG
INDIANS].
[Multigraphed], Washington, D.C., 17 pp., 1956.
Native Americans - dysfunctions - prevention - treatment   D-1594.

1232. Unkovic, Charles M.; Adler, Rudolf J.; and Miller, Susan E.
A CONTEMPORARY STUDY OF JEWISH ALCOHOLISM.
Unpublished report: 19 pp., 1975.
United States - Jews - epidemiology - sociocultural   D-1126.

1233. Urbanowicz, Charles F.
DRINKING IN THE POLYNESIAN KINGDOM OF TONGA.
Ethnohistory, 22(1): 33-50, 1975.
Polynesia - Tonga - class - kava - stereotype   D-0958.

1234. Vachon, André
L'EAU-DE-VIE DANS LA SOCIETE INDIENNE. [Distilled
beverages in Indian society.] [Fre]
Canadian Historical Association Annual Report: 22-32, 1960.
Canada - Native Americans - history, pre-1900 - review   D-0959.

1235. Valee, B[ert] L.
ALCOHOL METABOLISM AND METALLOENZYMES.
Therapeutic Notes, 14: 71-74, 1966.
metabolism - "race"   D-0961.

1236. Valenzuela Rojas, Bernardo
APUNTES BREVES DE COMIDAS Y BEBIDAS DE LA REGION DE CARAHUE.
[Brief notes on food and drink in Carahue region.] [Spa]
Archivo Folklórico, 8: 90-105, 1957.

Chile - Mapuche - customs - homebrew   D-0960.

1237. Vallee, Frank G.
STRESSES OF CHANGE AND MENTAL HEALTH AMONG THE CANADIAN ESKIMOS.
Archives of Environmental Health, 17: 565-570,   1968.
Canada - Eskimos - anomie - psychiatric problems - stress   D-0962.

1238. Vanderkooi, Ronald C[harles]
SKID ROW AND ITS MEN: AN EXPLORATION OF SOCIAL STRUCTURE, BEHAVIOR AND ATTITUDES.
Unpublished report: Michigan State University, Institute for Community Development (Technical Bulletin B-39), Kalamazoo, MI,   1963.
United States - Skid Row - attitudes - social organization   D-1215.

1239. Vanderkooi, Ronald Charles
SKID ROWERS: THEIR ALIENATION AND INVOLVEMENT IN COMMUNITY AND SOCIETY.
Ph.D. Dissertation, Michigan State University, Department of Sociology and Anthropology, 271 pp.,   1966.
United States - Skid Row - anomie - economics - social organization - sociocultural - stress   D-0290.

1240. Vanderyst, Hyac
LE VIN DE PALM OU MALAFU. [Palm wine ("malafu").] [Fre]
Bulletin Agricole du Congo Belge, 8(11): 219-224,   1920.
Congo - homebrew - manufacture   D-0963.

1241. Van Onselen, Charles
RANDLORDS [SIC] AND ROTGUT, 1886-1903: AN ESSAY ON THE ROLE OF ALCOHOL IN THE DEVELOPMENT OF EUROPEAN IMPERIALISM AND SOUTH AFRICAN CAPITALISM.
History Workshops, 2:   1976.
South Africa - economics - history, pre-1900   D-1182.

1242. Varlet, F.
FABRICATION ET COMPOSITION DE L'ALCOOL DE BANGUI. [The manufacture and composition of Bangui palm-wine.] [Fre]
Notes Africaines, 71: 74-75,   1956.
Africa - Bangui - homebrew - manufacture   D-0964.

1243. Varma, S.C.
PROBLEM OF DRINKING IN THE PRIMITIVE TRIBES.
Eastern Anthropologist, 12: 252-256,   1959.
Cross-ethnic - India - change - economics - homebrew - moonshine - religion - social organization - temperance   D-0965.

1244. Vasconcelos, R.
EL ALCOHOLISMO Y SUS CONSECUENCIAS SOCIOMEDICAS: II.
LO SOCIOCULTURAL. [Alcoholism and its sociomedical
consequences: II. The sociocultural.] [Spa]
Gaceta Médica de México, 107: 182-195, 1974.
review - sociocultural D-0069.

1245. Vasev, C., and Milosavčević, V.
ALKOHOLIZAM KOD CIGANA. [Alcoholism among Gypsies.]
[Ser-Cro]
Alkoholizam, 10: 47-57, 1970.
Yugoslavia - Gypsies - pathology D-0966.

1246. Vázquez, Mario C.
LA CHICHA EN LOS PAISES ANDINOS. [Chicha in the Andean
countries.] [Spa]
América Indígena, 27: 265-282, 1967.
Andean - customs - functions - homebrew - ritual -
social organization - sociocultural D-0967.

1247. Vedder, H.
NOTES ON THE BREWING OF KAFFIR BEER IN SOUTH WEST AFRICA.
South West Africa Scientific Society Journal, 8: 41-43, 1951.
Cross-ethnic - South Africa - Herrero - Nama - change -
economics - homebrew - manufacture - nutrition - political -
prohibition - social organization - sociocultural D-0968.

1248. Velapatiño Ortega, Alfredo
SUMMARY OF AN ALCOHOLISM STUDY IN THE APURIMAC-AYACUCHO
RIVER VALLEY, PERU.
In: Everett, Michael W.; Waddell, Jack O.; and Heath,
Dwight B., ed. Cross-cultural approaches to the study
of alcohol: An interdisciplinary perspective. The Hague:
Mouton, pp. 209-212, 1976.
Peru - Quechua D-0969.

1249. Velasco Muñoz-Ledo, María del Pilar
PATRONES DE INGESTION DEL ALCOHOL EN RELACION CON ALGUNAS
CARACTERISTICAS ETNOGRAFICAS DE UNA COMUNIDAD INDIGENA
DE LA SIERRA NORTE DE PUEBLA, MEXICO. [Patterns of
alcohol consumption in relation to some ethnographic
characteristics of an Indian community in the northern
highlands of Pueblo, Mexico.] [Spa]
Unpublished paper: Society for Applied Anthropology,
Mérida, Mexico, 1978.
Mexico D-1596.

1250. Verrall, F.M.
THE CATHOLIC CHURCH AND THE ENGLISH INN.
Catholic World, 144: 606-610, 1937.
England - bar - political - religion D-0248.

162.

1251. Verster, J.P.
BASIESE BEHANDELING. THE PERSONALITY AND TREATMENT OF THE ALCOHOLIC IN SOUTH AFRICA: REPORT OF THE PROJECT ALCOHOLISM, VOLUME 7, HOOFSTUK 1. [Afr]
Pretoria: Department of Social Welfare and Pensions, Republic of South Africa,
South Africa - psychiatric problems
1971.
D-1120.

1252. Vilkuna, Kustaa
OLET I DET FORNFINSKA SAMHALLET. [Beer in ancient Finnish society.] [Fin]
Alkoholpolitik, 17(3): 69-73,
Finland - beer - folklore - history, pre-1500 - homebrew
1954.
D-0070.

1253. Viñas Tello, Eduardo
LA COMPOSICION QUIMICA DE LAS DIFERENTES VARIEDADES DE CHICHA QUE SE CONSUMEN EN EL PERU. [The chemical composition of different varieties of chicha consumed in Peru.] [Spa]
Unpublished report: Ministerio de Salud Pública y Asistencia Social, Departamento de Nutrición, Lima,
Peru - homebrew - manufacture
1951.
D-1597.

1254. Vinchon, Jean
NOTES SUR L'HISTOIRE DE L'ALCOOLISME DANS L'ISLAM. [Notes on the history of alcoholism in Islam.] [Fre]
Mémoires de la Société Français d'Histoire de la Médecine et de ses Filiales, 2: 21-24,
Islam - Persians, ancient - literature - norms - prohibition - religion - temperance
1946.
D-0071.

1255. Viqueira, Carmen, and Palerm, Angel
ALCOHOLISMO BRUJERIA Y HOMICIDIO EN DOS COMUNIDADES RURALES DE MEXICO. [Alcoholism, witchcraft, and murder in two rural Mexican communities.] [Spa]
América Indígena, 14: 7-36,
Cross-ethnic - Mexico - Totonac - aggression - murder - social organization - sociocultural
1954.
D-0970.

1256. Vlok, A.
BEDRYFSIELKUNDIGE ASPEKTE: DIE PROBLEEMDRINKER EN SY WERKGEWER. THE PERSONALITY AND TREATMENT OF THE ALCOHOLIC IN SOUTH AFRICA: REPORT OF THE PROJECT ALCOHOLISM, VOLUME 4. [Afr]
Pretoria: Department of Social Welfare and Pensions, Republic of South Africa,
South Africa - dysfunctions
1971.
D-1121.

1257. [Voorst, John van]
CUPS AND THEIR CUSTOMS.
London: John van Voorst, Paternoster Row, 62 pp.,
1869.

World survey - customs - history, pre-1500 - history,
pre-1900 - review   D-0249.

1258.   Vrey, J.D.
        OPVOEDING TER VOORKOMING VAN ALKOHOLISME. THE
        PERSONALITY AND TREATMENT OF THE ALCOHOLIC IN SOUTH
        AFRICA: REPORT OF THE PROJECT ALCOHOLISM, VOLUME 13.
        [Afr]
        Pretoria: Department of Social Welfare and Pensions,
        Republic of South Africa,   1971.
        South Africa   D-1122.

1259.   Wacko, William J.
        OBSERVATIONS AND RECOMMENDATIONS RESPECTING ALCOHOL
        AND DRUGS IN THE NORTHWEST TERRITORIES.
        Unpublished report: Department of Social Development,
        Government of the Northwest Territories, Yellowknife,
        68 pp.,   1973.
        Canada - Native Americans - epidemiology - prevention -
        treatment   D-1201.

1260.   Wacko, William J.
        INDIAN ALCOHOL AND DRUG USE IN ALBERTA.
        Unpublished report: Department of Indian Affairs and
        Northern Development, Alberta Region,   1974.
        Canada - Native Americans - consumption - drugs   D-1919.

1261.   Waddell, Jack O.
        "DRINK, FRIEND!" SOCIAL CONTEXTS OF CONVIVIAL DRINKING
        AND DRUNKENNESS AMONG PAPAGO INDIANS IN AN URBAN SETTING.
        In: Chafetz, Morris, E., ed. Research on alcoholism:
        Clinical problems and special populations. Proceedings
        of the 1st Annual Institute on Alcohol Abuse and
        Alcoholism. Held June 25-26, 1971 in Washington, D.C.
        Rockville, MD: National Institute on Alcohol Abuse and
        Alcoholism (NTIS order no. PB 257-354), pp. 237-251,   1973.
        United States - Native Americans - Papago - ambivalence -
        bar - self - social organization - stereotype   D-0971.

1262.   Waddell, Jack O.
        FOR INDIVIDUAL POWER AND SOCIAL CREDIT: THE USE OF
        ALCOHOL AMONG TUCSON PAPAGOS.
        Human Organization, 34(1): 9-15,   1975.
        United States - Native Americans - Papago - functions -
        power - social organization - urbanization   D-0972.

1263.   Waddell, Jack O.
        FROM TANK TO TOWNHOUSE: PROBING THE IMPACT OF A LEGAL
        REFORM ON THE DRINKING STYLES OF URBAN PAPAGO INDIANS.
        Urban Anthropology, 5: 187-198,   1976.
        United States - Native Americans - Papago - change -
        urbanization   D-0974.

164.

1264. WADDELL, Jack O.
       THE ROLE OF THE CACTUS WINE RITUAL IN THE PAPAGO
       INDIAN ECOSYSTEM.
       In: Bharati, Agehananda, ed. Rituals, cults,
       shamanism: The realm of the extra-human, Volume 2:
       Ideas and actions. The Hague: Mouton, pp. 213-228,   1976.
       United States - Native Americans - Papago - economics -
       functions - homebrew - ritual - social organization   D-0973.

1265. Walker, Constance G.
       INFLUENCE OF PARENTAL DRINKING BEHAVIOR ON THAT OF
       ADOLESCENT NATIVE AMERICANS.
       M.S. Thesis, University of Washington,   1976.
       United States - Native Americans - enculturation -
       family - youth   D-0975.

1266. Wallace, Anthony F.C.
       THE INSTITUTIONALIZATION OF CATHARTIC AND CONTROL
       STRATEGIES IN IROQUOIS RELIGIOUS PSYCHOTHERAPY.
       In: Opler, Marvin K., ed. Culture and mental health.
       New York, NY: Macmillan, pp. 63-96,   1959.
       United States - Native Americans - Iroquois - change -
       Church - conversion - treatment   D-0072.

1267. Wallgren, Henrik
       THE ALCOHOLISM PROBLEM AS A CULTURAL QUESTION.
       Oy Alkoholiliike Ab:n Keskuslaboratorio, Report No. 7086,
       21 pp.,   1960.
       review - sociocultural   D-1206.

1268. Wallis, Wilson D., and Wallis, Ruth Sawtell
       CULTURE LOSS AND CULTURE CHANGE AMONG THE MICMAC OF
       THE CANADIAN MARITIME PROVINCES.
       Kroeber Anthropological Society Papers, 8-9: 100-129,   1953.
       Canada - Native Americans - Micmac - acculturation -
       anomie - stress   D-0250.

1269. Walsh, D.
       CULTURAL INFLUENCES IN PSYCHIATRIC ILLNESSES IN THE IRISH.
       Journal of the Irish Medical Association, 50(297):
       62-68,   1962.
       Ireland - family - folklore - psychiatric problems -
       stress - sociocultural   D-0976.

1270. Wanberg, Kenneth, and Horn, John L.
       ALCOHOLISM SYNDROMES RELATED TO SOCIOLOGICAL
       CLASSIFICATIONS.
       International Journal of the Addictions, 8(1): 99-120, 1973.
       United States - class - diagnosis   D-0977.

1271. Wang, Richard P.
A STUDY OF ALCOHOLISM IN CHINATOWN.
International Journal of Social Psychiatry, 14: 260-267, 1968.
United States - Overseas Chinese - acculturation - norms - social organization
D-0978.

1272. Wanner, Eric
POWER AND INHIBITION: A REVISION OF THE MAGICAL POTENCY THEORY.
In: McClelland, David C.; Davis, William N.; Kalin, Rudolf; and Wanner, Eric. The drinking man. New York, NY: Free Press, pp. 73-98, 1972.
power - self
D-0979.

1273. Warner, Rebecca H., and Rosett, Henry L.
EFFECTS OF DRINKING ON OFFSPRING: AN HISTORICAL SURVEY OF THE AMERICAN AND BRITISH LITERATURE.
Journal of Studies on Alcohol, 36(11): 1395-1420, 1975.
United States - England - attitudes - history, pre-1900 - pathology
D-0251.

1274. Washburne, Chandler
ALCOHOL, SELF AND THE GROUP.
Quarterly Journal of Studies on Alcohol, 17: 108-123, 1956.
functions - self - social organization
D-0980.

1275. Washburne, Chandler
PRIMITIVE DRINKING: A STUDY OF THE USES AND FUNCTIONS OF ALCOHOL IN PRELITERATE SOCIETIES.
New Haven, CT: College and University Press, 282 pp., 1961.
World survey - Cross-cultural - attitudes - customs - dysfunctions - functions - stress
D-0981.

1276. Washburne, Chandler
PRIMITIVE RELIGION AND ALCOHOL.
International Journal of Comparative Sociology, 9: 97-105, 1968.
functions - possession - religion - stress
D-0982.

1277. Watney, J.
MOTHER'S RUIN: A HISTORY OF GIN.
London: Peter Owen, 1976.
World survey - economics - history, pre-1900 - moonshine - political
D-0423.

1278. Weast, Donald E.
PATTERNS OF DRINKING AMONG INDIAN YOUTH: THE CASE OF A WISCONSIN TRIBE.
Ph.D. Dissertation, University of Wisconsin, 1969.
United States - Native Americans - Oneida - anomie - attitudes - consumption - youth
D-0983.

1279. Weathersbee, P.S.; Olsen, L.K.; and Lodge, J.R.
SELECTED BEVERAGE CONSUMPTION PATTERNS AMONG MORMON
AND NON-MORMON POPULATIONS FROM THE SAME GEOGRAPHIC
LOCATION.
American Journal of Clinical Nutrition, 30: 1162-1165, 1977.
Cross-ethnic - Protestants - cancer - Church -
consumption
D-0984.

1280. Webb, S., and Webb, B.
THE HISTORY OF LIQUOR LICENSING IN ENGLAND,
PRINCIPALLY FROM 1700 TO 1830.
London: Longmans, Green, 162 pp., 1903.
England - bar - change - economics - history, pre-1900 -
political
D-0252.

1281. Wechsler, H.; Demone, H.W., Jr.; Thum, D.; and Kasey, E.H.
RELIGIOUS-ETHNIC DIFFERENCES IN ALCOHOL CONSUMPTION.
Journal of Health and Social Behavior, 11: 21-29, 1970.
Cross-ethnic - Jews - Protestants - Church -
consumption
D-0985.

1282. Weigand, Phil C.
MOONSHINING IN SOUTHERN ILLINOIS.
In: Arens, William, and Montague, Susan, ed. The
American dimension: Cultural myths and social realities.
Sherman Oaks, CA: Alfred, 1976.
United States - economics - manufacture - moonshine
D-0986.

1283. Weil, Andrew, and de Rios, Marlene Dobkin
CROSS-CULTURAL COMPARISONS OF ALCOHOLISM AND DRUG ABUSE.
Unpublished paper: Conference on Alcoholism and Drug
Abuse, University of California, San Francisco, CA, 1976.
Cross-ethnic - drugs
D-1598.

1284. Werlin, J.
WEINREZEPTE AUS EINER SUDTIROLER SAMMELHANDSCHRIFT.
[Wine recipes from a South Tyrolian manuscript.] [Ger]
Archiv für Kulturgeschichte, 45: 243-252, 1963.
Tyrol - folklore - manufacture - wine
D-1233.

1285. West, Louis J.
A CROSS-CULTURAL APPROACH TO ALCOHOLISM.
Annals of the New York Academy of Sciences,
197: 214-216, 1972.
Mexico - Tarahumara - binge - functions - homebrew -
social organization
D-0987.

1286. Westermeyer, Joseph J.
ALCOHOL RELATED PROBLEMS AMONG OJIBWAY PEOPLE IN
MINNESOTA: A SOCIAL PSYCHIATRIC STUDY.
Ph.D. Dissertation, University of Minnesota, 1970.
United States - Native Americans - Ojibwa - dysfunctions -
epidemiology - prevention - psychiatric problems -

sociocultural   D-0988.

1287.   Westermeyer, Joseph J.
        USE OF ALCOHOL AND OPIUM BY THE MEO OF LAOS.
        American Journal of Psychiatry, 127: 1019-1023,   1971.
        Laos - Meo - binge - drugs - family - ritual - social
        organization   D-0989.

1288.   Westermeyer, Joseph J.
        OPTIONS REGARDING ALCOHOL USE AMONG THE CHIPPEWA.
        American Journal of Orthopsychiatry, 42: 398-403,   1972.
        United States - Native Americans - Chippewa - abstainers -
        aggression - change - functions - norms - sex - social
        organization   D-0990.

1289.   Westermeyer, Joseph J., and Brantner, John
        VIOLENT DEATH AND ALCOHOL USE AMONG THE CHIPPEWA IN
        MINNESOTA.
        Minnesota Medicine, 55: 749-752,   1972.
        United States - Native Americans - Chippewa - accidents -
        dysfunctions   D-0996.

1290.   Westermeyer, Joseph J.
        CROSS-CULTURAL STUDIES OF ALCOHOLISM IN THE CLINICAL
        SETTING.
        American Journal of Drug and Alcohol Abuse, 1: 89-105,   1974.
        Cross-ethnic - research methods - review   D-0991.

1291.   Westermeyer, Joseph [J.]
        THE "DRUNKEN INDIAN": MYTH AND REALITIES.
        Psychiatric Annals, 4: 29 ff,   1974.
        Native Americans - review - stereotype   D-0992.

1292.   Westermeyer, Joseph J., and Lang, Gretchen
        ETHNIC DIFFERENCES IN USE OF ALCOHOLISM FACILITIES.
        International Journal of the Addictions, 10(3): 513-520, 1975.
        Cross-ethnic - United States - Native Americans - Whites -
        treatment   D-0997.

1293.   Westermeyer, Joseph J.
        CLINICAL GUIDELINES FOR THE CROSS-CULTURAL TREATMENT OF
        CHEMICAL DEPENDENCY.
        American Journal of Drug and Alcohol Abuse, 3: 315-322,   1976.
        sociocultural - treatment   D-0995.

1294.   Westermeyer, Joseph J.
        CROSS-CULTURAL STUDIES OF ALCOHOLISM IN THE CLINICAL
        SETTING: A REVIEW AND EVALUATION.
        In: Everett, Michael W.; Waddell, Jack O.; and Heath,
        Dwight, B., ed. Cross-cultural approaches to the study
        of alcohol: An interdisciplinary perspective. The Hague:
        Mouton, pp. 359-377,   1976.
        Cross-ethnic - research methods - review   D-0994.

168.

1295. Westermeyer, Joseph J.
       USE OF A SOCIAL INDICATOR SYSTEM TO ASSESS ALCOHOLISM
       AMONG INDIAN PEOPLE IN MINNESOTA.
       American Journal of Drug and Alcohol Abuse,
       3(3): 447-456,   1976.
       United States - Native Americans - dysfunctions -
       epidemiology - research methods   D-0993.

1296. Wever, Oswald Raymond
       ALCOHOLISM IN ARUBA.
       Groningen: Drukkerij van Denderen, 308 pp.,   1977.
       West Indies - Alcoholics Anonymous - alcoholism -
       diagnosis - epidemiology   D-0073.

1297. Wheeler, Daniel
       EFFECTS OF THE INTRODUCTION OF ARDENT SPIRITS AND
       IMPLEMENTS OF WAR AMONG THE NATIVES OF THE SOUTH SEA
       ISLANDS AND NEW SOUTH WALES.
       London: Harvey and Darton,   1839.
       Oceania - Australia - change - distribution - history,
       pre-1900 - temperance   D-0998.

1298. White, Mervin Forrest
       DRINKING BEHAVIOR AS SYMBOLIC INTERACTION.
       Ph.D. Dissertation, University of Kentucky, 277 pp.,   1971.
       Cross-ethnic - Hawaiian Islands - stereotype   D-0999.

1299. White, Robert
       THE LOWER-CLASS "CULTURE OF EXCITEMENT" AMONG THE
       CONTEMPORARY SIOUX.
       In: Nurge, Ethel, ed. The modern Sioux: Social
       systems and reservation culture. Lincoln, NB:
       University of Nebraska Press, pp. 175-199,   1970.
       United States - Native Americans - Sioux - attitudes -
       class - norms   D-1000.

1300. Whitehead, Paul C.
       TOWARD A NEW PROGRAMMATIC APPROACH TO THE PREVENTION
       OF ALCOHOLISM: A RECONCILIATION OF THE SOCIO-CULTURAL
       AND DISTRIBUTION OF CONSUMPTION APPROACHES.
       Unpublished paper: Presented at the 30th International
       Congress on Alcoholism and Drug Dependence. Held
       September 4-9, 1972 in Amsterdam. 21 pp.,   1972.
       consumption - epidemiology - prevention - sociocultural   D-1207.

1301. Whitehead, Paul C., and Harvey, Cheryl
       EXPLAINING ALCOHOLISM: AN EMPIRICAL TEST AND
       REFORMULATION.
       Journal of Health and Social Behavior, 15: 57-65,   1974.
       World survey - Cross-cultural - ambivalence - consumption -
       norms   D-1001.

1302. Whittaker, James O.
       ALCOHOL AND THE STANDING ROCK SIOUX TRIBE: I. THE
       PATTERN OF DRINKING.
       Quarterly Journal of Studies on Alcohol, 23: 468-479,   1962.
       United States - Native Americans - Sioux - aggression -
       binge - change - consumption - economics - female -
       functions - norms - responsibility - sociocultural -
       stress   D-1527.

1303. Whittaker, James O.
       ALCOHOL AND THE STANDING ROCK SIOUX TRIBE: II.
       PSYCHODYNAMIC AND CULTURAL FACTORS IN DRINKING.
       Quarterly Journal of Studies on Alcohol, 24: 80-90,   1963.
       United States - Native Americans - Sioux - aggression -
       binge - change - consumption - economics - female -
       functions - norms - responsibility - sociocultural -
       stress   D-1002.

1304. Whittaker, J[ames] O.
       THE PROBLEM OF ALCOHOLISM AMONG AMERICAN RESERVATION
       INDIANS.
       Alcoholism, 2(2): 141-146,   1966.
       United States - Native Americans - Sioux - functions -
       norms - sociocultural - stress   D-1003.

1305. Whittet, M.M.
       AN APPROACH TO THE EPIDEMIOLOGY OF ALCOHOLISM: STUDIES
       IN THE HIGHLANDS AND ISLANDS OF SCOTLAND.
       British Journal of Addiction, 65: 325-339,   1970.
       Scotland - epidemiology   D-1004.

1306. Wicks, A.C.B.
       ALCOHOL: A CAUSE OF DIABETES IN RHODESIA.
       South African Medical Journal, 48: 1115-1117,   1974.
       Rhodesia - homebrew - pathology   D-1005.

1307. Wilkes, H. Garrison
       INTERESTING BEVERAGES OF THE EASTERN HIMALAYAS.
       Economic Botany, 22: 347-353,   1968.
       India - Tibet - homebrew - manufacture   D-0271.

1308. Wilkinson, Rupert
       THE PREVENTION OF DRINKING PROBLEMS: ALCOHOL CONTROL
       AND CULTURAL INFLUENCES.
       New York, NY: Oxford University Press, 301 pp.,   1970.
       United States - customs - history, pre-1900 - norms -
       prevention - review - sociocultural   D-1006.

1309. Williams, Brett
       SERVING UP SELVES AND PRESERVING THE SELF: WAITRESSES
       AT WORK.
       Journal of the Steward Anthropological Society, 6(2):
       90-117,   1975.

170.

	United States - bar - occupation	D-1007.
1310.	Williams, C.V. TAVERNERS, TAPSTERS AND TOPERS: A STUDY OF DRINKING AND DRUNKENNESS IN THE LITERATURE OF THE ENGLISH RENAISSANCE. Ph.D. Dissertation, Louisiana State University, 500 pp., England - bar - customs - history, pre-1900 - literature	1969. D-1008.
1311.	Williams, John R. A COMPARISON OF THE SELF-CONCEPTS OF ALCOHOLIC AND NON-ALCOHOLIC MALES OF INDIAN AND NON-INDIAN ANCESTRY IN TERMS OF SCORES ON THE TENNESSEE SELF CONCEPT SCALE. Ed.D. Dissertation, University of South Dakota, Cross-ethnic - Native Americans - Whites - self	1975. D-1009.
1312.	Wilson, [George] Carter EXPRESSION OF PERSONAL RELATIONS THROUGH DRINKING. In: Siverts, Henning, ed. Drinking patterns in highland Chiapas. Bergen: Universitetsforlaget, pp. 121-146, Mexico - Chamula - customs - functions - social organization	1972. D-1010.
1313.	Wilson, G.B. THE LIQUOR PROBLEM IN ENGLAND AND WALES: A SURVEY FROM 1860 TO 1935. British Journal of Inebriety, 38(4): 141-165, England - Wales - change - consumption - dysfunctions - economics - history, pre-1900 - pathology	1941. D-0074.
1314.	Wilson, George C[arter] DRINKING AND DRINKING CUSTOMS IN A MAYAN COMMUNITY. Unpublished paper: (Cornell-Columbia-Harvard Illinois Summer Field Studies Program in Mexico), Harvard University, Cambridge, MA, 101 pp., Mexico - Chamula - customs - functions - religion - ritual - social organization - sociocultural	1963. D-1240.
1315.	Wilson, J.R.; McClearn, G.E.; and Johnson, R.C. ETHNIC VARIATION IN USE AND EFFECTS OF ALCOHOL. Drug and Alcohol Dependence, 3: 147-151, Cross-ethnic - "race"	1978. D-0253.
1316.	Wilson, Lawrence, and Shore, James H. EVALUATION OF A REGIONAL INDIAN ALCOHOL PROGRAM. American Journal of Psychiatry, 132(3): 255-258, United States - Native Americans - treatment	1975. D-1011.
1317.	Wilson, R.L. EVIDENCE IN EMPTY BOTTLES. El Palacio, 66: 120-123, United States - customs - history, pre-1900 - research methods	1959. D-0254.

1318.   Winkler, Allan M.
        DRINKING ON THE AMERICAN FRONTIER.
        Quarterly Journal of Studies on Alcohol, 29: 413-445,   1968.
        United States - change - customs - economics - history,
        pre-1900   D-1012.

1319.   Winn, W.
        AMERICAN INDIAN ALCOHOLISM: ETIOLOGY AND IMPLICATIONS
        FOR EFFECTIVE TREATMENT.
        Alaska Medicine, 20(3): 30-32,   1978.
        United States - Native Americans - acculturation - etiology
        - self - sociocultural - stress   D-0255.

1320.   Wiseman, Jacqueline P.
        STATIONS OF THE LOST: THE TREATMENT OF SKID ROW ALCOHOLICS.
        Englewood Cliffs, NJ: Prentice-Hall, 346 pp.,   1970.
        United States - Skid Row - Church - customs - economics -
        norms   D-1013.

1321.   Wiseman, Jacqueline P.
        THE ALCOHOLIC'S RETURN TO SOCIETY.
        In: Rubington, Earl, and Weinberg, Martin S., ed. Deviance,
        the interactionist perspective: Text and readings in the
        sociology of deviance. (2nd ed.). New York, NY: Macmillan,
        pp. 414-427,   1973.
        United States - leisure - norms - treatment   D-1014.

1322.   Wiswe, H.
        DIE BRANNTWEINKALSCHALE: STUDIEN UM EIN SPEISEBRAUCHTUM.
        [A draft of cold brandy: Studies on a food custom.] [Ger]
        Beitraege zür Deutschen Volks- und Altertumskunde,
        8: 61-86,   1964.
        customs   D-1927.

1323.   Wolcott, Harry F.
        THE AFRICAN BEER GARDENS OF BULAWAYO: INTEGRATED
        DRINKING IN A SEGREGATED SOCIETY.
        New Brunswick, NJ: Rutgers Center of Alcohol Studies
        (Monograph No. 10), 261 pp.,   1974.
        Rhodesia - bar - beer - customs - dysfunctions - functions -
        political - social organization - sociocultural   D-1015.

1324.   Wolcott, Harry F.
        FEEDBACK INFLUENCES ON FIELDWORK; OR, A FUNNY THING
        HAPPENED ON THE WAY TO THE BEER GARDEN.
        In: Kileff, C., and Pendleton, W., ed. Urban man in
        Southern Africa. Gwelo (Rhodesia): Mambo Press,
        pp. 99-125,   1975.
        Rhodesia - research methods - sociocultural   D-1016.

1325.   Wolfe, Julie C., and Mauss, Armand C.
        DRINKING AS A "NON-DETERMINANT" OF SKID ROW REHABILITATION
        POTENTIAL.

Unpublished paper: Society for the Study of Social
Problems, Chicago, IL, 1977.
Skid Row - treatment D-1917.

1326. Wolff, Peter H.
ETHNIC DIFFERENCES IN ALCOHOL SENSITIVITY.
Science, 175(4020): 449-450, 1972.
Cross-ethnic - Orientals - Whites - metabolism -
"race" D-1017.

1327. Wolff, Peter H.
VASOMOTOR SENSITIVITY TO ALCOHOL IN DIVERSE MONGOLOID
POPULATIONS.
American Journal of Human Genetics, 25(2): 193-199, 1973.
Cross-ethnic - Native Americans - Orientals - Whites -
metabolism - "race" D-1018.

1328. Wolin, Steven J.; Bennett, Linda A.; and Noonan, Denise [L.]
RITUAL AND MYTH: THEIR ROLE IN THE INTERGENERATIONAL
CONTINUITY OF FAMILY IDENTITY.
Unpublished paper: National Council on Family Relations,
Theory Construction Workshop, New York, NY, 12 pp., 1976.
United States - family - folklore - ritual D-1599.

1329. Wolman, Carol
GROUP THERAPY IN TWO LANGUAGES, ENGLISH AND NAVAJO.
American Journal of Psychotherapy, 24: 677-685, 1970.
United States - Native Americans - Navaho - disulfiram -
treatment D-1019.

1330. Woodside, Arch G.; Bearden, William O.; and Ronkainen,
Ilkka
IMAGES ON SERVING MARIJUANA, ALCOHOLIC BEVERAGES, AND
SOFT DRINKS.
Journal of Psychology, 96: 11-14, 1977.
United States - attitudes - youth D-0256.

1331. Wright, Anne
THE BAR SCENE: GENDER DIFFERENCES IN NONVERBAL
BEHAVIOR.
Unpublished paper: American Anthropological Association,
Houston, TX, 12 pp., 1977.
United States - bar - female - research methods - social
organization - space D-1908.

1332. Wright-St. Clair, R.E.
BEER IN THERAPEUTICS: AN HISTORICAL ANNOTATION.
New Zealand Medical Journal, 61: 512-513, 1962.
World survey - beer - homebrew - history, pre-1500 -
history, pre-1900 - medical D-1020.

1333. Yamamuro, Bufo
       NOTES ON DRINKING IN JAPAN.
       Quarterly Journal of Studies on Alcohol, 15: 491-498,   1954.
       Japan - Buddhism - change - customs - history, pre-1500 -
       history, pre-1900 - prehistory - religion - ritual -
       social organization   D-1021.

1334. Yamamuro, Bufo
       JAPANESE DRINKING PATTERNS: ALCOHOLIC BEVERAGES IN
       LEGEND, HISTORY AND CONTEMPORARY RELIGIONS.
       Quarterly Journal of Studies on Alcohol, 19: 482-490,   1958.
       Japan - Buddhism - ambivalence - change - customs -
       history, pre-1500 - history, pre-1900 - prehistory -
       religion - ritual - social organization   D-1022.

1335. Yamamuro, Bufo
       FURTHER NOTES ON JAPANESE DRINKING.
       Quarterly Journal of Studies on Alcohol, 25: 150-153,   1964.
       Japan - folklore - medical - prohibition   D-1023.

1336. Yamamuro, Bufo
       ORIGINS OF SOME JAPANESE DRINKING CUSTOMS.
       Quarterly Journal of Studies on Alcohol, 29: 979-982,   1968.
       Japan - customs - folklore - history, pre-1500   D-1024.

1337. Yarshater, E.
       THE THEME OF WINE-DRINKING AND THE CONCEPT OF THE BELOVED
       IN EARLY PERSIAN POETRY.
       Studia Islamica, 7(13): 43-53,   1960.
       Persians, ancient - attitudes - history, pre-1500 -
       literature - wine   D-0075.

1338. Yawney, Carole D.
       THE COMPARATIVE STUDY OF DRINKING PATTERNS IN PRIMITIVE
       CULTURES.
       Toronto, Ont.: Addiction Research Foundation, Substudy
       No. 301, 21 pp.,   1967.
       World survey - Cross-ethnic - acculturation - change -
       dysfunctions - functions - review - sociocultural   D-1208.

1339. Yawney, Carole D.
       DRINKING PATTERNS AND ALCOHOLISM IN TRINIDAD.
       McGill Studies in Caribbean Anthropology Occasional
       Papers, 5: 34-48,   1969.
       Cross-ethnic - Trinidad - Blacks - Overseas Indians -
       ambivalence - customs - dysfunctions - functions - norms -
       sociocultural   D-1025.

1340. Younger, William
       GODS, MEN AND WINE.
       Cleveland, OH: World, 516 pp.,   1966.
       World survey - Classical peoples - containers - history,
       pre-1500 - manufacture - prehistory - religion   D-1026.

1341.   Zeiner, Arthur R.; Paredes, Alfonso; and Cowden,
        Lawrence
        PHYSIOLOGIC RESPONSES TO ETHANOL AMONG TARAHUMARA
        INDIANS.
        Annals of the New York Academy of Sciences,
        273: 151-158,   1976.
        Mexico - Tarahumara - metabolism   D-1028.

1342.   Zeiner, Arthur R.; Paredes, Alfonso; Musicant, Robert A.;
        and Cowden, Lawrence
        RACIAL DIFFERENCES IN PSYCHOPHYSIOLOGICAL RESPONSES TO
        ETHANOL AND PLACEBO.
        In: Seixas, Frank A., ed. Currents in alcoholism,
        Volume 1: Biological, biochemical, and clinical topics.
        New York, NY: Grune & Stratton, pp. 271-286,   1977.
        Cross-ethnic - Tarahumara - Whites - metabolism -
        "race"   D-1029.

1343.   Zeiner, Arthur R., and Paredes, Alfonso
        RACIAL DIFFERENCES IN CIRCADIAN VARIATION OF ETHANOL
        METABOLISM.
        Alcoholism: Clinical and Experimental Research,
        2: 71-76,   1978.
        Cross-ethnic - metabolism - "race"   D-1027.

1344.   Zentner, Henry
        FACTORS IN THE SOCIAL PATHOLOGY OF A NORTH AMERICAN
        INDIAN SOCIETY.
        Anthropologica, 5: 119-130,   1963.
        Canada - Native Americans - Iroquois - Alcoholics
        Anonymous - dysfunctions - norms   D-1030.

1345.   Zimberg, Sheldon
        SOCIOPSYCHIATRIC PERSPECTIVES ON JEWISH ALCOHOL ABUSE:
        IMPLICATIONS FOR THE PREVENTION OF ALCOHOLISM.
        American Journal of Drug and Alcohol Abuse, 4(4): 571-579, 1977.
        United States - Jews - change - enculturation - norms -
        prevention   D-0082.

1346.   Zingg, Robert M.
        THE GENUINE AND SPURIOUS VALUES IN TARAHUMARA CULTURE.
        American Anthropologist, 44: 78-92,   1942.
        Mexico - Tarahumara - functions - dysfunctions -
        religion - social organization   D-1031.

1347.   Zitzen, E.G.
        DER WEIN IN DER WORT- UND WIRTSCHEFTGESCHICHTE. [Wine
        in literature and history.] [Ger]
        Bonn: [no publisher],   1952.
        Europe - history, pre-1500 - history, pre-1900 -
        literature - wine   D-1216.

1348.   Zurukzoglu, S.
           DER ALKOHOLISMUS ALS KULTURSCHADEN. [Alcoholism as a
           culture fault.]   [Ger]
           Praxis, 53: 917-918,   1964.
           Germany - dysfunctions   D-0076.

1349.   Zwick, Gwen
           PROHIBITION IN THE CHEROKEE NATION, 1820-1907.
           M.A. Thesis, University of Oklahoma,   1940.
           United States - Native Americans - Cherokee - change -
           economics - history, pre-1900 - prohibition   D-1032.

APPENDIX:

RESEARCH IN PROGRESS

Alcohol Use and World Cultures Escalante, Fernando

1. Aiyappan, A.
   [RESEARCH IN PROGRESS: ALCOHOL AND ANXIETY IN ORISSA, INDIA.] (n.d.)
   India - stress D-1974.

2. Blume, Sheila
   [RESEARCH IN PROGRESS: DRINKING AMONG JEWS IN CONTEMPORARY U.S.A.] (n.d.)
   United States - Jews D-1975.

3. Brown, Donald N.
   DRINKING AS AN INDICATOR OF COMMUNITY DISHARMONY: THE PEOPLE OF TAOS PUEBLO.
   In: Waddell, Jack O., and Everett, Michael W., ed. Drinking behavior among Southwestern Indians. Tucson, AZ: University of Arizona Press, [expected 1980] (n.d.)
   United States - Native Americans - Taos - dysfunctions - norms - social organization D-1976.

4. Cardi, Jeanne
   [RESEARCH IN PROGRESS: DRINKING PATTERNS IN JAPAN.] (n.d.)
   Japan D-1977.

5. Carlson, Katherine A.
   [IN PREPARATION: STRANGERS IN FAMILIAR PLACES: BAR INTERACTION AND PUBLIC DRINKING.] (n.d.)
   United States - bar D-1978.

6. Charest, Paul
   [RESEARCH IN PROGRESS: FUNCTIONS OF ALCOHOLIC BEVERAGES AMONG THE AFRICAN MANDINGOLU.] (n.d.)
   Africa - Mandingolu D-1979.

7. Cooley, Richard
   NATIVE AMERICANS AND ALCOHOL PROGRAMS.
   In: Waddell, Jack O., and Everett, Michael W., ed. Drinking behavior among Southwestern Indians. Tucson, AZ: University of Arizona Press, [expected 1980] (n.d.)
   United States - Native Americans - attitudes - norms - sociocultural - treatment D-1980.

8. De Lima, Florence
   [RESEARCH IN PROGRESS: DRINKING HABITS OF EAST INDIANS IN CUREPE.] (n.d.)
   Overseas Indians - West Indies D-1993.

9. Escalante, Fernando
   GROUP PRESSURE AND EXCESSIVE DRINKING AMONG NATIVE AMERICANS: A NATIVE AMERICAN'S PERSPECTIVE.
   In: Waddell, Jack O., and Everett, Michael W., ed. Drinking behavior among Southwestern Indians. Tucson, AZ: University of Arizona Press, [expected 1980] (n.d.)
   United States - Native Americans - attitudes - dysfunctions -

norms - social organization D-1981.

10. Everett, Michael W.
DRINKING AS A MEASURE OF PROPER BEHAVIOR: THE WHITE
MOUNTAIN APACHES.
In: Waddell, Jack O., and Everett, Michael W., ed.
<u>Drinking behavior among Southwestern Indians</u>. Tucson, AZ:
University of Arizona Press, [expected 1980] (n.d.)
United States - Native Americans - Apache - attitudes -
functions - norms - social organization - youth D-1982.

11. Gailfus, Patricia T.
[RESEARCH IN PROGRESS: HEAVY DRINKING AMONG TURTLE
MOUNTAIN INDIANS.] (n.d.)
Native Americans D-1983.

12. Glotzer, Richard
[RESEARCH IN PROGRESS: DRINKING IN BLACK TOWNSHIPS IN
NATAL, SOUTH AFRICA.] (n.d.)
South Africa - Natal - urbanization D-1984.

13. Graves, Theodore D.
[RESEARCH IN PROGRESS: DRINKING AND VIOLENCE IN TAVERNS
IN URBAN NEW ZEALAND.] (n.d.)
New Zealand - aggression - bar D-1985.

14. Hamer, John H., and Steinbring, Jack, ed.
[ALCOHOL AND THE NORTH AMERICAN INDIAN: EXAMPLES FROM
THE SUB-ARCTIC.] (n.d.)
Native Americans D-1986.

15. Heath, Dwight B.; Waddell, Jack O.; and Topper, Martin, D., ed.
<u>CULTURAL ASPECTS OF ALCOHOL USE AND TREATMENT</u>.
New Brunswick, NJ: Center of Alcohol Studies, Rutgers
University, [expected 1980] (n.d.)
United States - Cross-ethnic - Native Americans - Blacks -
Hispanos - functions - norms - sociocultural - treatment D-1987.

16. Johnson, Ronald C.
[RESEARCH IN PROGRESS: ETHNIC DIFFERENCES IN ALCOHOL
RELATED BEHAVIORS.] (n.d.)
Cross-ethnic - family - "race" D-1988.

17. King, Doris E.
[RESEARCH IN PROGRESS: ROLE OF TAVERNS IN THE AMERICAN
REVOLUTION] (n.d.)
United States - bar - history, pre-1900 - political D-1989.

18. Lawrence, Robert
[RESEARCH IN PROGRESS: DIFFERENTIAL DRINKING ATTITUDES
AND BEHAVIOR AMONG WOLOF CASTES IN SENEGAL, WEST AFRICA.] (n.d.)
Senegal - Wolof - attitudes - caste - customs D-1990.

19. Levy, Robert I.
    [IN PREPARATION: DRINKING AMONG THE NEWARS OF
    NEPAL.] (n.d.)
    Nepal - Newar D-1991.

20. Lewis, Robert F.
    [RESEARCH IN PROGRESS: ZUNI ALCOHOLISM PROGRAM.] (n.d.)
    United States - Native Americans - Zuni - treatment D-1992.

21. Long, Joseph K.
    [IN PREPARATION: DRINKING AND WITCHCRAFT AS INDICES
    OF TENSION IN LATIN AMERICA.] (n.d.)
    Cross-ethnic - Latin America - stress D-1994.

22. Lundberg, Greta
    [IN PREPARATION: SOCIOCULTURAL CHANGE AND DRINKING
    PATTERNS IN BRITISH HONDURAS.] (n.d.)
    Belize D-1995.

23. Maha Patra, Shri S.K.
    [IN PREPARATION: ALCOHOL AND ALCOHOLISM AMONG TRIBAL
    COMMUNITIES IN ORISSA, INDIA.] (n.d.)
    India - customs D-1996.

24. Malen, Vernon D.
    [IN PREPARATION: VALUE ORIENTATIONS AND ALCOHOLISM ON
    THE PINE RIDGE SIOUX RESERVATION.] (n.d.)
    United States - Native Americans - Sioux - norms D-1997.

25. McCall, Grant
    [IN PREPARATION: DRINKING PATTERNS OF THE BASQUES.] (n.d.)
    Spain - Basques - customs D-1998.

26. McCloy, Sandra G.
    [IN PREPARATION: DRINKING PATTERNS AND RELIGION IN THE
    OUTER HEBRIDES.] (n.d.)
    Scotland - Hebrides Islands - conversion D-1999.

27. Miller, Maurice W., and Ostendorf, Don
    NATIVE AMERICANS AND MENTAL HEALTH PROGRAMS.
    In: Waddell, Jack O., and Everett, Michael W., ed.
    Drinking behavior among Southwestern Indians. Tucson, AZ:
    University of Arizona Press, [expected 1980] (n.d.)
    United States - Native Americans - psychiatric problems -
    treatment D-2000.

28. Nissly, Charles M.
    [IN PREPARATION: CHICHA IN PERU.] (n.d.)
    Peru - homebrew D-2001.

29. Nolan, Riall W.
    [IN PREPARATION: BEER AMONG THE BASSARI OF SENEGAL,
    WEST AFRICA.] (n.d.)

	Senegal - Bassari - change - economics - functions - homebrew - manufacture - possession - ritual - social organization - sociocultural	D-2002.
30.	Owen, Roger C. [IN PREPARATION: ALCOHOL IN SEVERAL BRAZILIAN POPULATION SEGMENTS: AN EVOLUTIONARY APPROACH.] Brazil - class - social organization	(n.d.) D-2003.
31.	Paredes, Alfonso, and Khalil, S. [RESEARCH IN PROGRESS: SOCIAL CONTROLS OF DRINKING BEHAVIOR IN ISLAM.] Islam - norms	(n.d.) D-2004.
32.	Popham, Robert E. [IN PREPARATION: NOTES ON THE TAVERN IN CONTEMPORARY LIFE; EXPECTED 1980.] World survey - bar - functions - sociocultural	(n.d.) D-2005.
33.	Quarcoo, A.K. [IN PREPARATION: ALCOHOL AND TRADITIONAL RELIGIONS IN GHANA.] Ghana - Cross-ethnic - religion	(n.d.) D-2006.
34.	Rao, M.S.A. [IN PREPARATION: A RELIGIOUS TEMPERANCE MOVEMENT AND ITS IMPACT ON A TODDY-TAPPING CASTE IN KERALA, INDIA.] India - caste - change - conversion - occupation	(n.d.) D-2007.
35.	Raskin, Neil H. [IN PREPARATION: ETHNIC AND INDIVIDUAL VARIATIONS IN ETHANOL METABOLISM.] Cross-ethnic - Native Americans - Orientals - Whites - metabolism - "race"	(n.d.) D-2008.
36.	Reimer, Toni T. [RESEARCH IN PROGRESS: DIFFERENCES IN ALCOHOL METABOLISM IN THREE HUMAN POPULATIONS.] metabolism - "race"	(n.d.) D-2009.
37.	Sanders, Andrew [RESEARCH IN PROGRESS: ALCOHOL AND ALIENATION AMONG GUYANESE INDIANS.] Guiana	(n.d.) D-2010.
38.	Schmidt, J.J. [IN PREPARATION: DRINKING PATTERNS IN AN URBAN BANTU COMMUNITY.] Africa - Bantu	(n.d.) D-2011.
39.	Segal, Boris M. [IN PREPARATION: CONTEMPORARY AND HISTORICAL STUDIES OF ALCOHOL USE IN THE SOVIET UNION.]	(n.d.)

Soviet Union - change - customs - economics -
history, pre-1500 - history, pre-1900 - norms -
political - sociocultural   D-2012.

40. Smith, Valene
[RESEARCH IN PROGRESS: RELATIONSHIP BETWEEN HYPOGLYCEMIA,
DIET, AND ALCOHOLISM AMONG AMERICAN INDIANS AND ESKIMOS.]   (n.d.)
Eskimos - Native Americans - hypoglycemia   D-2013.

41. Topper, Martin D.
DRINKING AS AN EXPRESSION OF STATUS: NAVAJO MALE
ADOLESCENTS.
In: Waddell, Jack O., and Everett, Michael W., ed.
Drinking behavior among Southwestern Indians. Tucson, AZ:
University of Arizona Press, [expected 1980]   (n.d.)
United States - Native Americans - Navaho - stereotype -
youth   D-2014.

42. Vogt, Evon Z.
[IN PREPARATION: ALCOHOLISM IN TWO MEXICAN INDIAN
COMMUNITIES.]   (n.d.)
Cross-ethnic - Mexico - Chamula - Zinacantan - change -
sociocultural   D-2015.

43. Waddell, Jack O.
ALCOHOLIC INTOXICATION AS A COMPONENT OF THE PAPAGO
INDIAN SYSTEM OF EXPERIENTIAL REALITY.
Ultimate Reality and Meaning, 1(3): [expected 1980]   (n.d.)
United States - Native Americans - Papago - customs -
intoxication - norms   D-2016.

44. Waddell, Jack O.
DRINKING AS A MEANS OF ARTICULATING SOCIAL AND CULTURAL
VALUES: PAPAGOS IN AN URBAN SETTING.
In: Waddell, Jack O., and Everett, Michael W., ed.
Drinking behavior among Southwestern Indians. Tucson, AZ:
University of Arizona Press, [expected 1980]   (n.d.)
United States - Native Americans - Papago - functions -
norms - social organization - sociocultural - urbanization   D-2017.

45. Waddell, Jack O., and Everett, Michael W., ed.
DRINKING BEHAVIOR AMONG SOUTHWESTERN INDIANS.
Tucson, AZ: University of Arizona Press, [expected 1980]   (n.d.)
United States - Native Americans   D-2018.

46. Waddell, Jack O.
SIMILARITIES AND VARIATIONS IN ALCOHOL USE IN FOUR
NATIVE AMERICAN SOCIETIES IN THE SOUTHWEST.
In: Waddell, Jack O., and Everett, Michael W., ed.
Drinking behavior among Southwestern Indians. Tucson, AZ:
University of Arizona Press, [expected 1980]   (n.d.)
United States - Native Americans - Cross-ethnic   D-2019.

A47   Appendix

47.   Waddell, Jack O.
         THE USE OF INTOXICATING BEVERAGES AMONG NATIVE PEOPLES
         OF THE ABORIGINAL GREATER SOUTHWEST.
         In: Waddell, Jack O., and Everett, Michael W., ed.
         Drinking behavior among Southwestern Indians. Tucson, AZ:
         University of Arizona Press, [expected 1980]   (n.d.)
         United States - Native Americans - distribution -
         history, pre-1900   D-2020.

48.   Webe, Gosta
         [IN PREPARATION: A DISTRIBUTIONAL STUDY OF DRINKING
         AMONG SOUTH AMERICAN INDIANS.]   (n.d.)
         South America - customs - distribution - homebrew -
         manufacture - sociocultural   D-2021.

49.   Wood, Ron
         URBAN NATIVE AMERICANS AND ALCOHOLISM PROGRAMS.
         In: Waddell, Jack O., and Everett, Michael W., ed.
         Drinking behavior among Southwestern Indians. Tucson, AZ:
         University of Arizona Press, [expected 1980]   (n.d.)
         United States - Native Americans - treatment   D-2022.

INDEX OF AUTHORS

The purpose of this index is to help anyone who wants to find the work of a particular individual. The alphabetic organization of the list of citations is helpful in finding works that are written by a single author, or those of which the individual in question is the "senior author" (i.e., the author whose name is listed first, and who is presumed to have played a major role in the research and/or writing). But it is often useful also to find books or articles of which a person is a "junior author"; one obvious reason would be that a subject, concept, theory, or approach that was addressed by an author in one context is likely to recur, whether in updated or otherwise revised form, in other writings by that person.

In this index, the names of all of the authors whose works are cited appear, in alphabetic sequence by surname. Those numbers following each name are the numbers of individual references in the list of "Citations" rather than page-numbers within this volume. Numbers that are underlined indicate the items of which that individual is sole or senior author.

Editorials and other unsigned publications are listed under "Anonymous", regardless of the source in which they appear.

AUTHOR INDEX

Aalto, P.
  1
Abad, V.
  2
Ablon, J.
  3-8
Abu-Laban, B.
  9
Ackerman, L.A.
  10
Adair, J.
  11
Adandé, A.
  12, 13
Adaranijo, H.
  56
Ade, G.
  14
Adis Castro, G.
  566
Adler, N.
  15
Adler, R.J.
  1232
Adomakoh, C.C.
  16
Adriaens, E.L.
  17, 18
Adrian, J.
  937
Aguilar, G.Z.
  19
Ahlström-Laakso, S.
  20
Aiyappan, A.
  A1
Alba, M.D.
  21
Albaugh, B.
  22
Albrecht, S.L.
  1134
Alday, R.K.
  23
Aldo, P.
  922
Alhava, A.
  24
Allardt, E.
  25, 26

Allen, H.W.
  27
Allman, L.P.
  28
Almeida V., M.
  29
Almeida Vargas, M.
  219
Alonso Fernández, F.
  30, 31
Amar, A.M.
  32
Amark, C.
  33
Amsel, Z.
  34
Anderson, B.G.
  35
Anderson, P.O.
  22
Anderson, R.K.
  36
Ando, H.
  37
Andorka, R.
  38
András Falvy, B.
  39
Angrosino, M.V.
  40-42
Anonymous
  43-55
Anumonye, A.
  56, 57
Apostle, R.
  58
Appia, M.G.
  59
Arnold, J.P.
  60
Askwith, G.R.
  61
Asmundsson, G.
  529
Austin, W.K.
  448
Ayats, H.
  278, 279, 309
Azayem, G.M.
  62

Azrin, N.H.
575

Babcock, C.G.
63
Babor, T.F.
64
Babow, I.
65
Bacon, M.K.
66-71, 104, 246, 247
Bacon, S.D.
72-77
Baddeley, F.J.
78
Badri, M.B.
79
Baha, C.J.
369
Bahr, H.M.
80-84
Baird, E.G.
85-89
Baker, J.L.
90
Baker, J.M.
91
Baker, O.
92
Baldus, H.
93
Bales, R.F.
94
Balikci, A.
95
Banay, R.S.
96
Banks, E.
97
Barber, K.
802
Barclay, W.S.
1090
Bard, J.
98
Barlett, P.F.
99
Barnett, M.L.
100
Barrera Vásquez, A.
101

Barrow, M.V.
102
Barry, E.
103
Barry, H., III
66, 67, 104-106, 246, 247
Barter, E.R.
107
Barter, J.T.
107
Basserman Jordan, F.V.
108
Beals, R.L.
109
Bearden, W.O.
1330
Beaubrun, M.H.
110-115
Beckett, J.
116
Beckley, R.E.
237
Beede, L.I.
117
Begleiter, H.
663
Beidelman, T.O.
118
Bejarano, J.
119
Bell, M.
120
Bellmann, H.
121
Belmont, F.V. de
122
Belshaw, C.S.
509
Benjamin, R.
123
Bennett, L.
124, 125
Bennett, L.A.
1328
Bennion, L.J.
126
Benos, J.
127
Berg, C.
128
Bergman, R.L.
162

Bernier, G.
  129, 130
Berreman, G.D.
  131
Berruecos, L.A.
  132
Bett, W.R.
  133
Bickerton, Y.J.
  134, 135
Billiard, R.
  136
Billings, A.G.
  137, 138
Bismuth, H.
  139-140
Bissonette, R.
  141
Bitsuie, D.
  183
Bittker, T.E.
  142, 143
Blacker, E.
  144
Blacker, H.
  145, 146
Blane, H.T.
  147, 148
Blaney, R.
  149
Blehr, O.
  150
Bleichsteiner, R.
  151
Blevans, S.A.
  152
Blignaut, F.W.
  153
Blom, F.
  154
Bloom, J.D.
  155
Blum, E.M.
  156, 157
Blum, R.H.
  156-158
Blume, S.
  A2
Blyth, W.
  159
Boalt, G.
  160

Boatman, J.F.
  161
Bock, G.E.
  162
Bollinger, J.
  683
Bolton, R.
  163
Bonfiglio, G.
  164
Bose, D.K.
  165
Botha, E.M.
  166
Bourguignon, E.E.
  167, 168
Bourke, J.G.
  169, 170
Boutilier, L.R.
  1226
Boyatzis, R.E.
  171, 172
Boyce, G.A.
  173
Boyer, L.B.
  174, 175
Braidwood, R.J.
  176
Branson, H.
  177
Brantner, J.
  1289
Bratrude, A.P.
  1193
Bregenzer, J.M.
  1052
Brelsford, G.
  178
Brettler, P.
  179
Brod, T.M.
  180
Brody, H.
  181
Brown, D.N.
  A3
Brown, E.M.
  1193
Brown, J.
  430
Brown, J.H.
  182

189.

Brown, R.C.
183
Brown, R.M.
578
Brown, W.L.
184
Brown, W.R., III
185
Brownlee, F.
186
Bruman, H.J.
187-189
Bruun, K.
190-192
Bubenik, V.
193
Buchanan, W.M.
194
Buchwald, C.
104
Buckland, A.W.
195
Buckley, P.L.
196
Buda, B.
38
Buehlmann, J.
197
Bullemer, K.
198
Bunzel, R.
199, 200
Burgstaller, E.
201
Burns, M.
202
Burton-Bradley, B.G.
203, 204
Busch, C.E.
205
Butterfass, T.O.
206
Butterworth, D.S.
207

Cagol, A.
208
Cahalan, D.
209-214
Calderón Narvaez, G.
215, 216

Calkins, R.
217
Calvo, J.
36
Campillo-Serrano, C.
314
Canelos, S.P.
218
Caplow, T.
82
Caravedo Carranza, B.
219
Cardenas, M.
297
Cardi, J.
A4
Cardinal, D.J.
220
Cardinal, H.
221
Carlson, K.A.
222, A5
Carpenter, E.S.
223
Carr, L.G.
224
Carson, G.
225
Carstairs, G.M.
226
Carter, C.
854
Carter, W.E.
227
Cartwright, A.K.
228
Cassava, N.
229
Castetter, E.F.
230
Catanzaro, R.J.
956
Cavan, S.
231
Certhoux, A.
1011
Cervantes, G.E.
232
Cevallos, R.
218
Chadwick, B.A.
81

Chafetz, M.E.
    <u>233</u>, <u>234</u>
Chaiaramonte, J.
    <u>235</u>
Chakravarty, T.
    <u>236</u>
Chalfant, H.P.
    <u>237</u>
Chalke, H.D.
    <u>238</u>
Chambers, C.D.
    1115
Charest, P.
    <u>239</u>, <u>A6</u>
Chattopadhya, A.
    <u>240</u>
Chavira, J.A.
    <u>241</u>, 1221
Chegwidden, M.
    <u>242</u>
Cheinisse, L.
    <u>243</u>
Chen, S.-H.
    1160
Cherrington, E.H.
    <u>244</u>
Chiappe, M.
    <u>245</u>
Child, I.L.
    66, 67, 104, <u>246</u>, <u>247</u>
Cho, H.C.
    <u>248</u>
Chopra, G.S.
    249
Chopra, J.C.
    249
Chopra, R.N.
    249
Chowenhill, R.C.
    1182
Christoffel, K.
    <u>250</u>
Chu, G.
    <u>251</u>
Cinquemani, D.K.
    <u>252</u>
Cisin, I.H.
    209, 212, <u>253</u>
Clairmont, D.H.
    <u>254</u>, <u>255</u>
Clark, N.H.
    <u>256</u>

Clark, W.B.
    <u>257-259</u>
Clarke, F.
    <u>260</u>
Claudian, J.
    <u>261</u>
Clemmesen, C.
    <u>262</u>
Clinard, M.N.
    <u>263</u>
Clinebell, H.J., Jr.
    <u>264</u>
Cobb, J.C.
    455
Cockerham, W.
    <u>265</u>
Cockerham, W.C.
    <u>266</u>, <u>267</u>
Coffey, T.G.
    <u>268</u>, <u>269</u>
Cohen, H.H.
    <u>270</u>
Cohen, R.
    <u>271</u>
Collard, J.
    <u>272</u>
Collett, J.
    <u>273</u>
Collins, T.
    <u>274</u>, <u>275</u>
Collis, C.H.
    <u>276</u>, <u>277</u>
Collomb, H.
    <u>278</u>, <u>279</u>, 309
Connell, K.H.
    <u>280</u>
Connor, W.D.
    <u>281</u>, <u>282</u>
Conrad, R.D.
    <u>283</u>
Cook, P.
    <u>284</u>
Cook, P.J.
    276, 277
Cooley, R.
    <u>A7</u>
Cooney, J.G.
    <u>285</u>
Cooper, J.M.
    <u>286</u>
Cornwall, E.E.
    <u>287</u>

Covington, J.W.
288
Cowden, L.
1341, 1342
Crahan, M.E.
289
Cramer, J.O.
649
Crawford, M.
830
Crawfurd, J.
290
Crawley, A.E.
291, 292
Cromwell, W.O.
293
Crossley, H.M.
209
Crothers, T.D.
294
Csikszentmihalyi, M.
295
Curley, R.T.
296
Cutler, H.C.
297
Cutler, R.
298
Cutler, R.E.
299
Cutter, H.S.G.
300
Cutter, T.
301
Cuzent, G.
302

Dabney, J.E.
303
Dailey, R.C.
304-306
Daily, J.M.
202
D'Albuquerque, I.L.
452
Danielou, J.
307
Dann, J.L.
308
Da Piedade, J.
309

Davies, C.S.
310
Davis, W.
832
Davis, W.N.
311, 628, 833, 834
Dawson, W.R.
312
Day, R.C.
81
Declay, E.
369
Defer, B.
313
De la Fuente, R.
314
De Lejarza, F.
315
De Lima, F.
A8
De Lint, J.
316, 430
Delk, J.L.
626
Delle Monache, F.
452
De Mello, J.F.
452
Demerdash, A.
317
Demone, H.W., Jr.
1281
Dennis, P.A.
318
De Rios, M.D.
319, 320, 1283
Desai, A.V.
321
Dessirier, R.
322
Dettori, R.G.
323
Devenyi, P.
324
Devereux, G.
325, 326
Dewar, R.
327
Dight, S.E.
328

Dinitz, S.
 329
Diop, M.
 279
Disselhoff, H.D.
 330
Djenda, M.
 331
Dobyns, H.F.
 332
Dodson, J.
 275
Dodson, J.W.
 333
Donnelly, J.P.
 334
Dorman, N.
 492
Dosman, E.J.
 335
Doughty, P.L.
 336
Douyon, E.
 337
Doxat, J.
 338
Dozier, E.P.
 339
Drilling, V.
 340
Driver, H.E.
 341, 342
Drower, E.S.
 343
Duennebier, S.A.
 344
Duffy, J.
 953
Duka, N.
 345
Dumett, R.E.
 346
Dumont, M.P.
 347
Duncan, E.
 348
Durand, D.
 349
Durand, L.
 350
Durgin, E.
 351

Du Toit, B.M.
 352
Dwyer, E.
 353
Ebrahimi, F.
 881
Eddy, R.
 354
Edgerton, R.B.
 355, 773
Edzard, D.O.
 356
Efron, V.
 357, 358
Eguchi, P.K.
 359
Eis, G.
 360
Eldar, P.
 361
Elwin, V.
 362
Emboden, W.
 363
Emerson, E.R.
 364
Endfield, M.R.
 369
Eriksson, K.
 365
Erlich, V.S.
 366
Ervin, A.M.
 367
Escalante, F.
 A9
Evangelista, A.E.
 368
Everett, M.W.
 369-371, 681, 729, A10, A45
Ewing, J.A.
 372
Eyolfson, C.
 348
Ezell, P.H.
 373
F., H.
 374

Fairbanks, R.A.
375
Fallding, H.
376
Falli, S.
164
Farris, J.J.
377, 378
Favre, H.
379
Fazey, C.
380
Feinhandler, S.
492
Feldman, D.J.
319, 320
Feldman, W.M.
381, 382
Feldstein, A.
383
Felice, Ph. de
384
Feliciano, R.T.
385
Fenasse, J.M.
386
Fenna, D.
387
Ferguson, F.N.
388-392
Ferrant, J.-P.
64
Ferreira, A.G.
393
Field, P.B.
394
Figueroa-Rosales, R.
395
Finkler, H.W.
396
Finney, F.F.
397
Firebaugh, W.C.
398, 399
Firth, H.
112
Fiume, S.
400
Flaherty, B.J.
242
Foreman, J.K.
276, 277

Forslund, M.A.
265
Fort, J.
401
Fortuine, R.
102
Foulks, E.F.
402
Fouquet, P.
403
Franke, C.O.
404
Frederick, C.J.
405
Frederikson, O.F.
406
French, R.V.
407
Frese, W.
1027, 1028
Freund, P.
408
Friedman, G.D.
664
Fritz, W.B.
409
Frøland, B.
410, 826
Fromm, E.
411
Fuente, R. de la, see
De la Fuente, R.
Fukui, K.
412
Fukui, M.
413, 1160
Futterman, S.
929, 930

Gabe, R.C.
414
Gadourek, I.
415
Gaete, J.
1197
Gai, B.M.
416
Gaileus, P.T.
All
Galan, F.J.
417

Galang, R.C.
  418
Gallagher, M.M.
  479
Gallagher, O.R.
  419
García Alcaraz, A.
  420
Gardner, R.E.
  421
Garland, M.A.
  422
Garrett, G.R.
  84
Gayre, G.R.
  423
Geertz, C.
  424
Gelfand, M.
  425, 426
Geralin, H.
  427
Gerard, M.J.
  664
Ghosh, S.K.
  428
Gibbins, R.J.
  999, 1000
Giesbrecht, N.
  429-431
Giffen, P.J.
  429
Gilbert, J.A.L.
  387, 432
Gilbert, M.J.
  433
Gilder, D.D.
  434
Gill, M.
  435
Gillin, J.
  436
Gillis, L.S.
  437
Girard, G.
  438
Girouard, M.
  439
G.-Kiss, J.
  38
Glad, D.D.
  440

Glatt, M.M.
  441-443
Glick, C.
  444
Glotzer, R.
  A12
Glover, E.
  445
Gluckman, L.K.
  446
Goffman, E.
  447
Gold, R.S.
  448
Golder, G.M.
  752
Goldman, I.
  449
Goleman, D.
  15
Gomberg, C.
  656
Gomberg, C.A.
  137, 138
Gómez Huamán, N.
  450
Gonçalves de Lima, O.
  451, 452
Goodenough, E.R.
  453
Goodwin, D.W.
  454, 1106
Gorad, S.L.
  455
Gordon, A.J.
  456, 457
Górski, J.
  458
Goshen, C.E.
  459
Gottleib, D.
  460
Gould, L.L.
  461
Grace, V.
  462
Gracia, M.F.
  463
Grandoit, G.
  464
Graves, T.D.
  465-467, 607, A13

195.

Gravière, E. la, see
    La Gravière, E.
Gray, J.H.
    468
Greeley, A.M.
    469
Gregory, D.
    470
Gregson, R.E.
    471
Grmek, M.D.
    472
Groff, J.
    473
Guiart, J.
    474
Gunson, N.
    475
Gurunanjappa, B.S.
    183
Gusfield, J.
    476
Gusfield, J.R.
    477
Gutman, I.
    674
Guze, S.B.
    454

Haavio-Manilla, E.
    478
Hackenberg, R.A.
    479
Hackwood, F.W.
    480
Hagaman, B.L.
    481
Hage, P.
    482
Hahn, D.S.
    483
Hale, L.
    641
Halpern, B.
    674
Halsweig, M.
    930
Hamer, J.H.
    484, 485, A14
Hampson, J.L.
    1113

Hanna, J.M.
    486, 487
Hansen, E.C.
    488, 489
Hanson, R.C.
    607
Harding, W.M.
    490
Harford, C.F.
    491
Harford, T.C.
    492
Harford-Battersby, C.F.
    493
Harman, M.S.
    927
Harper, F.D.
    494, 495
Harrison, B.
    496
Harrison, B.H.
    497
Hartman, L.F.
    498
Hartmann, G.
    499-501
Hartocollis, P.
    502
Harvey, C.
    1301
Harwood, A.
    503
Hasan, K.A.
    504, 505
Hasegawa, E.
    37
Hatcher, E.R.
    506
Hauser, S.F.
    507
Havard, V.
    508
Hawk, R.J.
    183
Hawthorn, H.B.
    509
Hays, T.E.
    510
Heaston, M.D.
    511
Heath, D.B.
    370, 371, 512-525, A15

Heidenreich, C.A.
526, 527
Helgason, T.
528, 529
Hellman, E.
530
Helmick, E.F.
531
Helwig, R.
532
Henderson, N.B.
533, 534
Henk, M.L.
535
Hennigh, L.
696
Hentig, H. Von
536
Herick, F.A.
537
Herrero, M.
538
Hes, J.P.
539
Hill, T.W.
540, 541
Hippler, A.E.
542
Hirsch, J.
543
Hirvonen, K.
544
Hittman, M.
545
Hitz, D.
546
Hocherman, I.
34
Hocking, R.B.
547
Hoff, E.C.
548
Hoffman, M.
549
Hoffmann, H.
550-553
Hole, L.W.
1090
Holloway, R.
554
Holmberg, A.R.
555

Honigmann, I.
556, 560, 562, 563
Honigmann, J.J.
556-564
Horn, J.L.
1270
Horton, D.J.
565
Horwitz, J.
566, 567
Houlett, W.
568
Howard-Craft, A.
569
Howay, F.W.
570
Howland, J.W.
571
Howland, R.W.
571
Hrdlička, A.
572
Hsien Rin
573
Hudolin, V.
574
Hunt, G.M.
575
Hunt, H.J.
576
Hurt, W.R.
577, 578
Hutchinson, B.
579
Hutchison, H.
580
Hyman, E.
1217

Indian Brotherhood of the
  Northwest Territories
581
Indian Health Service Task
  Force on Alcoholism
582
International Labor Office
583
Irgens-Jensen, O.
584, 585
Ivey, T.
586

Jabour, C.
587
Jackson, C.
588
Jackson, D.N.
550, 551
Jackson, M.
589
Jacobs, R.
590
Jacobs, W.R.
591
Jacobsen, E.
592
James, B.J.
593
Jamieson, S.M.
509
Jansen, G.H.
594
Jarvis, D.H.
595
Jastrow, M., Jr.
596
Jay, E.J.
597
Jay, M.
598
Jeanselme, E.
599
Jeffreys, M.D.W.
600
Jellinek, E.M. (see also 971, 972)
601-605
Jepson, W.W.
606
Jessor, R.
607, 608
Jessor, S.L.
607, 608
Jilek, W.G.
609, 610
Jilek-Aal, L.
611, 612
Jochelson, W.
613
Johannsen, E.
614
Johnson, J.
454
Johnson, L.V.
615

Johnson, R.C.
1315, A16
Johnston, T.F.
616-619
Jones, A.D.
620
Jones, B.M.
377, 378
Jones, W.C.
300
Jorgensen, J.G.
621
Joyce, K.
622
Juhász, P.
623
Jupp, G.A.
624, 625

Kahn, M.W.
283, 626
Kaiser, W.
627
Kalant, H.
999-1001
Kalin, R.
628, 832-834
Kamien, M.
629-631
Kane, S.L.
632
Kant, I.
633
Kaplan, B.
634
Kapur, B.M.
1000
Karayannis, A.D.
635
Kärkkäinen, K.
365
Karp, I.
636
Kasey, E.H.
1281
Katz, S.H.
402
Kearney, M.
637
Keast, H.
638

198.

Keast, T.J.
1159
Keehn, J.D.
639, 640
Kelbert, M.
641
Kelepouris, M.B.
635
Keller, M.
642-647
Kellner, E.
648
Kelly, R.E.
649
Kemnitzer, L.S.
650
Kennedy, E.
651
Kennedy, J.G.
652, 653
Kerketta, K.
654
Kermorgant, A.
655
Kessler, M.
137, 138, 656
Key, J.C.
300
Khalil, S.
A31
Kim, S.D.
657
Kim, Y.
658
Kim, Y.S.
659
King, D.E.
A17
King, F.A.
660
Kingsdale, J.M.
661
Kinzie, J.D.
1113
Kircher, K.
662
Kissin, B.
663
Klatsky, A.L.
664
Klausner, S.Z.
665

Kmet, J.
666
Knisley, E.R.
667
Knupfer, G.
668, 669
Köbben, A.J.
670
Kolodney, R.
1106
Koolage, W.W., Jr.
671
Koplowitz, I.
672
Kotarba, J.A.
673
Krasilowsky, D.
674, 1114
Kraus, R.
675
Krause, M.L.
676
Kreitman, N.
953
Kriek, J.J.
677
Krige, E.J.
678
Kruger, J.J.
679
Kubodera, I. (see also 967)
680
Kunitz, S.J.
681-684, 729-733
Kuttner, R.E.
685, 686
Kylmälä, T.
687

La Barre, W.
688-691
Laforest, L.
692
La Gravière, E.
693
Lambert, S.
429, 430
Lambrecht, A.
129, 130
Lane, E.W.
694

Lang, G.
  1292
Lang, G.M.
  695
Langness, L.L.
  696
Larkins, J.R.
  697
Larni, M.
  698
Larsen, D.E.
  9
Larsson, O.
  802
Latronico, N.
  699
Laubach, F.D.
  700
Lavenaire, A.
  1011
Lawrence, R.
  A18
Leacock, S.
  701
Le Berre, S.
  937
Lechnyr, R.J.
  702
Ledermann, S.
  703, 704
Lee, C.K.
  659
Legnaro, A.
  705
Leibowitz, J.O.
  706
Leis, P.E.
  707
Lejarza, F. de, see
  De Lejarza, F.
Leland, J.H.
  708-711
LeMasters, E.E.
  712, 713
Lemert, E.M.
  714-723
Lender, M.E.
  724, 725
Lenoir, R.
  726
Levine, H.G.
  727

Levy, H.
  728
Levy, J.E.
  681, 683, 684, 729-733
Levy, R.I.
  734, A19
Lewis, H.
  735
Lewis, J.
  437
Lewis, R.F.
  A20
Lewis, R.G.
  736
Leyburn, J.G.
  737
Li, T.-K.
  126
Lickiss, J.N.
  738
Liebenau, Th. von
  739
Lieber, C.S.
  740
Lima, F. de. see
  De Lima, F.
Lindner, P.
  741
Lint, J. de, see
  De Lint, J.
Listiak, A.
  742
Little, M.A.
  743
Littman, G.
  744, 745
Lobban, M.C.
  746
Lockhard, R.
  747
Locklear, H.H.
  748
Lodge, J.R.
  1279
Loeb, E.M.
  749, 750
Loedolff, J.F.
  751
Lolli, G.
  752, 753, 1061
Lomnitz, L.
  754-757

Long, J.K.
    A21
Lookout, M.
    758
Lorenzo, A.M.
    759
Lorincz, A.B.
    685
Lotterhos, J.F.
    760
Lovald, K.A.
    761
Lozet, F.
    17
Lubart, J.M.
    762
Lucia, S.P.
    763-765
Ludovici, A.M.
    766
Lumsden, D.P.
    767
Lundberg, G.
    A22
Lurie, N.O.
    768, 769
Lutes, S.V.
    770
Lutz, H.F.
    771
Luzzatto-Fegiz, P.
    752
Lynge, I.
    772

MacAndrew, C.
    773
Maccoby, M.
    411, 774
MacLeod, W.C.
    775, 776
Macrory, B.E.
    777
Madsen, C.
    780
Madsen, W.
    778-783
Maha Patra, S.S.K.
    A23
Mahboubi, E.
    666

Maher, C.
    454
Mahoney, F.B.
    784
Mail, P.D.
    785-787
Mäkelä, K.
    788, 789
Malen, V.D.
    A24
Malik, M.O.A.
    790
Mandel, W.
    34
Mandelbaum, D.C.
    791
Mangin, E.
    792
Mann, B.
    793, 794
Mann, B.J.
    1157
Manning, F.E.
    795-797
Marconi, J.
    566, 567, 798, 859
Mare, C.
    98
Mariani, C.
    799
Mariátegui, J.
    800
Maril, R.L.
    801
Marini-Bettolo, G.B.
    452
Marinovich, N.
    802
Maritz, F.A.
    803
Marlatt, G.A.
    804
Marrison, L.W.
    805
Marroquín, J.
    806
Marrus, M.R.
    807
Marshall, L.B.
    809, 811
Marshall, M.
    408, 808-814

Marshall, W.E.
815
Martin, D.
1214
Martín del Campo, R.
816
Masanes, P.
64
Mason, C.
34
Massicotte, E.Z.
817
Mass Observation
818
Matre, M.
615
Matthias, L.
34
Maurizio, A.
819
Mauss, A.C.
1325
Maxwell, M.
940
May, J.
820-822, 996
May, P.A.
823-825
Maynard, E.
826-829
McBeth, K.C.
830
McCabe, T.R.
64
McCall, G.
A25
McCarthy, R.G.
831, 1179
McClearn, G.E.
1315
McClelland, D.C.
628, 832-834
McCloy, S.G.
A26
McClure, W.T.
531
McCourt, W.F.
455
McCready, W.C.
469
McDonald, D.R.
787

McFarland, K.
835
McGlashan, N.D.
836, 1007
McGonegal, J.
837
McGoodwin, J.R.
838
McGregor, H.G.
839
McGunigle, E.
840
McKinlay, A.P.
841-853
McLaughlin, D.
854
McNair, C.N.
855
McNeill, F.M.
856
Mears, A.R.R.
857
Medical Practitioner, A
858
Medina C.
859
Menage, C.
139, 140
Mendelsohn, O.A.
860
Metzger, D.G.
861
Metzner, R.J.
142
Meza y Posada, S.A.
862
Micev, M.
863
Midgley, J.
864
Milaković, I.
961
Miles, J.D.
865
Millar, L.L.
866
Miller, M.W.
A27
Miller, S.E.
1232
Miller, T.-I.
953

Miller, V.P.
58
Milosavčević, V.
1245
Minguell, J.
1197
Miranda, I.
1197
Mitchell, P.M.
531
Mitra, B.R.
867
Mix, L.
387
Mizruchi, E.H.
868
Modi, J.J.
869
Mohatt, G.
870
Monckton, H.A.
871
Montell, G.
872
Montoya y F., J.B.
873
Moore, E.C.
874
Moore, M.
875
Mora de Jaramillo, V.
876
Morewood, S.
877
Morgan, J.P.
878
Morice, R.D.
879
Morote Best, E.
880
Morris, J.
881
Morrison, N.
298
Moser, J.
882
Mosher, J.F.
883
Moskowitz, H.
202
Moss, F.E.
884

Mossman, B.M.
885
Muelle, J.C.
886
Mulas, L.
1056
Muñoz, C.
1197
Mununggurr, D.
1006
Murcia Valcarcel, E.
887
Murphy, H.B.M.
888
Murray, R.F., Jr.
889
Musicant, R.A.
1342
Myerson, A.
890, 891

Nagler, M.
892
Naroll, R.
893
Nash, B.H.
138
Nason, J.D.
894
Nastrucci, M.
895
Nathan, P.E.
28
National Institute on Alcohol
Abuse and Alcoholism
896
Negrete, J.C.
897-900
Nelson, G.K.
901
Nelson, L.
902
Netting, R. McC
903
Neulinger, J.
128
Nicholson, G.E.
904
Nickerson, G.
905
Nicolich, M.J.
1183

Nida, E.A.
906
Nightingale, K.W.
907
Niiniluoto, Y.
908
Nissly, C.M.
A28
Niswander, J.D.
102
Noem, A.A.
552, 553
Nolan, R.W.
A29
Noonan, D.L.
124, 125, 1328
Nordland, O.
909, 910
Norelle Lickiss, F.
911
Norick, F.A.
912
Norman, A.J.
913
Novellie, L.
901, 914

Obayemi, A.M.U.
915
O'Connor, J.
916, 917
Odoroff, C.L.
683
Ogan, E.
918
Oki, G.
429
Olsen, L.K.
1279
O'Meara, J.E.
919
Omoniwa, N.
56
Onselen, C.V., see
Van Onselen, C.
Opler, M.E.
230
Oppenheim, A.L.
498
Orellana, G.
1197

Ossenberg, R.J.
920
Ostendorf, D.
A27
Otélé, A.
921
Otsyula, W.
922
Owen, R.C.
A30

Pacini, A.
164
Pagés Larraya, F.
923
Palerm, A.
1255
Palframan, J.F.
276, 277
Pan, L.
924
Paredes, A.
925, 926, 1178, 1341-1343,
A31
Parker, D.A.
927
Parkin, D.J.
928
Pascarosa, P.
929, 930
Patnaik, N.
931
Patrick, C.H.
932
Patton, W.
933
Payne, G.
36
Peeke, H.L.
934
Pellizzari, E.D.
372
Pelto, P.J.
935
Pendered, A.
936
Pérez, G.
1197
Perisse, J.
937
Perkins, N.
301

Perrucci, R.
  868
Pertold, O.
  938
Peterson, D.M.
  1115
Peterson, W.J.
  939, 940
Pfautz, H.W.
  941
Phelps, G.H.
  414
Piechochi, W.
  627
Piedade, J. da, see
  Da Piedade, J.
Piga Pascual, A.
  942, 943
Pilgrim, K.
  944
Pinto, L.J.
  945
Pitt, P.
  946
Pittman, D.J.
  947-952, 1140, 1167, 1219
Plant, M.A.
  953
Platt, B.S.
  954
Plaut, T.F.A.
  955
Podlewski, H.
  956
Poikolainen, K.
  957
Poirier, J.
  958, 959
Pollnac, R.B.
  960, 1018
Polovina, H.
  961
Poot, A.
  962
Popham, H.E.
  963
Popham, R.E.
  964-974, 1087-1089, A32
Pozas Arciniegas, R.
  975
Poznanski, A.
  976

Prakash, O.
  977
Preller, A.C.N.
  978
Prestan Simon, A.
  979
Preuss, K. Th.
  980
Price, J.A.
  981, 982
Price, P.H.
  889
Prins, S.J.
  983
Purchase, I.F.H.
  614

Quarcoo, A.K.
  A33
Quichaud, J.
  984

Raboin, R.M.
  265
Radke, G.
  985
Radović, B.
  986
Raman, A.C.
  987
Rankin, J.G.
  1000
Rao, C.R.P.
  988
Rao, M.S.A.
  A34
Rao, S.S.V.V.
  988
Rappaport, A.
  454
Rashad, M.H.
  854
Raskin, N.H.
  A35
Rasmussen, C.
  826, 989
Ravi Varma, L.A.
  990
Ray, R.B.J.-C.
  991-993
Raymond, I.W.
  994

Reader, D.H.
901, 995, 996
Redding, C.
997
Reed, R.E.
998
Reed, T.E.
999-1002
Regier, M.C.
1003
Reiche C., C.E.
1004
Reid, J.B.
1005
Reid, J.C.
1006
Reilly, C.
1007
Reilly, J.
1008
Reimer, T.T.
A36
Rerat, A.
937
Resavac, S.
961
Reuband, K.-H.
1009
Reuning, H.
901
Rhuneaud, G.
1010
Ribstein, M.
1011
Richard-Molard, J.
1012, 1013
Richards, C.E.
1014
Riches, D.
1015
Riffenburgh, A.S.
1016
Rios, M.D. de, see
De Rios, M.D.
Rios-Osoria, J. de los
1033
Rip, C.M.
1017
Robbins, M.C.
960, 1018, 1019
Robbins, R.H.
1020-1022

Robinson, D.
1023
Roca W., D.
1024
Rodríguez Sandoval, L.
1025
Roebuck, J.B.
1026-1028
Rohner, E.C.
1029
Rohner, R.P.
1029
Rohrmann, C.A.
1030
Rojas, U.
1031
Rojas González, F.
1032
Rojas-Mackenzie, R.
1033
Rolleston, J.D.
1034-1036
Romanucci-Ross, L.
1095
Ronkainen, I.
1330
Room, R.
211, 669, 1037-1043
Rooney, J.F.
1044
Rorabaugh, W.J.
1045
Rosett, H.L.
1273
Roth, W.E.
1046
Rothstein, E.
300
Rotman, A.E.
1047
Rotter, H.
1048
Roueché, B.
1049-1051
Roufs, T.G.
1052
Rouse, B.A.
372
Rubington, E.
1053-1055
Ruck, J.A.
414

Rudas, N.
1056
Rüden, E.
1057
Rühmland, R.
1058
Rühmland, U.
1058
Ruiz Moreno, A.
1059
Ryan, J.
1200

Sachs, H.
901
Sadler, P.
1060
Sadoun, R.
1061
Saiki, J.H.
1194
Saint, E.G.
1062
Salo, K.
1063
Salone, E.
1064
Salonen, A.
1065, 1066
Sams, G.K.
1067
Samuelson, J.
1068
Sanders, A.
A37
Sangree, W.H.
1069
Sapper, K.
1070
Sargent, M.J.
1071-1073
Sariola, S.
1074-1077
Sasaki, T.
1078
Savard, R.J.
1079, 1080
Savishinsky, J.S.
1081, 1082
Sawi, O.
790

Sayres, W.C.
1083
Schaefer, J.M.
1084, 1085
Schaefer, O.
387, 432
Scheper-Hughes, N.
1086
Schmidt, J.J.
A38
Schmidt, W.
1087-1089
Schmitt, N.
1090
Schmitthenner, E.
1091
Schmitthenner, H.
1091
Schreiber, G.
1092, 1093
Schultze, R.
1094
Schwartz, T.
1095
Sclare, A.B.
1096
Seekirchner, A.
1097
Segal, B.M.
1098, A39
Selby, H.
1099, 1100
Selby, K.
369
Selley, E.
1101
Seltman, C.
1102
Semple, B.M.
1103
Serebro, B.
1104
Serianni, E.
752
Serrano, G.
36
Sescovitch, S.
1197
Setälä, V.
1105
Seto, A.
1106

207.

Shadwell, A.
1107
Shalloo, J.P.
1108
Shanks, P.
1217
Shaw, S.J.
228
Sheen, J.R.
1109
Sheldon, M.
1110, 1111
Shore, J.H.
1112, 1113, 1316
Shuval, R.
1114
Siegel, H.A.
1115, 1116
Siegelaub, A.
664
Sievers, M.L.
1117
Siliceo Pauer, P.
1118
Silverman, M.
1061
Simboli, B.J.
1119
Simeone, C.M.
1120
Simmons, O.G.
1121-1123
Singer, K.
1124-1126
Singh, S.
1127
Sišnik, L.
1128
Siverts, H.
1129, 1130
Skirrow, J.
1131
Skolnik, J.H.
1132
Skorzyski, L.
1133
Slabbert, M.
437
Slater, A.D.
1134
Slotkin, J.S.
1135

Smith, V.
A40
Smythe, D.W.
1136
Snow, C.C.
925
Snyder, C.R.
66, 947, 1137-1141
Sølling, L.
1142-1144
Solms, H.
1145
Sommer, R.
327, 1146, 1147
Sommerschield, F.E.
1148
Sousa, M.
452
Sparling, R.
1110
Spaulding, P.
1149
Specht, F.A.
1150
Spencer, E.
1151
Spiller, B.
1152
Spindler, G.D.
1153
Spitulnik, K.
1154
Spradley, J.P.
1155-1158
Spray, S.L.
1026
Stage, T.B.
1159
Stamatoyannopoulous, G.
1160
Stanbury, W.T.
1161
Stanislawski, D.
1162
Stanley, G.F.G.
1163
Steffenhagen, R.A.
1164
Steigelmann, W.
1165
Steinbring, J.
1166, A14

Sterne, M.A.
1167
Stevens, J.A.
1168
Stewart, E.R.
1169
Stewart, O.C.
1170, 1171
Stivers, R.A.
1172-1175
Stolte, E.
1176
Storm, T.
299
Stratton, J.
1177
Stratton, R.
1178
Straus, R.
1179-1181
Street, P.B.
1182, 1217
Streit, F.
1183
Strübing, E.
1184
Stuart, C.
1111
Stull, D.D.
1185, 1186
Suarez, J.
2
Súkeník, L.
1187
Sullivan, T.
1106
Suolahti, J.
1188-1191
Suuronen, K.
1192
Swanson, D.W.
1193
Szuter, C.F.
1194
Szwed, J.F.
1195

Tadesse, E.
1196
Talman, J.J.
422

Tapia, I.
1197
Taussig, C.W.
1198
Taylor, H.A.
28
Taylor, W.B.
1199
Termansen, P.E.
1200
Theron, J.S.
1201, 1202
Thomas, A.E.
1203
Thorner, I.
1204
Thudichum, G.
1205
Thum, D.
1281
Thune, C.E.
1206
Tihon, L.
1207
Tillhagen, C.-H.
1208
Timberlake, J.
1209
Toerian, I.
1210
Toit, B.M. du, see
  Du Toit, B.M.
Tongue, A.
1211
Topper, M.D.
1212, 1213, A15, A41
Torres, M.
1214
Toulouse, J.H.
1215
Towle, L.H.
1216
Treiman, B.R.
1217
Treviño M.
1218
Trice, H.M.
1219
Tricomi, S.
1106
Trinder, B.
497

Trotter, R.T., II
1220, 1221
Trudell, J.
1222
Tulloss, T.C.
878
Turner, E.S.
1223
Twiss, G.
828
Tzu-Ch^cing, H.
1224

Udvalget For Samfundsforskning
I Grønland
1225
Uecker, A.E.
1226
Ullman, A.D.
1227
Umunna, I.
1228
United States, Department of
Health, Education and Welfare
1229
United States, Department of
Health, Education and Welfare,
Indian Health Service
1230
United States, Department of
the Interior, Bureau of
Indian Affairs
1231
Unkovic, C.M.
1232
Urbanowicz, C.F.
1233

Vachon, A.
1234
Vadnal, N.J.
147
Valee, B.L.
1235
Valenzuela Rojas, B.
1236
Vallee, F.G.
1237
Vanderkooi, R.C.
1238, 1239
Vanderyst, H.
1240

Van Onselen, C.
1241
Varlet, F.
1242
Varma, S.C.
1243
Vasconcelos, R.
1244
Vasev, C.
1245
Vázquez, M.C.
1246
Vedder, H.
1247
Velapatiño Ortega, A.
1248
Velasco Muñoz-Ledo, M.D.P.
1249
Verrall, F.M.
1250
Verster, J.P.
1251
Vilkuna, K.
1252
Vinas Tello, E.
1253
Vinchon, J.
1254
Viqueira, C.
1255
Vlok, A.
1256
Vogt, E.Z.
A42
Von Fumetti, B.
1112
Voorst, J.V.
1257
Vrey, J.D.
1258

Wacko, W.J.
1259, 1260
Waddell, J.O.
370, 371, 1261-1264, A15,
A43-A47
Wakasugi, C.
413
Walker, C.G.
1265
Wallace, A.F.C.
1266

Wallgren, H.
   1267
Wallis, R.S.
   1268
Wallis, W.D.
   1268
Walsh, D.
   1269
Wanberg, K.
   1270
Wang, R.P.
   1271
Wanner, E.
   832-834, 1272
Warner, R.H.
   1273
Washburne, C.
   1274-1276
Watney, J.
   1277
Weast, D.E.
   1278
Weathersbee, P.S.
   1279
Webb, B.
   1280
Webb, S.
   1280
Webe, G.
   A48
Wechsler, H.
   1281
Weigand, P.C.
   1282
Weil, A.
   1283
Weiner, S.
   137, 138
Werlin, J.
   1284
West, L.J.
   925, 1285
Westermeyer, J.J.
   1286-1295
Wever, O.R.
   1296
Wheeler, D.
   1297
White, M.F.
   1298
White, R.
   1299

Whitehead, P.C.
   1300, 1301
Whittaker, J.O.
   1302-1304
Whittet, M.M.
   1305
Whop, J.
   651
Wicks, A.C.B.
   1306
Wilkes, H.G.
   1307
Wilkinson, R.
   1308
Williams, B.
   1309
Williams, C.
   98
Williams, C.V.
   1310
Williams, J.R.
   1311
Wilson, C. (see also Wilson, G.C.)
   1312
Wilson, G.B.
   1313
Wilson, G.C. (see also Wilson, C.)
   1314
Wilson, J.R.
   1315
Wilson, L.
   1316
Wilson, R.L.
   1317
Winkler, A.M.
   1318
Winn, W.
   1319
Wiseman, J.P.
   1320, 1321
Wiswe, H.
   1322
Wolcott, H.F.
   1323, 1324
Wolfe, J.C.
   1325
Wolff, P.H.
   1326, 1327
Wolin, S.J.
   124, 125, 1328
Wolman, C.
   1329

Wolpaw, I.
98
Wong, M.
1125
Wood, R.
A49
Wood, R.C.
1182
Woodside, A.G.
1330
Wright, A.
1331
Wright-St. Clair, R.E.
1332

Yamamuro, B.
1333-1336
Yarrow, A.
1103
Yarshater, E.
1337
Yawney, C.D.
967, 968, 1338, 1339
Yiin-Ts'ung, C.
1224
Younger, W.
1340

Zamora, M.D.
885
Zavaleta, A.
801
Zeiner, A.
1178
Zeiner, A.R.
1341-1343
Zentner, H.
1344
Zimberg, S.
1345
Zimmerli, W.H.
448
Zinberg, N.E.
490
Zingg, R.M.
1346
Zitzen, E.G.
1347
Zurukzoglu, S.
1348
Zwick, G.
1349

Zwingelstein, J.
278

INDEX OF SUBJECTS

The purpose of this index is to help anyone who wants to find works that deal with a particular concept, theory, or topic on the one hand, or with a particular area, nation, tribe, or other special population on the other. Ample use of cross-references marked "see..." is intended to guide users to key-words, in recognition of the fact that terminology differs from time to time just as it differs among users with different backgrounds. Cross-references marked "see also..." indicate that some of the entries under the alternative entry or entries will probably also be relevant. Scope-notes are included (in parentheses, following the key-word) in those instances when it seems appropriate to limit, specify, qualify, or otherwise explain more fully the meaning of a term in its usage as a key-word in this context.

The numbers following each entry are the numbers of individual references in the list of "Citations" rather than page-numbers within this volume.

SUBJECT INDEX

A.A.
see Alcoholics Anonymous
Aborigines
(refers specifically to native peoples of Australia; for aboriginal peoples of other areas, see names of nations and regions; names of peoples)
116, 242, 301, 576, 629-631, 651, 738, 802, 879, 911, 1006
abstainers
(refers to persons and/or populations who do not drink alcoholic beverages, for whatever reasons)
see also Church; prohibition; Protestants
454, 553, 1099, 1170, 1204, 1288
Abyssinia
see also Ethiopia
895
accidents
(including all kinds)
10, 33, 115, 145, 183, 298, 427, 431, 438, 479, 606, 652, 675, 703, 704, 824, 957, 1090, 1178, 1185, 1289
acculturation
(refers to changes in a sociocultural system that come about largely because of contact with another; usually, but not always, the changes are described as occurring within a smaller and/or dependent population, under the impact of a larger dominant one)
see also change; urbanization
3, 5, 19, 43, 81, 116, 131, 147, 148, 180, 221, 255, 296, 305, 313, 315, 320, 339, 346, 351, 361, 375, 388-392, 402, 406, 430, 431, 436, 446, 465, 474, 479, 484, 509, 539, 545, 565, 570, 579, 593, 610, 611, 657, 667, 671, 674, 682, 714, 717, 738, 745, 746, 762, 773, 775, 778, 779, 814, 815, 829, 840, 883, 911, 912, 923, 943, 958, 960, 1015, 1018, 1021, 1022, 1032, 1059, 1064, 1081, 1082, 1114, 1119, 1166, 1173, 1185, 1268, 1271, 1319, 1338
addiction
(refers to an individual's apparent dependence, whether physiological or psychological, on alcoholic beverages)
77, 727
adolescents
see youth
Africa
(some sources deal with the entire continent; others deal with nations, regions, or peoples, with various degrees of specificity)
names of nations and regions that are specifically cited in the sources include the following (see individual index-entries): Abyssinia; Congo; Dahomey; Egypt; Ethiopia; Ghana; Guinea; Kenya; Madagascar; Malawi; Morocco; Mozambique; Nigeria; Reunion; Rhodesia; Ruanda; Senegal; South Africa; Sudan; Tanganyika; Togo; Transvaal; Uganda; Upper Volta; Zambia
names of peoples that are specifically cited in the sources include the following (see individual index-entries): Akan; Ama; Amhara; Bakoena; Balobedu; Bangui; Bantu; Bapedi; Bapende; Baraguru; Bassari; Biblical peoples; Bomuana; Buganda; Cape Coloured;

Dahomey; Diola; Egyptians,
ancient; Fingo; Giriama;
Henga; Herrero; Hide; Ibibio;
Ijaw; Iraqu; Islam; Iteso;
Kaguru; Katanga; Kelabit;
Kofyar; Kwango; Malagache;
Mandingolu; Moba; Nama;
Natal; Pondomi; Safwa; Thonga;
Tiriki; Tsonga; Ubangi-Chari;
Wolof; Xosa; Yoruba
16, 59, 139, 140, 145, 276,
277, 284, 346, 359, 425, 481,
491, 493, 598, 693, 836, 924,
987, 1012, 1013, 1097, 1242,
A6, A38

Afro-Americans
see Blacks

Afro-Brazilians
see Batuque

aged
see elderly

aggression
(as a sequel of drinking)
see also fighting; murder;
rape; suicide
3, 95, 98, 145, 163, 171,
175, 190, 199, 239, 246,
252, 304, 306, 406, 410,
411, 556, 560, 565, 572,
593, 606, 629, 631, 634,
716, 717, 855, 912, 935,
946, 1030, 1079, 1255,
1288, 1302, 1303, A13

Agringado
see Hispanos

Ainu
(Japan)
680, 967

Akan
(Ghana)
346

Alaskan Natives
see Aleuts; Eskimos; Native
Americans; names of peoples

Albanians
(in Yugoslavia)
863

alcohol
(in view of the fact that
all entries in this volume
refer to some aspect of
alcohol in relation to
human behavior, it would
be pointless to index this
word; however, for specific
beverages, see beer;
brandy; homebrew; whiskey;
wine; for techniques of
production, see manufacture;
etc.)

Alcoholics Anonymous
22, 40, 112, 506, 552, 569,
611, 612, 744, 781, 782,
1060, 1166, 1206, 1296,
1344

alcoholism
(indicates only that the
source includes discussion
of "alcoholism"; the
definition is often not
specified, or is specified
in a unique way; the
compilers have not
attempted to impose a
uniform definition)
see also addiction;
definition; diagnosis;
dysfunctions; pathology;
psychiatric problems
30, 31, 102, 210, 211, 551,
602, 603, 706, 708, 955,
995, 1113, 1125, 1179,
1296

ale
see beer

Aleuts
(northwestern North
America)
52, 53, 102, 131, 402,
582, 667, 675

Algonquian/Algonquin/Algonkian/
Algonkin
(northeastern North
America)
304

Ama
(South Africa)
see also Bomuana
310

ambivalence
(refers specifically

to situations in which
members of a population
share conflicting favorable
and fearful or otherwise
unfavorable attitudes toward
alcoholic beverages and/or
their effects)
26, 112, 144, 175, 324,
505, 560, 562, 563, 668,
734, 890, 891, 961, 995,
1042, 1071, 1122, 1227,
1261, 1301, 1334, 1339

America, Central
see Central America
America, Middle
see Central America
America, North
see Aleuts; Canada; Eskimos;
Native Americans; United
States; names of peoples (North
America)
America, South
see South America
Americans, Native
see Native Americans; names
of peoples (North America)

Amhara
(Ethiopia)
1196

Ami
(Taiwan; includes Nan Shi)
573

Andean
(referring to highland
Indians of South America)
see also Bolivia; Colombia;
Ecuador; Peru
1246

anomie/anomia
(refers to that kind of
stress that results from an
individual's inability to
achieve what he/she considers
appropriate; or from an
individual's inability to
reconcile conflicting norms)
19, 22, 74, 80-84, 116,
131, 155, 161, 180, 181,
221, 243, 254, 255, 258,
296, 301, 304, 335, 339,
351, 367, 388-392, 406,
417, 430, 436, 465, 467,
484, 509, 510, 610, 615,
667, 692, 717, 730, 738,
744, 745, 778, 815, 855,
912, 918, 923, 1032, 1086,
1111, 1139, 1149, 1161,
1237, 1239, 1268, 1278

Apache
(southwestern North
America)
174, 175, 230, 296, 369,
510, 572, 732, 785, 786,
1112, A10

Arabs
see Islam; Near East;
names of nations and
regions

Arapaho
22, 265-267, 275, 333,
375, 929

archeology
see prehistory

Arctic
see Aleuts; Eskimos;
Native Americans; names of
peoples

Argentina
923

arrests
see crime

ascetic Protestants
see Protestants

Asia
(includes the continent
and outlying islands;
some sources refer to the
entire continent, and
others to specific nations,
regions, or peoples) names
of nations and regions that
are specifically cited in
the sources include the
following (see individual
index-entries): Bahrein;
Bengal; Ceylon; Chaldea;
China; India; Iran;
Israel; Japan; Korea;
Kuwait; Laos; Mesopotamia;
Mongolia; Near East;
Nepal; Philippines;
Sarawak; Soviet Union;
Taiwan; Tibet

names of peoples that are
specifically cited in the
sources include the
following (see individual
index-entries): Ainu; Ami;
Bhils; Biblical peoples;
Bukidnon; Bulsar; Classical
peoples; Dyak; Eskimos;
Gond; Islam; Kayan;
Loi-Manipuri; Meo; Murut;
Newar; Oraon; Persians,
ancient; Reddi; Subanun;
Suraf; Tagalog; Yakut;
Yemenites
234, 399
Assiniboin
see Canada
Athabascan/Athapascan
(a linguistic group of
Native Americans, widely
distributed in Sub-Arctic,
northwestern and south-
western North America)
178, 542, 1120
attitudes
(toward alcoholic beverages
and/or drinking and its
sequelae)
see also norms
11, 26, 37, 94, 100, 127,
142, 156, 157, 184, 191,
209, 211, 214, 223, 225,
250, 256, 265, 266, 281,
282, 289, 321, 353, 367,
393, 415, 424, 429, 440,
454, 459, 461, 468, 496,
512-514, 543, 549, 554,
557, 558, 571, 579, 592,
597, 602, 604, 605, 635,
637, 669, 684, 710, 713,
727, 744, 864, 875, 897,
988, 1072, 1073, 1124,
1137, 1164, 1167, 1177,
1226, 1227, 1238, 1273,
1275, 1278, 1299, 1330,
1337, A7, A9, A10, A18
Australia
see also Aborigines
116, 242, 301, 576, 629-631,
651, 738, 802, 879, 911,
1006, 1062, 1072, 1297

Austria
see also Tyrol
201, 482, 557, 558
aversion therapy
see treatment
Aymara
see also Qolla
227, 517
Aztec
(Mexico)
154, 926

Bahama Islands
956
Bahrein
50
Bakoena
(South Africa)
186
Balobedu
(South Africa)
678
Bangui
(west Africa)
1242
Bantu
(South Africa)
78, 179, 530, 579, 614,
865, 1104, A38
Bantu beer
see Bantu; homebrew
Bapedi
(Transvaal)
208
Bapende
(Congo)
962
bar
(any public establishment
selling alcoholic beverages
to be consumed on the
premises, including beer-
hall, cafe, cocktail lounge,
pub, tavern, etc.)
3, 14, 61, 78, 118, 120,
137, 141, 146, 177, 217,
222, 231, 259, 263, 293,
295, 299, 308, 312, 320,
327, 329, 347, 357, 367,
393, 398, 399, 421, 439,
447, 456, 460, 480, 488,
489, 492, 502, 530, 557,

558, 598, 594, 623, 624,
638, 656, 657, 660, 661,
673, 685, 700, 712, 713,
738, 739, 742, 762, 777,
793-795, 807, 817, 818,
835, 855, 874, 886, 920,
953, 963, 966, 973, 974,
982, 1006, 1008, 1014,
1026-1028, 1039, 1063,
1101, 1146, 1147, 1154,
1157, 1167, 1176, 1203,
1223, 1250, 1261, 1280,
1309, 1310, 1323, 1331,
A5, A13, A17, A32

Baraguru
(Tanganyika)
118

Basques
A25

Bassari
(Senegal)
A29

Batuque
(Brazil)
701

beer
(includes fermented beverages
with base of grain, honey
or vegetables, such as ale,
beer, chicha, Kaffir-beer,
mead, etc.)
see also homebrew
60, 78, 186, 198, 338,
423, 482, 532, 549, 642,
805, 871, 909, 910, 1010,
1152, 1187, 1252, 1323,
1332

beer-garden
see bar

Belize
A22

Bengal
236

Bermuda
795, 796,

beverages
see beer; brandy; homebrew;
moonshine; whiskey; wine;

Bhils
(India)
938

Biblical peoples
(includes the several
ancient populations
referred to in the Holy
Bible, comprising both
Old and New Testaments)
see also Egyptians,
ancient; Jews; Mesopotamia;
Romans, ancient
270, 287, 307, 343, 356,
382, 386, 399, 434, 453,
543, 596, 672, 933, 976,
1066, 1165

bibliography
(indicates that a major
portion of the source
consists of biblio-
graphical references to
other sources on the
subject)
see also review
53, 80, 102, 380, 408, 448,
644, 646, 787, 808, 896,
905, 968, 1038, 1131, 1183,
1217, 1221

binge
(refers to a behavioral
pattern characterized by
sporadic episodes of
heavy drinking)
19, 99, 131, 178, 208,
254, 255, 262, 296, 301,
315, 352, 449, 513, 514,
537, 556, 616, 617, 619,
620, 630, 637, 650, 714,
755, 792, 894, 903, 918,
1074-1076, 1081, 1090,
1094, 1120, 1150, 1228,
1285, 1287, 1302, 1303

Blackfeet
(central and northwestern
North America)
824, 1168

Blacks
(sometimes referred to as
Afro-Americans, Negroes,
et al.)
see also Africa; Batuque;
names of nations and
regions; names of peoples
120, 123, 159, 414, 470,
494, 495, 590, 664, 697,

Blacks
  735, 736, 795, 1167,
  1339, A15
blood-sugar
  see hypoglycemia
Bolivia
  227, 297, 373, 513, 514,
  516, 517, 923, 1076
Bomuana
  (South Africa)
  see also Ama
  310
Bosnia
  see also Yugoslavia
  961
bout
  see binge
boys
  see youth
brandy
  122, 338, 805, 986,
  1128, 1163
Brazil
  see also Batuque
  93, 701, A30
Buddhism
  (wherever it occurs)
  165, 1333, 1334
Buganda
  (Uganda)
  960, 1018, 1019
Bukidnon
  (Philippine Islands)
  418
Bulsar
  (India)
  321

cafe
  see bar
Camba
  (Bolivia)
  513, 514, 516, 517
Canada
  see also Eskimos; Native
  Americans; names of peoples
  (North America)
  58, 95, 102, 122, 181, 196,
  220, 221, 235, 239, 254,
  255, 271, 298, 299, 304,
  306, 335, 348, 367, 396,
  409, 422, 429-431, 468,
  509, 554, 556, 560-563,
  570, 581, 610, 624, 658,
  671, 692, 742, 746, 762,
  797, 815, 855, 882, 892,
  919, 920, 970, 982, 1015,
  1020-1022, 1029, 1064,
  1087, 1088, 1090, 1146,
  1149, 1161, 1163, 1166,
  1195, 1200, 1234, 1237,
  1259, 1260, 1268, 1344
cancer
  (as presumed to be affected
  by drinking of alcoholic
  beverages)
  276, 277, 284, 836, 1279
Cape Coloured
  (offspring of "racially
  mixed" parentage in South
  Africa)
  437
carcinoma
  see cancer
cargo cult
  see conversion
Caribbean Islands
  see West Indies; names of
  nations and regions
  (Central America)
caste
  (refers to relatively
  rigid and endogamous
  social categories; contrast
  class)
  40, 226, 504, 842, 931,
  958, A18, A34
Catalonia
  488, 489, 887
Caucasoid
  see Whites

causes (of problem drinking,
  etc.)
  see etiology
Central America
  (as used here, includes
  Mexico, Belize, and the
  Caribbean Islands as well
  as the Central American
  nations; names of nations
  and regions that are
  specifically cited in the
  sources include the
  following (see individual

index-entries): Bahama
Islands; Belize; Bermuda;
Dominica; Dominican Republic;
Guatemala; Haiti; Jamaica;
Martinique; Mexico; Panama;
Puerto Rico; Tobago; Trinidad;
West Indies
names of peoples that are
specifically cited in the
sources include the following
(see individual index-entries):
Aztec; Blacks; Chamula; Chichicastenango; Cuna; Huichol; Kekchi;
Maya; Mestizos; Mexica; Mixtec;
Otomí; Oxchuc; Tarahumara;
Tarascan; Tojolabal; Totonac;
Zapotec; Zinacantan
286

Ceylon
(Sri Lanka)
133

Chaco
(a region of plains in
Argentina, Bolivia, Chile,
and Paraguay)
923

Chaldea
see also Biblical peoples
294

Chamula
(Mexico)
199, 200, 379, 975, 1312,
1314, A42

change
(specifically with respect to
drinking patterns)
see also acculturation; history;
urbanization
19, 31, 32, 46, 56, 57, 59, 73,
76, 81, 132, 147, 148, 164,
165, 203, 207, 214, 223, 256,
262, 268, 274, 304-306, 322,
327, 352, 357, 419, 422, 427,
429-431, 441-443, 456, 457,
459, 461, 468, 474, 475, 480,
484, 496, 497, 502, 515-517,
539, 545, 547, 549, 560, 570,
571, 579, 589, 592, 598, 604,
623, 627, 641, 660, 674, 684,
697, 707, 719, 723, 734, 756,
757, 773, 775, 779, 791, 807,
809-811, 814, 821, 823, 824,
830, 867, 883, 892, 894,
902, 903, 916, 918, 923,
928, 934, 944, 958, 960,
984, 1003, 1006, 1016,
1018, 1032, 1045, 1059,
1064, 1066, 1068, 1069,
1071, 1095, 1107, 1119,
1142, 1173, 1175, 1181,
1188, 1192, 1196, 1199,
1208, 1212, 1229, 1243,
1247, 1263, 1266, 1280,
1288, 1297, 1302, 1303,
1313, 1318, 1333, 1334,
1338, 1345, 1349, A29, A34,
A39, A42

Cherokee
(southwestern North
America)
1349

Cheyenne
(central North
America)
22, 375, 586, 824

Chicanos
see Hispanos

chicha
see beer; homebrew

Chichicastenango
(Guatemala)
199, 200

child/children
see youth

Chile
19, 754-757, 798, 799,
859, 1197, 1236

China
see also Taiwan; Tibet;
names of peoples (Asia)
444, 690, 698, 875, 1224

Chipewyan
(northwestern North
America)
671

Chippewa
(central North
America)
436, 552, 606, 695, 1288,
1289

chronic police offenders
see Skid Row

Church
(includes references to

Coptic, Greek Orthodox,
Mormon, Native American,
Nestorian, Protestants,
and Russian Orthodox
Churches)
99, 264, 315, 343, 353,
421, 474, 627, 669, 724,
796, 919, 929, 930, 943,
994, 1031, 1059, 1132,
1204, 1266, 1279, 1281,
1320

cirrhosis
see liver

class
(refers to socioeconomic,
or other social strati-
fication)
see also caste
111, 113, 114, 117, 209,
211, 212, 226, 262, 361,
373, 415, 417, 437, 441,
460, 466, 559, 560, 578,
627, 661, 692, 712, 713,
751, 811, 872, 918, 920,
940, 1026, 1095, 1167,
1175, 1233, 1270, 1299,
A30

Classical peoples
(includes "classic" Greeks,
"imperial" Roman, and
other literate populations,
roughly 500 B.C. to 1000 A.D.)
85-89, 108, 136, 184, 238,
250, 287, 354, 363, 364,
399, 462, 472, 543, 544,
604, 605, 706, 849, 869,
933, 976, 1034, 1102,
1184, 1189, 1340

cocktail lounge
see bar

Colombia
119, 873, 876, 1033,
1077, 1083

comparative studies
see Cross-cultural;
Cross-ethnic; Cross-
national; World survey

Congo
(Zaire)
17, 18, 129, 130, 616,
921, 962, 1207, 1240

consumption
(refers to specific data
on quantities of alcoholic
beverages consumed in
various contexts)
34, 58, 115, 209-211, 323,
328, 345, 393, 463, 492,
562, 563, 584, 592, 664,
703, 704, 711, 788, 789,
800, 804, 927, 944, 1089,
1104, 1132, 1144, 1260,
1278, 1279, 1281, 1300-1303,
1313

containers
(of beverages, including
paraphernalia used in
production, storage, or
consumption)
13, 92, 276, 277, 284,
365, 423, 462, 480, 613,
836, 1007, 1215, 1340

contents
(of alcoholic beverages)
see manufacture

conversion
(in a religious sense,
whether to a nativistic
movement or to a formal
international religion)
339, 411, 513, 514, 542,
545, 637, 781, 879, 1060,
1099, 1166, 1266, A26, A34

conviviality
see functions

Cook Islands
(Polynesia)
717, 720, 723

Coptic Church
see Church

Cree
see Canada

crime
(as a presumed concomitant
of drinking)
see also fighting; murder;
rape
10, 74, 117, 133, 145,
254, 388, 389, 391, 396,
414, 426, 429, 467, 470,
529, 533, 534, 536, 547,
560, 562, 563, 649, 658,
673, 716, 785, 823, 824, 1016,

1156, 1158, 1171, 1177,
1178, 1199
Croatia
see also Yugoslavia
574
Cross-cultural
(refers to a comparison
of two or more markedly
different and historically
unrelated sociocultural
systems, usually including
non-literate peoples)
see also Cross-ethnic;
Cross-national; World
survey
15, 63, 66-69, 71, 98,
104, 106, 246, 247, 311,
394, 565, 585, 628, 665,
670, 708, 832, 833, 893,
974, 1030, 1038, 1084,
1186, 1275, 1301
Cross-ethnic
(refers to a comparison
of two or more different
populations, not necessarily
historically unrelated, and
often sub-groups within a
larger literate society)
see also Cross-cultural;
Cross-national; World
survey
94, 97, 109, 111, 113,
117, 118, 126, 134, 135,
159, 191, 196, 199, 200,
213, 226, 239, 242, 265,
267, 272, 275, 304, 313,
324, 342, 343, 358, 371,
372, 377, 378, 381, 387,
401, 414, 424, 428, 432,
456, 465, 469, 470, 486,
487, 517, 533, 550, 552,
556, 562, 563, 590, 607,
608, 664, 669, 671, 683,
685, 696, 714, 716, 717,
719, 720, 726, 732, 733,
736, 780, 802, 809, 811,
824, 854, 855, 857, 868,
889, 920, 923, 924, 958,
959, 987, 988, 998-1000,
1037, 1040, 1072, 1083,
1108, 1110, 1112, 1114,
1117, 1129, 1132, 1133,

1149, 1167, 1178, 1184,
1226, 1243, 1247, 1255,
1279, 1281, 1283, 1290,
1292, 1294, 1298, 1311,
1315, 1326, 1327, 1338,
1339, 1342, 1343, A15,
A16, A21, A33, A35, A42,
A46
Cross-national
(refers to a comparison of
the populations of two or
more nation-states)
see also Cross-cultural;
Cross-ethnic; World survey
20, 64, 112, 295, 373,
523, 566, 567, 602, 603,
703-705, 882, 916, 957,
971, 972, 982, 994, 1008,
1038, 1098, 1175
Crow
(central North
America)
824
Cubeo
(Venezuela)
449
culture
see sociocultural
Cuna
(Panama)
979
customs
(with respect to drinking)
31, 97, 100, 103, 127,
131, 147, 148, 150, 156,
157, 164, 178, 182, 184,
192, 196, 201, 209, 211,
214, 216, 229, 239, 246,
248-250, 286, 289, 291, 292,
295, 306, 310, 315, 323,
325, 327, 328, 342, 343,
351, 354, 356, 359, 364,
366, 368, 386, 393, 407,
415, 419, 422, 424, 431,
443, 450, 458, 459, 464,
472, 480, 482-484, 499,
502, 505, 507, 512-515,
527, 537, 543, 549, 555,
557, 558, 578, 602-604,
607, 613, 615, 636, 658,
659, 676, 682, 683, 685,
687, 690, 691, 694, 697,

698, 710, 713, 714, 719,
723, 727, 734, 745, 752-
754, 759, 766, 774, 780,
786, 792, 806, 814, 821,
822, 827, 831, 855, 856,
860, 863-865, 872, 875,
901, 902, 908-910, 915,
916, 939, 943, 944, 954,
974, 988, 996, 1033,
1058, 1061-1063, 1066,
1068, 1069, 1072, 1074-
1076, 1079, 1083, 1091-
1093, 1098, 1109, 1121,
1123, 1124, 1126, 1128, 1129,
1137, 1138, 1150, 1155,
1165, 1167, 1173-1175,
1187, 1188, 1192, 1198,
1208, 1211, 1212, 1228,
1236, 1246, 1257, 1275,
1308, 1310, 1312, 1314,
1317, 1318, 1320, 1322,
1323, 1333, 1334, 1336,
1339, A18, A23, A25,
A39, A43, A48

Czechoslovakia
see also Slovakia
233, 1128

Dahomey
12, 140
Dakota
(central North America)
5
definition
(of "alcoholism", problem
drinking, etc.)
30, 144, 209-212, 260,
602, 603, 703, 704, 708,
727, 955, 965, 995, 1179
Denmark
150, 192, 772, 957, 1142,
1144, 1225
dependence
see addiction
dependency
(as a psychological and/or
sociological characteristic,
referring to social relations)
see also power; for
physiological and/or psychological dependence on alcohol,
see addiction

4, 63, 67, 69, 98, 105,
106, 311, 485, 738, 1193
detribalization
see acculturation
deviance
see responsibility
diagnosis
(of "alcoholism", problem
drinking, etc.)
706, 708, 727, 990, 1023,
1270, 1296
Diola
(Africa)
13
disease concept
(of alcoholism)
184, 209-211, 571, 603,
727, 782
distillation
see manufacture
distilled beverages
see brandy; moonshine;
whiskey
distribution
(geographic, with reference
to alcoholic beverages, or
drinking patterns; includes
Cross-cultural, Cross-
ethnic, Cross-national, and
World survey comparative
studies; not economic
analyses)
97, 103, 109, 121, 139,
187, 189, 195, 276, 277,
284, 286, 290-292, 338,
341, 342, 364, 499-501,
508, 688, 749, 750, 791,
805, 809, 836, 877, 1097,
1099, 1135, 1152, 1162,
1297, A47, A48
disulfiram
162, 388, 389, 745, 1080,
1194, 1329
Dominica
(West Indies)
588
Dominican Republic
457
drinking bouts
see binge
drinking customs/patterns
see customs

drinking groups
    see social organization
drugs
    (other than alcohol)
    32, 114, 204, 219, 226,
    265, 267, 272, 279, 286,
    313, 415, 441, 442, 445,
    504, 505, 527, 539, 545,
    617, 620, 630, 750, 815,
    899, 945, 952, 1072, 1117,
    1126, 1164, 1182, 1260,
    1283, 1287
drunken comportment/drunkenness
    see intoxication; responsibility
Dyak
    (Sarawak; includes both Land and Sea Dyaks)
    97
Dynastic Egyptians
    see Egyptians, ancient
DWI/drinking while impaired/intoxicated
    see accidents
dysfunctions
    (unfavorable outcomes of drinking, whether in social, economic, psychological, or other terms)
    see also alcoholism; pathology; psychiatric problems; et al.
    10, 45, 48, 65, 73, 76,
    77, 81, 97, 166, 175,
    202, 210, 211, 218, 228,
    232, 260, 268, 281, 282,
    293, 315, 339, 367, 376,
    395, 406, 411, 425, 427,
    438, 491, 527, 530, 534,
    538, 560, 565, 573, 582,
    583, 592, 602, 607, 608,
    629, 631, 632, 651, 658,
    696, 705, 714, 716, 720,
    775, 783, 806, 821, 827,
    828, 868, 902, 922, 942,
    945, 955, 958, 959, 981,
    983, 1012, 1013, 1023,
    1059, 1098, 1134, 1136,
    1167, 1222, 1229-1231,
    1256, 1275, 1286, 1289,
    1295, 1313, 1323, 1338,
    1339, 1344, 1346, 1348,
    A3, A9

East Indians
    see India; Overseas Indians; names of peoples (Asia)
economics
    (refers to cost- and exchange-values of alcoholic beverages)
    115, 118, 122, 130, 155,
    178, 185, 186, 206, 268,
    280, 288, 303, 306, 333, 334,
    336, 345, 346, 354, 359, 367,
    393, 397, 402, 406, 410,
    411, 415, 419, 430, 438,
    471, 477, 481, 484, 489,
    493, 503, 511, 530, 538,
    559, 565, 568, 570, 591,
    604, 623, 627, 629, 637,
    652-654, 660, 678, 685,
    692, 695, 697, 703, 704,
    707, 728, 733, 738, 754-
    757, 759, 761, 811, 827-
    829, 839, 871, 874, 902,
    903, 919, 924, 925, 928,
    937, 954, 958, 973, 1021,
    1022, 1025, 1029, 1044,
    1052, 1053, 1065, 1068,
    1077, 1115, 1116, 1120,
    1121, 1123, 1134, 1142,
    1145, 1157, 1162, 1163,
    1169, 1173, 1175, 1179,
    1190, 1192, 1198, 1212,
    1228, 1239, 1241, 1243,
    1247, 1264, 1277, 1280,
    1282, 1302, 1303, 1313,
    1318, 1320, 1349, A29, A39
Ecuador
    99, 218, 410, 826, 827,
    989, 1025
education
    see enculturation
ego
    see self
Egypt
    (modern)
    62
Egyptians, ancient
    287, 294, 942, 1184
elderly
    215, 1069

enculturation
(refers to the teaching
of youth, by their elders,
of beliefs and behaviors
about alcohol)
see also norms
9, 35, 38, 67, 124,
125, 469, 490, 553, 560,
673, 685, 837, 868,
890, 891, 916, 1009,
1017, 1061, 1122, 1137,
1265, 1345
England
see also United Kingdom
61, 92, 112, 146, 268,
312, 407, 439, 441, 443,
480, 496, 497, 589, 638,
818, 839, 860, 871, 908, 916,
963, 1023, 1035, 1063,
1101, 1107, 1223, 1250,
1273, 1280, 1310, 1313
epidemiology
(refers to the incidence
and/or prevalence of
drinking problems,
"alcoholism", and/or
related pathologies in
specific populations)
31, 33, 49, 64, 111, 115,
132, 153, 209-212, 219,
313, 314, 316, 328, 415,
431, 470, 483, 525, 526,
528, 566, 567, 574, 587,
629, 669, 681, 683, 703,
704, 786, 789, 854, 887,
898, 899, 922, 927, 956,
959, 1037, 1089, 1098,
1103, 1104, 1113, 1134,
1178, 1232, 1259, 1286,
1295, 1296, 1300, 1305
Eskimos
52, 53, 102, 254, 255,
262, 367, 387, 396, 402,
430, 431, 537, 559-563,
582, 595, 667, 671, 675,
746, 762, 772, 815, 912,
1015, 1142, 1225, 1237,
A40
Ethiopia
see also Abyssinia
1196
ethnic/ethnicity/ ethnic groups
see Cross-ethnic studies;
names of regions; names of peoples

ethnography
see names of specific
populations;
see also customs;
research methods
ethnohistory
see history
ethnology
see Cross-cultural studies;
distribution; World survey
ethnoscience/ethnosemantics
see semantics
etiology
(presumed causes of
drinking problems,
"alcoholism", etc.)
30, 38, 64, 110, 111, 264,
440, 531, 575, 603, 685,
732, 825, 840, 1108, 1319
Europe
(includes the entire
continent and offshore
islands) names of nations
and regions that are
specifically cited in the
sources include the
following (see individual
index-entries): Austria;
Bosnia; Catalonia; Croatia;
Czechoslovakia; Denmark;
England; Faroe Islands;
Finland; France; Germany;
Greece; Greenland; Hebrides
Islands; Herzegovina;
Hungary; Iceland; Illyria;
Ireland; Italy; Netherlands;
Norway; Poland; Portugal;
Scandinavia; Scotland;
Serbia; Slovakia; Soviet
Union; Spain; Sweden;
Switzerland; Tyrol; United
Kingdom; Wales; Yugoslavia
names of peoples that are
specifically cited in the
sources include the
following (see individual
index-entries): Albanians;
Basques; Biblical peoples;
Classical peoples; Greeks,
ancient; Gypsies; Irish-
Americans; Italian-Americans;
Lapps; Romans, ancient
20, 92, 108, 136, 250, 398,

399, 403, 423, 544, 705,
1034, 1036, 1091, 1094,
1102, 1347

family
see also heredity; kinship;
social organization
6-8, 10, 57, 112, 124,
125, 149, 411, 481, 553,
575, 685, 837, 902, 1017,
1265, 1269, 1287, 1328,
A16

Faroe Islands
150

female
(includes detailed information
specifically on girls and/or
women)
67, 71, 84, 247, 257, 349,
435, 456, 481, 711, 843,
891, 1110, 1111, 1142,
1214, 1302, 1303, 1331

fighting
(as a sequel to drinking)
see also aggression
150, 252, 254, 367, 426,
478, 530, 537, 767, 1066

Fingo
(South Africa)
857

Finland
see also Lapps
24-26, 191, 192, 365, 478,
935, 957, 1074, 1075, 1192,
1252

firewater myth
see Native Americans;
"race"; stereotype

flushing
see "race"

folklore
(attitudes and usages of
alcoholic beverages as
reflected in songs, tales,
and other folk and popular
media)
120, 235, 237, 245, 250,
360, 362-364, 403, 423,
435, 458, 478, 506, 549,
600, 616, 618, 619, 628,
799, 832, 833, 878, 938,
941, 961, 980, 1010, 1036,
1092, 1093, 1150, 1184,
1192, 1196, 1252, 1269,
1284, 1328, 1335, 1336

food
see nutrition

France
35, 64, 441, 599, 687,
807, 817, 1061

functions
(favorable outcomes of
drinking)
15, 65, 70, 71, 77, 94,
96, 97, 100, 122, 146,
156, 157, 160, 180, 181,
199, 203, 217, 223, 227,
231, 241, 255, 263, 293,
296, 300, 304-306, 308,
318, 320, 325, 326, 329,
336, 347, 359, 376, 394,
398, 399, 412, 421, 449,
450, 455, 456, 471, 484,
485, 503, 506, 512-517,
527, 530, 537, 555-558,
564, 565, 585, 594, 597,
607, 608, 611, 624, 636,
637, 640, 645, 650, 652-
655, 658, 661, 673, 676,
678, 682, 685, 690, 696,
700, 712, 714, 716, 717,
720, 726, 734, 738, 745,
749, 754, 755, 765, 766,
768, 769, 774, 777, 782,
783, 792, 807, 821, 825,
827-829, 832-834, 855,
872, 874, 892, 894, 901,
903, 915, 918, 923, 935,
945, 948, 958, 960, 963,
966, 974, 975, 979, 989,
995, 996, 1004, 1011,
1014, 1019, 1020, 1025,
1027-1029, 1033, 1039,
1044, 1061, 1069, 1071, 1072,
1081-1083, 1098, 1101,
1120-1124, 1129, 1143,
1154, 1155, 1164, 1167,
1170, 1179, 1184, 1203,
1223, 1228, 1246, 1262,
1264, 1274-1276, 1285,
1288, 1302-1304, 1312,
1314, 1323, 1338, 1339,
1346, A10, A15, A29, A32,
A44

fundamentalists
    see Protestants

gambling
    15, 203, 251, 1066
genetics
    see heredity
geriatrics
    see elderly
Germany
    198, 360, 532, 627,
    819, 1010, 1058,
    1092, 1093, 1150,
    1348
Ghana
    767, A33
Giriama
    (Kenya)
    928
girls
    see female; youth
Gond
    (India, includes Maria
    Gond)
    362, 597
Greece
    (modern)
    127, 156, 157, 502,
    635
Greek Orthodox Church
    see Church
Greeks, ancient
    see also Classical peoples
    399, 842, 852, 853,
    1034, 1184, 1189
Greenland
    262, 772, 1142, 1144,
    1225
groups
    see social organization
Guatemala
    199, 200, 1004, 1070
Guiana
    (unspecified)
    1046, A37
Guinea
    140, 984
Gypsies
    1208, 1245

Haida
    (northwestern North
    America)
    714

Haiti
    167, 337
Hare
    (northwestern North
    America)
    351, 1081, 1082
Hawaiian Islands
    134, 135, 719, 854, 1298
Hebrews
    see Jews
Hebrides Islands
    (Scotland)
    A26
Henga
    (Malawi)
    471
heredity
    see family; "race"
Herrero
    (South Africa)
    1247
Herzegovina
    see also Yugoslavia
    961
Hide
    (West Africa)
    359
Hinduism
    see also caste; India
    165, 226, 240, 434, 867,
    938, 977, 987
Hispanos
    (Spanish-speakers in the
    United States, including
    immigrants from Latin
    America, as well as
    Chicanos, Mexican-Americans,
    etc.)
    42, 241, 320, 417, 424, 433,
    456, 457, 465, 590, 607,
    608, 615, 736, 778, 801,
    1111, 1214, 1217, 1218,
    1221, A15
history, pre-1500
    (reference to alcoholic
    beverages, prior to 1500
    A.D.)
    see also Biblical peoples;
    Classical peoples;
    prehistory; names of nations
    and regions; names of
    peoples
    1, 27, 60, 61, 79, 85-89,
    92, 101-103, 108, 109, 118,

119, 136, 146, 154, 165,
184, 187, 195, 201, 215,
216, 236, 238, 240, 250,
261, 270, 287, 291, 292,
294, 306, 307, 338, 341,
342, 345, 354, 356, 357,
360, 363, 364, 382, 386,
398, 399, 403, 407, 416,
423, 434, 443, 446, 451-
453, 458, 462, 472, 480,
498, 502, 532, 543, 544,
549, 589, 596, 599, 604,
627, 642, 643, 645, 647,
660, 672, 694, 706, 725,
741, 749, 763-765, 771,
776, 805, 806, 816, 839,
841-849, 851-853, 862,
867, 869, 871, 875, 877,
926, 933, 942, 963, 973,
974, 976, 977, 985, 986,
990, 992-994, 997, 1032,
1034, 1035, 1049, 1051,
1058, 1065, 1068, 1092-
1094, 1102, 1109, 1135,
1148, 1150, 1151, 1165,
1184, 1187-1191, 1205,
1211, 1224, 1252, 1257,
1332-1334, 1336, 1337,
1340, 1347, A39
  history, pre-1900
    (reference to alcoholic
    beverages between 1500
    and 1900 A.D.)
    14, 27, 33, 60, 61, 85-89,
    91, 92, 102, 103, 109,
    118, 119, 122, 131, 146,
    154, 170, 182, 184, 185,
    187, 189, 195, 201, 206,
    223, 225, 236, 238, 239,
    250, 256, 261, 263, 268,
    280, 288, 289, 291, 292,
    303-306, 312, 322, 325,
    334, 338, 342, 346, 353,
    354, 357, 360, 364, 375,
    397, 406, 407, 422, 439,
    441, 443, 446, 458, 459,
    468, 474, 475, 477, 478,
    480, 484, 496, 497, 502,
    511, 521, 532, 538, 545,
    549, 568, 570-572, 578,
    579, 589, 591, 592, 605,
    641, 643, 647, 650, 660,

672, 684, 697, 714, 717,
724, 725, 727, 729, 730,
732, 739, 747, 756, 757,
760, 763, 764, 773, 775,
776, 779, 805-807, 809,
811, 817, 830, 839, 840,
856, 860, 862, 870, 871,
877, 883, 890, 908, 919,
923, 924, 934, 943, 963,
973, 974, 976, 986, 997,
1031, 1032, 1037, 1045,
1049, 1051, 1058, 1059,
1062, 1064, 1068, 1092-
1094, 1097, 1109, 1135,
1142, 1150, 1151, 1154,
1163, 1169, 1175, 1187,
1192, 1198, 1199, 1205,
1209, 1211, 1215, 1229,
1234, 1241, 1257, 1273,
1277, 1280, 1297, 1308,
1310, 1313, 1317, 1318,
1332-1334, 1347, 1349,
A17, A39, A47
homebrew
    (refers to non-vinous
    fermented beverages
    produced on a relatively
    small scale, including
    beers, chicha, mead,
    palm-wine, pulque, etc.)
    12, 13, 17, 18, 21, 36,
    47, 56, 57, 60, 97, 101,
    119, 129-131, 133, 139,
    165, 170, 176, 179, 182,
    187, 189, 193-195, 201,
    205, 208, 224, 229, 230,
    249, 255, 262, 276, 277,
    284, 286, 290, 297, 302,
    331, 338, 341, 342, 351,
    356, 362, 364, 368, 374,
    412, 418-420, 423, 450-
    452, 472, 481, 491, 498-
    500, 503, 504, 530, 532,
    536, 555, 556, 572, 597,
    600, 613, 614, 652-654,
    658, 678, 680, 688, 716,
    717, 720, 723, 734, 737,
    741, 755, 762, 771, 792,
    805, 806, 811, 816, 836,
    839, 849, 857, 867, 871,
    876, 880, 886, 895, 901,
    904, 907, 909, 910, 914,

921, 928, 936, 937, 946,
954, 958, 962, 967, 979,
985, 1007, 1010, 1018,
1019, 1024, 1025, 1046,
1052, 1059, 1067, 1069,
1070, 1077, 1094, 1097,
1109, 1118, 1135, 1148,
1152, 1187, 1191, 1192,
1196, 1207, 1224, 1228,
1236, 1240, 1242, 1243,
1246, 1247, 1252, 1253,
1264, 1285, 1306, 1307,
1332, A28, A29, A48
homeless persons
see Skid Row
homicide
see murder
Hong Kong
1124-1126
Hopi
(southwestern North
America)
683, 702, 730, 732, 733
Hottentot
see Nama
Huichol
(Mexico)
188
Hungary
38, 39, 623
hypoglycemia
(in relation to drunken
comportment)
see also aggression
163, A40

Ibibio
(Nigeria)
600
Iceland
528, 529
Ijaw
(Nigeria)
707
Illyria
(ancient area now
in Yugoslavia)
472
incidence
(of problem drinking,
"alcoholism", etc.)
see epidemiology

India
see also names of peoples
1, 165, 226, 236, 240,
249, 321, 362, 419, 428,
491, 504, 505, 597, 654,
741, 759, 867, 931, 938,
977, 988, 990-993, 1085,
1127, 1243, 1307, A1, A23,
A34
Indians, American
see Native Americans;
names of peoples (North
America)
infants
see youth
ingredients
see manufacture
integration
(of alcoholic beverages
into sociocultural systems),
see functions; (as a
positive social outcome of
drinking),
see functions; social
organization
international
see Cross-national; World
survey
intoxication
(including descriptions of
drunken comportment)
67, 69, 77, 90, 97, 122,
131, 145, 156, 171, 172,
178, 190, 199, 246, 254,
255, 272, 286, 304, 410,
455, 620, 716, 718, 773,
861, 1020, 1095, A43
Inuit
see Eskimos
Iran
see also Persians, ancient
416, 666
Iraqu
(Tanganyika)
412
Ireland
see also United Kingdom
94, 149, 280, 285, 888,
916, 1008, 1086, 1174,
1175, 1269
Irish-Americans
440, 456, 669, 888, 1037,

1173, 1175
Iroquois
(northeastern North America)
223, 304, 306, 641, 1266, 1344
Islam
(regardless of location)
see also Near East
50, 62, 79, 234, 317, 416, 434, 694, 864, 958, 984, 987, 1065, 1066, 1105, 1254, A31
Israel
see also Jews
361, 539, 674, 1114
Italian-Americans
147, 148, 196, 752, 1037, 1119
Italy
164, 323, 400, 752, 1056
Iteso
(Kenya)
636

Jamaica
111, 113, 114
Japan
see also Ainu
37, 413, 680, 967, 1071, 1072, 1078, 1160, 1333-1336, A4
Jews
(regardless of nationality)
55, 94, 243, 270, 361, 382, 440, 442, 453, 596, 645, 669, 672, 674, 837, 868, 891, 1037, 1072, 1087, 1088, 1114, 1132, 1137, 1138, 1141, 1232, 1281, 1345, A2
Jicarilla
see Apache
job
see occupation

Kaffir beer
see homebrew
Kaguru
(Tanganyika)
118
Kalderaša
see Gypsies

Kaska
(northwestern North America)
855
Katanga
(Congo)
129, 130
kava
(made from piper methysticum in Oceania; does not contain ethynol, but its use and effects are so similar to those of homebrew that some observers have historically treated it as an alcoholic beverage)
408, 547, 723, 808, 812, 1233
Kayan
(Sarawak)
97
Kekchi
(Guatemala)
1070
Kelabit
(Kenya)
97
Kenya
636, 922, 928
Kenyah
(Sarawak)
97
kinship
see family; social organization
Klamath
(northwestern North America)
352
Kofyar
(Nigeria)
903
Koran
see Islam
Korea
248, 483, 657, 659
Kutchin
(northwestern North America)
95
Kuwait
317
Kwakiutl
(northwestern North America)
714, 1029

Kwango
    (Dahomey)
    18
labeling
    (in the sociological sense,
    relating to symbolic inter-
    actionist analyses, self-
    fulfilling stereotypes, etc.)
    see also stereotype
    77, 684, 705, 965
ladino
    see Mestizos
language
    (linguistic evidence for
    historical relations among
    peoples, meanings of alcohol-
    related terminology, etc.)
    see also semantics
    101, 711, 838, 1010
Laos
    1287
Lapps
    24, 935, 1074, 1075
Latin America
    (as used here, includes
    Mexico, Central America, all
    Caribbean Islands, and South
    America, regardless of
    predominant language or
    culture; some sources
    include general discussion,
    but most deal with selected
    populations)
    for Spanish-speakers in the
    United States, see Hispanos;
    see also names of nations
    and regions; names of peoples
    (Central America; South
    America)
    32, 43, 315, 332, 341, 519,
    566, 567, 688, 800, 898-900,
    943, 1031, A21
learning
    see enculturation
learning theory
    (as a basis for therapy)
    see treatment
leisure
    (role of alcoholic beverages in)
    120, 128, 296, 304, 305,
    388, 419, 530, 577, 578,
    623, 649, 658, 734, 737,
    795, 892, 912, 1081, 1181,
    1193, 1321
literature
    (allusions to alcoholic
    beverages in)
    see also folklore
    165, 184, 382, 416, 434,
    441, 451, 453, 549, 596,
    850, 851, 853, 860, 875,
    908, 941, 961, 1066, 1254,
    1310, 1337, 1347
liver
    (especially disorders
    resulting from heavy
    drinking)
    413, 681, 683, 730, 732,
    824, 1061, 1117, 1178
Loi-Manipuri
    (Assam)
    1127
lounge
    see bar
LSD
    see peyote
Madagascar
    958, 959
Malagache
    (Madagascar)
    958
Malawi
    471
Mandingolu
    (west Africa)
    A6
manufacture
    (methods of producing
    alcoholic beverages,
    including recipes,
    procedures of fermentation,
    distillation, etc.)
    see also containers
    13, 17, 18, 21, 47, 60,
    121, 129, 130, 139, 169,
    170, 179, 182, 186, 188,
    193, 195, 215, 230, 239,
    276, 277, 280, 284, 297,
    302, 303, 338, 342, 350,
    356, 362, 363, 374, 385,
    412, 418, 420, 423, 491,
    498, 499, 501, 508, 530,

549, 572, 600, 613, 614,
648, 660, 678, 680, 688,
747, 771, 805, 836, 867,
871, 872, 876, 877, 880,
886, 895, 904, 909, 910,
914, 921, 936-938, 946,
954, 962, 967, 985, 986,
991, 997, 1007, 1046, 1052,
1068, 1118, 1127, 1135,
1148, 1151, 1162, 1191,
1196, 1207, 1224, 1240,
1242, 1247, 1253, 1282,
1284, 1307, 1340, A29,
A48
Manus
   (Melanesia)
   1095
Maohi
   (Polynesia)
   734
Maori
   (New Zealand)
   446
Mapuche
   (Chile)
   754-757, 798, 859,
   1236
Maria Gond
   see Gond
Martinique
   (West Indies)
   1011
matériél
   (associated with
   manufacture and
   drinking)
   see containers
Maya
   (includes not only pre-
   Columbian but also
   contemporary Maya-
   speakers) (Central
   America)
   101, 154, 452, 1129
mead
   see beer; homebrew
meanings
   see semantics; symbols
medical
   (uses of alcoholic
   beverages for medicinal
   purposes, ideas about

their prophylactic or
therapeutic values, etc.)
103, 133, 156, 165, 186,
203, 205, 261, 360, 416,
450, 472, 504, 537, 543,
557, 635, 642, 643, 699,
763-765, 839, 849, 869,
912, 946, 975, 976, 990,
1025, 1034, 1083, 1093,
1118, 1124, 1137, 1184,
1196, 1332, 1335
Melanesia
   see also Oceania;
   especially names of nations
   and regions; names of
   peoples
   236, 918, 1095
Meo
   (Laos)
   1287
mescal/mescaline
   see peyote
Mesoamerica
   see Central America
Mesopotamia
   356, 498
messianic movements
   see conversion
Mestizos
   see also Métis
   373, 411, 513, 514, 517,
   555, 780, 1077, 1083,
   1121-1123
metabolism
   (of alcoholic beverages)
   see also "race"
   126, 372, 377, 378, 383,
   387, 432, 487, 740, 802,
   889, 999-1002, 1085, 1106,
   1160, 1235, 1326, 1327,
   1341-1343, A35, A36
methodology/methods of
   research
   see research methods
Métis
   (Canada)
   335, 554, 855, 1149
Mexica
   (Mexico)
   780
Mexican-Americans
   see Hispanos

Mexico
21, 36, 101, 109, 132,
154, 169, 187-189, 199,
200, 207, 215, 216, 232,
252, 314, 318, 373, 379,
395, 411, 420, 435, 451,
637, 652, 653, 770, 774,
779, 780, 816, 861, 882,
925, 926, 975, 980, 1032,
1052, 1118, 1129, 1130,
1135, 1199, 1249, 1255,
1285, 1312, 1314, 1341,
1346, A42
Micmac
(northeastern North America)
1268
Micronesia
see also Oceania; especially names of nations and regions; names of peoples
51, 784, 809-811, 814, 894,
Middle East
see Near East
migration
see urbanization
minority
see Blacks; Cross-ethnic; elderly; Hispanos; names of peoples
Mixtec
(Mexico)
207
Moba
(Togo)
937
modernization
see acculturation; change; urbanization
Mohammedanism
see Islam
Mohave
(southwestern North America)
325, 326
Mongolia
151, 872
Mongoloid
see Native Americans; Orientals; "race"
moonshine
(illicitly distilled alcoholic beverages, regardless of the base raw material)
47, 57, 121, 189, 239, 280,
303, 321, 350, 385, 419,
504, 556, 568, 595, 597,
648, 666, 707, 747, 790,
836, 878, 938, 986, 991,
1007, 1019, 1127, 1128, 1192,
1243, 1277, 1282
Mormon
see also Church
424
Morocco
313
Mozambique
617-619
murder
see also aggression; crime
90, 362, 379, 405, 426,
729, 730, 790, 824, 1077,
1178, 1199, 1255
Murut
(Sarawak)
97
music
(as associated with drinking)
see also folklore
237, 616, 618, 619, 878,
980
Muslim
see Islam

Nama
(South Africa; includes Hottentot)
1247
names of nations and regions/ names of peoples
see alphabetical listings, under those two headings for major world-areas (Africa; Asia, Central America; Europe; North America; Oceania; South America)
Nan-Shi
see Ami
Nasioi
(Melanesia)
918

Naskapi
    (northeastern North
    America)
    1020-1022
Natal
    (South Africa)
    A12
national drinking patterns
    see names of nations;
    see also Cross-national;
    World survey
Native Alaskans
    see Aleuts; Eskimos;
    Native Americans; names
    of peoples (North America)
Native American Church
    see Church; peyote
Native Americans
    (generic name for
    populations in North
    America often referred to
    as "American Indians"; when
    used without a modifier,
    refers to general or unspeci-
    fied populations)
    see also Aleuts; Eskimos;
    names of peoples (North
    America)
    3-5, 10, 11, 22, 23, 45,
    48, 52, 53, 58, 81, 90,
    91, 95, 102, 107, 117,
    122, 126, 142, 143, 159,
    161, 162, 170, 173-175,
    178, 180, 181, 183, 185,
    196, 197, 202, 206, 220,
    221, 223, 224, 230, 254,
    255, 260, 265-267, 269,
    271, 274, 275, 283, 288,
    296, 298, 304-306, 308,
    325, 326, 333-335, 339-
    342, 348, 351, 352, 369,
    375, 377, 378, 387-392,
    397, 402, 405, 406, 409,
    414, 421, 430, 431, 436,
    456, 463, 465-467, 470,
    479, 484, 485, 507-512,
    515, 526, 527, 531, 533-
    537, 540-542, 545, 550,
    551, 553, 554, 556, 561-
    563, 569, 570, 572, 577,
    578, 580-582, 586, 591,
    593, 606-612, 622, 626,
    632, 634, 641, 649, 650,
    658, 667, 671, 675, 676,
    681-686, 688, 689, 695,
    696, 702, 708-711, 714,
    716, 729-733, 736, 744,
    745, 748, 758, 768, 769,
    773, 775, 785-787, 815,
    823-825, 828-830, 840,
    855, 870, 881, 883, 884,
    892, 902, 905, 912, 919,
    920, 929, 930, 945, 970,
    981, 982, 1016, 1020-1022,
    1029, 1047, 1064, 1079-
    1082, 1090, 1112, 1113,
    1117, 1120, 1131, 1134,
    1159, 1161, 1163, 1166,
    1168, 1169, 1171, 1177,
    1178, 1182, 1183, 1185,
    1193, 1194, 1200, 1212,
    1213, 1216, 1222, 1226,
    1229-1231, 1234, 1259-1266,
    1268, 1278, 1286, 1288,
    1289, 1291, 1292, 1295,
    1299, 1302-1304, 1311,
    1316, 1319, 1327, 1329,
    1344, 1349, A3, A7, A9-A11,
    A14, A15, A20, A24, A27,
    A35, A40, A41, A43-A47,
    A49
Native Canadians
    see Canada; Eskimos;
    Native Americans; names of
    peoples (North America)
nativistic movements
    see conversion
Navaho/Navajo
    (southwestern North
    America)
    11, 183, 388-392, 424,
    466, 467, 512, 515, 533-
    535, 634, 649, 681-684,
    729, 730, 732, 733, 1047,
    1079, 1080, 1177, 1212,
    1213, 1329, A41
Near East
    see also names of nations
    and regions; names of
    peoples (Asia)
    108, 136, 176, 193, 234,
    250, 270, 343, 356, 403,
    453, 543, 544, 642, 645,
    771, 869, 933, 985, 1066,

235.

1067, 1102, 1114, 1165
negative outcomes of drinking
    see dysfunctions
Negroid
    see Africa; Blacks
Nepal
    946, A19
Nestorian Church
    see Church
Netherlands
    415, 944
Newar
    (Nepal)
    A19
New Guinea
    see also Papua New Guinea
    46
New Hebrides
    (Micronesia)
    474, 547
New Zealand
    see also Maori
    446, A13
Nez Perce
    (central and northwestern
    North America)
    10, 830
Nigeria/Niger
    56, 57, 140, 600, 707,
    903, 915, 1228
non-literate peoples
    see names of peoples
Nootka
    (northwestern North
    America)
    714
norms
    (with respect to drinking,
    drunkenness, and drunken
    comportment)
    see also customs;
    enculturation; responsibility
    9, 26, 31, 57, 77, 85-89, 94,
    100, 105, 111, 144, 165,
    190, 214, 215, 220, 231,
    351, 352, 382, 390, 392,
    396, 434, 440, 453, 457,
    465, 467, 490, 510, 512-
    514, 520, 522, 537, 540-
    543, 545, 575, 579, 580,
    596, 607, 608, 634, 635,
    637, 652, 657, 669, 682,
683, 705, 707, 713-715,
718, 720, 721, 724, 730,
732, 752, 780, 831, 837,
850, 858, 867, 868, 890,
891, 894, 897, 912, 916,
926, 931, 941, 948, 957,
981, 983, 987, 988, 994,
1006, 1015, 1041, 1042,
1048, 1055, 1056, 1072,
1082, 1092, 1099, 1105,
1111, 1122, 1124, 1137,
1138, 1174, 1192, 1195,
1204, 1218, 1227, 1254,
1271, 1288, 1299, 1301-
1304, 1308, 1320, 1321,
1339, 1344, 1345, A3, A7,
A9, A10, A15, A24, A31,
A39, A43, A44
North America
    names of nations and regions
    see Canada; United States;
    names of peoples see Aleuts;
    Algonquian; Apache; Arapaho;
    Athabascan; Blackfeet;
    Blacks; Cherokee; Cheyenne;
    Chipewyan; Chippewa; Crow;
    Dakota; Eskimos; Haida;
    Hare; Hispanos; Hopi;
    Irish-Americans; Iroquois;
    Italian-Americans; Kaska;
    Klamath; Kutchin; Kwakiutl;
    Métis; Micmac; Mohave;
    Naskapi; Native Americans;
    Navaho; Nez Perce; Nootka;
    Ojibwa; Omaha; Oneida;
    Osage; Paiute; Papago;
    Pomo; Ponca; Potawatomi;
    Salish; Santee; Shoshone;
    Sioux; Tahltan; Taos;
    Tsimshian; Ute; Winnebago;
    Yakima; Zuni
Northeast
    see Native Americans;
    names of peoples (North
    America)
Northwest
    see Native Americans;
    names of peoples (North
    America)
Norway
    192, 584, 909

nutrition
   (includes ideas about
   alcoholic beverages
   in relation to nutrition;
   some sources are detailed
   "scientific" analyses
   and others reflect folk
   beliefs, which may be
   markedly discrepant)
   35, 36, 130, 156, 186,
   307, 600, 613, 678, 737,
   763, 857, 901, 903, 907, 921,
   954, 962, 1019, 1118,
   1247

observation
   see research methods
occupation
   (refers to specific
   occupational groups,
   some of which are noted
   as having distinctive
   patterns of drinking
   and/or risks of alcohol-
   related problems)
   226, 313, 546, 719,
   760, 797, 811, 859,
   931, 1157, 1185, 1215,
   1309, A34
Oceania
   (refers to populated
   islands of the Pacific
   Ocean, including Australia)
   names of nations and regions
   that are specifically cited
   in the sources include the
   following (see individual
   index-entries): Australia;
   Cook Islands; Hawaiian
   Islands; Manus; Maohi;
   Melanesia; Micronesia;
   New Guinea; New Hebrides;
   New Zealand; Papua New
   Guinea; Samoa; Society
   Islands; Tahiti, Truk
   names of peoples that
   are specifically cited in
   the sources include the
   following (see individual
   index-entries): Aborigines;
   Maori; Nasioi; Tonga
   54, 145, 322, 408, 474,
   475, 547, 723, 734, 808,
   812, 1297
Oglala/Oglalla
   see Sioux
Ojibwa/Ojibway
   (northeastern and central
   North America)
   593, 999, 1000, 1166,
   1286
Omaha
   (central North America)
   685
Oneida
   (central North America)
   1278
Oraon
   (India)
   419, 654
Orientals
   (sometimes used as a
   generic term in reference
   to Chinese, Japanese,
   Koreans, and/or other
   Mongoloid populations)
   see also "race"; names of
   nations and regions;
   names of peoples (Asia)
   664, 999, 1000, 1106,
   1326, 1327, A35
Osage
   (central and southwestern
   North America)
   397, 689
Otomí
   (Mexico)
   36
Ouray Indians
   see Ute
Overseas Chinese
   (endogamous enclaves of
   Chinese-speakers in
   countries other than China)
   100, 111, 113, 251, 958,
   1072, 1124-1126, 1271
Overseas Indians
   (endogamous enclaves of
   East Indian-speakers in
   countries other than India)
   40, 110-112, 866, 958,
   1339, A8

Oxchuc
(Mexico)
1130

Pacific Ocean
see Oceania
Paiute
(southwestern North
America)
545
palm-wine
see homebrew
Panama
979
Papago
(southwestern North
America)
283, 479, 1185, 1261-
1264, A43, A44
Papua New Guinea
see also New Guinea
203, 204
Paraguay
923, 1059
paraphernalia
see containers;
manufacture
participant-observation
see research methods
pathology
(as used here, refers
specifically to medical
complications associated
with heavy drinking)
see also liver; psychiatric
problems
194, 205, 218, 278, 425,
582, 583, 587, 664, 666,
675, 703, 704, 782, 839,
857, 858, 907, 946, 1037,
1113, 1230, 1245, 1273,
1306, 1313
Persians, ancient
see also Mesopotamia;
Near East
416, 741, 869, 1254, 1337
personality
114, 550, 551
Peru
see also Andean
29, 163, 205, 219, 227,
229, 245, 330, 336, 450,
538, 555, 743, 792, 806,
880, 886, 904, 1024, 1121-
1123, 1248, 1253, A28
peyote
see also Church; conversion;
drugs
22, 689, 929, 930
pharmacology
see drugs; intoxication
phases
(of "alcoholism" as a
progressive disease)
29, 242, 329, 1047, 1181
Philippines
368, 385, 404, 418
physiological effects
see intoxication;
metabolism; pathology
Pine Ridge Indians
see Sioux
Plains
see Native Americans
play
see leisure
poison
see suicide
Poland
233, 458
police
see crime
political
(includes not only controls
on access, but also ways in
which alcoholic beverages
are an adjunct to other
political activities,
e.g., among tribal populations)
23, 118, 185, 186, 353,
461, 477, 488, 591, 623,
697, 728, 756, 757, 792,
810, 869, 973, 974, 1068,
1173, 1175, 1190, 1198,
1209, 1247, 1250, 1277,
1280, 1323, A17, A39
poly-drug use/addiction
see drugs
Polynesia
see also Oceania, especially
names of nations and regions;
names of peoples
717, 720, 1233

Pomo
    (southwestern North America)
    507
Ponca
    (central North America)
    685
Pondomi
    (South Africa)
    857
popular culture
    see folklore
Portugal
    393, 1162
possession
    (in the religious sense; includes vision-quest)
    167, 168, 215, 223, 304-306, 384, 403, 445, 485, 609, 612, 701, 796, 906, 923, 926, 1076, 1276, A29
positive outcomes of drinking
    see functions
Potawatomi
    (central North America)
    484, 485
power
    see also dependency
    173, 300, 311, 349, 601, 612, 628, 832-834, 870, 1025, 1143, 1196, 1262, 1272
prehistory
    1, 60, 85-89, 101, 103, 108, 109, 158, 176, 188, 193, 195, 215, 216, 238, 261, 287, 291, 292, 294, 341, 354, 356, 363, 364, 399, 403, 407, 451, 452, 498, 544, 549, 605, 642, 643, 647, 749, 765, 771, 776, 816, 974, 977, 992, 993, 1032, 1049, 1051, 1067, 1094, 1109, 1135, 1205, 1211, 1333, 1334, 1340
prevalence
    (of problem drinking, "alcoholism", etc.)
    see epidemiology

prevention
    (of "alcoholism", problem drinking, etc.)
    65, 85-89, 155, 214, 281, 282, 316, 339, 354, 401, 405, 427, 430, 431, 438, 476, 526, 586, 693, 725, 786, 788, 789, 803, 884, 902, 927, 955, 981, 1089, 1103, 1112, 1218, 1230, 1231, 1259, 1286, 1300, 1308, 1345
primitive peoples
    see names of peoples
problems resulting from drinking
    see alcoholism; dysfunctions; liver; pathology; psychiatric problems
production
    see manufacture
prohibition
    (not only in U.S. history, but as a legal stance against alcoholic beverages)
    see also temperance
    59, 79, 85-89, 165, 185, 256, 296, 315, 321, 385, 406, 416, 461, 468, 493, 515, 530, 556, 571, 609, 672, 766, 775, 806, 810, 811, 823, 824, 858, 878, 879, 883, 918, 1012, 1031, 1065, 1066, 1079, 1095, 1099, 1107, 1169, 1209, 1247, 1254, 1335, 1349
Protestants
    (usually, but not exclusively, ascetic sects)
    see also Church; conversion; Mormon
    454, 669, 724, 796, 868, 1132, 1204, 1279, 1281
proxemics
    see space
psychiatric problems
    (as associated with drinking)
    19, 28, 56, 107, 143, 180, 218, 402, 409, 411, 427, 437, 550, 551, 610, 623, 631, 675, 677, 706, 772, 774, 782, 888, 987,

1011, 1086, 1113, 1125,
1200, 1230, 1237, 1251,
1269, 1286, A27
psychoanalysis
see etiology; treatment
psychopharmacological effects
of alcohol
see intoxication
psychotherapy
see treatment
pub
see bar
Pueblo
see Hopi; Zuni
Puerto Rico
2
pulque
see homebrew

Qolla
(Bolivia, Peru)
see also Andean; Aymara
163
Quechua
(Bolivia, Colombia, Ecuador, Peru)
see also Andean
99, 330, 336, 410, 743,
792, 826, 827, 886, 989,
1025, 1083, 1248

"race"
(use of quotation-marks
indicates the compilers'
view that, although this
term is often used in ways
that imply biological
classification, criteria
are more often social than
genetic)
see also Blacks; Cross-
ethnic; Native Americans;
Orientals; names of nations
and regions; names of
peoples
44, 111, 113, 126, 272,
304, 372, 377, 378, 381,
383, 387, 413, 432, 470,
486, 487, 522, 622, 708,
740, 743, 802, 840, 854,
855, 889, 999-1002, 1057,
1085, 1106, 1160, 1235,
1315, 1326, 1327, 1342,
1343, A16, A35, A36
rape
see also aggression; sex
326
recipes
see manufacture
recreation
see leisure
Reddi
(India)
1085
religion
(includes attitudes about
alcoholic beverages, as
well as their uses and
meanings, in various
religions, including many
tribal religions)
see also Church; conversion;
Islam; Jews; Mormon;
Protestants; ritual; symbols;
names of peoples
10, 79, 99, 151, 165, 167,
168, 215, 216, 223, 250,
264, 294, 304-307, 315,
343, 363, 364, 382, 384,
403, 416, 434, 451-454,
474, 543, 545, 555, 596,
597, 605, 613, 635, 637,
638, 645, 652-654, 662,
665, 672, 678, 694, 697,
701, 728, 749, 781, 841,
858, 867, 869, 926, 975,
980, 987, 994, 1034, 1065,
1069, 1076, 1083, 1092,
1105, 1137, 1204, 1243,
1250, 1254, 1276, 1314,
1333, 1334, 1340, 1346,
A33
research methods
(includes details on
methods by which data were
collected)
8, 34, 66, 72, 75, 93,
104, 115, 137, 138, 174,
200, 213, 246, 253, 299,
319, 365, 369, 371, 433,
462, 492, 520-523, 533,
565, 607, 621, 628, 641,
646, 656, 664, 670, 682,
710, 722, 731, 733, 752,

759, 782, 783, 788, 794,
804, 818, 838, 893, 927,
953, 964, 972, 1001, 1002,
1005, 1018, 1040, 1043,
1054, 1073, 1084, 1089,
1129, 1130, 1146, 1158,
1181, 1186, 1197, 1213,
1215, 1219, 1290, 1294,
1295, 1317, 1324, 1331
responsibility
(of the individual,
including discussions of
alcohol as diminishing;
includes discussions of
"deviance", "time-out",
etc.)
255, 296, 305, 306, 318,
320, 326, 363, 379, 426,
455, 484, 510, 540, 541,
593, 629, 634, 742, 753,
773, 810, 875, 902, 920
958, 1004, 1020, 1199,
1302, 1303
Reunion
(island east of Africa)
145, 598
review
(indicates that the source
includes a fairly broad
review of the literature
on a given topic or area,
whether in analytic or
synthetic terms)
see also bibliography;
Cross-cultural; socio-
cultural; World survey
7, 16, 20, 44, 70, 72,
75, 105, 144, 152, 158,
180, 244, 258, 324, 332,
340, 355, 371, 401, 476,
486, 518-523, 525, 527,
647, 663, 703, 704, 709,
722, 731, 740, 745, 763,
764, 773, 776, 782, 783,
788, 791, 805, 812, 813,
825, 831, 844, 847, 877,
888, 900, 917, 923, 924,
932, 945, 947-952, 964,
974, 977, 995, 1001,
1002, 1005, 1050, 1073,
1100, 1139-1141, 1151,
1172, 1180, 1187, 1219,
1221, 1234, 1244, 1257,
1267, 1290, 1291, 1294,
1308, 1338
revitalization movements
see conversion
Rhodesia
47, 374, 426, 820-822,
913, 936, 996, 1306,
1323, 1324
ritual
(emphasizes roles of
alcohol in various kinds of
rituals, or highly
patterned behavior associated
with the use of alcoholic
beverages themselves)
67, 100, 109, 124, 125,
151, 156, 199, 227, 235,
241, 243, 279, 337, 343,
359, 384, 403, 410, 445,
452, 490, 513, 514, 539,
617, 652-654, 662, 665,
678, 691, 717, 754, 903,
928, 938, 975, 980, 989,
1025, 1069, 1071, 1078,
1083, 1120, 1121, 1123,
1137, 1138, 1192, 1228,
1246, 1264, 1287, 1314,
1328, 1333, 1334, A29
Romans, ancient
see also Classical peoples
399, 604, 706, 841, 843,
845, 846, 848, 850, 851,
1034, 1188-1191
Ruanda
17
rum
see moonshine; whiskey
Russia
see Soviet Union
Russian Orthodox Church
see Church

Safwa
(Tanganyika)
503
sailors
see occupation
Salish
(northwestern North
America)
196, 609-612, 714, 716, 1193

241.

Samoa
717, 720
San Carlos Indians
see Apache
Santee
(central North America)
541
Sarawak
97
Saulteaux Indians
see Canada
Scandinavia
see also Lapps;
names of nations and
regions (Europe)
592, 910, 1148
Scotland
see also Hebrides Islands;
United Kingdom
328, 344, 656, 747, 856,
882, 953, 1096, 1103,
1305, A26
self
96, 110, 181, 534, 612,
634, 702, 1021, 1022,
1206, 1261, 1272, 1274,
1311, 1319
semantics
see also symbols
270, 353, 404, 482, 710,
793, 861, 939, 1054,
1129, 1130, 1155, 1213
Senegal
13, 140, 278, 279, 309,
A18, A29
sensitivity to alcohol
see metabolism
Serbia
see also Yugoslavia
986
sex
(association of alcohol
with sexual behavior)
see also rape; for
specific information on
females, see female
2, 175, 177, 325, 326,
556, 686, 855, 912,
1026, 1066, 1288
Shangana-Tsonga
see Tsonga

Shoshone
(central and southwestern
North America)
265-267, 275, 333, 733
Sioux
(central North America)
197, 577, 578, 650, 685,
828, 829, 870, 1299, 1302-
1304, A24
Skid Row/Skid Road
(as a type of community
of urban nomads, regardless
of specific location)
41, 80, 82-84, 181, 308,
335, 347, 429, 685, 686,
744, 761, 939, 940, 1003,
1044, 1053-1055, 1115,
1116, 1155, 1156, 1158,
1179, 1238, 1239, 1320,
1325
Slovakia
see also Czechoslovakia
345
socialization
see enculturation; norms
social organization
(patterns of social
relationship, as affecting
and affected by the use of
alcoholic beverages; includes
drinking-groups)
see also caste; class;
elderly; family; female;
functions;kinship;occupation;
youth
6-8, 26, 28, 31, 40, 42, 70,
71, 73, 74, 76, 77, 80, 82-
84, 94, 95, 100, 111, 118,
124, 131, 149, 155, 217,
227, 243, 293, 296, 299,
320, 327, 336, 344, 352,
376, 394, 412, 437, 447,
449, 471, 478, 481, 484,
488, 489, 510, 512-517, 530,
537, 555, 561, 577-579, 584,
623, 636, 640, 645, 650,
652-654, 676, 678, 682, 690,
695, 714, 716, 717, 720, 721,
726, 732, 749, 751, 754,
755, 761, 793, 797, 810,
811, 834, 874, 888, 894,
903, 925, 928, 931, 935,

939, 954, 963, 974, 975,
979, 1019-1022, 1025,
1027-1029, 1033, 1037,
1044, 1053, 1055, 1060,
1061, 1069, 1071, 1074-
1076, 1080, 1081, 1083,
1086, 1113, 1116, 1120-
1124, 1136, 1138, 1154,
1155, 1157, 1166, 1174,
1176, 1179, 1192, 1203,
1212, 1219, 1223, 1228,
1238, 1239, 1243, 1246,
1247, 1255, 1261, 1262,
1264, 1271, 1274, 1285,
1287, 1288, 1312, 1314,
1323, 1331, 1333, 1334,
1346, A3, A9, A10, A29,
A30, A44

Society Islands
(Polynesia)
717, 720, 734

sociocultural
(indicates that the
source explicitly
emphasizes social and/or
cultural factors in
discussing the interrelations
of alcohol and human
behavior; some such sources
are primarily theoretic,
whereas others are descriptive
and a few are reviews)
see also Cross-cultural;
Cross-ethnic; World survey
23, 30, 41, 44, 64, 68, 70,
72, 73, 75, 76, 94, 96,
105, 110, 132, 142, 144,
152, 157, 160, 173, 174,
191, 199, 200, 203, 204,
212, 228, 269, 309, 316,
319, 324, 325, 351, 355,
358, 370, 371, 393, 399-
401, 411, 415, 430, 450,
456, 465, 476, 490, 512-
525, 527, 530, 533, 541,
546, 548, 550, 555-558,
560, 562-564, 567, 575,
585, 594, 597, 603, 607,
608, 620, 621, 625, 633,
652-654, 658, 663, 668,
676, 678, 682, 696, 697,
709, 714-718, 720, 722,
727, 728, 730, 745, 752,
755, 760, 768, 769, 778,
780, 789, 791, 792, 798,
800, 814, 815, 827, 828,
836, 861, 882, 885, 888,
897, 898, 903, 915, 917,
924, 927, 932, 939, 947-
952, 964, 965, 969-972,
974, 979, 988, 995, 998,
1006, 1007, 1009, 1018,
1019, 1023, 1029, 1030,
1042, 1050, 1056, 1069,
1083, 1100, 1108, 1120-
1123, 1129, 1137-1141,
1145, 1153, 1155, 1168,
1172, 1180, 1192, 1195,
1197, 1211, 1219, 1220,
1227, 1232, 1239, 1244,
1246, 1247, 1255, 1267,
1269, 1286, 1293, 1300,
1302-1304, 1308, 1314,
1319, 1323, 1324, 1338,
1339, A7, A15, A29, A32,
A39, A42, A44, A48

sociology
see bar; class; occupation;
research methods;
sociocultural

song
see folklore; music

South Africa
(compilers have not
attempted to standardize
varied usage which refers
sometimes to the nation
and sometimes to the region)
see also names of nations
and regions; names of
peoples (Africa)
49, 78, 153, 166, 179,
186, 194, 208, 310, 437,
500, 530, 579, 587, 614,
620, 677-679, 737, 751,
803, 857, 864-866, 901,
907, 914, 954, 978, 983,
1017, 1069, 1104, 1201,
1202, 1210, 1241, 1247,
1251, 1256, 1258, A12

South America
(includes the entire
continent) names of
nations and regions that

243.

South America

are specifically cited in
the sources include the
following (see individual
index-entries): Andean;
Argentina; Bolivia; Brazil;
Chaco; Chile; Colombia;
Ecuador; Guiana; Paraguay;
Peru
names of peoples that are
specifically cited in the
sources include the
following (see individual
index-entries): Aymara;
Batuque; Camba; Cubeo;
Mapuche; Mestizos; Qolla;
Quechua
286, 297, 499, 501, 583,
726, A48
Southeast
see Native Americans;
names of peoples (North
America)
Southwest
see Native Americans;
names of peoples (North
America)
Soviet Union
(Union of Soviet Socialist
Republics)
233, 281, 282, 357, 613,
1098, 1133, A39
space
(not "outer space", but
refers to ways in which
the placement of people
and things affect and are
affected by drinking)
231, 295, 835, 1028, 1147,
1157, 1331
Spain
31, 488, 489, 887, A25
Sri Lanka
see Ceylon
stages
see phases
Standing Rock Indians
see Sioux
stereotype
(refers to ethnic or
"racial" stereotyping)
see also labeling
44, 91, 181, 231, 255,
304, 419, 455, 478, 533,
534, 536, 564, 576, 580,
593, 612, 622, 639, 676,
708, 716, 768, 769, 773,
855, 918, 1013, 1095, 1120,
1149, 1156, 1173, 1175,
1182, 1233, 1261, 1291,
1298, A41
still
see manufacture; moonshine
stress
(in a broad psychological
and/or sociological sense)
see also acculturation;
anomie; occupation
3-5, 19, 28, 31, 38, 67, 84,
94, 105, 107, 112, 116,
131, 160, 180, 191, 221,
254, 255, 301, 305, 320,
321, 339, 388-392, 402,
417, 436, 466, 467, 479,
484, 511, 537, 545, 553,
565, 584, 592, 610-612,
629-631, 641, 658, 667,
674, 762, 767, 778, 815,
829, 855, 870, 892, 893,
911, 912, 942, 944, 945,
958, 981, 1015, 1030, 1071,
1076, 1079, 1081-1084,
1104, 1114, 1134, 1136,
1164, 1179, 1181, 1185,
1193, 1237, 1239, 1268,
1269, 1275, 1276, 1302-
1304, 1319, A1, A21
students
see youth
Subanun
(Philippine Islands)
404
Sub-Arctic
see Arctic; names of peoples
(North America)
Sub-Saharan Africa
see Africa; especially
names of nations and regions;
names of peoples
suicide
283, 298, 326, 405, 634,
675, 730, 785, 815, 824,
1161, 1178

Suraf
   (India)
   321
Sweden
   see also Gypsies
   33, 192, 273, 957,
   1208
Switzerland
   739
symbolic interaction
   see labeling; stereotype
symbols/symbolism
   (refers to symbolic forms,
   ideas, and behaviors
   that are associated with
   alcoholic beverages;
   including, but not
   restricted to, religious
   symbols)
   270, 291, 292, 294, 307,
   343, 363, 376, 386, 403,
   434, 453, 543, 579, 601,
   605, 612, 662, 665, 749,
   806, 870

Tagalog
   (Philippine Islands)
   368
Tahiti
   145
Tahltan
   (northwestern North
   America)
   855
Taiwan
   see also Ami
   573
Tanganyika
   118, 412, 503
Taos
   (southwestern North
   America)
   A3
Tarahumara
   (Mexico)
   652, 653, 925, 1285,
   1341, 1342, 1346
Tarascan
   (Mexico)
   169
tavern
   see bar

techniques of research
   see research methods
technology
   see containers; manufacture
teenagers
   see youth
temperance
   (refers to attitudes and
   norms that oppose intoxication;
   including, but not restricted
   to, political movements in
   the history of Western
   nations)
   see also attitudes; norms;
   prohibition; responsibility
   33, 43, 133, 165, 225,
   322, 353, 354, 422, 427,
   443, 468, 474, 477, 496,
   497, 502, 571, 592, 627,
   645, 725, 845, 846, 848,
   852, 858, 943, 1013, 1059,
   1175, 1189, 1243, 1254,
   1297
tension/tension-reduction hypothesis
   see stress
therapy
   see treatment
Thonga
   (South Africa)
   see also Tonga; Tsonga
   620
Tibet
   1307
time-out
   see responsibility
Tiriki
   (South Africa)
   1069
Tobago
   (West Indies)
   see also Trinidad
   110, 115
Togo
   937
Tojolabal
   (Mexico)
   861
tolerance
   see addiction; metabolism
Tonga
   (Polynesia)
   see also Thonga; Tsonga
   1233

Totonac
    (Mexico)
    1255
toxicology
    see pathology
Transvaal
    617
treatment
    (includes various modalities
    for the amelioration of
    different kinds of problems
    associated with drinking)
    see also Alcoholics Anonymous
    22, 33, 42, 52, 83, 91,
    110, 113, 141-143, 153,
    162, 184, 214, 220, 242,
    245, 269, 281, 282, 294,
    301, 361, 375, 388-390,
    392, 393, 502, 526, 533,
    535, 542, 552, 569, 574,
    576, 581, 582, 609, 626,
    639, 640, 695, 733, 748,
    778, 881, 884, 885, 902,
    929, 930, 955, 956, 970,
    1036, 1080, 1112, 1159,
    1194, 1201, 1202, 1206,
    1210, 1216, 1230, 1231,
    1259, 1266, 1292, 1293,
    1316, 1321, 1325, 1329,
    A7, A15, A20, A27, A49
tribes
    see names of peoples
Trinidad
    (also includes Trinidad/
    Tobago)
    see also Tobago
    40, 110, 112, 113, 115,
    1339
Truk
    (Micronesia)
    810, 814
Tsimshian
    (northwestern North
    America)
    714
Tsonga/Tsongo
    (Congo)
    616-619
Tyrol
    (Europe)
    1284

Tzotzil
    see Chamula
Ubangi-Chari
    (Africa)
    921
Uganda
    960, 1018, 1019
Uintah Indians
    see Ute
United Kingdom
    see also England; Ireland;
    Scotland; Wales
    660, 1203
United States
    (of America)
    see also Blacks; Hispanos;
    Native Americans; names of
    peoples (North America)
    3-5, 10, 11, 14, 22, 23, 41,
    42, 52, 53, 64, 65, 80-84,
    90, 91, 100, 102, 107, 120,
    123-125, 128, 131, 137,
    142, 143, 147, 148, 159, 161,
    162, 170, 171, 173-175,
    177, 178, 182, 183, 185,
    197, 202, 206, 209-212,
    214, 217, 222, 224, 225,
    230, 231, 237, 241, 256,
    257, 259, 263, 265-267,
    274, 275, 283, 288, 289,
    293, 296, 303, 308, 320,
    325-327, 329, 333, 334,
    339, 340, 347, 350, 351,
    353, 369, 375, 388-392,
    397, 405, 406, 414, 417,
    424, 433, 436, 440, 447,
    454, 456, 457, 459-461,
    463, 465-467, 469, 470,
    477, 479, 484, 485, 490,
    492, 494, 495, 507, 510-
    512, 515, 533-535, 540-542,
    545, 550-553, 568, 571, 572,
    577, 578, 586, 590, 593,
    606-608, 615, 626, 632,
    634, 648-650, 661, 664,
    667, 669, 673, 675, 676,
    681-686, 689, 691, 695, 697,
    700, 702, 711-713, 724, 727,
    729, 730, 732, 733, 735,
    736, 752, 753, 760, 761,
    777, 778, 782, 785, 786,

793, 801, 823, 824, 828-
830, 870, 874, 878, 884,
890, 902, 929, 934, 939-
941, 955, 982, 1003,
1008, 1014, 1026-1028,
1037, 1041, 1044, 1045,
1047, 1053-1055, 1098,
1108, 1110, 1111, 1115,
1116, 1119, 1120, 1132,
1137, 1154-1158, 1164,
1167-1169, 1173, 1175,
1176, 1179, 1181, 1185,
1194, 1198, 1209, 1212-
1218, 1221, 1232, 1238,
1239, 1261-1266, 1270,
1271, 1273, 1278, 1282,
1286, 1288, 1289, 1292,
1295, 1299, 1302-1304,
1308, 1309, 1316-1321,
1328-1331, 1345, 1349,
A2, A3, A5, A7, A9, A10,
A15, A17, A20, A24, A27,
A41, A43-A47, A49
Upper Volta
   140
urbanization
   (includes rural-to-
   urban migration)
   3-5, 32, 78, 107, 202,
   207, 252, 268, 308, 335,
   340, 367, 393, 402, 421,
   466, 467, 479, 530, 540,
   541, 563, 569, 577, 649,
   671, 685, 686, 744, 745,
   754, 759, 820-822, 859,
   892, 911, 982, 996, 1161,
   1178, 1262, 1263, A12,
   A44
urban nomads
   see Skid Row
U.S.A.
   see United States
U.S.S.R.
   see Soviet Union
Ute
   (southwestern North
   America)
   275, 465, 607, 608, 884,
   1112

values
   (of drinking)
   see functions

vasodilation
   see "race"
vessels
   see containers
violence
   see aggression; fighting;
   murder; rape; suicide
vision-quest
   see possession
vocabulary
   (of drinking)
   see language; semantics

Wales
   see also United Kingdom
   1313
West Indies
   see also names of nations
   (Central America)
   2, 40, 286, 337, 588, 795,
   956, 1011, 1296, A8
whiskey/whisky
   see also moonshine
   303, 338, 468, 747, 805
White Mountain Indians
   see Apache
Whites
   (a category, ostensibly
   biological but more
   accurately social; used
   in Cross-ethnic studies,
   in contrast with Blacks,
   Native Americans, Orientals,
   and/or other "races")
   126, 159, 265, 267, 377,
   378, 387, 414, 424, 465,
   470, 550, 552, 556, 562,
   563, 590, 607, 608, 664,
   679, 736, 742, 802, 855,
   920, 999, 1000, 1167,
   1226, 1292, 1311, 1326,
   1327, 1342, A35
Wind River Indians
   see Arapaho; Cheyenne
wine
   (usually refers to fermented
   grape juice) for palm-
   wine and other fermented
   beverages, see beer;
   homebrew
   27, 39, 103, 240, 250,
   323, 338, 343, 345, 363,

wine
386, 416, 444, 453, 472,
473, 538, 596, 599, 604,
642, 662, 687, 694, 699,
763, 764, 771, 805, 849,
869, 875, 933, 997, 1065,
1066, 1092-1094, 1102,
1109, 1162, 1165, 1184,
1191, 1205, 1224, 1284,
1337, 1347
Winnebago
(central North
America)
541, 685
Wolof
(Senegal)
A18
women
see female
words
see language; semantics
work
see leisure; occupation
World survey
(indicates that the
source includes data
from a fairly broad
sample of sociocultural
systems, on more than
two continents; often,
but not always, many of
the societies are non-
Western)
see also Cross-cultural;
Cross-ethnic
60, 67, 70, 71, 85-89,
98, 103, 104, 106, 121,
144, 158, 168, 184, 195,
238, 244, 246, 247, 261,
290-292, 302, 338, 354,
364, 394, 427, 434, 438,
520, 522, 549, 565, 601,
605, 643, 655, 663, 670,
728, 749, 763-766, 776,
788, 791, 805, 813, 831,
844, 847, 858, 862, 877,
893, 932, 948, 952, 972-
974, 976, 995, 997, 1030,
1038, 1049, 1051, 1068,
1084, 1099, 1109, 1140,
1151, 1187, 1205, 1211,
1257, 1275, 1277, 1301,
1332, 1338, 1340, A32

Xosa
(South Africa
857
Yakima
(northwestern North
America)
676
Yakut
(Siberia)
613
Yemenites
(in Israel)
539
Yoruba
(Nigeria)
915
youth
(includes infants, children,
adolescents, and students,
of both sexes)
10, 11, 35, 67, 117, 161,
173, 265-267, 301, 369,
440, 529, 531, 537, 540,
541, 554, 608, 682, 755,
784, 912, 916, 918, 945,
1112, 1164, 1167, 1193,
1212, 1265, 1278, 1330,
A10, A41
Yugoslavia
see also Albanians; Bosnia;
Croatia; Herzegovina;
Serbia
366, 472, 574, 863, 961,
986, 1245

Zaire
see Congo
Zambia
882, 1007
Zapotec
(Mexico)
318, 637
Zinacantan
(Mexico)
A42
Zuni
(southwestern North
America)
424, 533, 902, A20